TERRORISM

Commentary on Security Documents

VOLUME 103

TERRORISM

Commentary on Security Documents

VOLUME 103

GLOBAL ISSUES

Kristen E. Boon, Professor
Seton Hall School of Law

Aziz Huq, Professor
University of Chicago School of Law

Douglas C. Lovelace, Jr., Esquire
Senior National Securities Strategist

OXFORD
UNIVERSITY PRESS

OXFORD
UNIVERSITY PRESS

Oxford University Press, Inc., publishes works that further Oxford University's objective of excellence in research, scholarship, and education.

Published by Oxford University Press, Inc.
198 Madison Avenue, New York, New York 10016

Cataloging-in-Publication information is available from the Library of Congress.

ISSN 1062-4007
Terrorism: Commentary on Security Documents

ISBN 978-0-19-539807-6 (v. 103)

Note to Readers:
This publication is designed to provide accurate and authoritative information in regard to the subject matter covered. It is based upon sources believed to be accurate and reliable and is intended to be current as of the time it was written. It is sold with the understanding that the publisher is not engaged in rendering legal, accounting, or other professional services. If legal advice or other expert assistance is required, the services of a competent professional person should be sought. Also, to confirm that the information has not been affected or changed by recent developments, traditional legal research techniques should be used, including checking primary sources where appropriate.

(Based on the Declaration of Principles jointly adopted by a Committee of the American Bar Association and a Committee of Publishers and Associations.)

TABLE OF CONTENTS

VOLUME 103

GLOBAL ISSUES

DOCUMENTS

PREFACE

GLOBAL, REGIONAL, STRATEGIC, ECONOMIC, AND INTELLIGENCE TRENDS IN TERRORISM

By
Douglas C. Lovelace Jr.

Volumes 103 and 104 provide timely updates in five key trend areas regarding terrorism and efforts to defeat it. Just as the names ascribed to this epic battle have changed over time, so has the struggle itself. The "Global War on Terror," "Long War," "Fight against al Qaeda and Affiliated Movements," "Era of Persistent Conflict," and the new name that will almost certainly be given by the Obama administration signals that the effort itself, or at least perceptions of it, continues to change in important ways, as the pitted adversaries continue to adapt and adjust to gain relative advantage and achieve their respective goals. Upon leaving office under a hail of criticism over many of his administration's policies and programs, George W. Bush emphasized a salient point: the United States has not suffered a terrorist attack since September 11, 2001. Some commentators go so far as to say al Qaeda has been defeated for all practical purposes. Others argue that it would be very imprudent for the United States to become sanguine over the terrorist threat because even in its apparent dormancy, it remains virulent.

Part of the problem with assessing the extent to which the terrorist threat has been diminished is the lack of objective measures of success. Some might count the number of attacks worldwide, which was the most frequently used indicator prior to September 11, 2001. Some argue that calculating and aggregating the effects of terrorist attacks is the most important metric, since it better describes the overall harm done and, thus, better exposes the threat posed to society. Still others, like former President Bush, would prefer measures that combine frequency of attack with severity of the consequences. For example, proponents of that approach point out that even a ten-year hiatus in terrorist activity would still represent a catastrophic failure of counterterrorism strategy were the period brought to its close by an act of weapons-of-mass-destruction terrorism, a topic covered extensively by the most recent volume of this series.

Another problem with discerning trends associated with terrorism is the impossibility of determining the efficacy of deterrent measures; i.e., of proving a negative—why attacks did not occur. For all these reasons and others, logic and prudence preclude us from declaring "mission accomplished," the end of the war against terrorists, or even claiming that we are winning the war. In all probability, neither the United States nor any other country will ever describe the terrorist threat as eliminated. The best we can do is to assess the trends associated with terrorism periodically and derive whatever conclusions we may from them. By presenting key update documents, Volumes 103 and 104 are designed to assist us in doing so.

INTRODUCTION

GLOBAL AND REGIONAL TRENDS IN TERRORISM

By
Douglas C. Lovelace Jr.

The documents presented in this volume update key trends associated with terrorism in two broad topical areas. The documents are not intended to describe the topics comprehensively, but only to provide useful, pacesetting insights. Likewise, the topical areas are but a few that could be included in periodic assessments of terrorism trends. Nonetheless, the documents provide the reader valuable information as to how the international struggle to reduce, if not eliminate, terrorism is progressing, as well as how terrorists are adapting in the face of constantly evolving and improving counterterrorism and anti-terrorism measures.

The first topical area addressed in this volume is a global trend analysis. A single, but very comprehensive document, *Global Trends 2025: A Transformed World,* is presented to provide an overarching trend context within which to assess trends associated with terrorism and measures to thwart it. The document describes trends that might foster terrorism and identifies potentially new partners in combating it.

Next, the volume moves to descriptions and assessments of terrorism and efforts to combat it in key regions and states. *Combating Terrorism: The United States Lacks Comprehensive Plan to Destroy the Terrorist Threat and Close the Safe Haven in Pakistan's Federally Administered Tribal Areas* and *Securing, Stabilizing, and Developing Pakistan's Border Area with Afghanistan: Key Issues for Congressional Oversight*, and *War in Afghanistan: Strategy, Military Operations and Issues for Congress* focus on the most critical region of the world with respect to the war against terrorists.

Latin America: Terrorism Issues reminds us that a significant threat of terrorism exists in the western hemisphere, is evolving over time, and warrants greater attention by the nations of the hemisphere. *U.S.-China Counterterrorism Cooperation: Issues for U.S. Policy* surveys the uneven history of

China's support to the war against terrorists and assesses the trends in U.S.-Sino cooperation to defeat terrorists. This section of the volume concludes with a Congressional Research Service report on the *Terrorist Attacks in Mumbai, India, and Implications for U.S. Interests.* The report provides a very useful look into India-Pakistan-United States relations as they relate to the war against terrorists.

A. GLOBAL TRENDS IN TERRORISM

COMMENTARY

GLOBAL TRENDS IN TERRORISM

By
Douglas C. Lovelace Jr.

The first document presented in this volume, *Global Trends 2025: A Transformed World,* in large measure sets the overall context for all the documents that follow. It is a November 2008 report prepared by the National Intelligence Council "to stimulate strategic thinking about the future by identifying key trends, the factors that drive them, where they seem to be headed, and how they might interact." It surveys and discusses the factors likely to shape the global security environment, rather than attempt to predict what the future environment will be. In doing so, it uses the familiar technique of presenting illustrative scenarios, while not claiming that any will eventuate or are even likely. The report is necessary reading for anyone interested in understanding the transnational and geostrategic contexts with which the terrorist threat will be defined.

The report posits an international system in 2025 strikingly different from that which has evolved since the end of World War II. The "multi-polar" international system will be one in which the United States remains a powerful nation but no longer able to dominate the international order that emerged after the collapse of the Soviet Union. The report speaks of emerging BRIC countries (Brazil, Russia, India, and China) propelled by continued globalization of the world economy, the unprecedented transfer of wealth from the West to South and East Asia, and the increased influence of non-state entities such as businesses, tribes, religious organizations, and large criminal enterprises. The report suggests that the era of American exceptionalism will be at an end.

The report also acknowledges that the most salient transnational issues will change due to demographics, energy demands, water and food shortages, and climate change. The report concludes that in spite of these challenges, the world will continue to enjoy an age of prosperity. However, the relative prosperity will also likely be accompanied by competition and perhaps conflict over trade, capital, technology, and possible arms races, territorial expansion, and military adventures. The belief by many that the United States is the "indispensable nation" will be seriously challenged, as rising powers such as China exert greater regional and global influence. The United States will have to come to grips with an ever-increasing insistence on multilateral cooperation in addressing transnational issues.

The report cites disproportionate economic growth as the major factor in producing new powers that will compete with the United States, speaking particularly of the BRIC countries. However, one is left with the impression that the report's authors may not have thoroughly addressed issues that may slow down such growth. For example, the historically high prices of petroleum and natural gas experienced last summer breathed new life into the Russian economy. Emboldened by its economic success, Russia assumed more confrontational positions vis-à-vis the United States on many international issues, signaling a more nationalistic future in which a Russian-led block will challenge the West as the former Soviet Union did last century. However, when one looks inside the Russian state, one sees several impediments to sustained economic growth. The criminal culture that has blossomed in post-Soviet Russia has and will limit economic development due not only to profiteering but also to inadequate long-term investments in the nation's economic infrastructure. Additionally, Russia has unaddressed environmental and ecological challenges remaining from its irresponsible and unrestrained competition with the West during the Cold War. They are so severe that significant financial investments and regulatory constraints will be necessary to address them adequately. Another vulnerability of the Russian economy is that it is becoming overly dependent on oil and natural gas exports. It needs to serve a more diversified export market if it is not to be upset by long-term reductions in demand for those primary exports, which may prove catastrophic if alternative energy breakthroughs should occur.

As for China, it is quite possible that its so-called "state capitalism" that the report suggests could be a more attractive and effective model than a liberal free-market economy, will come under severely increased pressure as China's middle class grows and more and more of the peasantry seek to enter it. Some view the state capitalism model only as an intermediate step, and that China's government will ultimately be faced with the choice of accepting slower economic growth or liberalizing its political processes and apparatus in order to become more democratic. Certainly, internal pressures emanating from China's heartland, much of which is barely governed, will have to be addressed. That will serve to slow China's economic growth. Additionally, like Russia, China has severe environmental issues it cannot ignore much longer. From an ecological perspective, China's economic growth over the past three decades has been irresponsible, as well. The air in major Chinese cities, Beijing included, is almost unbreathable;

the wearing of surgical masks by persons walking the streets is a familiar sight. Air quality in manufacturing villages is significantly worse. Virtually none of China's water supply is potable. Health care for the peasantry is extremely poor and the gap between the super rich and miserably poor is widening, notwithstanding an incipient middle class. Additionally, China's disregard for the global impact of its environmental recklessness, as it seeks double-digit economic growth, will eventually bring orchestrated international condemnation and possibly retaliatory action. These factors and others will eventually exact a price on China and slow its economic growth.

More germane to the issue of terrorism is the likelihood that many states will become even more dangerous breeding grounds for terrorists, as the countries fall further behind the developed world. The report correctly notes that Sub-Saharan Africa will be the most worrisome region in this regard due to economic disruption, population growth and concomitant stresses, civil conflict, and political instability. The report correctly concludes that terrorism will remain a key concern out to at least 2025. Although the report adopts the premise that the allure of terrorism can be mitigated by economic advances, reductions in unemployment among youth, and greater legitimate political participation, it also soberly notes that many potential terrorists are motivated by other factors such as radicalism and martyrdom. Disturbing but accurate, the report notes that the acquisition and use of weapons of mass destruction by terrorists will become increasingly likely in the years ahead. The pursuit of nuclear weapons by a terrorist-sponsoring state such as Iran increases the possibility of biological, radiological, or nuclear weapons falling into the hands of terrorists. Additionally, the possibility of fragile states like Pakistan and North Korea failing and allowing the proliferation of weapons of mass destruction to terrorists, although remote, is very worrisome. Added to this witch's brew is the probability that terrorists in possession of weapons of mass destruction are not likely to be deterred from using them.

In total, the report paints the picture of an exceedingly more complex global security environment in 2025. That environment could well be punctuated by disharmony among traditional states, movements, ideologies, businesses, and other non-state actors. The report provides a substantial basis for its suggestion that the future will bring major discontinuities, shocks, and surprises to the global security environment. They may include a precipitous decline in Western influence, large increase in the power of non-state actors, natural or manmade pandemics, nuclear detonations, disruptive transition to alternative energy sources, and major state-on-state conflict over resources. Clearly, terrorism will remain a key threat to global security in the years ahead. Nonetheless, as the report notes, much can be done to reduce that threat.

DOCUMENT NO. 1

GLOBAL TRENDS 2025: A TRANSFORMED WORLD

The Office of the Director of National Intelligence and The National Intelligence Council NIC 2008-003

November 2008

We prepared ***Global Trends 2025: A Transformed World*** to stimulate strategic thinking about the future by identifying key trends, the factors that drive them, where they seem to be headed, and how they might interact. It uses scenarios to illustrate some of the many ways in which the drivers examined in the study (e.g., globalization, demography, the rise of new powers, the decay of international institutions, climate change, and the geopolitics of energy) may interact to generate challenges and opportunities for future decisionmakers. The study as a whole is more a description of the factors likely to shape events than a prediction of what will actually happen.

By examining a small number of variables that we judge probably will have a disproportionate influence on future events and possibilities, the study seeks to help readers to recognize signposts indicating where events are headed and to identify opportunities for policy intervention to change or lock in the trajectories of specific developments. Among the messages we hope to convey are: "If you like where events seem to be headed, you may want to take timely action to preserve their positive trajectory. If you do not like where they appear to be going, you will have to develop and implement policies to change their trajectory." For example, the report's examination of the transition out of dependence on fossil fuels illustrates how different trajectories will entail different consequences for specific countries. An even more important message is that leadership matters, no trends are immutable, and that timely and well-informed intervention can decrease the likelihood and severity of negative developments and increase the likelihood of positive ones.

Global Trends 2025 is the fourth installment in the National Intelligence Council-led effort to identify key drivers and developments likely to shape world events a decade or more in the future. Both the product and the process used to produce it benefited from lessons learned in previous iterations. Each edition of *Global Trends* has tapped larger and more diverse communities of experts. Our first effort, which looked out to 2010, relied primarily on expertise within the US Intelligence Community. There was some outreach to other elements of the United States Government and the American academic community. For *Global Trends 2015*, we engaged more numerous and more varied groups of non-US Government experts, most of whom were American citizens.

For the third iteration, *Global Trends* 2020, we greatly expanded the participation of non-American specialists by convening six seminars on five continents. We also increased the number and varied the format of meetings in the United States. These sessions enhanced our understanding of both specific trends and drivers and the ways these factors were perceived by experts in different regions of the world.

Each past iteration produced an even more interesting and influential report. Indeed, the worldwide response to *Global Trends 2020* was extraordinary. The report has been translated into several languages, debated in government offices, discussed in university courses, and used as a point of departure in community meetings on international affairs. The report was closely read and constructively criticized by myriad experts and members of the public.

Seeking to capitalize on the interest generated by previous reports and to capture even wider circles of expertise, we modified our processes yet again to produce *Global Trends 2025*. In addition to increasing still more the participation of non-USG experts from the United States and abroad to develop the framework for the current study, we shared several drafts with participants via the Internet and a series of discussion sessions across the US and in several other countries. This iteration of *Global Trends* is the most collaborative yet produced; that collaboration has made it a better product and we are extremely grateful for the time and intellectual energy that literally hundreds of people have devoted to this effort.

As was the case with our previous looks at global trends that will shape the future, the process and spin-off benefits of preparing *Global Trends 2025* were as important as the final product. The ideas generated and insights gained during the preparation of the accompanying report have enriched the work of countless analysts and been incorporated into numerous analytic products published by the National Intelligence Council and other Intelligence Community agencies. Anecdotal evidence indicates they have also influenced the thinking and work of many participants in the process who do not work for the United States Government. We are pleased by and proud of these ancillary benefits and look forward to reaping many more when others have a chance to read and react to this edition of ***Global Trends***.

Many people contributed to the preparation of ***Global Trends 2025***, but no one contributed more than did Mathew Burrows. His intellectual gifts and managerial abilities were critical to the production of this report and everyone involved owes him a huge debt of gratitude. Mat's own note of appreciation on the following page lists others who made especially noteworthy contributions. Many others also made important contributions. We could not have produced this edition of ***Global Trends*** without the support of everyone who participated and we are deeply grateful for the partnerships and the friendships that facilitated and resulted from this collaborative effort.

C. Thomas Fingar

Chairman, National Intelligence Council

Acknowledgements

In preparing this work the National Intelligence Council received immeasurable help from numerous think tanks, consulting firms, academic institutions, and literally hundreds of experts inside and outside governments here in the United States and overseas. We cannot possibly name all the institutions and individuals we consulted but would like to acknowledge a number for their important contributions.

The Atlantic Council of the United States and the Stimson Center were both important for opening doors to institutions abroad and viewpoints that we would not easily have gathered for this project. Dr. William Ralston, Dr. Nick Evans and their team at SRI Consulting Business Intelligence provided needed S & T expertise and guidance. Dr. Alexander Van de Putte of PFC Energy International put together a series of meetings in three regional hubs across the globe to help us begin the process of conceiving and constructing the scenarios. Others involved in that effort include Professor Jean-Pierre Lehmann of the Evian Group at IMD in Lausanne and Peter Schwartz and Doug Randall at the Monitor Group's Global Business Network in San Francisco. Professor Barry Hughes of the University of Denver contributed notably in the scenario construction process and in plotting out the possible trajectories of major powers. Dr. Jacqueline Newmyer and Dr. Stephen Rosen from the Long Term Strategy Group organized three workshops that were critical to advancing our thinking on the complexities of the future security environment and the changing character of conflict. Several individuals and institutions helped organize roundtables to critique drafts or delve deeply into various aspects, including Dr. Geoff Dabelko at the Wilson Center; Dr. Greg Treverton of RAND; Sebastian Mallaby at the Council on Foreign Relations; Carlos Pascual at Brookings; Dr. Michael Auslin at AEI; Professor Christopher Layne at Texas A&M University; Professor Sumit Ganguly at Indiana University and Dr. Robin Niblett and Jonathan Paris at Chatham House in London. Professor John Ikenberry from Princeton's Woodrow Wilson School organized several workshops of prominent international relations scholars, helping us with changing geopolitical trends. Two workshops—one organized by Professor Lanxin Xiang and hosted by CICIR in Beijing, the other organized and hosted by Dr. Bates Gill at SIPRI in Stockholm—were particularly instrumental in gathering international perspectives on strategic challenges facing the world.

Within the United States government, special thanks goes to Julianne Paunescu from the State Department's Bureau of Intelligence and Research (INR). In helping us at every step of the way, she and her team fulfilled their mandate spearheading intelligence community outreach to nongovernmental experts in an outstanding manner. Marilyn Maines and her experts at NSA provided essential expertise on S&T and organized workshops with Toffler Associates to delve more deeply into future trends. The NIC's Analysis and Production staff, including Elizabeth Arens' deft editorial hand, provided essential support.

The 2025 Global Landscape

Relative Certainties	Likely Impact
A global multipolar system is emerging with the rise of China, India, and others. The relative power of nonstate actors—businesses, tribes, religious organizations, and even criminal networks—also will increase.	By 2025 a single "international community" composed of nation-states will no longer exist. Power will be more dispersed with the newer players bringing new rules of the game while risks will increase that the traditional Western alliances will weaken. Rather than emulating Western models of political and economic development, more countries may be attracted to China's alternative development model.
The unprecedented shift in relative wealth and economic power roughly from West to East now under way will continue.	As some countries become more invested in their economic well-being, incentives toward geopolitical stability could increase. However, the transfer is strengthening states like Russia that want to challenge the Western order.
The United States will remain the single most powerful country but will be less dominant.	Shrinking economic and military capabilities may force the US into a difficult set of tradeoffs between domestic versus foreign policy priorities.

Relative Certainties	Likely Impact
Continued economic growth—coupled with 1.2 billion more people by 2025—will put pressure on energy, food, and water resources.	The pace of technological innovation will be key to outcomes during this period. All current technologies are inadequate for replacing traditional energy architecture on the scale needed.
The number of countries with youthful populations in the "arc of instability"[1] will decrease, but the populations of several youth-bulge states are projected to remain on rapid growth trajectories.	Unless employment conditions change dramatically in parlous youth-bulge states such as Afghanistan, Nigeria, Pakistan, and Yemen, these countries will remain ripe for continued instability and state failure.
The potential for conflict will increase owing to rapid changes in parts of the greater Middle East and the spread of lethal capabilities.	The need for the US to act as regional balancer in the Middle East will increase, although other outside powers—Russia, China and India—will play greater roles than today.
Terrorism is unlikely to disappear by 2025, but its appeal could lessen if economic growth continues in the Middle East and youth unemployment is reduced. For those terrorists that are active the diffusion of technologies will put dangerous capabilities within their reach.	Opportunities for mass-casualty terrorist attacks using chemical, biological, or less likely, nuclear weapons will increase as technology diffuses and nuclear power (and possibly weapons) programs expand. The practical and psychological consequences of such attacks will intensify in an increasingly globalized world.

Key Uncertainties	Potential Consequences
Whether an energy transition away from oil and gas—supported by improved energy storage, biofuels, and clean coal—is completed during the 2025 time frame.	With high oil and gas prices, major exporters such as Russia and Iran will substantially augment their levels of national power, with Russia's GDP potentially approaching that of the UK and France. A sustained plunge in prices, perhaps underpinned by a fundamental switch to new energy sources, could trigger a long-term decline for producers as global and regional players.
How quickly climate change occurs and the locations where its impact is most pronounced.	Climate change is likely to exacerbate resource scarcities, particularly water scarcities.
Whether mercantilism stages a comeback and global markets recede.	Descending into a world of resource nationalism increases the risk of great power confrontations.
Whether advances toward democracy occur in China and Russia.	Political pluralism seems less likely in Russia in the absence of economic diversification. A growing middle class increases the chances of political liberalization and potentially greater nationalism in China.

[1] Countries with youthful age structures and rapidly growing populations mark a crescent or "arc of instability" stretching from the Andean region of Latin America across Sub-Saharan Africa, the Middle East and the Caucasus, and through the northern parts of South Asia.

Key Uncertainties	Potential Consequences
Whether regional fears about a nuclear-armed Iran trigger an arms race and greater militarization.	Episodes of low-intensity conflict and terrorism taking place under a nuclear umbrella could lead to an unintended escalation and broader conflict.
Whether the greater Middle East becomes more stable, especially whether Iraq stabilizes, and whether the Arab-Israeli conflict is resolved peacefully.	Turbulence is likely to increase under most scenarios. Revival of economic growth, a more prosperous Iraq, and resolution of the Israeli-Palestinian dispute could engender some stability as the region deals with a strengthening Iran and global transition away from oil and gas.
Whether Europe and Japan overcome economic and social challenges caused or compounded by demography.	Successful integration of Muslim minorities in Europe could expand the size of the productive work forces and avert social crisis. Lack of efforts by Europe and Japan to mitigate demographic challenges could lead to long-term declines.
Whether global powers work with multilateral institutions to adapt their structure and performance to the transformed geopolitical landscape.	Emerging powers show ambivalence toward global institutions like the UN and IMF, but this could change as they become bigger players on the global stage. Asian integration could lead to more powerful regional institutions. NATO faces stiff challenges in meeting growing out-of-area responsibilities with declining European military capabilities. Traditional alliances will weaken.

Executive Summary

The **international system**—as constructed following the Second World War—will be almost unrecognizable by 2025 owing to the rise of emerging powers, a globalizing economy, an historic transfer of relative wealth and economic power from West to East, and the growing influence of nonstate actors. By 2025, the international system will be a **global multipolar one** with gaps in national power[2] continuing to narrow between developed and developing countries. Concurrent with the shift in power among nation-states, the relative power of various nonstate actors—including businesses, tribes, religious organizations, and criminal networks—is increasing. The players are changing, but so too are the scope and breadth of transnational issues important for continued global prosperity. Aging populations in the developed world; growing energy, food, and water

[2] National power scores, computed by the International Futures computer model, are the product of an index combining the weighted factors of GDP, defense spending, population, and technology.

constraints; and worries about climate change will limit and diminish what will still be an historically unprecedented age of prosperity.

Historically, emerging multipolar systems have been more unstable than bipolar or unipolar ones. Despite the recent financial volatility—which could end up accelerating many ongoing trends—we do not believe that we are headed toward a complete breakdown of the international system, as occurred in 1914–1918 when an earlier phase of globalization came to a halt. However, the next 20 years of transition to a new system are fraught with risks. Strategic rivalries are most likely to revolve around trade, investments, and technological innovation and acquisition, but we cannot rule out a 19th century-like scenario of arms races, territorial expansion, and military rivalries.

This is a story with **no clear outcome**, as illustrated by a series of vignettes we use to map out divergent futures. Although the United States is likely to remain the single most powerful actor, the United States' relative strength—even in the military realm—will decline and US leverage will become more constrained. At the same time, the extent to which other actors—both state and nonstate—will be willing or able to shoulder increased burdens is unclear. Policymakers and publics will have to cope with a growing demand for multilateral cooperation when the international system will be stressed by the incomplete transition from the old to a still-forming new order.

Economic Growth Fueling Rise of Emerging Players

In terms of size, speed, and directional flow, the transfer of **global wealth and economic power** now under way—roughly from West to East—is without precedent in modern history. This shift derives from two sources. First, increases in oil and commodity prices have generated windfall profits for the Gulf states and Russia. Second, lower costs combined with government policies have shifted the locus of manufacturing and some service industries to Asia.

Growth projections for Brazil, Russia, India, and China (the BRICs) indicate they will collectively match the original G-7's share of global GDP by 2040–2050. **China** is poised to have more impact on the world over the next 20 years than any other country. If current trends persist, by 2025 China will have the world's second largest economy and will be a leading military power. It also could be the largest importer of natural resources and the biggest polluter. **India** probably will continue to enjoy relatively rapid economic growth and will strive for a multipolar world in which New Delhi is one of the poles. China and India must decide the extent to which they are willing and capable of playing increasing global roles and how each will relate to the other. **Russia** has the potential to be richer, more powerful, and more self-assured in 2025 if it invests in human capital, expands and diversifies its economy, and integrates with global markets. On the other hand, Russia could experience a significant decline if it fails to take these steps and oil and gas prices remain in the $50–70 per barrel range. No other countries are projected to rise to the level of China, India, or Russia, and none is likely to match their individual global clout. We expect, however, to see the political and economic power of other countries—such as Indonesia, Iran, and Turkey—increase.

For the most part, China, India, and Russia are not following the Western liberal model for self-development but instead are using a different model, "**state capitalism.**" State capitalism is a loose term used to describe a system of economic management that gives a prominent role to the state. Other rising powers—South Korea, Taiwan, and Singapore—also used state capitalism to develop their economies. However, the impact of Russia, and particularly China, following this path is potentially much greater owing to their size and approach to "democratization." We remain optimistic about the *long-term* prospects for **greater democratization**, even though advances are likely to be slow and globalization is subjecting many recently democratized countries to increasing social and economic pressures with the potential to undermine liberal institutions.

Many other countries will fall further behind economically. **Sub-Saharan Africa** will remain the region most vulnerable to economic disruption, population stresses, civil conflict, and political instability. Despite increased global demand for commodities for which Sub-Saharan Africa will be a major supplier, local populations are unlikely to experience significant economic gain. Windfall profits arising from sustained increases in commodity prices might further entrench corrupt or otherwise ill-equipped governments in several regions, diminishing the prospects for democratic and market-based reforms. Although many of **Latin America's** major countries will have become middle income powers by 2025, others, particularly those such as Venezuela and Bolivia that have embraced populist policies for a protracted period, will lag behind—and some, such as Haiti, will have become even poorer and less governable. Overall, Latin America will continue to lag behind Asia and other fast-growing areas in terms of economic competitiveness.

Asia, Africa, and Latin America will account for virtually all **population growth** over the next 20 years; less than 3 percent of the growth will occur in the West. Europe and Japan will continue to far outdistance the emerging powers of China and India in per capita wealth, but they will struggle to maintain robust growth rates because the size of their working-age populations will decrease. The US will be a partial exception to the aging of populations in the developed world because it will experience higher birth rates and more immigration. The number of migrants seeking to move from disadvantaged to relatively privileged countries is likely to increase.

The number of countries with youthful age structures in the current "arc of instability" is projected to decline by as much as 40 percent. Three of every four youth-bulge countries that remain will be located in Sub-Saharan Africa; nearly all of the remainder will be located in the core of the Middle East, scattered through southern and central Asia, and in the Pacific Islands.

New Transnational Agenda

Resource issues will gain prominence on the international agenda. Unprecedented global economic growth—positive in so many other regards—will continue to put pressure on a number of **highly strategic resources**, including energy, food, and water, and demand is projected to outstrip easily available supplies over the next decade or so. For example, non-OPEC liquid hydrocarbon production—crude oil, natural gas liquids, and unconventionals such as tar sands—will not grow commensurate with demand. Oil and gas production of many traditional energy producers already is declining. Elsewhere—in China, India, and Mexico—production has flattened. Countries capable of significantly expanding production will dwindle; oil and gas production will be concentrated in unstable areas. As a result of this and other factors, the world will be in the midst of a fundamental energy transition away from oil toward natural gas, coal and other alternatives.

The World Bank estimates that **demand for food** will rise by 50 percent by 2030, as a result of growing world population, rising affluence, and the shift to Western dietary preferences by a larger middle class. Lack of access to stable supplies of water is reaching critical proportions, particularly for agricultural purposes, and the problem will worsen because of rapid urbanization worldwide and the roughly 1.2 billion persons to be added over the next 20 years. Today, experts consider 21 countries, with a combined population of about 600 million, to be either cropland or freshwater scarce. Owing to continuing population growth, 36 countries, with about 1.4 billion people, are projected to fall into this category by 2025.

Climate change is expected to exacerbate resource scarcities. Although the impact of climate change will vary by region, a number of regions will begin to suffer harmful effects, particularly water scarcity and loss of agricultural production. Regional differences in agricultural production are likely to become more pronounced over time with declines disproportionately concentrated in developing countries, particularly those in Sub-Saharan Africa. Agricultural losses are expected to mount with substantial impacts forecast by most economists by late this century. For many developing countries, decreased agricultural output will be devastating because agriculture accounts for a large share of their economies and many of their citizens live close to subsistence levels.

New technologies could again provide solutions, such as viable alternatives to fossil fuels or means to overcome food and water constraints. However, all current technologies are inadequate for replacing the traditional energy architecture on the scale needed, and new energy technologies probably will not be commercially viable and widespread by 2025. The pace of technological innovation will be key. Even with a favorable policy and funding environment for biofuels, clean coal, or hydrogen, the transition to new fuels will be slow. Major technologies historically have had an "adoption lag." In the energy sector, a recent study found that it takes an average of 25 years for a new production technology to become widely adopted.

Despite what are seen as long odds now, we cannot rule out the possibility of an **energy transition** by 2025 that would avoid the costs of an energy infrastructure overhaul. The greatest possibility for a relatively quick and inexpensive transition during the period comes from better renewable generation sources (photovoltaic and wind) and improvements in battery technology. With many of these technologies, the infrastructure cost hurdle for individual projects would be lower, enabling many small economic actors to develop their own energy transformation projects that directly serve their interests—e.g., stationary fuel cells powering homes and offices, recharging plug-in hybrid autos, and selling energy back to the grid. Also, energy conversion schemes—such as plans to generate hydrogen for automotive fuel cells from electricity in the homeowner's garage—could avoid the need to develop complex hydrogen transportation infrastructure.

Prospects for Terrorism, Conflict, and Proliferation

Terrorism, proliferation, and conflict will remain key concerns even as resource issues move up on the international agenda. Terrorism is unlikely to disappear by 2025, but its appeal could diminish if economic growth continues and youth unemployment is mitigated in the Middle East. Economic opportunities for youth and greater political pluralism probably would dissuade some from joining terrorists' ranks, but others—motivated by a variety of factors, such as a desire for revenge or to become "martyrs"—will continue to turn to violence to pursue their objectives.

In the absence of employment opportunities and legal means for political expression, conditions will be ripe for disaffection, growing radicalism, and possible recruitment of youths into **terrorist groups**. Terrorist groups in 2025 will likely be a combination of descendants of long-established groups—that inherit organizational structures, command and control processes, and training procedures necessary to conduct sophisticated attacks—and newly emergent collections of the angry and disenfranchised that become self-radicalized. For those terrorist groups that are active in 2025, the diffusion of technologies and scientific knowledge will place some of the world's most dangerous capabilities within their reach. One of our greatest concerns continues to be that terrorist or other malevolent groups might acquire and employ biological agents, or less likely, a nuclear device, to create mass casualties.

Although **Iran's** acquisition of nuclear weapons is not inevitable, other countries' worries about a nuclear-armed Iran could lead states in the region to develop new security arrangements with external powers, acquire additional weapons, and consider pursuing their own nuclear ambitions. It is not clear that the type of stable deterrent relationship that existed between the great powers for most of the Cold War would emerge naturally in the Middle East with a nuclear-weapons capable Iran. Episodes of low-intensity conflict taking place under a nuclear umbrella could lead to an unintended escalation and broader conflict if clear red lines between those states involved are not well established.

We believe **ideological conflicts** akin to the Cold War are unlikely to take root in a world in which most states will be preoccupied with the pragmatic challenges of globalization and shifting global power alignments. The force of ideology is likely to be strongest in the Muslim world—particularly the Arab core. In those countries that are likely to struggle with youth bulges and weak economic underpinnings—such as Pakistan, Afghanistan, Nigeria, and Yemen—the radical Salafi trend of Islam is likely to gain traction.

Types of **conflict** we have not seen for awhile—such as over resources—could reemerge. Perceptions of energy scarcity will drive countries to take actions to assure their future access to energy supplies. In the worst case, this could result in interstate conflicts if government leaders deem assured access to energy resources, for example, to be essential for maintaining domestic stability and the survival of their regimes. However, even actions short of war will have important geopolitical consequences. Maritime security concerns are providing a rationale for naval buildups and modernization efforts, such as China's and India's development of blue-water naval capabilities. The buildup of regional naval capabilities could lead to increased tensions, rivalries, and counterbalancing moves but it also will create opportunities for multinational cooperation in protecting critical sea lanes. With water becoming more scarce in Asia and the Middle East, cooperation to manage changing water resources is likely to become more difficult within and between states.

The risk of **nuclear weapon use** over the next 20 years, although remaining very low, is likely to be greater than it is today as a result of several converging trends. The spread of nuclear technologies and expertise is generating concerns about the potential emergence of new nuclear weapon states and the acquisition of nuclear materials by terrorist groups. Ongoing low-intensity clashes between India and Pakistan continue to raise the specter that such events could escalate to a broader conflict between those nuclear powers. The possibility of a future disruptive regime change or collapse occurring in a nuclear weapon state such as North Korea also continues to raise questions regarding the ability of weak states to control and secure their nuclear arsenals.

If nuclear weapons are used in the next 15–20 years, the international system will be shocked as it experiences immediate humanitarian, economic, and political-military repercussions. A future use of nuclear weapons probably would bring about significant geopolitical changes as some states would seek to establish or reinforce security alliances with existing nuclear powers and others would push for global nuclear disarmament.

A More Complex International System

The trend toward greater diffusion of authority and power that has been occurring for a couple decades is likely to accelerate because of the emergence of new global players, the worsening institutional deficit, potential expansion of regional blocs, and enhanced strength of nonstate actors and networks. The **multiplicity of actors** on the international scene could add strength— in terms of filling gaps left by aging post-World War II institutions—or further fragment the international system and incapacitate international cooperation. The diversity in type of actor raises the likelihood of fragmentation occurring over the next two decades, particularly given the wide array of transnational challenges facing the international community.

The rising BRIC powers are unlikely to challenge the international system as did Germany and Japan in the 19th and 20th centuries, but because of their growing geopolitical and economic clout, they will have a high degree of freedom to customize their political and economic policies rather than fully adopting Western norms. They also are likely to want to preserve their policy freedom to maneuver, allowing others to carry the primary burden for dealing with such issues as terrorism, climate change, proliferation, and energy security.

Existing multilateral institutions—which are large and cumbersome and were designed for a different geopolitical order—will have difficulty adapting quickly to undertake new missions, accommodate changing memberships, and augment their resources.

Nongovernmental organizations (NGOs)—concentrating on specific issues—increasingly will be a part of the landscape, but NGO networks are likely to be limited in their ability to effect change in the absence of concerted efforts by multilateral institutions or governments. Efforts at greater inclusiveness—to reflect the emergence of the newer powers—may make it harder for international organizations to tackle transnational challenges. Respect for the dissenting views of member nations will continue to shape the agenda of organizations and limit the kinds of solutions that can be attempted.

Greater **Asian regionalism**—possible by 2025—would have global implications, sparking or reinforcing a trend toward three trade and financial clusters that could become quasi-blocs: North America, Europe, and East Asia. Establishment of such quasi-blocs would have implications for the ability to achieve future global World Trade Organization (WTO) agreements. Regional clusters could compete in setting trans-regional product standards for information technology, biotechnology, nanotechnology, intellectual property rights, and other aspects of the "new economy." On the other hand, an absence of regional cooperation in Asia could help spur competition among China, India, and Japan over resources such as energy.

Intrinsic to the growing complexity of the overlapping roles of states, institutions, and nonstate actors is the **proliferation of political identities**, which is leading to establishment of new networks and rediscovered communities. No one political identity is likely to be dominant in most societies by 2025. Religion-based networks may be quintessential issue networks and overall may play a more powerful role on many transnational issues such as the environment and inequalities than secular groupings.

The United States: Less Dominant Power

By 2025 the US will find itself as one of a number of important actors on the world stage, albeit still the most powerful one. Even in the military realm, where the US will continue to possess considerable advantages in 2025, advances by others in science and technology, expanded adoption of irregular warfare tactics by both state and nonstate actors, proliferation of long-range precision weapons, and growing use of cyber warfare attacks increasingly will constrict US freedom of action. A more constrained US role has implications for others and the likelihood of new agenda issues being tackled effectively. Despite the recent rise in anti-Americanism, the US probably will continue to be seen as a much-needed regional balancer in the Middle East and Asia. The US will continue to be expected to play a significant role in using its military power to counter global terrorism. On newer security issues like climate change, US leadership will be widely perceived as critical to leveraging competing and divisive views to find solutions. At the same time, the multiplicity of influential actors and distrust of vast power means less room for the US to call the shots without the support of strong partnerships. Developments in the rest of the world, including internal developments in a number of key states—particularly China and Russia—are also likely to be crucial determinants of US policy.

2025—What Kind of Future?

The above trends suggest major **discontinuities**, shocks, and surprises, which we highlight throughout the text. Examples include nuclear weapons use or a pandemic. In some cases, the surprise element is only a matter of **timing**: an energy transition, for example is inevitable; the only questions are when and how abruptly or smoothly such a transition occurs. An energy transition from one type of fuel (fossil fuels) to another (alternative) is an event that historically has only happened once a century at most with momentous consequences. The transition from wood to coal helped trigger industrialization. In this case, a transition—particularly an abrupt one—out of fossil fuels would have major repercussions for energy producers in the Middle East and Eurasia, potentially causing permanent decline of some states as global and regional powers.

Other discontinuities are less predictable. They are likely to result from an interaction of several trends and depend on the quality of leadership. We put uncertainties such as whether China or Russia becomes a democracy in this category. China's growing middle class increases the chances but does not make such a development inevitable. Political pluralism seems less likely in Russia in the absence of economic diversification. Pressure from below may force the issue, or a leader might begin or enhance the democratization process to sustain the economy or spur economic growth. A sustained plunge in the price of oil and gas would alter the outlook and increase prospects for greater political and economic liberalization in Russia. If either country were to democratize, it would represent another wave of democratization with wide significance for many other developing states.

Also **uncertain** are the outcomes of demographic challenges facing Europe, Japan, and even Russia. In none of these cases does demography have to spell destiny with less regional and global power an inevitable outcome. Technology, the role of immigration, public health improvements, and laws encouraging greater female participation in the economy are some of the measures that could change the trajectory of current trends pointing toward less economic growth, increased social tensions, and possible decline.

Whether global institutions adapt and revive—another key uncertainty—also is a function of leadership. Current trends suggest a dispersion of power and authority will create a global governance deficit. Reversing those trend lines would require strong leadership in the international community by a number of powers, including the emerging ones.

Some uncertainties would have greater consequences—should they occur—than would others. In this work, we emphasize the overall potential for greater conflict—some forms of which could threaten globalization. We put WMD terrorism and a Middle East nuclear arms race in this category. The key uncertainties and possible impacts are discussed in the text and summarized in the textbox on page vii. In the four fictionalized scenarios, we have highlighted new challenges that could emerge as a result of the ongoing global transformation. They present new situations, dilemmas, or predicaments that represent departures from recent developments. As a set, they do not cover all possible futures. ***None of these is inevitable or even necessarily likely***; but, as with many other uncertainties, the scenarios are potential game-changers.

- In ***A World Without the West***, the new powers supplant the West as the leaders on the world stage.
- ***October Surprise*** illustrates the impact of inattention to global climate change; unexpected major impacts narrow the world's range of options.
- In ***BRICs' Bust-Up***, disputes over vital resources emerge as a source of conflict between major powers—in this case two emerging heavyweights—India and China.
- In ***Politics is Not Always Local***, nonstate networks emerge to set the international agenda on the environment, eclipsing governments.

Introduction

The international system—as constructed following the Second World War—will be almost unrecognizable by 2025. Indeed, "international system" is a misnomer as it is likely to be more ramshackle than orderly, its composition hybrid and heterogeneous as befits a transition that will still be a work in progress in 2025. The transformation is being fueled by a globalizing economy, marked by an historic shift of relative wealth and economic power from West to East, and by the increasing weight of new players—especially China and India. The US will remain the single most important actor but will be less dominant. As was true of the United States in the 19th and 20th centuries, China and India will at times be reticent and at other times impatient to assume larger roles on the world stage. In 2025, both will still be more concerned about their own internal development than changing the international system.

Concurrent with the shift in power among nation-states, the ***relative*** power of various nonstate actors—including businesses, tribes, religious organizations, and even criminal networks—will continue to increase. Several countries could even be "taken over" and run by criminal networks. In areas of Africa or South Asia, states as we know them might wither away, owing to the inability of governments to provide for basic needs, including security.

By 2025, the international community will be composed of many actors in addition to nation-states and will lack an overarching approach to global governance. The "system" will be multipolar with many clusters of both state and nonstate actors. Multipolar international systems—like the Concert of Europe—have existed in the past, but the one that is emerging is unprecedented because it is global and encompasses a mix of state and nonstate actors that are not grouped into rival camps of roughly equal weight. The most salient characteristics of the "new order" will be the shift from a unipolar world dominated by the United States to a relatively unstructured hierarchy of old powers and rising nations, and the diffusion of power from state to nonstate actors.

History tells us that rapid change brings many dangers. Despite the recent financial volatility, which could end up accelerating many ongoing trends, we do not believe that we are headed toward a complete breakdown—as occurred in 1914–1918 when an earlier phase of globalization came to a halt. However, the next 20 years of transition toward a new international system are fraught with risks—more than we envisaged when we published ***Mapping the Global Future***[3] in 2004. These risks include the growing prospect of a nuclear arms race in the Middle East and possible interstate conflicts over resources. The breadth of transnational issues requiring attention also is increasing to include issues connected with resource constraints in energy, food, and water; and worries about climate change. Global institutions that could help the world deal with these transnational issues and, more generally, mitigate the risks of rapid change currently appear incapable of rising to the challenges without concerted efforts by their leaders.

[3] See ***Mapping the Global Future: Report of the National Intelligence Council's 2020 Project,*** National Intelligence Council, December 2004, which can be found at: www.dni.gov/nic/NIC_2020_project.html.

Comparison Between *Mapping the Global Future: Report of the Intelligence Council's 2020 Project* and *Global Trends 2025: A Transformed World*

The most dramatic difference between ***Mapping the Global Future: Report of the Intelligence Council's 2020 Project*** and ***Global Trends 2025: A Transformed World*** is the latter's assumptions of a multipolar future, and therefore dramatic changes in the international system. The 2025 report describes a world in which the US plays a prominent role in global events, but the US is one among many global actors who manage problems. In contrast, the 2020 report projects continued US dominance, positing that most major powers have forsaken the idea of balancing the US.

The two documents also differ in their treatment of energy supply, demand, and new alternative sources. In 2020, energy supplies "in the ground" are considered "sufficient to meet global demand." What is uncertain, according to the earlier report, is whether political instability in producer countries, supply disruptions, or competition for resources might deleteriously affect international oil markets. Though 2020 mentions the global increase in energy consumption, it emphasizes the domination of fossil fuels. In contrast, 2025 sees the world in the midst of a transition to cleaner fuels. New technologies are projected to provide the capability for fossil fuel substitutes and solutions to water and food scarcity. The 2020 report acknowledges that energy demands will influence superpower relations, but the 2025 report considers energy scarcity as a driving factor in geopolitics.

Both reports project probable strong global economic growth—fueled by the rise of Brazil, Russia, India, and China, absent major shocks. The 2025 report, however, assesses the likelihood of major discontinuities to be high, emphasizing that "no single outcome seems preordained" and that the next 20 years of transition toward a new international system are fraught with risks, such as a nuclear arms race in the Middle East and possible interstate conflicts over resources.

The scenarios in both reports address the future of globalization, the future structure of the international system, and the dividing lines among groups that will cause conflict or convergence. In both reports, globalization is seen as a driver so pervasive that it will reorder current divisions based on geography, ethnicity, and religious and socio-economic status.

More Change than Continuity

The rapidly changing international order at a time of growing geopolitical challenges increases the likelihood of discontinuities, shocks, and surprises. No single outcome seems preordained: the Western model of economic liberalism, democracy, and secularism, for example, which many assumed to be inevitable, may lose its luster—at least in the medium term.

In some cases, the surprise element is only a matter of timing: an energy transition, for example, is inevitable; the only questions are when and how abruptly or smoothly such a transition occurs. Other discontinuities are less predictable. Recognizing that what may seem implausible today could become feasible or even likely by 2025, we have looked at a number of single development "shocks." Examples include the global impact of a nuclear arms exchange, a rapid replacement for fossil fuels, and a "democratic" China.

New technologies could provide solutions, such as viable alternatives to fossil fuel or means to overcome food and water constraints. A critical uncertainty is whether new technologies will be developed and commercialized in time to avert a significant slowdown in economic growth owing to resource constraints. Such a slowdown would jeopardize the rise of new powers and deal a serious blow to the aspirations of those countries not yet fully in the globalization game. A world in which shortages predominate could trigger behaviors diferent from one in which scarcities are overcome through technology or other means.

Alternative Futures

This study is organized into seven sections that examine:

- The Globalizing Economy.
- Demographics of Discord.
- The New Players.
- Scarcity in the Midst of Plenty.
- Growing Potential for Conflict.
- Will the International System Be Up to the Challenges?
- Power-Sharing in a Multipolar World.

As with our previous works, we will describe possible alternative futures that could result from the trends we discuss.[4] We see the next 15–20 years as one of those great historical turning points where multiple factors are likely to be in play. How such factors intersect with one another and the role of leadership will be crucial to the outcome.

[4] See *Global Trends 2015, A Dialogue About the Future with Nongovernment Experts,* National Intelligence Council, December 2000; and *Mapping the Global Future: Report of the National Intelligence Council's 2020 Project,* National Intelligence Council, December 2004. The reports can be found at www.dni.gov/nic/NIC_global trends 2015.html and www.dni.gov/nic/NIC_2020_project.html respectively.

In constructing these scenarios, we focused on critical uncertainties regarding the relative importance of the nation-state as compared with nonstate actors, and the level of global cooperation. In some of the scenarios, states are more dominant and drive global dynamics; in others, nonstate actors, including religious movements, nongovernmental organizations (NGOs), and super-empowered individuals play more important roles. In some of the scenarios, key players interact in competing groups, through partnerships and cross-border affiliations. Other scenarios envision more interaction as autonomous players operate independently and sometimes conflict with one another.

In all the ***fictionalized scenarios***, we highlight challenges that could emerge as a result of the ongoing global transformation. The scenarios present new situations, dilemmas, or predicaments that would cause upheavals in the global landscape, leading to very different "worlds." ***None of these is inevitable or even necessarily likely***; but, as with many other uncertainties, they are potential game-changers.

A World Without the West. In this world, described in a fictional letter from a future head of the Shanghai Cooperation Organization (SCO), new powers supplant the West as the leaders on the world stage. The US feels overburdened and withdraws from Central Asia, including Afghanistan; Europe will not step up to the plate and take the lead. Russia, China, and others are forced to deal with the potential for spillover and instability in Central Asia. The SCO gains ascendance while NATO's status declines. Anti-China antagonism in the US and Europe reaches a crescendo; protectionist trade barriers are put in place. Russia and China enter a marriage of convenience; other countries—India and Iran—rally around them. The lack of any stable bloc—whether in the West or the non-Western world—adds to growing instability and disorder, potentially threatening globalization.

October Surprise. In this world, depicted in a diary entry of a future US President, many countries have been preoccupied with achieving economic growth at the expense of safeguarding the environment. The scientific community has not been able to issue specific warnings, but worries increase that a tipping point has been reached in which climate change has accelerated and possible impacts will be very destructive. New York City is hit by a major hurricane linked to global climate change; the NY Stock Exchange is severely damaged and, in the face of such destruction, world leaders must begin to think about taking drastic measures, such as relocating parts of coastal cities.

BRICs' Bust-Up. In this world, conflict breaks out between China and India over access to vital resources. Outside powers intervene before the conflict escalates and expands into a global conflagration. The clash is triggered by

Chinese suspicion of efforts by others to threaten Beijing's energy supplies. Misperceptions and miscalculations lead to the clash. The scenario highlights the importance of energy and other resources to continued growth and development as a great power. It shows the extent to which conflict in a multipolar world is just as likely to occur between rising states as between older and newer powers.

Politics is Not Always Local. In this world, outlined in an article by a fictional ***Financial Times*** reporter, various nonstate networks—NGOs, religious groups, business leaders, and local activists—combine to set the international agenda on the environment and use their clout to elect the UN Secretary General. The global political coalition of nonstate actors plays a crucial role in securing a new worldwide climate change agreement. In this new connected world of digital communications, growing middle classes, and transnational interest groups, politics is no longer local and domestic and international agendas become increasingly interchangeable.

Long-Range Projections: A Cautionary Tale

In the 20th century, experts forecasting the next 20 years—roughly the time frame of this study—often missed major geopolitical events, basing their predictions largely on linear projections without exploring possibilities that could cause discontinuities. Before WW I, while tensions between European "great powers" were on the rise, few had an inkling of major changes in the offing, from the extent of mutual slaughter to the downfall of age-old empires. In the early 1920s, few envisioned the lethal situation about to unfold, ushered in by the Great Depression, Stalin's gulags, and an even more bloody world war encompassing multiple genocides. The postwar period saw the establishment of a new international system—many of whose institutions—the UN and Bretton Woods—remain with us. Although the bipolar and nuclear age did not lack war and conflict, it did provide a stable framework until the collapse of the Soviet Union. The development of a globalized economy in which China and India play major roles has opened a new era without clear outcomes.

Lessons from the last century, however, appear to suggest:

- **Leaders and their ideas matter.** No history of the past hundred years can be told without delving into the roles and thinking of such leaders as Vladimir Lenin, Josef Stalin, Adolf Hitler or Mao Zedong. The actions of dominating leaders are the hardest element to anticipate. At several junctures in the 20th century, Western experts thought liberal and market ideas had triumphed. As demonstrated by the impacts of Churchill, Roosevelt, and Truman, leadership is key even in societies where institutions are strong and the maneuvering room for wielding personal power is more constrained.

- **Economic volatility introduces a major risk factor.** Historians and social scientists have discovered a strong correlation between rapid economic change—both positive and negative—and political instability. The massive dislocation and economic volatility introduced by the end of the "first" globalization in 1914–1918 and the rise of protectionist barriers in the 1920s and 1930s, combined with the lingering resentments over the Versailles peace settlement, laid the groundwork for WW II. The collapse of multinational and ethnic empires—begun after WW I and continuing with the end of the colonial empires in the post-WW II period—also unleashed a long series of national and ethnic conflicts that reverberates today. Today's globalization also has spurred the movement of people, disrupting traditional social and geographic boundaries.
- **Geopolitical rivalries trigger discontinuities more than does technological change.** Many stress the role of technology in bringing about radical change and there is no question it has been a major driver. We—as others—have oftentimes underestimated its impact. However, over the past century, geopolitical rivalries and their consequences have been more significant causes of the multiple wars, collapse of empires, and rise of new powers than technology alone.

Chapter 1
The Globalizing Economy

In terms of size, speed, and directional flow, the global shift in relative wealth and economic power now under way—roughly from West to East—is without precedent in modern history. This shift derives from two key sources. First, sustained increases in oil and commodity prices have generated windfall profits for the Gulf states and Russia. Second, relatively low labor costs combined with certain government policies have shifted the locus of manufacturing and some service industries to Asia. Strong global demand for these products has made for wide economies of scale margins across Asia, particularly in China and India. These shifts in demand and supply are deep and structural, which suggests that the resulting transfer of economic power we are witnessing is likely to endure. These shifts are the driving force behind globalization that—as we underlined in our ***Mapping the Global Future*** report—is a meta-trend, transforming historic patterns of economic flows and underlying stocks, creating pressures for rebalancing that are painful for both rich and poor countries.

Although this transfer is not zero-sum, early losers such as most of Latin America (with the exception of Brazil and a few others) and Africa are receiving neither a stake in the initial asset transfer nor any significant inbound investment from the recipient countries. Certain industrialized states such as Japan also appear increasingly challenged by inchoate financial links among these emerging markets. The US and Eurozone are receiving much of this emerging market liquidity, but whether they will benefit relative to their current position depends on several factors, including the ability of Western countries to reduce oil consumption and demand, the ability of these states to capitalize on a favorable export climate in sectors of comparative strength, such as technology and services, and the domestic policies of recipient states, particularly on issues of monetary policy and openness to foreign investment.

Back to the Future

Asia's economic powerhouses—China and India—are restoring the positions they held two centuries ago when China produced approximately 30 percent and India 15 percent of the world's wealth. China and India, for the first time since the 18th century, are set to be the largest contributors to worldwide economic growth. These two countries will likely surpass the GDP of all other economies except the US and Japan by 2025, but they will continue to lag in per capita income for decades. The years around 2025 will be characterized by the "dual identity" of these Asian giants: powerful, but many individual Chinese or Indians feeling relatively poor compared to Westerners.

Growth projections for Brazil, Russia, India, and China have them collectively matching the original G-7's share of global GDP by 2040–2050. According to these same projections, the eight largest economies in 2025 will be, in descending order: the US, China, India, Japan, Germany, the UK, and France, and Russia.

China, especially, has emerged as a new financial heavyweight, claiming $2 trillion in foreign exchange reserves in 2008. Rapidly developing countries, including China and Russia, have created sovereign wealth funds (SWFs)[5] with the aim of using their hundreds of billions of dollars' worth of assets to achieve higher returns to help them weather economic storms. Some of these funds will return to the West in the form of investments, thereby promoting greater productivity and economic competitiveness.

[5] Sovereign wealth funds (SWFs) constitute capital generated from government surpluses and invested in private markets abroad. Since 2005, the number of states with SWFs has grown from three to over 40, and the aggregate sum under their control from around $700 billion to $3 trillion. The range of functions served by SWFs also has expanded, as many of the states that created them recently have done so out of a desire to perpetuate current account surpluses, or to cultivate intergenerational savings, rather than to buffer commodity market volatility. Should current trends hold, SWFs will swell to over $6.5 trillion within five years, and to $12-15 trillion within a decade, exceeding total fiscal reserves and comprising some 20 percent of all global capitalization.

However, foreign direct investment (FDI) by emerging powers in the developing world is increasing significantly.

A generation of globally competitive companies is emerging from the new powers, helping to further solidify their position in the global marketplace; from Brazil in agribusiness and offshore energy exploration; Russia in energy and metals; India in IT services, pharmaceuticals, and auto parts; and China in steel, home appliances, and telecommunications equipment. Of the top 100 new global corporate leaders from the non-OECD world listed in a 2006 report from The Boston Consulting Group, 84 were headquartered in Brazil, Russia, China and India.

Growing Middle Class

We are witnessing an unprecedented moment in human history: never before have so many been lifted out of extreme poverty as is happening today. A stunning 135 million people escaped dire poverty between 1999 and 2004 alone—more than the population of Japan and almost as many as live in Russia today.

Over the next several decades the number of people considered to be in the "global middle class" is projected to swell from 440 million to 1.2 billion or from 7.6 percent of the world's population to 16.1 percent, according to the World Bank. Most of the new entrants will come from China and India.

- However, there is a dark side to the global middle class coin: continued divergence at the extremes. Many countries—especially the landlocked and resource-poor ones in Sub Saharan Africa—lack the fundamentals for entering the globalization game. By 2025–2030, the portion of the world considered poor will shrink by about 23 percent, but the world's poor—still 63 percent of the globe's population—stand to become relatively poorer, according to the World Bank.

State Capitalism: A Post-Democratic Marketplace Rising in the East?

The monumental achievement of millions escaping extreme poverty underpins the rise of new powers—especially China and India—on the international scene but does not tell the whole story. Today wealth is moving not just from West to East but is concentrating more under state control. In the wake of the 2008 global financial crisis, the state's role in the economy may be gaining more appeal throughout the world.

With some notable exceptions like India, the states that are beneficiaries of the massive shift of wealth—China, Russia, and Gulf states—are non-democratic and their economic policies blur distinctions between public and private. These states are not following the Western liberal model for self-development but are using a different model—"state capitalism."

State capitalism is a loose term to describe a system of economic management that gives a prominent role to the state.

Regional Income Inequality: European Inequality Lower Than Most

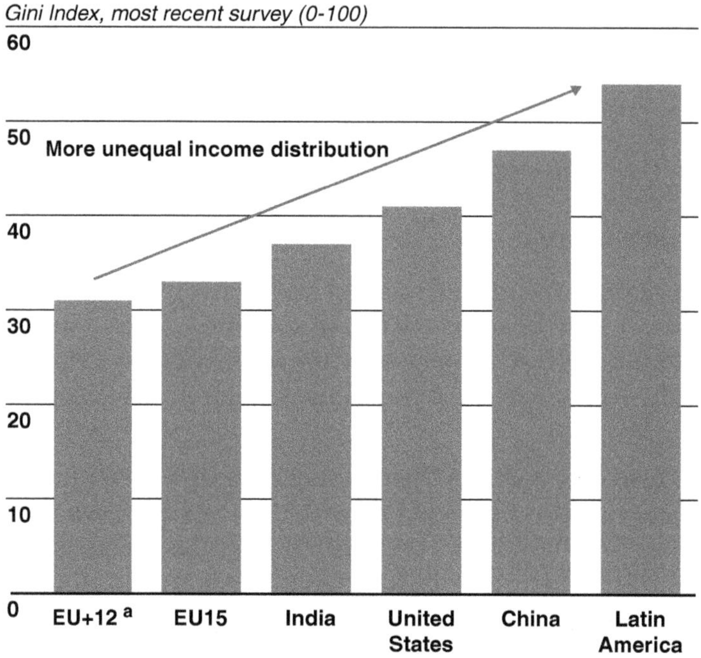

[a] European Union Nations that acceded in 2004 or later.
Source: UNDP, Human Development Report 2007/2008: World Bank.

Others—like South Korea, Taiwan, and Singapore—also chose state capitalism as they initially developed their economies. However, the impact of Russia, and particularly China, following this path is potentially greater given their weight on the world stage. Ironically, the major enhancement of the state role in Western economies now under way as a result of the current financial crisis may reinforce the emerging countries' preference for greater state control and distrust of an unregulated marketplace.

These states typically favor:

- ***An Open Export Climate.*** Given the wealth flowing into these states, their desire for a weak currency despite strong domestic economic performance requires heavy intervention in currency markets, leading to heavy official asset accumulation, typically until now in the form of US Treasury bonds.
- ***Sovereign Wealth Funds (SWFs) and Other State Investment Vehicles.*** Having amassed huge assets, Gulf Cooperation Council (GCC) and Chinese officials have increasingly used various forms of sovereign

investment. States entering private markets are doing so partly for the prospect of higher return. SWFs are the most widely publicized but only one of many sovereign investment vehicles.

Globalization at Risk with the 2008 Financial Crisis?

As with most of the trends discussed in this report, the impacts from the financial crisis will depend heavily on government leadership. Proactive fiscal and monetary policies probably will ensure the current panic and likely deep national recessions will not turn into an extended depression, although reduced economic growth could slow globalization's pace, increasing protectionist pressures and financial fragmentation.

The crisis is accelerating the global economic rebalancing. Developing countries have been hurt; several, such as Pakistan with its large current account deficit, are at considerable risk. Even those with cash reserves—such as South Korea and Russia—have been severely buffeted; steep rises in unemployment and inflation could trigger widespread political instability and throw emerging powers off course. However, if China, Russia, and Mideast oil exporters can avoid internal crises, they will be in a position to leverage their likely still sizeable reserves, buying foreign assets and providing direct financial assistance to still-struggling countries for political favors or to seed new regional initiatives. In the West, the biggest change—not anticipated before the crisis—is the increase in state power. Western governments now own large swaths of their financial sectors and must manage them, potentially politicizing markets.

The crisis has increased calls for a new "Bretton Woods" to better regulate the global economy. World leaders, however, will be challenged to renovate the IMF and devise a globally transparent and effective set of rules that apply to differing capitalisms and levels of financial institutional development. Failure to construct a new all-embracing architecture could lead countries to seek security through competitive monetary policies and new investment barriers, increasing the potential for market segmentation.

- *Renewed Efforts Toward Industrial Policy*. Governments that highly manage their economies often have an interest in industrial policy. China, Russia, and the Gulf states have state plans to diversify their economies and climb the value-added ladder into high technology and service sectors. The significant difference between today's efforts and those of earlier periods, however, is that these states now directly own the economic wherewithal to implement their plans and need not rely on incentivizing parties or luring foreign capital.
- *Rollback of Privatization and the Resurgence of State-Owned Enterprises (SOEs)*. In the early 1990s, many economists predicted

that SOEs would be a relic of the 20th century. They were wrong. SOEs are far from extinction, are thriving, and in many cases seek to expand beyond their own borders, particularly in the commodities and energy sectors. SOEs, especially national oil companies, are likely to attract investment for the surfeit of ready capital that these states are accumulating. Much like SWFs, SOEs serve a secondary function as pressure valves, helping to relieve inflation and currency appreciation pressures. They also can act as vehicles for increased political control. To the extent state-owned firms reach across state borders, they may become vehicles for geopolitical influence, particularly those dealing in key strategic resources such as energy.

The increasing role of the state as a player in emerging markets has contrasted until recently with nearly opposite trends in the West, where the state has struggled to keep pace with private financial engineering, such as derivatives and credit swaps. The seeds of this capital market's depth and complexity date to the 1980s but grew with rising asset prices and bull markets from the 1990s until recently. The financial engineering—based upon a magnitude of leverage unthinkable even a decade ago—in turn has injected an unprecedented degree of risk and volatility into global markets. Greater controls and international regulation—a possible outcome of the current financial crisis—could change this trajectory, although a gap on the role of the state in the economy is likely to remain between the West and the rapidly emerging economic powers.

Bumpy Ride in Correcting Current Global Imbalances

The refusal of emerging markets to allow currency appreciation despite booming economies, together with the willingness of the US to incur greater sums of debt, has created a mutually supporting, albeit ultimately unsustainable cycle of imbalances. Indeed, the Wall Street events of 2008 mark the opening chapters of a larger story of rebalancing and course correction from these imbalances. The righting of these imbalances will be bumpy as the global economy moves into realignment. The difficulties of global economic policy coordination—in part a byproduct of the growing political and financial multipolarity—increase the chances of a bumpy ride.

One of the following developments or a combination could cause an adjustment: a slowdown in US consumption and an attendant increase in the US savings rate, and an increase in demand from emerging Asian markets, particularly China and India. Whether imbalances stabilize or rebound out to 2025 depends in part on the particular lessons that the emerging powers choose to draw from the financial crisis. Some may interpret the crisis as a rationale for hoarding yet more in the way of a cushion, while others—in understanding that few if any emerging economies were immune from the widespread downturn—could come to regard the stockpiling of reserves as less of a priority.

Major financial disruptions and the needed economic and political readjustments have often spread beyond the financial arena. History suggests that this rebalancing will require long-term efforts to establish a new international system. Specific problems to be overcome include:

- *Greater Trade and Investment Protectionism.* Increasingly aggressive foreign acquisitions by corporations based in the rapidly emerging economies—many will be state-owned—will raise political tensions, potentially creating a public backlash in countries against foreign trade and investment. The perception of uneven benefits from globalization in the US may fuel protectionist forces.
- *An Accelerated Resource Grab.* The new powers increasingly will have the means to acquire commodities in an effort to ensure continued development. Russia, China, and India have linked their national security to increased state control of and access to energy resources and markets through their state-owned energy firms. Gulf states are interested in land leases and purchases elsewhere to ensure adequate food supplies.
- *Slowing Democratization.* China, particularly, offers an alternative model for political development in addition to demonstrating a different economic pathway. This model may prove attractive to underperforming authoritarian regimes, in addition to weak democracies frustrated by years of economic underperformance.
- *The Overshadowing of International Financial Institutions.* Sovereign wealth funds have injected more capital into emerging markets than the IMF and World Bank combined, and this trend could even continue with unwinding global imbalances. China already is beginning to couple SWF investment with direct aid and foreign assistance, often directly outbidding the World Bank on development projects. Such foreign investment by newly rich states such as China, Russia, and the GCC states will lead to diplomatic realignments and new relationships between these states and the developing world.
- *A Decline in the Dollar's International Role.* Despite recent inflows into dollar assets and the appreciation of the dollar, the dollar could lose its status as an unparalleled global reserve currency by 2025, and become a first among equals in a market basket of currencies. This may force the US to consider more carefully how the conduct of its foreign policy affects the dollar. Without a steady source of external demand for dollars, US foreign policy actions might bring exposure to currency shock and higher interest rates for Americans.

Growing use of the euro is already evident, potentially making it harder for the US in the future to exploit the unique role of the dollar in international trade and investment to freeze assets and disrupt the financial flows of its adversaries, such as it recently has accomplished with financial sanctions against the leadership in North Korea and Iran. Incentives and inclinations to move away from the dollar will be tempered, however, by uncertainties and instabilities in the international financial system.

Multiple Financial Nodes

Anchored by the US and EU in the West, Russia and the GCC states in Central Asia and the Middle East, and China and eventually India in the East, the financial landscape for the first time will be genuinely global and multipolar. Insomuch as the recent financial crisis heightens interest in less leveraged finance, Islamic finance may also see a boost. While such a global and multipolar financial order signals a relative decline for US power and a likely increase in market competition and complexity, these downsides are likely to be accompanied by many positives. Over time, and as they develop, these multiple financial centers may create redundancies that help insulate markets against financial shocks and currency crises, quelling their effects before global contagion takes hold. Similarly, as regions become more invested in their financial epicenters, incentives to preserve geopolitical stability to shelter these financial flows will increase. History suggests, however, that such a redirection toward regional financial centers could soon spill over into other areas of power. Rarely, if ever, have such "financiers of last resort" been content to limit their influence to strictly financial realms. Interregional tensions could divide the West with the US and EU having increasingly divergent economic and monetary priorities, complicating Western efforts to lead and jointly grow the global economy.

Science and Technology Leadership: A Test for the Emerging Powers

The relationship between achievements in science and technology and economic growth has been long established, but the path is not always predictable. More significant is the overall effectiveness of a nation's National Innovation System (NIS)—the process by which intellectual concepts are moved toward commercialization for the benefit of a national economy. According to a NIC-contracted global survey of scientific experts, the United States currently boasts a stronger innovation system than the developing economies of China and India.

- The idea of an NIS was first developed in the 1980s as an aid to understanding how some countries were proving better than others at turning intellectual concepts into commercial products that would boost their economies. The NIS model is evolving as information technology and the effect of increased globalization (and multinational corporations) influence national economies.

According to the NIC-commissioned study, nine factors can contribute to a modern NIS: fluidity of capital, flexibility of the labor pool, government receptivity to business, information communication technologies, private sector development infrastructure, legal systems to protect intellectual property rights, available scientific and human capital, marketing skills, and cultural propensity to encourage creativity.

China and India are expected in 10 years to achieve near parity with the US in two different areas: scientific and human capital (India) and government receptivity to business innovation (China). China and India will narrow significantly but not close the gap in all remaining factors. The United States is expected to remain dominant in three areas: protection for intellectual property rights, business sophistication to mature innovation, and encouragement of creativity.

Companies in China, India, and other major developing countries have unique opportunities to be the first to develop a host of emerging technologies. This is especially the case in those instances where companies are building new infrastructure and not burdened by historical patterns of development. Such opportunities include distributed electrical power generation, development of clean water sources, and the next generation of Internet and new information technologies (such as ubiquitous computing and the Internet of Things—see the foldout). Early and significant adoption of these technologies could provide considerable economic advantage.

Diverging Development Models, but for How Long?

The state-centric model in which the state makes the key economic decisions and, in the case of China and increasingly Russia, democracy is restricted, raises questions about the inevitability of the traditional Western recipe—roughly liberal economics and democracy—for development. Over the next 15–20 years, more developing countries may gravitate toward Beijing's state-centric model rather than the traditional Western model of markets and democratic political systems to increase the chances of rapid development and perceived political stability. While we believe a gap will remain, the enhanced role of the state in Western economies may also lessen the contrast between the two models.

In the Middle East, secularism, which also has been considered an integral part of the Western model, increasingly may be seen as out of place as Islamic parties come into prominence and possibly begin to run governments. As in today's Turkey, we could see both increased Islamization and greater emphasis on economic growth and modernization.

The lack of any overarching ideology and the mix-and-match of some of the elements—for example Brazil and India are vibrant market democracies—means the state-centric model does not yet constitute anything like an alternative system and, in our view, is unlikely ever to be one. Whether China liberalizes both politically and economically over the next two decades is a particularly critical test for the long-term sustainability of an alternative to the traditional Western model. Although democratization probably will be slow and may have its own Chinese character, we believe the emerging middle class will press for greater political influence and accountability of those in charge, particularly if the central government falters in its ability to sustain economic growth or is unresponsive to growing "quality of life" issues such as increasing pollution or the need for health and education services. The government's own efforts to boost S&T and establish a "high tech" economy will increase incentives for greater openness to develop human capital at home and attract expertise and ideas from outside.

Historical patterns evinced by other energy producers suggest deflecting pressures for liberalization will be easier for Russian authorities. Traditionally, energy producers also have been able to use revenues to buy off political opponents; few have made the transition to democracy while their energy revenues remain strong.

A sustained plunge in the price of oil and gas would alter the outlook and increase prospects for greater political and economic liberalization in Russia.

Latin America: Moderate Economic Growth, Continued Urban Violence

Many Latin American countries will have achieved marked progress in democratic consolidation by 2025, and some of these countries will have become middle income powers. Others, particularly those that have embraced populist policies, will lag behind—and some, such as Haiti, will have become even poorer and still less governable. Public security problems will continue to be intractable—and in some cases unmanageable. Brazil will become the leading regional power, but its efforts to promote South American integration will be realized only in part. Venezuela and Cuba will have some form of vestigial influence in the region in 2025, but their economic problems will limit their appeal. Unless the United States is able to deliver market access on a permanent and meaningful basis, the US could lose its traditionally privileged position in the region, with a concomitant decline in political influence.

Steady economic growth between now and 2025—perhaps as high as 4 percent—will fuel modest decreases in poverty levels in some countries and a gradual reduction of the informal sector. Progress on critical secondary reforms, such as education, regressive tax systems, weak property rights, and inadequate law enforcement will remain incremental and spotty. The relative growing importance of the region as a producer of oil, natural gas, biofuels, and other alternative energy sources will spur growth in Brazil, Chile, Colombia, and Mexico, but state ownership and political turmoil will impede efficient development of energy resources. The economic competitiveness of Latin America will continue to lag behind Asia and some other fast growing areas.

Population growth in the region will be relatively moderate, but the rural poor and indigenous populations will continue to grow at a faster rate. Latin America will have a graying population as the growth rate of adults aged 60 and over rises.

Parts of Latin America will continue to be among the world's most violent areas. Drug trafficking organizations, sustained in part by increased local drug consumption, transnational criminal cartels, and local crime rings and gangs, will continue to undermine public security. These factors, and persistent weaknesses in the rule of law, will mean that a few small countries, especially in Central America and the Caribbean, will verge on becoming failed states.

Latin America will continue to play a marginal role in the international system, except for its participation in international trade and some peacekeeping efforts.

US influence in the region will diminish somewhat, in part because of Latin America's broadening economic and commercial relations with Asia, Europe, and other blocs. Latins, in general, will look to the United States for guidance both globally and for relations with the region. An increasingly numerous Hispanic population will ensure greater US attention to, and involvement in, the culture, religion, economics, and politics of the region.

Women as Agents of Geopolitical Change

Economic and political empowerment of women could transform the global landscape over the next 20 years. This trend already is evident in the area of economics: ***The explosion in global economic productivity in recent years has been driven as much by fostering human resources—particularly through***

improvements in health, education, and employment opportunities for women and girls—as by technological advances.

- The predominance of women in Southeast Asia's export manufacturing sector is a likely key driver of that region's economic success; women agricultural workers account for half the world's food production—even without reliable access to land, credit, equipment, and markets.
- Over the next 20 years the increased entry and retention of women in the workplace may continue to mitigate the economic impacts of global aging.

Women in much of Asia and Latin America are achieving higher levels of education than men, a trend that is particularly significant in a human capital-intensive global economy.

- Demographic data indicate a significant correlation between a higher level of female literacy and more robust GDP growth within a region (e.g., the Americas, Europe, and East Asia). Conversely, those regions with the lowest female literacy rates (southern and western Asia; the Arab world; and Sub-Saharan Africa) are the poorest in the world.
- Improved educational opportunities for girls and women also are a contributing factor to falling birth rates worldwide—and by extension better maternal health. The long-term implications of this trend likely include fewer orphans, less malnutrition, more children in school, and other contributions to societal stability.

Although data on women's ***political*** involvement are less conclusive than those regarding economic participation, political empowerment of women appears to change governmental priorities. ***Examples as disparate as Sweden and Rwanda indicate that countries with relatively large numbers of politically active women place greater importance on societal issues such as healthcare, the environment, and economic development.*** If this trend continues over the next 15–20 years, as is likely, an increasing number of countries could favor social programs over military ones. Better governance also could be a spinoff benefit, as a high number of women in parliament or senior government positions correlates with lower corruption.

Nowhere is the role of women potentially more important for geopolitical change than in the Muslim World. Muslim women do far better assimilating in Europe than their male relatives, partly because they flourish in the educational system, which facilitates their entry into jobs in information or service industries. Sharply declining fertility rates among Muslims in Europe demonstrate this willingness to accept jobs outside the home and a growing refusal to conform to traditional norms. In the short term, the decline of traditional Muslim family structures may help explain the openness of many young Muslim men to radical Islamic messages. However, in rearing future generations, women might help show the way to greater social assimilation and reduce the likelihood of religious extremism. The impact of growing numbers of women in the workplace may also have an impact outside Europe. The modernizing countries of the Islamic Mediterranean have close ties to Europe, to which these countries have sent many migrants. Migrants return to visit or resettle and bring with them new ideas and expectations. These Islamic countries also receive foreign influences from European mass media, through satellite dishes and the Internet.

Higher Education Shaping the Global Landscape in 2025

As global business grows increasingly borderless and labor markets more seamless, education has become a key determinant of countries' economic performance and potential. Adequate primary education is essential, but the quality and accessibility of secondary and higher education will be even more important for determining whether societies successfully graduate up the value-added production ladder.

The US lead in highly skilled labor will likely narrow as large developing countries, particularly China, begin to reap dividends on recent investments in human capital, including education but also nutrition and healthcare. India faces a challenge because inadequate primary education is widespread in the poorer regions and top-flight educational institutions cater to a relatively privileged few. Funding as a proportion of GDP has grown to around 5 percent in most European countries, although few European universities are rated as world class. Spending on education in the Arab world is roughly on par with the rest of the world in absolute terms and surpasses the global mean as a percentage of GDP, lagging only slightly behind OECD high-income countries. UN data and research findings by other institutions suggest, however that training and education of Middle Eastern youth is not driven by the needs of employers, especially for science and technology. There are some signs of progress.

The US may be uniquely able to adapt its higher education and research system to rising global demand and position itself as a world education hub for the growing number of students that will enter the education market out to 2025. Although further opening of US classrooms and laboratories could mean greater competition for US students, the US economy would likely benefit because companies tend to base their operations near available human capital. Continued export of US educational models with the building of US campuses in the Middle East and Central Asia could boost the attractiveness and global prestige of US universities.

Chapter 2
The Demographics of Discord

Trends in birth, death, and migration are changing the absolute and relative size of young and old, rural and urban, and ethnic majority and minority populations within and among emerging and established powers. These demographic reconfigurations will offer social and economic opportunities for some powers and severely challenge established arrangements in others. The populations of more than 50 countries will increase by more than a third (some by more than two-thirds) by 2025, placing additional stresses on vital natural resources, services, and infrastructure. Two-thirds of these countries are in Sub-Saharan Africa; most of the remaining fast-growing countries are in the Middle East and South Asia.

Populations Growing, Declining, and Diversifying—at the Same Time

World population is projected to grow by about 1.2 billion between 2009 and 2025—from 6.8 billion to around 8 billion people. Although the global population increase is substantial—with concomitant effects on resources—the rate of growth will be slower than it was, down from levels that added 2.4 billion persons between 1980 and today. Demographers project that Asia and Africa will account for most of the population growth out to 2025 while less than 3 percent of the growth will occur in the "West"—Europe, Japan, the United States, Canada, Australia, and New Zealand. In 2025, roughly 16 percent of humanity will live in the West, down from the 18 percent in 2009 and 24 percent in 1980.

- The largest increase will occur in India, representing about one-fifth of all growth. India's population is projected to climb by around 240 million by 2025, reaching approximately 1.45 billion people. From 2009 to 2025, Asia's other giant, China, is projected to add more than 100 million to its current population of over 1.3 billion. (See graphic on page 41.)
- In aggregate, the countries of Sub-Saharan Africa are projected to add about 350 million people during the same period, while those in Latin America and the Caribbean will increase by about 100 million.
- Between now and 2025, Russia, Ukraine, Italy, almost all countries in Eastern Europe, and Japan are expected to see their populations decline by several percent. These declines could approach or exceed 10 percent of the current populations in Russia, Ukraine, and a few other Eastern European countries.
- The populations of the US, Canada, Australia, and a few other industrial states with relatively high immigration rates will continue to

grow—the US by more than 40 million, Canada by 4.5 million, and Australia by more than 3 million.

By 2025, the already diverse array of national population age structures promises to be more varied than ever, and the gap between the youngest and oldest profiles will continue to widen. The "oldest" countries—those in which people under age 30 form less than one-third of the population—will mark a band across the northern edge of the world map. In contrast, the "youngest" countries, where the under-30 group represents 60 percent of the population or more, will nearly all be located in Sub-Saharan Africa. (See the maps below.)

World Age Structure, 2005 and Projected 2025

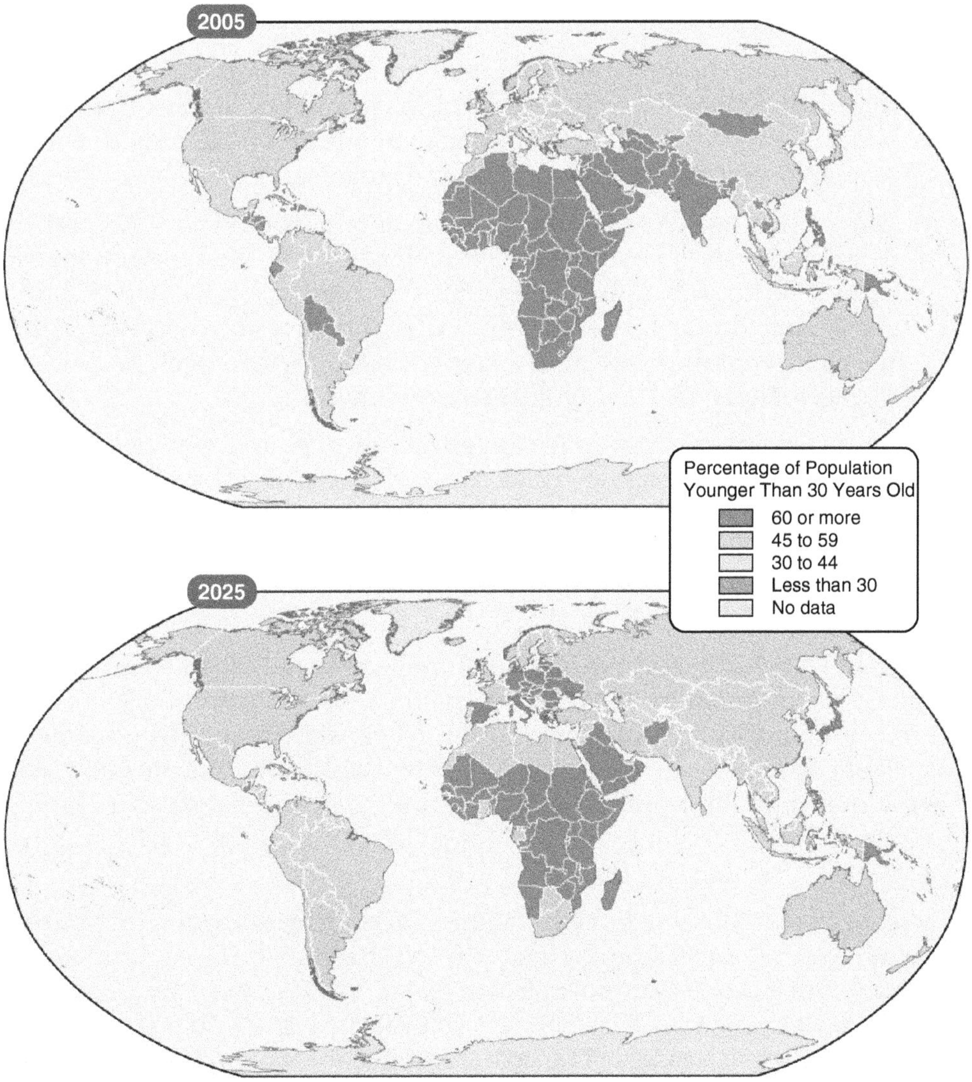

Source: US Census data.

The Pensioner Boom: Challenges of Aging Populations

Population aging has brought today's developed countries—with a few exceptions such as the US—to a demographic *"**tipping point**."* Today, nearly 7 out of every 10 people in the developed world are in the traditional working years (ages 15 to 64)—a high-tide mark. This number has never before been so high and, according to experts, in all likelihood will never be so high again.

In almost every developed country, the period of most rapid growth in the ratio of seniors (age 65 and older) to the working-age population will occur during the 2010s and 2020s, boosting the fiscal burden of old-age benefit programs. By 2010, there will be about one senior for every four working-age people in the developed world. By 2025, this ratio will have climbed to one to three, and possibly higher.

- Japan is in a difficult position: its working-age population has been contracting since the mid-1990s and its overall population since 2005. Today's projections envision a society in which, by 2025, there will be one senior for every two working-age Japanese.
- The picture for Western Europe is more mixed. The UK, France, Belgium, the Netherlands, and the Nordics will likely maintain the highest fertility rates in Europe but will remain below two children per woman. In the rest of the region, fertility probably will stay below 1.5 children per woman, on par with Japan (and well below the replacement level of 2.1 children per woman).

Large and sustained increases in the fertility rate, even if they began now, would not reverse the aging trend for decades in Europe and Japan. If fertility rose immediately to the replacement level in Western Europe, the ratio of seniors to people in their working years would continue to rise steadily through the late 2030s. In Japan, it would continue to rise through the late 2040s.

The annual level of net immigration would have to double or triple to keep working-age populations from shrinking in Western Europe. By 2025, non-European minority populations could reach significant proportions—15 percent or more—in nearly all Western European countries and will have a substantially younger age structure than the native population. Given growing discontent with current levels of immigrants among native Europeans, such steep increases are likely to heighten tensions.

The aging of societies will have economic consequences. Even with productivity increases, slower employment growth from a shrinking work force probably will reduce Europe's already tepid GDP growth by 1 percent. By the 2030s, Japan's GDP growth is projected to drop to near zero according to some models. The cost of trying to maintain pensions and health coverage will squeeze out expenditures on other priorities, such as defense.

Persistent Youth Bulges

Countries with youthful age structures and rapidly growing populations form a crescent stretching from the Andean region of Latin America across Sub-Saharan Africa, the Middle East and the Caucasus, and then through the northern parts of South Asia. By 2025, the number of countries in this "arc of instability" will have decreased by 35 to 40 percent owing to declining fertility and maturing populations. Three quarters of the three dozen "youth bulge countries" projected to linger beyond 2025 will be located in Sub-Saharan Africa. The remainder will be located in the Middle East and scattered across Asia and among the Pacific Islands.

Total Population

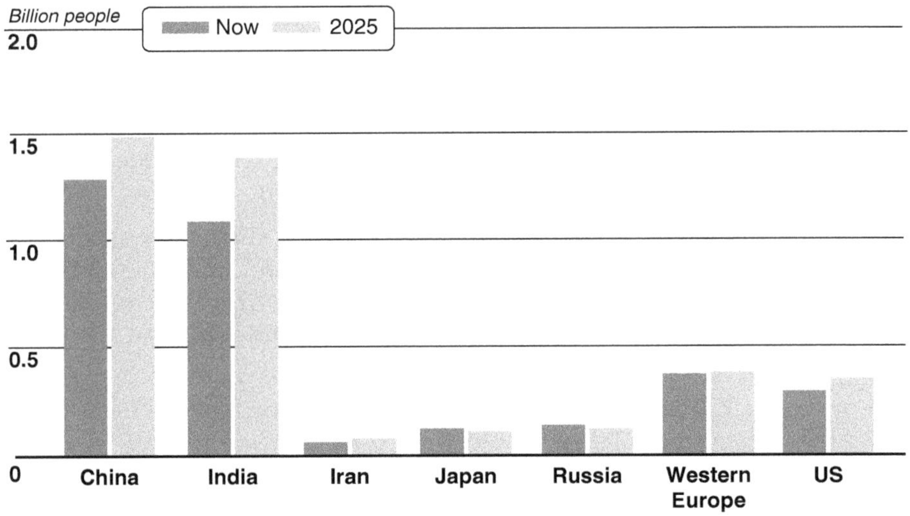

Source: US Census Data

- The emergence of new economic tigers by 2025 could occur where youth bulges mature into "worker bulges." Experts argue that this demographic bonus is most advantageous when the country provides an educated work force and a business-friendly environment for investment. Potential beneficiaries include Turkey, Lebanon, Iran, and the Maghreb states of North Africa (Morocco, Algeria and Tunisia), Colombia, Costa Rica, Chile, Vietnam, Indonesia, and Malaysia.
- The current youth bulges in the Maghreb states, Turkey, Lebanon, and Iran will diminish rapidly but those in the West Bank/Gaza, Iraq, Yemen, Saudi Arabia and adjacent Afghanistan and Pakistan will persist through 2025. Unless employment conditions change dramatically,

youth in weak states will continue to go elsewhere—externalizing volatility and violence.

The populations of already parlous youth-bulge states—such as Afghanistan, Democratic Republic of Congo (DROC), Ethiopia, Nigeria, Pakistan, and Yemen—are projected to remain on rapid-growth trajectories. Pakistan's and Nigeria's populations are each projected to grow by about 55 million people. Ethiopia and DROC will likely add about 40 million each, while the populations of Afghanistan and Yemen are projected to grow more than 50 percent larger than today's. All will retain age structures with large proportions of young adults, a demographic feature that is associated with the emergence of political violence and civil conflict.

The Impact of HIV/AIDS

Neither an effective HIV vaccine nor a self-administered microbicide, even if developed and tested before 2025, will likely be widely disseminated by then. Although prevention efforts and local behavioral changes will depress infection rates globally, experts expect HIV/AIDS to remain a global pandemic through 2025 with its epicenter of infection in Sub-Saharan Africa. Unlike today, the vast majority of people living with HIV will have access to life-extending antiretroviral therapies.

- If prevention efforts and effectiveness remain at current levels, the HIV-positive population is expected to climb to around 50 million by 2025—up from 33 million today (22 million in Sub-Saharan Africa). In this scenario, 25 million to 30 million people would need anti-retroviral therapy to survive during 2025.
- In another scenario assuming fully scaled-up prevention by 2015, the HIV-infected population would peak and then fall to near 25 million worldwide by 2025, bringing the number needing antiretroviral therapy to between 15 and 20 million people.

Changing Places: Migration, Urbanization and Ethnic Shifts

Moving Experiences. The net migration of people from rural to urban areas and from poorer to richer countries likely will continue apace in 2025, fueled by a widening gap in economic and physical security between adjacent regions.

- Europe will continue to attract migrants from younger, less developed, and faster growing African and Asian regions nearby. However, other emerging centers of industrialization—China and southern India and possibly Turkey and Iran— could attract some of this labor migration as growth among their working-age populations slows and wages rise.

- Labor migration to the United States probably will slow as Mexico's industrial base grows and its population ages—a response to rapid fertility declines in the 1980s and 1990s—and as competing centers of development arise in Brazil and the southern cone of South America.

Urbanization. If current trends persist, by 2025 about 57 percent of the world's population will live in urban areas, up from about 50 percent today. By 2025, the world will add another eight megacities to the current list of 19—all except one of these eight will be in Asia and Sub-Saharan Africa. Most urban growth, however, will occur in smaller cities of these regions, which are expanding along highways and coalescing near crossroads and coastlines, often without formal sector job growth and without adequate services.

Identity Demography. Where ethno-religious groups have experienced their transition to lower birth rates at varying paces, lingering ethnic youth bulges and shifts in group proportions could trigger significant political changes. Shifts in ethno-religious composition resulting from migration also could fuel political change, particularly where immigrants settle in low-fertility industrialized countries.

- Differing rates of growth among Israel's ethnic communities could abet political shifts in the Knesset (Israel's parliament). By 2025, Israeli Arabs, who currently comprise a fifth of the population, will comprise about a quarter of Israel's expected population of nearly 9 million. Over the same period, Israel's ultra-orthodox Jewish community could nearly double, becoming larger than 10 percent of the population.
- Irrespective of their political status in 2025, the populations of the West Bank, currently about 2.6 million people, and Gaza, now at 1.5 million, will have grown substantially: the West Bank by nearly 40 percent; Gaza by almost 60 percent. Their combined population in 2025—still youthful, growing, and approaching 6 million (or exceeding that figure, according to some projections)—promises to introduce further challenges to institutions hoping to generate adequate employment and public services, maintain sufficient availability of fresh water and food, and achieve political stability.

A number of other ethnic shifts between now and 2025 will have regional implications. For example, growing proportions of Native Americans in several Andean and Central American democracies are likely to continue to push governments in those countries toward populism. In Lebanon, ongoing fertility decline in the Shiite population, which currently lags ethnic neighbors in income and exceeds them in family size, will bring about a more mature age structure in this community—and could deepen Shiite integration into the mainstream of Lebanese economic and political life, easing communal tensions.

Western Europe has become the destination of choice for more than one million immigrants annually and home for more than 35 million foreign born—many from Muslim-majority countries in North Africa, the Middle East, and South Asia (see box on page 45). Immigration and integration politics, and confrontations with Muslim conservatives over education, women's rights, and the relationship between the state and religion are likely to strengthen right-of-center political organizations and splinter the left-of-center political coalitions that were instrumental in building and maintaining Europe's welfare states.

By 2025, international migration's human capital and technological transfer effects will begin to favor the most stable Asian and Latin American countries. Although the emigration of professionals probably will continue to deprive poor and unstable countries across Africa and parts of the Middle East of talent, the likely return of many wealthy and educated Asian and Latin Americans from the US and Europe will help boost the competitiveness of China, Brazil, India, and Mexico.

Demographic Portraits: Russia, China, India, and Iran

Russia*: *A Growing Multiethnic State? Currently a country with around 141 million people, Russia's demographically aging and declining population is projected to drop below 130 million by 2025. The chances of stemming such a steep decline over this period are slim: the population of women in their 20s—their prime childbearing years—will be declining rapidly, numbering around 55 percent of today's count by 2025.

Russia's high rate of male middle-age mortality is unlikely to change dramatically. Muslim minorities that have maintained higher fertility will comprise larger proportions of the Russian population, as will Turkic and Chinese immigrants. According to some more conservative projections, the Muslim minority share of Russia's population will rise from 14 percent in 2005 to 19 percent in 2030, and 23 percent in 2050. In a shrinking population, the growing proportion that are not Orthodox Slavs will likely provoke a nationalist backlash. Because Russia's fertility and mortality problems are likely to persist through 2025, Russia's economy—unlike Europe's and Japan's—will have to support the large proportion of dependents.

Antique China? By 2025, demographers expect China to have almost 1.4 billion people, nearly 100 million above its current population. The advantageous condition of having a relatively large working population and small proportions of both old-age and childhood dependents will begin to fade around 2015, when the size of China's working-age population will start to decline. Demographic aging—the onset of larger proportions of retirees and relatively fewer workers—is being accelerated by decades of policies that have limited childbirth and by a tradition of early retirement. By opting to slow population growth dramatically in order to dampen growing demand for energy, water, and food, China is hastening the aging of its population. By 2025, a large proportion of China's population will be retired or entering retirement. Although China may over time reverse its restrictive policies on childbearing to achieve birth cohorts more closely balancing infant girls and boys, marriage-age adults in 2025 will still experience a significant male-dominated imbalance that will create a large pool of unmarried males.

Muslims in Western Europe

Western Europe's Muslim population currently totals between 15 and 18 million. The largest proportions of Muslims—between 6 and 8 percent—are in France (5 million) and the Netherlands (nearly 1 million), followed by countries with 4 to 6 percent: Germany (3.5 million), Denmark (300,000), Austria (500,000), and Switzerland (350,000). The UK and Italy also have relatively large Muslim populations, 1.8 million and 1 million respectively, though constituting less overall proportions (3 percent and 1.7 percent respectively). If current patterns of immigration and Muslim residents' above-average fertility continue, Western Europe could have 25 to 30 million Muslims by 2025.

Countries with growing numbers of Muslims will experience a rapid shift in ethnic composition, particularly around urban areas, potentially complicating efforts to facilitate assimilation and integration. Economic opportunities are likely to be greater in urban areas, but, in the absence of growth in suitable jobs, the increasing concentration could lead to more tense and unstable situations, such as occurred with the 2005 Paris surburban riots.

Slow overall growth rates, highly regulated labor markets, and workplace policies, if maintained, will make it difficult to increase job opportunities, despite Europe's need to stem the decline of its working-age population. When coupled with job discrimination and educational disadvantage, these factors are likely to confine many Muslims to low-status, low-wage jobs, deepening ethnic cleavages. Despite a sizeable stratum of integrated Muslims, a growing number—driven by a sense of alienation, grievance, and injustice—are increasingly likely to value separation in areas with Muslim-specific cultural and religious practices.

Although immigrant communities are unlikely to gain sufficient parliamentary representation to dictate either domestic or foreign policy agendas by 2025, Muslim-related issues will be a growing focus and shaper of the European political scene. Ongoing societal and political tension over integration of Muslims is likely to make European policymakers increasingly sensitive to the potential domestic repercussions of any foreign policies for the Middle East, including aligning too closely with the US on policies seen as pro-Israeli.

Two Indias. India's current fertility rate of 2.8 children per woman masks vast differences between the low-fertility states of South India and the commercial hubs of Mumbai, Delhi, and Kolkata on the one hand, and the higher rates of populous states in the so-called Hindi-speaking belt across the north, where women's status is low and services lag. Largely owing to growth in India's densely populated northern states, its population is projected to overtake China's around 2025—just as China's population is projected to peak and begin a slow decline.

By then, India's demographic duality will have widened the gap between north and south. By 2025, much of India's work force growth will come from the most poorly educated, impoverished, and crowded districts of rural northern India. Although North Indian entrepreneurial families have lived for decades in southern cities, the arrival of whole communities of Hindi-speaking unskilled laborers looking for work could rekindle dormant animosities between India's central government and ethno-nationalist parties in the South.

Iran's Unique Trajectory. Having experienced one of the most rapid fertility declines in history—from more than six children per woman in 1985 to less than two today—Iran's population is destined for dramatic changes by 2025. The country's politically restless, job-hungry youth bulge will largely dissipate over the next decade, yielding more mature population and work force growth rates comparable to current rates in the US and China (near 1 percent per year). In this time frame, the working-age population will grow large relative to children, creating opportunities to accumulate savings, better educate, and eventually to shift to more technical industries and raise living standards. Whether Iran capitalizes on this demographic bonus depends on the country's political leadership, which at present is unfriendly to markets and private businesses, unsettling for investors, and more focused on oil revenues than on broader job creation.

Two additional demographic near-certainties are apparent: first, despite low fertility, Iran's population of 66 million will grow to around 77 million by 2025. Second, by then, a new youth bulge (an echo produced by births during the current one) will be ascending—but in this one, 15-to-24 year olds will account for just one-sixth of those in the working age group compared to one third today. Some experts believe this echo bulge signals a resurgence of revolutionary politics. Others speculate that, in the more educated and developed Iran of 2025, young adults will find career and consumption more attractive than extremist politics. Only one aspect of Iran's future is sure: its society will be more demographically mature than ever before and strikingly different than its neighbors.

Chapter 3
The New Players

By 2025, the United States will find itself in the position of being one of a number of important actors on the world stage, albeit still the most powerful one. The relative political and economic clout of many countries will shift by 2025, according to an International Futures model measuring GDP, defense spending, population, and technology for individual states.[6] Historically, *emerging* multipolar systems have been more unstable than bipolar or even unipolar ones; the greater diversity and growing power of more countries portends less cohesiveness and effectiveness for the international system. Most emerging powers already want a greater say and, along with many Europeans, dispute the notion of any one power having the right to be a hegemon. The potential for less cohesiveness and more instability also is suggested by the relatively steeper declines in national power of Europe and Japan.

Although we believe chances are good that China and India will continue to rise, their ascent is not guaranteed and will require overcoming high economic and social hurdles. Because of this, both countries are likely to remain inwardly focused and per capita wealth will lag substantially behind Western economies throughout the period to 2025 and beyond. Individuals in these emerging economic powerhouses are likely to feel still poor in relation to Westerners even though their collective GDP increasingly will outdistance those of individual Western states. For Russia, remaining in the top tier where it has been since its remarkable resurgence during the late 1990s and early part of the 21st century may be extremely difficult. Demography is not always destiny, but diversifying the economy so that Russia can maintain its standing after the world transitions away from dependence on fossil fuel will be central to its long-term prospects. Europe and Japan also will be confronting demographic challenges; decisions taken now are likely to determine their long-term trajectories.

Although the rise of no other state can equal the impact of the rise of such populous states as China and India, other countries with potentially high-performing economies—Iran, Indonesia, and Turkey, for example—could play increasingly important roles on the world stage and especially for establishing new patterns in the Muslim world.

Rising Heavyweights: China and India

China*: *Facing Potential Bumps in the Road. Few countries are poised to have more impact on the world over the next 15–20 years than China.

[6] National Power scores are the product of an index combining the weighted factors of GDP, defense spending, population, and technology. Scores are calculated by the International Futures computer model and are expressed as a state's relative share (percentage) of all global power.

If current trends persist, by 2025 China will have the world's second largest economy and will be a leading military power. It could also be the largest importer of natural resources and an even greater polluter than it is now.

- US security and economic interests could face new challenges if China becomes a peer competitor that is militarily strong as well as economically dynamic and energy hungry.

The pace of China's economic growth almost certainly will slow, or even recede, even with additional reforms to address mounting social pressures arising from growing income disparities, a fraying social safety net, poor business regulation, hunger for foreign energy, enduring corruption, and environmental devastation. Any of these problems might be soluble in isolation, but the country could be hit by a "perfect storm" if many of them demand attention at the same time. Even if the Chinese Government can manage to address these issues, it will not have the ability to assure high levels of economic performance. Most of China's economic growth will continue to be domestically driven, but key sectors rely on foreign markets, resources, and technology as well as globalized production networks. As a result, China's economic health will be affected by that of other economies—particularly the United States and the EU.

In addressing these challenges, Chinese leaders must balance the openness necessary to sustain economic growth—essential to public tolerance for the Communist Party's monopoly of political power—against the restrictions necessary to protect that monopoly. Facing so many social and economic changes, the Communist Party and its position are likely to undergo further transformations. Indeed, Communist Party leaders themselves talk openly about the need to find new ways to retain public acceptance of the Party's dominant role. So far, however, these efforts do not appear to include opening the system to free elections and a free press. Moreover, barring the "perfect storm" described above, we do not foresee social pressures forcing real democracy in China by 2025. That said, the country could be moving toward greater political pluralism and more accountable governance.

Chinese leaders could, however, continue managing tensions by achieving significant growth without jeopardizing the Party's political monopoly, as they have for the past three decades. Although a protracted slump could pose a serious political threat, the regime would be tempted to deflect public criticism by blaming China's woes on foreign interference, stoking the more virulent and xenophobic forms of Chinese nationalism.

- Historically, people who become accustomed to rising living standards react angrily when their expectations are no longer met, and few people have had grounds for such high expectations as do the Chinese.

- China's international standing is based partly on foreigners' calculations that it is "the country of the future." If foreigners treat the country less deferentially, nationalistic Chinese could respond angrily.

***India*: *A Complicated Rise*.** Over the next 15–20 years, Indian leaders will strive for a multipolar international system, with New Delhi as one of the poles and serving as a political and cultural bridge between a rising China and the United States. India's growing international confidence, derived primarily from its economic growth and its successful democratic record, now drives New Delhi toward partnerships with many countries. However, these partnerships are aimed at maximizing India's autonomy, not at aligning India with any country or international coalition.

India probably will continue to enjoy relatively rapid economic growth. Although India faces lingering deficiencies in its domestic infrastructure, skilled labor, and energy production, we expect the nation's rapidly expanding middle class, youthful population, reduced reliance on agriculture, and high domestic savings and investment rates to propel continued economic growth. India's impressive economic growth over the past 15 years has reduced the number of people living in absolute poverty, but the growing gap between rich and poor will become a more important political issue.

We believe Indians will remain strongly committed to democracy, but the polity could become more fragmented and fractious, with national power being shared across successive political coalitions. Future elections are likely to be multi-sided affairs yielding awkward coalitions with unclear mandates. The general direction of India's economic policymaking is unlikely to be reversed, but the pace and scale of reform will fluctuate.

Regional and ethnic insurgencies that have plagued India since independence are likely to persist, but they will not threaten India's unity. We assess New Delhi will remain confident that it can contain the Kashmiri separatist movement. However, India is likely to experience heightened violence and instability in several parts of the country because of the growing reach of the Maoist Naxalite movement.

Indian leaders do not see Washington as a military or economic patron and now believe the international situation has made such a benefactor unnecessary. New Delhi will, however, pursue the benefits of favorable US ties, partly, too, as a hedge against any development of hostile ties with China. Indian policymakers are convinced that US capital, technology, and goodwill are essential to India's continued rise as a global power. The United States will remain one of India's largest export destinations, the key to international financial institutions such as the World Bank and foreign commercial lending, and the largest source of remittances. The Indian diaspora—composed largely of highly skilled professionals—will remain a key element in deepening US-Indian ties. The Indian market for US goods will grow substantially as New Delhi reduces restrictions on trade and investment. India's military also will be eager to benefit from expanded defense ties with Washington. Indian leaders, however, probably will avoid ties that could resemble an alliance relationship.

Other Key Players

Russia's Path: Boom or Bust. Russia has the potential to be richer, more powerful, and more self-assured in 2025 if it invests in human capital, expands and diversifies its economy, and integrates with global markets. On the other hand, multiple constraints could limit Russia's ability to achieve its full economic potential. Chief among them are a shortfall in energy investment, key infrastructure bottlenecks, decaying education and public health sectors, an underdeveloped banking sector, and crime and corruption. A sooner-than-expected conversion to alternative fuels or a sustained plunge in global energy prices before Russia has the chance to develop a more diversified economy probably would constrain economic growth.

Russia's population decline by 2025 will force hard policy choices. By 2017, for example, Russia is likely to have only 650,000 18-year-old males from which to maintain an army that today relies on 750,000 conscripts. Population decline also could take an economic toll with severe labor force shortages, particularly if Russia does not invest more in its existing human capital, rebuild its S&T base, and employ foreign labor migrants.

If Russia diversifies its economy, it could develop a more pluralistic, albeit not democratic, political system—the result of institutional consolidation, a rising middle class, and the emergence of new stakeholders demanding a greater voice.

A more proactive and influential foreign policy seems likely, reflecting Moscow's reemergence as a major player on the world stage; an important partner for Western, Asian, and Middle East capitals; and a leading force in opposition to US global dominance. Controlling key energy nodes and links in the Caucasus and Central Asia—vital to its ambitions as an energy superpower—will be a driving force in reestablishing a sphere of influence in its Near Abroad. Shared perceptions regarding threats from terrorism and Islamic radicalism could align Russian and Western security policies more tightly, notwithstanding disagreements on other issues and a persisting "values gap."

The range of possible futures for Russia remains wide because of starkly divergent forces—liberal economic trends and illiberal political trends. The tension between the two trends—together with Russia's sensitivity to potential discontinuities sparked by political instability, a major foreign policy crisis, or other wild cards—makes it impossible to exclude alternative futures such as a nationalistic, authoritarian petro-state or even a full dictatorship, which is an unlikely but nevertheless plausible future. Less likely, Russia could become a significantly more open and progressive country by 2025.

***Europe*: *Losing Clout in 2025*.** We believe Europe by 2025 will have made slow progress toward achieving the vision of current leaders and elites: a cohesive, integrated, and influential global actor able to employ independently a full spectrum of political, economic, and military tools in support of European and Western interests and universal ideals. The European Union would need to resolve a perceived democracy gap dividing Brussels from European voters and move past the protracted debate about its institutional structures.

The EU will be in a position to bolster political stability and democratization on Europe's periphery by taking in additional new members in the Balkans, and perhaps Ukraine and Turkey. However, continued failure to convince skeptical publics of the benefits of deeper economic, political, and social integration and to grasp the nettle of a shrinking and aging population by enacting painful reforms could leave the EU a hobbled giant distracted by internal bickering and competing national agendas, and less able to translate its economic clout into global influence.

The drop-off in working-age populations will prove a severe test for Europe's social welfare model, a foundation stone of Western Europe's political cohesion since World War II. Progress on economic liberalization is likely to continue only in gradual steps until aging populations or prolonged economic stagnation force more dramatic changes—a crisis point that may not hit before some time in the next decade and might be pushed off even further. There are no easy fixes for Europe's demographic deficits except likely cutbacks in health and retirement benefits, which most states have not begun to implement or even to contemplate. Defense expenditures are likely to be cut further to stave off the need for serious restructuring of social benefits programs. The challenge of integrating immigrant, especially Muslim, communities will become acute if citizens faced with a sudden lowering of expectations resort to more narrow nationalism and concentrate on parochial interests, as happened in the past.

Europe's strategic perspective is likely to remain narrower than Washington's, even if the EU succeeds in making reforms that create a "European President" and "European Foreign Minister" and develops greater institutional capacity for crisis management. Divergent threat perceptions within Europe and the likelihood that defense spending will remain uncoordinated suggest the EU will not be a major military power by 2025. The national interests of the bigger powers will continue to complicate

EU foreign and security policy and European support for NATO could erode.

The question of Turkey's EU membership will be a test of Europe's outward focus between now and 2025. Increasing doubts about Turkey's chances are likely to slow its implementation of political and human rights reforms. Any outright rejection risks wider repercussions, reinforcing arguments in the Muslim world—including among Europe's Muslim minorities—about the incompatibility of the West and Islam. Crime could be the gravest threat inside Europe as Eurasian transnational organizations—flush from involvement in energy and mineral concerns—become more powerful and broaden their scope. One or more governments in Eastern or Central Europe could fall prey to their domination.

Europe will remain heavily dependent on Russia for energy in 2025, despite efforts to promote energy efficiency and renewable energy and lower greenhouse gas emissions. Varying levels of dependence, differing perspectives on Russia's democratic maturity and economic intentions, and failure to achieve consensus on Brussels' role are hampering nascent efforts to develop common EU polices on energy diversification and security. In the absence of a collective approach that would reduce Russia's leverage, this dependence will foster constant attentiveness to Moscow's interests by key countries, including Germany and Italy, who see Russia as a reliable supplier. Europe could pay a price for its heavy dependence, especially if Russian firms are unable to fulfill contract commitments because of underinvestment in their natural gas fields or if growing corruption and organized criminal involvement in the Eurasian energy sector spill over to infect Western business interests.

***Japan*: *Caught Between the US and China*.** Japan will face a major reorientation of its domestic and foreign policies by 2025 yet maintain its status as an upper middle rank power. Domestically, Japan's political, social, and economic systems will likely be restructured to address its demographic decline, an aging industrial base, and a more volatile political situation. Japan's decreasing population may force authorities to consider new immigration policies like a long-term visa option for visiting workers. The Japanese, however, will have difficulty overcoming their reluctance to naturalize foreigners. The aging of the population also will spur development in Japan's healthcare and housing systems to accommodate large numbers of dependent elderly.

The shrinking work force—and Japan's cultural aversion to substantial immigrant labor—will put a major strain on Japan's social services and tax revenues, leading to tax increases and calls for more competition in the domestic sector to lower the price of consumer goods. We anticipate continued restructuring of Japan's export industries, with increased emphasis on high technology products, value-added production, and information technologies. The shrinking of Japan's agricultural sector will continue, perhaps down to just 2 percent of the labor force, with a corresponding increase in payments for food imports. The working-age population, declining in absolute numbers, includes a large number of unemployed and untrained citizens in their late teens and 20s. This could lead to a shortage of white collar workers.

With increasing electoral competition, Japan's one-party political system probably will fully disintegrate by 2025. The Liberal Democratic Party may split into a number of contending parties, but it is more likely that Japan will witness a continual splitting and merging of competing political parties, leading to policy paralysis.

On the foreign front, Japan's policies will be influenced most by the policies of China and the United States, where four scenarios are possible.

- In the first scenario, a China that continues its current economic growth pattern will be increasingly important to Japan's economic growth, and Tokyo will work to maintain good political relations and increase market access for Japanese goods. Tokyo may seek a free trade agreement with Beijing well before 2025. At the same time, China's military power and influence in the region will be of increasing concern to Japanese policymakers. Their likely response will be to draw closer to the United States, increase their missile defense and antisubmarine warfare capabilities, seek to develop regional allies such as South Korea, and push for greater development of international multilateral organizations in East Asia, including an East Asian Summit.
- In a second scenario, China's economic growth falters or its policies become openly hostile toward countries in the region. In response, Tokyo would likely move to assert its influence, in part by seeking to rally democratic states in East Asia, and in part by continuing to develop its own national power through advanced military hardware. Tokyo would assume strong support from Washington in this circumstance and would move to shape political and economic forums in the region to isolate or limit Chinese influence. This would cause states in the region to make a difficult choice between their continued unease with Japanese military strength and a China that has the potential to dominate nearly all nations near its borders. As a result, Japan might find itself dealing with an ad-hoc nonaligned movement of East Asian states seeking to avoid being entrapped by either Tokyo or Beijing.
- In a third scenario, should the United States' security commitment to Japan weaken or be perceived by Tokyo as weakening, Japan may decide to move closer to Beijing on regional issues and ultimately

consider security arrangements that give China a de facto role in maintaining stability in ocean areas near Japan. Tokyo is highly unlikely to respond to a loss of the US security umbrella by developing a nuclear weapons program, short of clearly aggressive intent by China toward Japan.

- A fourth scenario would see the United States and China move significantly toward political and security cooperation in the region, leading to US accommodation of a Chinese military presence in the region and a corresponding realignment or drawdown of US forces there. In this case, Tokyo almost certainly would follow the prevailing trend and move closer to Beijing to be included in regional security and political arrangements. Similarly, others in the region, including South Korea, Taiwan, and ASEAN members likely would follow such a US lead, putting further pressure on Tokyo to align its policies with those of the other actors in the region.

Brazil: Solid Foundation for an Enhanced Leadership Role. By 2025 Brazil probably will be exercising greater regional leadership, as first among equals in South American fora, but aside from its growing role as an energy producer and its role in trade talks, it will demonstrate limited ability to project beyond the continent as a major player in world affairs. Its progress in consolidating democracy and diversifying its economy will serve as a positive regional model.

The country's maturing commitment to democracy is on a secure footing with fair and open electoral processes and smooth transitions having become routine. The current President, Lula da Silva, has a strong socialist orientation and has pursued a moderate policy course domestically and internationally, setting a positive precedent for his successors. Brazilian views about the importance of playing a key role as both a regional and world leader have largely become ingrained in the national consciousness and transcend party politics.

Economically, Brazil has established a solid foundation for steady growth based on political stability and an incremental reform process. The growing consensus for responsible fiscal and monetary policy is likely to lessen the disruptions from crises that have plagued the country in the past. Dramatic departures from the current economic consensus in Brazil, either a radical turn toward a free-market and free trade-oriented economic model or a heavy-handed statist orientation, appear to be unlikely by 2025.

Brazil's recent preliminary finds of new, possibly large offshore oil deposits have the potential to add another dynamic to an already diversified economy and put Brazil on a more rapid economic growth path. The oil discoveries in the Santos Basin—potentially holding tens of billions of barrels of reserves—could make Brazil after 2020 a major oil exporter when these fields are fully exploited. Optimistic scenarios, which assume a legal and regulatory framework attractive to foreign investment, project oil rising to a 15 percent share of GDP by 2025; even then, petroleum would only complement existing sources of national wealth.

Progress on social issues, such as reducing crime and poverty, will likely play a decisive role in determining Brazil's future leadership status. Without advances in the rule of law, even rapid economic growth will be undercut by the instability that results from pervasive crime and corruption. Mechanisms to incorporate a growing share of the population into the formal economy also will be needed to buttress Brazil's status as a modernizing world power.

Up-and-Coming Powers

Owing to the large populations and expansive landmasses of the new powers like India and China, another constellation of powerhouses is unlikely to erupt on the world scene over the next decade or two. However, up-and-coming developing states could account for an increasing proportion of the world's economic growth by 2025. Others also will play a dynamic role in their own neighborhoods.

Indonesia, **Turkey** and a post-clerically run **Iran**—states that are predominantly Islamic, but which fall outside the Arab core—appear well-situated for growing international roles. A growth-friendly macro-economic policy climate would allow their natural economic endowments to flourish. In the case of Iran, radical political reform will be necessary.

Indonesia's performance will depend upon whether it can replicate its success at political reform with measures to spur the economy. In the past decade, Indonesians have transformed their once-authoritarian country into a democracy, turning the vast archipelago into a place of relative calm where support for moderate political solutions is strong, separatist movements are largely fading away, and terrorists, finding little public support, are increasingly found and arrested. With abundant natural resources and a large population of potential consumers (it is the world's fourth most populous country), Indonesia could rise economically if its elected leaders take steps to improve the investment climate, including strengthening the legal system, improving the regulatory framework, reforming the financial sector, reducing fuel and food subsidies, and generally lowering the cost of doing business.

Looking at **Iran**—a state rich in natural gas and other resources and high in human capital—political and economic reform in addition to a stable investment climate could fundamentally redraw both the way the world perceives the country and also the way in which Iranians view themselves. Under those circumstances, economic resurgence could take place quickly in Iran and embolden a latent cosmopolitan, educated, at times secular Iranian middle-class. If empowered, this portion of the population could broaden the country's horizons, particularly eastward and away from decades of being mired in the Arab conflicts of the Middle East.

Turkey's recent economic track record of increased growth, the vitality of Turkey's emerging middle class and its geostrategic locale raise the prospect of a growing regional role in the Middle East. Economic weaknesses such as its heavy dependence on external energy sources may help to spur it toward a greater international role as Turkish authorities seek to develop their ties with energy suppliers—including close neighbors Russia and Iran—and bolster its position as a transit hub. Over the next 15 years, Turkey's most likely course involves a blending of Islamic and nationalist strains, which could serve as a model for other rapidly modernizing countries in the Middle East.

Global Scenario I: *A World Without the West*

In this fictionalized account, the new powers supplant the West as leaders on the world stage. This is not inevitable nor the only possible outcome of the rise of new states. Historically the rise of new powers—such as Japan and Germany in the late 19th and early 20th centuries—presented stiff challenges to the existing international system, all of which ended in worldwide conflict. More plausible in our minds than a direct challenge to the international system is the possibility that the emerging powers will assume a greater role in areas affecting their vital interests, particularly in view of what may be growing burden fatigue for Western countries.

Such a coalition of forces could be a competitor to institutions like NATO, offering others an alternative to the West. As detailed, we do not see these alternative coalitions as necessarily permanent fixtures of the new landscape. Indeed, given their diverse interests and competition over resources, the newer powers could as easily distance themselves from each other as come together. Although the emerging powers are likely to be preoccupied with domestic issues and sustaining their economic development, increasingly, as outlined in this chapter, they will have the capacity to be global players.

Preconditions for this scenario include:

- Lagging Western growth prompts the US and Europe to begin taking protectionist measures against the faster-growing emerging powers.
- Different models of state-society relationships help underpin the powerful (albeit fragile) Sino-Russia coalition.
- Tensions between the principal actors in the multipolar world are high as states seek energy security and strengthened spheres of influence. The Shanghai Cooperation Organization (SCO), especially,

seeks reliable and dependable clients in strategic regions—and Central Asia is in both Russia's and China's backyards.

Simulated Document: ***NOT*** **AN ACTUAL DOCUMENT**

The Shanghai Cooperation Organisation

Letter from Head of Shanghai Cooperation Organization to Secretary-General of NATO

June 15, 2015

I know we meet tomorrow to inaugurate our strategic dialogue, but I wanted to share with you beforehand my thoughts about the SCO and how far we have come. Fifteen to 20 years ago, I would never have imagined the SCO to be NATO's equal—if not (patting myself on the back) an even somewhat more important international organization. Just between ourselves, we were not destined for "greatness" except for the West's stumbling.

I think it is fair to say it began when you pulled out of Afghanistan without accomplishing your mission of pacifying the Taliban. I know you had little choice. Years of slow or no growth in the US and West had decimated defense budgets. The Americans felt overstretched and the Europeans were not going to stay without a strong US presence. The Afghan situation threatened to destabilize the whole region, and we could not stand idly by. Besides Afghanistan, we had disturbing intelligence that some "friendly" Central Asian governments were coming under pressure from radical Islamic movements and we continue to depend on Central Asian energy. The Chinese and Indians were very reluctant to throw their hats into the ring with my homeland—Russia—but they did not have better options. None of us wanted the other guy to be in charge: we were so suspicious of each other and, if truth be told, continue to be.

The so-called SCO "peacekeeping" action really put the SCO on the map and got us off the ground. Before that, it was an organization where "cooperation" was a bit of a misnomer. It would have been more aptly called the "Shanghai Organization of Mutual Distrust." China did not want to offend the US, so it did not go along with Russia's anti-American efforts. India was there to keep an eye on both China and Russia. The Central Asians thought they could use the SCO for their own purpose of playing the neighboring big powers off against one another. Iran's Ahmedi-Nejad would have joined anything with a whiff of anti-Americanism.

Still, even with these operations, the SCO would not have become a "bloc" if it had not been for the rising antagonism shown by the US and Europe toward China. China's strong ties to the US had oddly enough provided Beijing with legitimacy. China also benefited from a strong US presence in the region; Beijing's Asian neighbors would have been much more worried about China's rise if they had not had the US as a hedge. China and India were content with the status quo and did not want to get into a strong alliance with us Russians for fear of antagonizing the US. As long as that status quo held, the SCO's prospects as a "bloc" were limited.

Then came the growing protectionist movements in the US and Europe led by a coalition of forces from left to right along the political spectrum. Chinese investments came under greater scrutiny and increasingly were denied. The fact that China and India became first adopters of so many new technologies—next generation Internet, clean water, energy storage, biogerontechnology, clean coal, and biofuels—only added to the economic-driven frustration. Protectionist trade barriers were put up. Somebody other than "the West" had to pay a price for that recession which dragged on there but not so much elsewhere. China's military modernization was seen as a threat and there was a lot of loose talk in the West about the emerging powers piggy-backing off the United States' protection of the sea lanes. Needless to say, the West's antagonism sparked a nationalistic movement in China.

Interestingly, we Russians watched this from the sidelines without knowing what to do. We were pleased to see our good friends in the West take an economic drubbing. It was still nothing like what we went through in the 1990s and, of course, we took a hit as energy prices sagged with the recession in the West. But we had accumulated a lot of reserves before then.

In the end, these events were a godsend because they forced Russia and China into each other's arms. Before, Russia had been more distrustful of China's rise than the United States. Yes, we talked big about shifting all our energy supplies eastward to scare the Europeans from time to time. But we also played China off against Japan, dangling possibilities and then not following through. Our main worry was China. Fears about China's overrunning Russia's Far East were a part of it, but I think the bigger threat from our standpoint was of a more powerful China—for example, one that would not forever hide behind Russia's skirts at the UN. The Soviet-China split was always lurking too. I personally was angered by endless Chinese talk about not repeating Soviet mistakes. That hurt. Not that the Chinese weren't right, but to admit we had failed when they might succeed—that struck at Russian pride.

But now this is all behind us. Having technology that allowed for the clean use of fossil fuels was a godsend. Whether the West gave it to us, or as we were accused of doing, we stole it, is immaterial. We saw a chance to cement a strong tie—offering the Chinese opportunities for a secure energy supply and less reliance on seaborne supplies from the Middle East. They reciprocated with long-term contracts. We also learned how to cooperate in Central Asia instead of trying to undermine each other by our actions with various regimes. Seeing a strong Sino-Russian partnership arise, the others—India, Iran, etc.—did not want to be left out of the picture and have rallied around us. Of course, it helps that US and European protectionists lumped India with China, so there really was not much left for them to do.

How stable is our relationship? Don't quote me, but this is not a new Cold War. Sure, we talk a great game about state capitalism and authoritarianism, but it is no ideology like Communism. And it is in our mutual interests that democracy not break out in Central Asia as China and Russia would be the targets of any such uprisings. I can't say that we Russians and Chinese really like each other much more than before. In fact, both of us have to worry about our respective nationalisms getting in the way of mutual interests. Let's put it this way: the Russian and Chinese peoples are not enamored with one another. Russians want to be respected as Europeans, not Eurasians, and China's elites are still in their hearts geared toward the West. But temporary expedients have been known to grow into permanence, you know?

Chapter 4
Scarcity in the Midst of Plenty?

The international system will be challenged by growing resource constraints at the same time that it is coping with the impact of new players. Access to relatively secure and clean energy sources and management of chronic food and water shortages will assume increasing importance for a growing number of countries during the next 15–20 years. Adding well over a billion people to the world's population by 2025 will itself put pressure on these vital resources. An increasing percentage of the world's population will be moving from rural areas to urban and developed ones to seek greater personal security and economic opportunity. Many—particularly in Asia—will be joining the middle class and will be seeking to emulate Western lifestyles, which involve greater per capita consumption of all these resources. Unlike earlier periods when resource scarcities loomed large, the significant growth in demand from emerging markets, combined with constraints on new production—such as the control exerted now by state-run companies in the global energy market—limits the likelihood that market forces alone will rectify the supply-and-demand imbalance.

The already stressed resource sector will be further complicated and, in most cases, exacerbated by climate change, whose physical effects will worsen throughout this period. Continued escalation of energy demand will hasten the impacts of climate change. On the other hand, forcibly cutting back on fossil fuel use before substitutes are widely available could threaten continued economic development, particularly for countries like China whose industries have not yet achieved high levels of energy efficiency. Technological advances and policy decisions around the world germane to greenhouse gas emissions over the next 15 years are likely to determine whether the globe's temperature ultimately rises more than

2 degree centigrade—the threshold at which effects are thought to be no longer manageable.

Food and water also are intertwined with climate change, energy, and demography. Rising energy prices increase the cost for consumers and the environment of industrial-scale agriculture and application of petrochemical fertilizers. A switch from use of arable land for food to fuel crops provides a limited solution and could exacerbate both the energy and food situations. Climatically, rainfall anomalies and constricted seasonal flows of snow and glacial melts are aggravating water scarcities, harming agriculture in many parts of the globe. Energy and climate dynamics also combine to amplify a number of other ills such as health problems, agricultural losses to pests, and storm damage. The greatest danger may arise from the convergence and interaction of many stresses simultaneously. Such a complex and unprecedented syndrome of problems could overload decisionmakers, making it difficult for them to take actions in time to enhance good outcomes or avoid bad ones.

The Dawning of a Post-Petroleum Age?

By 2025 the world will be in the midst of a fundamental energy transition—in terms of both fuel types and sources. Non-OPEC liquid hydrocarbon production (i.e., crude oil, natural gas liquids, and unconventionals such as tar sands) will not be able to grow commensurate with demand. The production levels of many traditional energy producers—Yemen, Norway, Oman, Colombia, the UK, Indonesia, Argentina, Syria, Egypt, Peru, Tunisia—are already in decline. Others' production levels—Mexico, Brunei, Malaysia, China, India, Qatar—have flattened. The number of countries capable of meaningfully expanding production will decline. Only six countries—Saudi Arabia, Iran, Kuwait, the UAE, Iraq (potentially), and Russia—are projected to account for 39 percent of total world oil production in 2025. The major producers increasingly will be located in the Middle East, which contains some two-thirds of world reserves. OPEC production in the Persian Gulf countries is projected to grow by 43 percent during 2003–2025. Saudi Arabia alone will account for almost half of all Gulf production, an amount greater than that expected from Africa and the Caspian area combined.

A partial consequence of this growing concentration has been increased control of oil and gas resources by national oil companies. When the Club of Rome made its famous forecast of looming energy scarcities, the "Seven Sisters" still had a strong influence on global oil markets and production.[7] Driven by shareholders, they responded to price signals to

[7] The "Seven Sisters" refers to seven Western oil companies that dominated mid-20th century oil production, refining, and distribution. With the formation and establishment of OPEC in the 1960s and 1970s, the Western oil companies' influence and clout declined.

explore, invest, and promote technologies necessary to increase production. By contrast, national oil companies have strong economic and political incentives to limit investment in order to prolong the production horizon. Keeping oil in the ground provides resources for future generations in oil states that have limited their economic options.

The number and geographic distribution of oil producers will decrease concurrent with another energy transition: the move to cleaner fuels. The prized fuel in the shorter term likely will be natural gas. By 2025, consumption of natural gas is expected to grow by about 60 percent, according to DoE/Energy Information Agency projections. Although natural gas deposits are not necessarily co-located with oil, they are highly concentrated. Three countries—Russia, Iran, and Qatar—hold over 57 percent of the world's natural gas reserves. Considering oil and natural gas together, two countries—Russia and Iran—emerge as energy kingpins. Nevertheless, North America (the US, Canada, and Mexico) is expected to produce an appreciable proportion—18 percent—of total world production by 2025.

Even though the use of natural gas is likely to grow steadily in absolute terms, coal may be the fastest growing energy source despite being the "dirtiest." Rising prices for oil and natural gas would put a new premium on energy sources that are cheap, abundant, and close to markets. Three of the largest and fastest-growing energy consumers—the US, China, and India—and Russia possess the four largest recoverable coal reserves, representing 67 percent of known global reserves. Increased coal production could extend non-renewable carbon-based energy systems for one or even two centuries. China will still be very dependent on coal in 2025 and Beijing is likely to be under increasing international pressure to use clean technologies to burn it. China is overtaking the US in the amount of carbon emissions it puts in the atmosphere despite its much smaller GDP.

The use of nuclear fuel for electrical power generation is expected to expand, but the increase will not be sufficient to fill growing demand for electricity. Third-generation nuclear reactors have lower costs of power generation, improved safety characteristics, and better waste and proliferation management features than previous reactor designs. Third-generation nuclear reactors are economically competitive at present electricity prices and are beginning to be deployed around the world. Although most nuclear power plants are currently in industrialized countries, growing demand for electricity in China, India, South Africa and other rapidly growing countries will increase the demand for nuclear power.

Breakdown of Likely Energy Sources

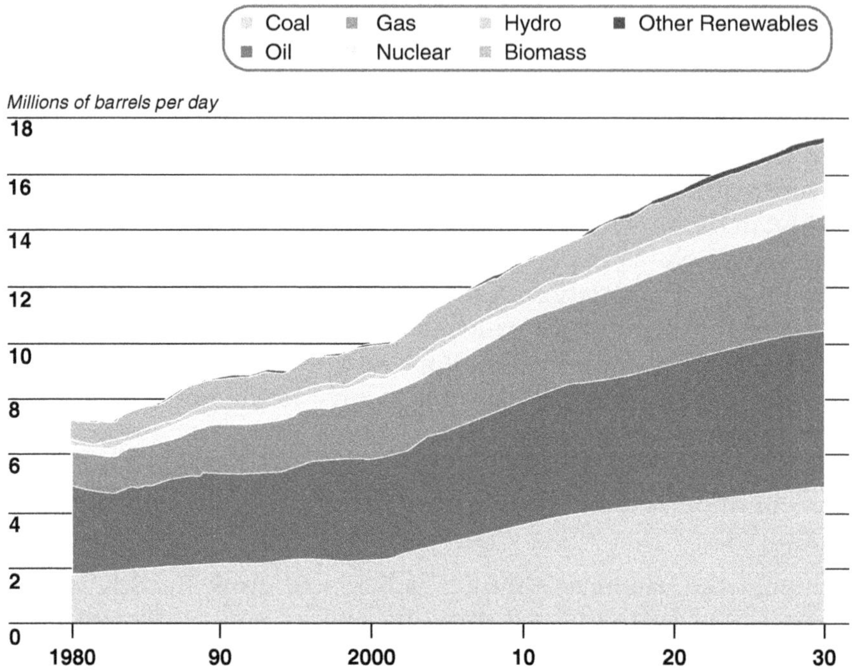

Note: Global demand grows by more than half over the next quarter of a century, with coal use rising in absolute terms.

Source: PFC Energy International.

The supply of uranium, which is the principal feedstock for nuclear power, is unlikely to limit the future deployment of nuclear power. Available uranium is likely to be sufficient to support the expansion of nuclear energy without reprocessing well into the second half of the century. If uranium should prove to be in short supply, reactors capable of breeding nuclear fuels, along with recycling of used fuels, could continue to support the global expansion of nuclear energy.

However, because of its infrastructure requirements, concern over proliferation of nuclear expertise and material, and uncertainty over licensing and spent fuel processing, expansion of nuclear power generation by 2025 to cover anywhere near the increasing demand would be virtually impossible. The infrastructure (human and physical), legal (permitting), and construction hurdles are just too big. Only at the end of our 15–20 year period are we likely to see a serious ramp up of nuclear technologies.

Timing is Everything

All current technologies are inadequate for replacing traditional energy architectures on the scale needed, and new energy technologies probably will not be commercially viable and widespread by 2025 (see foldout). The present generation of biofuels is too expensive to grow, would further boost food prices, and their manufacture consumes essentially the same amount of energy they produce. Other ways of converting nonfood biomass resources to fuels and chemical products should be more promising, such as those based on high-growth algae or agricultural waste products, especially cellulosic biomass. Development of clean coal technologies and carbon capture and storage is gaining momentum and—if such technologies were cost-competitive by 2025—would enable coal to generate more electricity in a carbon-constrained regulatory environment. Long-lasting hydrogen fuel cells have potential, but they remain in their infancy and are at least a decade away from commercial production. Enormous infrastructure investment might be required to support a "hydrogen economy." An Argonne National Laboratory study found that hydrogen, from well to tank, is likely to be at least twice as costly as gasoline.

Even with the favorable policy and funding environment that would be needed for biofuels, clean coal, or hydrogen, major technologies historically have had an "adoption lag." A recent study found that in the energy sector, it takes an average of 25 years for a new production technology to become widely adopted. A major reason for this lag is the need for new infrastructure to handle major innovation. For energy in particular, massive and sustained infrastructure investments made for almost 150 years encompass production, transportation, refining, marketing, and retail activities. Adoption of natural gas, a fuel superior to oil in many respects, illustrates the difficulty of a transition to something new. Technologies to use natural gas have been widely available since at least the 1970s, yet natural gas still lags crude oil in the global market because the technical and investment requirements for producing and transporting it are greater than they are for oil-based fuels.

Simply meeting baseline energy demand over the next two decades is estimated to require more than $3 trillion of investment in traditional hydrocarbons by companies built up over more than a century and with market capitalizations in the hundreds of billions of dollars. Because a new form of energy is highly unlikely to use existing infrastructure without modifications, we expect any new form of energy to demand similarly massive investment.

Despite what are seen as long odds now, we cannot rule out the possibility of a transition by 2025 that would avoid the costs of an infrastructure overhaul. The greatest possibility for a relatively quick and inexpensive transition during that period comes from better renewable generation sources (photovoltaic and wind) and improvements in battery technology. With many of these technologies, the infrastructure cost hurdle for individual projects would be lower, enabling many small economic actors to develop their own energy transformation projects that directly serve their interests—e.g., stationary fuel cells powering homes and offices, recharging plug-in hybrid autos, and selling energy back to the grid. Also, energy conversion schemes—such as plans to generate hydrogen for automotive fuel cells from electricity in a homeowner's garage—could avoid the need to develop complex hydrogen transportation infrastructure. Similarly, non-ethanol biofuels derived from genetically modified feed stocks may be able to leverage the considerable investment in liquid petroleum transport and distribution infrastructure.

The Geopolitics of Energy

Both high and low energy price levels would have major geopolitical implications and, over the course of 20 years, periods of both could occur. DoE's Energy Information Administration and several leading energy consultants believe higher price levels are likely, at least to 2015, because of plateauing supply and growing demand. These causes are unlike the case in 1970s and early 1980s when high oil prices were caused by an intentional restriction in supply. Even with the overall secular rise in energy costs, prices well below $100 a barrel are periodically likely with the expected increased volatility and need not come about as a result of technological breakthroughs and rapid commercialization of a substitute fuel. Plausible scenarios for a downward shift and change in market psychology include slowing global growth; increased production in Iraq, Angola, Central Asia, and elsewhere; and greater energy efficiencies with currently available technology.

Even at prices below $100 a barrel, financial transfers connected with the energy trade produce clear winners and losers. Most of the 32 states that import 80 percent or more of their energy needs are likely to experience significantly slower economic growth than they might have achieved with lower oil prices. A number of these states have been identified by outside experts as at risk of state failure—the Central African Republic, DROC, Nepal, and Laos, for example. States characterized by high import dependence, low GDP per capita, high current account deficits, and heavy international indebtedness form a particularly perilous state profile. Such a profile includes most of East Africa and the Horn. Pivotal yet problem-beset countries, such as Pakistan, will be at risk of state failure.

With *higher prices*, more stable countries fare better but their prospects for economic growth would drop somewhat and political turbulence could occur. Efficient, service-sector oriented OECD economies are not immune but are harmed the least. China, though cushioned by its massive financial reserves, would be hit by higher oil prices, which would make lifting millions more out of poverty more difficult. China also would need to mine and transport more domestic coal, build more nuclear power plants, and seek to improve energy end-use efficiencies to offset the higher priced imports.

With high prices, major exporters such as Russia and Iran would have the financial resources to increase their national power. The extent and modalities of steps to increase their power and influence would depend on how they used their profits to invest in human capital, financial stabilization, and economic infrastructure. Judicious application of Russia's increased revenues to the economy, social needs, and foreign policy instruments would likely more than double Russia's standing as measured by an academic national power index.

A *sustained plunge in oil prices* would have significant implications for countries relying on robust oil revenues to balance the budget or build up domestic investment. For Iran, a drop in oil prices to the $55–60 range or below would put significant pressure on the regime to make painful choices between subsidizing populist economic programs and sustaining funding for intelligence and security operations and other programs designed to extend its regional power. The notion that state-dominated economies, apparently able to achieve economic growth absent political freedoms or a fully free market, are a credible alternative to Western notions of free markets and liberal democracy could be badly dented, particularly since history suggests the US and other Western states adapt more quickly and effectively to unexpected changes in energy markets.

Winners and Losers in a Post-Petroleum World

We believe the most likely occurrence by 2025 is a technological breakthrough that will provide an alternative to oil and natural gas, but implementation will lag because of the necessary infrastructure costs and need for longer replacement time. However, whether the breakthrough occurs within the 2025 time frame or later, the geopolitical implications of a shift away from oil and natural gas will be immense.

- Saudi Arabia will absorb the biggest shock, as its leaders will be forced to tighten up on the costs of the royal establishment. The regime could face new tensions with the Wahabi establishment as Riyadh seeks to promote a series of major economic reforms—including women's full participation in the economy—and a new social contract with its public as it tries to institute a work ethic to accelerate development plans and diversify the economy.
- In Iran, the drop in oil and gas prices will undermine any populist economic policies. Pressure for economic reform will increase, potentially putting pressure on the clerical governing elite to loosen its grip. Incentives to open up to the West in a bid for greater foreign investment, establishing or strengthening ties with Western partners—including with the US—will increase.

Iranian leaders might be more willing to trade their nuclear policies for aid and trade.

For Iraq, emphasis on investing in non-oil sectors of its economy will increase. The smaller Gulf states, which have been making massive investments designed to transform themselves into global tourist and transport hubs, are likely to manage the transition well, bolstered by their robust sovereign wealth funds (SWFs). Across the Arab world, SWFs are being deployed to develop non-oil sectors of the economy in a race against oil as a diminishing asset.

Outside the Middle East, Russia will potentially be the biggest loser, particularly if its economy remains heavily tied to energy exports, and could be reduced to middle power status. Venezuela, Bolivia, and other petro-populist regimes could unravel completely, if that has not occurred beforehand because of already growing discontent and decreasing production. Absent support from Venezuela, Cuba might be forced to begin China-like market reforms.

Early oil decline states—those exporters which had peaked or were declining as is currently the case with Indonesia and Mexico—may be better prepared to shift the focus of their economic activities and diversify into non-energy sectors.

Under any scenario energy dynamics could produce a number of new alignments or groupings with geopolitical significance:

- Russia, needing Caspian area natural gas in order to satisfy European and other contracts, is likely to be forceful in keeping Central Asian countries within Moscow's sphere, and, absent a non-Russia-controlled outlet, has a good chance of succeeding.
- China will continue to seek to buttress its market power by cultivating political relationships designed to safeguard its access to oil and gas. Beijing's ties with Saudi Arabia will strengthen, as the Kingdom is the only supplier capable of responding in a big way to China's petroleum thirst.
- Beijing will want to offset its growing reliance on Riyadh by strengthening ties to other producers. Iran will see this as an opportunity to solidify China's support for Tehran, which probably would strain Beijing's ties to Riyadh. Tehran may also be able to forge even closer ties with Russia.
- We believe India will scramble to ensure access to energy by making overtures to Burma, Iran, and Central Asia. Pipelines to India transiting restive regions may connect New Delhi to local instabilities.

Water, Food, and Climate Change

Experts currently consider 21 countries with a combined population of about 600 million to be either cropland or freshwater scarce. Owing to

Technology Breakthroughs[a] by 2025

Probable · Possible · Plausible

What Is the Technology?	**Ubiquitous computing** will be enabled by widespread tagging and networking of mundane objects (the Internet of Things) such as food packages, furniture, room sensors, and paper documents. Such items will be located and identified, monitored, and remotely controlled through enabling technologies—including Radio Frequency Identifications, sensor networks, tiny embedded servers, and energy harvesters—connected via the next-generation Internet using abundant, low cost, and high-power computing.	**Clean water technologies** comprise a range of technologies that enable faster and more energy efficient treatment of fresh water and waste water, and desalination of brackish and sea water, to provide sustainable and diverse water sources useable for domestic, agricultural, and industrial purposes. The technologies include advances in existing technologies such as membrane bioreactors and a range of materials' substitutions and advances in other separation and purification technologies driven by the unique chemical and physical properties of nanoparticles and nanofibers.	**Energy storage technology** encompasses a wide range of materials and techniques for storing energy, a necessity for the viability of many alternatives to fossil-fuel energy sources. Included are battery materials, ultracapacitors and hydrogen storage materials (particularly for fuel cells). Efficient energy storage will enable the on-demand energy component of a variety of systems such as hydrogen-based energy systems, a host of renewable (but intermittent) energy sources such as wind and solar, and low-emission transport vehicles.	**"Biogerontechnology"** is the science related to the study of the cellular and molecular basis of disease and aging applied to the development of new technological means for identifying and treating diseases and disabilities associated with old age. Supporting technologies include improvements in biosensors for real-time monitoring of human health, robust information technology, ubiquitous DNA sequencing and DNA-specific medicine, and fully targeted drug-delivery mechanisms.	**Clean coal technologies** include various combinations of carbon capture sequestration (CCS) to prohibit CO_2—a byproduct of burning coal—from entering the atmosphere; coal conversion into syngas (gasification); and processes to convert syngas to hydrocarbons. CCS can reduce or possibly eliminate greenhouse gas emissions from a coal plant. Coal gasification improves efficiency when generating electricity and emits fewer pollutants relative to coal burning plants. The syngas also can be a feedstock for transportation fuels and industrial chemicals that replace petroleum-derived products.
What Are Drivers and Barriers?	**Key Drivers:** Demand for greater efficiency in a wide variety of applications from food safety to more efficient supply chains and logistics. Corporations, governments, and individuals will benefit in areas such as energy efficiency and security, quality of life, and early warning of equipment maintenance needs. **Key Barriers:** Implementation depends on availability of power for small, maintenance-free devices, development of profitable business models, and addressing likely major privacy and security concerns.	**Key Drivers:** Clean water is set to become the world's scarcest but most-needed natural resource because of new demands resulting from population increases and expectations that climate changes will reduce natural fresh water sources in some areas. Demand will increase for water for domestic use, as well as for agriculture (including new biopharma and biofuel crops) and industry processes. **Key Barriers:** The demand for sustainable clean water supplies will only be met if both large- and small-scale systems can overcome cost constraints—both in terms of energy requirements and infrastructure costs.	**Key Drivers:** High fossil fuel energy prices, the desire to reduce dependency on foreign energy sources, and pressure to increase renewable energy sources drive the development of these technologies. **Key Barriers:** Development and deployment of the technologies are restricted by material science, the unknown cost of large-scale manufacturing, and infrastructure investment costs.	**Key Drivers:** Aging populations, increasingly expensive medical costs, and the desire to keep older workers in the work force drive the development of these technologies. **Key Barriers:** Cost of development, lengthy human trials, privacy concerns, possible difficulties of insurance, and religious and social concerns will inhibit their development.	**Key Drivers:** The desire to reduce dependence on foreign energy sources drives interest in expanding the use of available coal reserves, while pressure for clean energy production requires development of CCS methods. **Key Barriers:** Substantial technology and cost barriers exist for CCS scale-up and implementation for coal power plants, while uncertainties in both the oil market and environmental regulatory landscape preclude investment in expensive coal gasification plants (even without CCS).
Why Is the Technology a Game-Changer?	These technologies could radically accelerate a range of enhanced efficiencies, leading to integration of closed societies into the information age and security monitoring of almost all places. Supply chains would be streamlined with savings in costs and efficiencies that would reduce dependence upon human labor.	Although the Earth contains a plentiful supply of water, only 1 percent is fit or available for human consumption and some 20 percent of the world's population does not have access to fresh drinking water. Regions experiencing water scarcity will increase as the global population increases and as climate change induced droughts occur. Both developing and developed countries will be affected. Various industries increasingly will compete for water, including agriculture, food, and beverage processing plants as well as chemical, pharmaceutical, and semiconductor industries. First movers to develop and deploy cheap energy-efficient clean-water technologies could gain huge geopolitical advantage.	The ability to store and use energy on demand from a combination of alternative energy sources offers a significant potential to lead a paradigm shift away from fossil fuels, resulting in significant global economic and social advantages to first commercializers. With widespread deployment, the result could be destabilizing to rentier economies dependant upon fossil fuels.	Deployment would shift the cost, allocation, and use of healthcare resources. Nations will be challenged as a result of the changing demographic structures and new psychologies, behaviors and activity patterns of aging yet healthy citizens and the concomitant need to formulate new national economic and social policies.	A successful accelerated and rapid deployment of clean coal technology could pose a major challenge to other hydrocarbon (predominately oil) energy markets and nascent renewable energy markets. This would change the dependency of coal rich/oil poor nations on imported oil/gas with a resulting significant shift in national interests.

[a]These breakthroughs are categorized based upon the development and initial deployment of the technology. In some cases, full deployment may lag significantly due to infrastructure requirements.

Source: SRI Consulting Business Intelligence and Toffler Associates.

Technology Breakthroughs[a] by 2025

Probable | Possible | Plausible

What Is the Technology?	**Human strength augmentation technologies** involve mechanical and electronic systems that supplement human physical capabilities. They include wearable exoskeletons with mechanical actuators at hips, elbows, and other skeletal joints. At the extreme an exoskeleton could resemble a wearable humanoid robot that uses sensors, interfaces, power systems, and actuators to monitor and respond to arm and leg movements, providing the wearer with increased strength and control.	**Biofuels technology** is used to produce ethanol from crops such as corn and sugarcane and biodiesel from crops such as grapeseed and soy. Next-generation processes will convert lignocellulosic materials to fuels. Significant potential also exists to cultivate high-growth microalgae for conversion to biodiesel and other biofuels.	**Service robotics** comprise robots and unmanned vehicles for non-manufacturing applications, using a large number of enabling technologies including hardware (e.g. sensors, actuators, power systems) and software platforms (advanced systems might incorporate behavioral algorithms and artificial intelligence). These technologies would enable a wide variety of remote controlled, semiautonomous (with human intervention), and completely autonomous robotic systems.	**Human cognitive augmentation technologies** include drugs, implants, virtual learning environments, and wearable devices to enhance human cognitive abilities. Training software exploits neuroplasticity to improve a person's natural abilities, and wearable and implantable devices promise to improve vision, hearing, and even memory. Bio and information technologies promise enhanced human mental performance at every life stage.
What Are Drivers and Barriers?	**Key Drivers:** Demand for enhanced strength, endurance, and physical security for assisting the handicapped and elderly, and for reducing reliance on manual labor drive these technologies. **Key Barriers:** The cost of manufacturing and the uncertain economic payoff, challenges with portable power sources, and humans' ability to accept and use the technology all constrain development and deployment of the technologies.	**Key Drivers:** High crude oil prices, the desire to reduce dependency on foreign oil sources, and government policies to increase renewable energy sources drive these technologies. **Key Barriers:** Development and deployment of the technologies are restricted by land use, water availability, competition from food applications, and the challenge of scaling up for large-scale production. Biofuels under development today are more sustainable, but production costs are still too high.	**Key Drivers:** Security and safety applications, healthcare or home care for aging populations, and the desire to improve manufacturing productivity and reduce demand for service labor drive these technologies. **Key Barriers:** Development of viable business models, cost, uncertain technology reach (portable power sources and especially artificial intelligence), and integration issues (e.g. IT, robot standards), inhibit the deployment of service robots.	**Key Drivers:** Desires for improved military planning, combatant performance, treatment of Alzheimer's disease, increasing education effectiveness, enhanced personal entertainment, and improving job performance could spur the development of these technologies. **Key Barriers:** Cultural hesitancy to go down an "unnatural" path of human development, and fears of unknown effects could slow down development and deployment. Major scientific and medical research challenges would need to be overcome.
Why Is the Technology a Game-Changer?	Biomechanical devices promise to give a person superhuman strength and endurance or restore a disabled person's capabilities. The widespread use of the technology would greatly improve labor productivity by reducing the number of humans needed for a task or increasing the amount of work a single human can accomplish, while enabling unassisted activity by the disabled or elderly. Such technologies also could greatly improve the combat effectiveness of ground combat forces.	A large-scale move to energy-efficient biofuels could reduce demand for oil and ease international competition for world oil supplies and reserves. In addition, widespread use of biofuels would fundamentally alter the energy dependence of some nations upon imported fossil fuels thereby shifting national interests. Emerging biofuels technologies that avoid significant land-use changes—using feedstocks such as agricultural waste products, native grasses, and biofuels from algae, could significantly reduce net CO_2 emissions to the atmosphere.	In domestic settings, widespread use of the technology could leverage manpower, disrupt unskilled labor markets and immigration patterns, and change care for a growing elderly population. As early adopters, governments could provide increased security and project combat power with reduced levels of manpower and system life-cycle costs.	The uneven deployment of these technologies could quickly reshape economic and military advantages between nations. Early and robust adopters could see significant benefits, while nations and societies hesitant to employ the technologies may find themselves disadvantaged. International pressure to regulate the technologies could likewise be disruptive as some cultures may welcome the changes to obtain quick benefits, while others loathe their "un-human" character.

[a]These breakthroughs are categorized based upon the development and initial deployment of the technology. In some cases, full deployment may lag significantly due to infrastructure requirements.

Source: SRI Consulting Business Intelligence and Toffler Associates.

continuing population growth, 36 countries, home to about 1.4 billion people, are projected to fall into this category by 2025. Among the new entrants will be Burundi, Colombia, Ethiopia, Eritrea, Malawi, Pakistan, and Syria. Lack of access to stable supplies of **water** is reaching unprecedented proportions in many areas of the world (see map on page 72) and is likely to grow worse owing to rapid urbanization and population growth. Demand for water for agricultural purposes and hydroelectric power generation also will expand. Use of water for irrigation is far greater than for household consumption. In developing countries, agriculture currently consumes over 70 percent of the world's water. The construction of hydroelectric power stations on major rivers may improve flood control, but it might also cause considerable anxiety to downstream users of the river who expect continued access to water.

The World Bank estimates that demand for food will rise by 50 percent by 2030, as a result of growing world population, rising affluence, and shifts to Western dietary preferences by a larger middle class. The global food sector has been highly responsive to market forces, but farm production probably will continue to be hampered by misguided agriculture policies that limit investment and distort critical price signals. Keeping food prices down to placate the urban poor and spur savings for industrial investment has distorted agricultural prices in the past. If political elites are more worried about urban instability than rural incomes—a safe bet in many countries—these policies are likely to persist, increasing the risk of tight supplies in the future. The demographic trend for increased urbanization—particularly in developing states—underscores the likelihood that failed policies will continue.

Two Climate Change Winners

Russia has the potential to gain the most from increasingly temperate weather. Russia has vast untapped reserves of natural gas and oil in Siberia and also offshore in the Arctic, and warmer temperatures should make the reserves considerably more accessible. This would be a huge boon to the Russian economy, as presently 80 percent of the country's exports and 32 percent of government revenues derive from the production of energy and raw materials. In addition, the opening of an Arctic waterway could provide economic and commercial advantages. However, Russia could be hurt by damaged infrastructure as the Arctic tundra melts and will need new technology to develop the region's fossil energy.

Canada will be spared several serious North American climate-related developments—intense hurricanes and withering heat waves—and climate change could open up millions of square miles to development. Access to the resource-rich Hudson Bay would be improved, and being a circumpolar power ringing a major portion of a warming Arctic could be a geopolitical and economic bonus. Additionally, agricultural growing seasons will lengthen, net energy demand for heating/cooling will likely drop, and forests will expand somewhat into the tundra. However, not all soil in Canada can take advantage of the change in growing season, and some forest products are already experiencing damage due to changes in pest infestation enabled by warmer climates.

Between now and 2025, the world will have to juggle competing and conflicting energy security and food security concerns, yielding a tangle of difficult-to-manage consequences. In the major grain exporters (the US, Canada, Argentina, and Australia), demand for biofuels—enhanced by government subsidies—will claim larger areas of cropland and greater volumes of irrigation water, even as biofuel production and processing technologies are made more efficient. This "fuel farming" tradeoff, coupled with periodic export controls among Asian producers and rising demand for protein among growing middle classes worldwide, will force grain prices in the global market to fluctuate at levels above today's highs. Some economists argue that, with international markets settling at lower grain volumes, speculation—invited by expectations of rising fuel costs and more erratic, climate change-induced weather patterns—could play a greater role in food prices.

A consortium of large agricultural producers—including India and China, along with the US and EU partners—is likely to work to launch a second Green Revolution, this time in Sub-Saharan Africa, which could help dampen price volatility in worldwide grain markets. By 2025, increases in African grain yields probably will be substantial, but the increases will be confined principally to states in the southern and eastern regions of the continent, which will have deepened trade and security relations with East and South Asian states. Elsewhere south of the Sahara, civil conflict and the political and economic focus on mining and petroleum extraction are likely to foil most of the consortium's attempts to upgrade irrigation and rural transportation networks and to extend credit and investment, allowing population growth to outpace gains in agricultural productivity.

In addition to the currently projected scarcities of freshwater and cropland, the UK Treasury-commissioned Stern Report estimates that by the middle of the century 200 million people may be permanently displaced "climate migrants"—representing a ten-fold increase over today's entire documented refugee and internally displaced populations. Although this is considered high by many experts, broad agreement exists about the risks of large scale migration and the need for better preparation. Most displaced persons traditionally relocate within their home countries, but in the future many are likely to find their home countries have diminishing capabilities to accommodate them. Thus the number of migrants seeking to move from disadvantaged into relatively privileged countries is likely to increase. The largest inflows will mirror many current migratory patterns—from North Africa and Western Asia into Europe, Latin America into the US, and Southeast Asia into Australia.

Strategic Implications of an Opening Arctic

Estimates vary as to when the Arctic is likely to be ice free during the summer. The National Snow and Ice Data Center suggests a seasonally ice-free Arctic by 2060; more current research suggests the date could be as soon as 2013. The two most important implications of an opening Arctic are improved access to likely vast energy and mineral resources and potentially shorter maritime shipping routes.

Transiting the Northern Sea Route above Russia between the North Atlantic and the North Pacific would trim about 5,000 nautical miles and a week's sailing time off a trip compared with use of the Suez Canal. Voyaging between Europe and Asia through Canada's Northwest Passage would trim some 4,000 nautical miles off of a trip using the Panama Canal.

Resource and shipping benefits are unlikely to materialize by 2025. The US National Petroleum Council has said that some of the technology to exploit oil from the heart of the Arctic region may not be ready until as late as 2050. Nonetheless, these potential riches and advantages are already perceptible to the United States, Canada, Russia, Denmark, and Norway—as evidenced by the emergence of competing territorial claims, such as between Russia and Norway, and Canada and Denmark.

Although serious near-term tension could result in small-scale confrontations over contested claims, the Arctic is unlikely to spawn major armed conflict. Circumpolar states have other major ports on other bodies of water, so the Arctic does not pose any lifeblood blockade dangers. Additionally, these states share a common interest in regulating access to the Arctic by hostile powers, states of concern, or dangerous nonstate actors; and by their shared need for assistance from high-tech companies to exploit the Arctic's resources.

The greatest strategic consequence over the next couple of decades may be that relatively large, wealthy, resource-deficient trading states such as China, Japan, and Korea will benefit from increased energy resources provided by any Arctic opening and shorter shipping distances.

Over the next 20 years, worries about climate change effects may be more significant than any physical changes linked to climate change. Perceptions of a rapidly changing environment may cause nations to take unilateral actions to secure resources, territory, and other interests. Willingness to engage in greater multilateral cooperation will depend on a number of factors, such as the behavior of other countries, the economic context, or the importance of the interests to be defended or won.

Many scientists worry that recent assessments underestimate the impact of climate change and misjudge the likely time when effects will be felt. Scientists currently have limited capability to predict the likelihood or magnitude of extreme climate shifts but believe—based on historic precedents—that it will not occur gradually or smoothly. Drastic cutbacks in allowable CO_2 emissions probably would disadvantage the rapidly emerging economies that are still low on the efficiency curve, but large-scale users in the developed world—such as the US—also would be shaken and the global economy could be plunged into a recession or worse.

Projected Global Water Scarcity, 2025

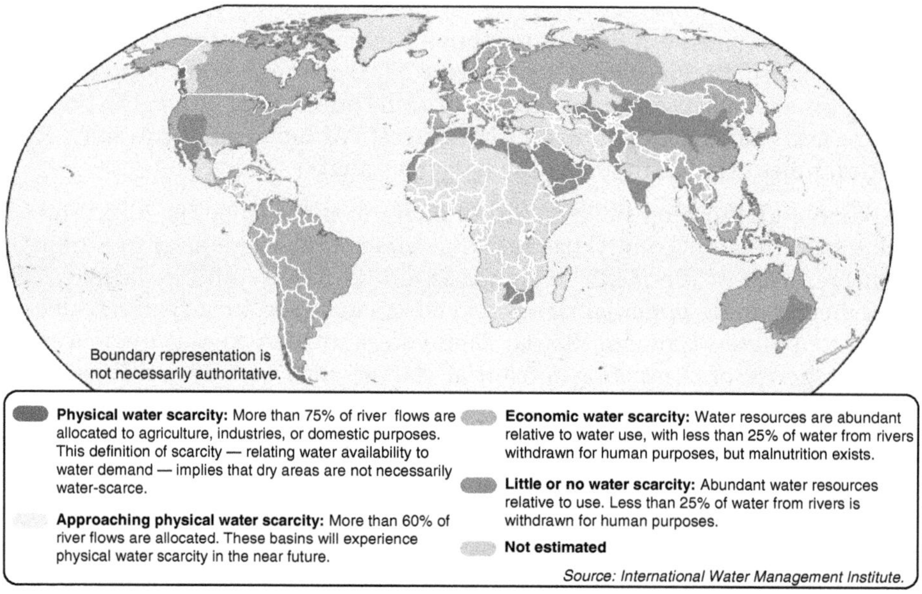

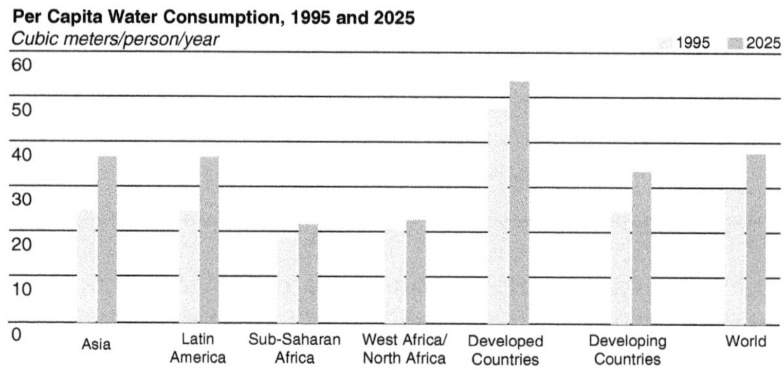

Source: International Food Policy Research Institute , Global Water Outlook to 2025.

Sub-Saharan Africa: More Interactions with the World and More Troubled

In 2025, Sub-Saharan Africa will remain the most vulnerable region on Earth in terms of economic challenges, population stresses, civil conflict, and political instability. The weakness of states and troubled relations between states and societies probably will slow major improvements in the region's prospects over the next 20 years unless there is sustained international engagement and, at times, intervention. Southern Africa will continue to be the most stable and promising sub-region politically and economically.

Sub-Saharan Africa will continue to be a major supplier of oil, gas, and metals to world markets and increasingly will attract the attention of Asian states seeking access to commodities, including China and India. However, despite increased global demand for commodities, increased resource income may not benefit the majority of the population or result in significant economic gains. Poor economic policies—rooted in patrimonial interests and incomplete economic reform—will likely exacerbate ethnic and religious divides as well as crime and corruption in many countries. Ruling elites are likely to continue to accrue greater income and wealth, while poverty will persist or worsen in rural areas and sprawling urban centers. The divide between elite and non-elite populations is likely to widen, reinforcing conditions that could generate divisive political and religious extremism.

By 2025, the region's population is expected to reach over one billion, notwithstanding the effects of HIV/AIDS. Over one-half of the population will be under age 24, and many will be seeking economic opportunity or physical safety via out-migration owing to conflict, climate change, or widespread unemployment. The earliest global effects of climate change, including water stress and scarcity, will begin to occur in Sub-Saharan Africa by 2025.

Today almost one-half (23 of 48) of the countries in Sub-Saharan Africa are classed as democracies, and the majority of African states are on a democratic path, but the most populous states in the region and those with high population growth could backslide.

Although Africa is already assuming more of its own peacekeeping responsibilities, the region will be vulnerable to civil conflict and complex forms of interstate conflict—with militaries fragmented along ethnic or other divides, limited control of border areas, and insurgents and criminal groups preying on unarmed civilians in neighboring countries. Central Africa contains the most troubling of these cases, including Congo-Kinshasa, Congo-Brazzaville, Central African Republic, and Chad.

In contrast to other regions of the world, African attitudes toward the US will remain positive, although many African governments will remain critical of US policies on issues like the Middle East, Cuba, and global trade. Africa will continue to push for UN reform and for permanent representation on the UN Security Council.

Global Scenario II: *October Surprise*

In the following fictionalized account, global inattention to climate change leads to major unexpected impacts, thrusting the world into a new level of vulnerability. Scientists are currently uncertain whether we already have hit a tipping point at which climate change has accelerated and whether there is little we can do—including reducing emissions—that will mitigate effects even over the longer term. Most scientists believe we will not know whether we have hit a tipping point until it is too late. Uncertainties about the pace and specific vulnerabilities or impacts from climate change are likely to persist over the next 15–20 years even if our knowledge about climate change deepens, according to many scientists.

An extreme weather event—as described in this scenario—could occur. Coping with the greater frequency of such events, coupled with other physical impacts of climate change such as growing water scarcities and more food crises, may preoccupy policymakers even while options for solving such problems dwindle. In this example, relocating the New York Stock Exchange to a less vulnerable location is considered, but serious consideration also would be given to relocating other institutions to ensure continuity of operations. Although this scenario focuses on an event that occurs in the US, other governments have been caught by surprise with different types of environmental disasters and have suffered a loss of standing. Mitigation efforts—further cutbacks in carbon emissions—are unlikely to make any difference, at least in the short run, according to this account. Such a world involving potentially major dislocations could threaten both developed and developing countries.

Preconditions assumed in this scenario include:

- Nations adopt a "growth-first" mentality leading to widespread environmental neglect and degradation.
- Governments, particularly those lacking transparency, lose legitimacy as they fail to cope with environmental and other disasters.
- Despite significant technological progress, no technological "silver bullet" is found to halt the effects of climate change.
- National solutions to environmental problems are short term and inadequate.

Simulated Document: *NOT* AN ACTUAL DOCUMENT

The White House

Presidential Diary Entry

October 1, 2020

The term "October Surprise" keeps recurring in my mind . . . I guess we had it coming, but it was a rude shock. Some of the scenes were like the stuff from the World War II newsreels, only this time it was not Europe but Manhattan. Those images of the US aircraft carriers and transport ships evacuating thousands in the wake of the flooding still stick in my mind. Why does hurricane season have to coincide with the UNGA in New York? It's bad enough that this had to happen; it was doubly embarrassing that half the world's leaders were here to witness it—and a fair number of them had to be specially airlifted or spirited away for their safety.

I guess the problem was that we counted on this not happening, at least not yet. Most scientists assumed the worst effects of climate change would occur later in the century. Still, enough warned there was always a chance of an extreme weather event coming sooner and, if it hit just right, one of our big urban centers could be knocked out. As I remember, most of my advisors thought the chances were pretty low after the last briefing we got on climate change. But we were warned that we needed to decentralize our energy generation and improve the robustness of our infrastructure to withstand extreme weather events. Tragically, we did not heed this advice.

We'll survive, but Wall Street really has taken a blow and I don't think we will get the NY Stock Exchange back up and running as quickly as we did after 9/11. There is a question whether it will continue to be the NY Stock Exchange to begin with; it might have to change its name to the "Garden State (New Jersey) Stock Exchange"—wouldn't that be a blow to New Yorkers' pride!

It's not as if this is just happening to us. Truth be told, the problem has been our whole attitude about globalization. When I say "our," I really mean in this context the elite or even the little knot of leaders around the world. We all have been focused on boosting or maintaining greater economic growth. We have a lot to be proud of too in that regard. We have avoided giving in to protectionist urges and managed to reenergize the trade rounds. But we have not prepared sufficiently for the toll that irresponsible growth is having on the environment. The New York disaster may not have been preventable with any measures we could have taken 20 years ago, but what are we laying in store for future generations by ignoring the signs? We all assume technology will come to the rescue, but so far we have not found the silver bullet and carbon emissions continue to climb.

What we did not understand is that the general publics in several countries appear to be ahead of leaders in understanding the urgency or at least they have had a better sense of the need for trade-offs. They have become early adopters for energy generation from renewables, the use of clean water technologies, and using improved Internet connectivity to avoid the concentration of people that make them vulnerable to extreme weather events. The Europeans, of course, have been out in the lead on energy efficiency, but they have been too ready to sacrifice growth, and without economic growth, they have not been able to generate high-paying jobs.

In China, it's the opposite—too much crony capitalism. It's not clear, for example, that China's Communist Party (CCP) will survive the scandal over burst dams and the devastation that followed. A couple of decades ago, I would have thought it possible. At that time, the public there was so grateful for the material benefits accruing from China's hell-bent efforts to modernize that the Chinese people forgave the leaders almost everything. Now it is different. The middle class wants clean air and water. They don't like the environmental devastation that was the price of rapid modernization or corruption that winks at the turning off of US provided carbon capture equipment in their coal fired electrical plants. The Party is split too. Half worry about a slowdown from more sustainable, environmentally prudent growth that could be politically devastating if jobs are not generated to the same degree. The other half understands the hardships and is more attuned to changing middle class priorities. I would not be surprised if the 100,000 who perished in the recent dam disaster turn out to be the straw that breaks the CCP's legitimacy, coming as it does on the heels of those corruption allegations against high party officials.

The poorest countries have suffered the most from our hands-off approach to globalization. I know we have talked for some time about not all boats being lifted and the need to do something about it. But I think we thought it best that Bill Gates, NGOs, and others handle the problem. Of course, everyone has to get involved. NGOs can't mount peacekeeping operations. States at some point have to take responsibility. Most of these countries did not have a chance without strong outside intervention. The fact that we had clean water technology and could not find a way to get it delivered to the most needy only made the bad impacts of climate change worse.

With the climate changing rapidly, we are facing more problems—though not insuperable—in maintaining adequate agricultural production. More challenging than boosting agricultural yields overall is that changing weather patterns mean certain areas can't sustain themselves. People migrate to the cities but the infrastructure is insufficient to support such burgeoning populations. This in turn sows the seeds for social conflict which impedes any steps toward good governance and actually digging out from a long downward cycle. I count about 20 countries in this condition.

The problem is that some of these are not small, geopolitically insignificant countries. Some—like Nigeria—we in the developed world rely on for needed resources. Because of the encroaching desertification in the north, the religious clash between Muslims and Christians is heating up. Another Biafra-like civil war—only this time along North-South lines—is not inconceivable.

We talk a lot about these problems at the G-14 summits and in fact have started to engage in joint scenario exercises, but doing anything about an impending storm cloud is still beyond us. My last thought for the diary before I have to greet the dignitaries being airlifted onto the aircraft carrier for the UNGA reception: the growth projection figures are really bad. The cumulation of disasters, needed cleanups, permafrost melting, lower agricultural yields, growing health problems, and the like are taking a terrible toll, much greater than we anticipated 20 years ago.

Chapter 5
Growing Potential for Conflict

We now assess the potential for conflict—both interstate and intrastate—over the next 15–20 years to be greater than we anticipated in ***Mapping the Global Future***, particularly in the greater Middle East. Large parts of the region will become less volatile than today and more like other parts of world, such as East Asia, where economic goals predominate, but other portions of the region remain ripe for conflict. The combination of increasingly open economies and persistently authoritarian politics creates the potential for insurgencies, civil war, and interstate conflict. By 2025, Iran's nuclear ambitions are likely to be clear in one way or the other and the region will either be swept up in an arms race or have found another way to try to establish regional security. Although we believe the appeal of al-Qa'ida and other international terrorist groups will diminish over the next 15–20 years, pockets of support will remain, ensuring a continuing threat, particularly as lethal technology is expected to become more accessible.

A Shrinking Arc of Instability by 2025?

In our previous study, ***Mapping the Global Future***, we assessed that those states most susceptible to conflict are in a great arc of instability stretching from Sub-Saharan Africa through North Africa, into the Middle East, the Balkans, the Caucasus, and South and Central Asia, and parts of Southeast Asia. Today, parts of this arc are experiencing increasing economic activity, including moderate to high levels of GDP growth, slow but perceptible economic reform, improved regulatory performance, deepening financial markets, high levels of outside and intra-regional investment and related technology transfers, and development of new trade corridors. In the medium-to-longterm, increased rates of growth are likely to be sustained if energy prices remain high, but not so high that they depress growth in other regions. Awareness of increasing vulnerability to systemic changes in world energy markets also may act as a goad to further economic reform, including greater diversification in energy-rich states.

For regimes, managing economic change will involve a delicate balancing act between the imperatives of fostering economic growth and maintaining authoritarian rule. Although some regimes may succeed, the odds are that only one or two will become genuine democracies and one or two will end up with civil disorder and conflict because rulers miscalculate the tradeoffs or take gambles that don't pay off.

Growing Risk of a Nuclear Arms Race in the Middle East

A number of states in the region are already thinking about developing or acquiring nuclear technology useful for development of nuclear weaponry. Over the next 15–20 years, reactions to the decisions Iran makes about its nuclear program could cause a number of regional states to intensify these efforts and consider actively pursuing nuclear weapons. This will add a new and more dangerous dimension to what is likely to be increasing competition for influence within the region, including via proxies—Shia in Iran's case and Sunnis for most of its neighbors—and a competition among outside powers anxious to preserve their access to energy supplies and to sell sophisticated conventional weaponry in exchange for greater political influence and energy agreements.

Not Inevitable... Historically, many states have had nuclear weapons ambitions but have not gone the distance. States may prefer to retain the technological ability to produce nuclear weapons rather than to develop actual weapons. Technological impediments and a desire to avoid political isolation and seek greater integration into the global economy could motivate Tehran to forego nuclear weaponization. However, even an Iranian *capacity* to develop nuclear weapons might prompt regional responses that could be destabilizing.

If Iran does develop nuclear weapons, or is seen in the region as having acquired a latent nuclear weapons capability, other countries in the region may decide *not* to seek a corresponding capability. It is more likely, however, that a few of Iran's neighbors will see Iran's development of nuclear weapons or a latent weapons capability as an existential threat or as resulting in an unacceptable, fundamental shift of power in the region, and therefore will seek offsetting capabilities. Security guarantees from existing nuclear powers that regional states find credible may be regarded by them as a sufficient offset to an Iranian nuclear weapons capability, but it could be a tall order to expect such guarantees to satisfy all of those concerned about a nuclear Iran.

A Non-nuclear Korea?

We see a unified Korea as likely by 2025—if not as a unitary state, then in some form of North-South confederation. While diplomacy working to end North Korea's nuclear weapons program continues, the final disposition of the North's nuclear infrastructure and capabilities at the time of reunification remain uncertain. A new, reunified Korea struggling with the large financial burden of reconstruction will, however, be more likely to find international acceptance and economic assistance by ensuring the denuclearization of the Peninsula, perhaps in a manner similar to what occurred in Ukraine post-1991. A loosely confederated Korea might complicate denuclearization efforts. Other strategic consequences are likely to flow from Korean unification, including prospects for new levels of major power cooperation to manage new and enduring challenges, such as denuclearization, demilitarization, refugee flows, and financing reconstruction.

...But Potentially More Dangerous than the Cold War. The prospect that nuclear weapons will embolden Iran, lead to greater instability, and trigger shifts in the balance of power in the Middle East appears to be the key concern of the Arab states in the region and may drive some to consider acquiring their own nuclear deterrent. Iran's growing nuclear capabilities are already partly responsible for the surge of interest in nuclear energy in the Middle East, fueling concern about the potential for a nuclear arms race. Turkey, United Arab Emirates, Bahrain, Saudi Arabia, Egypt, and Libya are or have expressed interest in building new nuclear power facilities. Future Iranian demonstrations of its nuclear capabilities that reinforce perceptions of its intent and ability to develop nuclear weapons potentially would prompt additional states in the region to pursue their own nuclear weapons programs.

It is not certain that the type of stable deterrent relationship that existed for most of the Cold War would emerge naturally in the Middle East with multiple nuclear-weapons capable states. Rather than episodes of suppressing or shortening low-intensity conflicts and terrorism, the possession of nuclear weapons may be perceived as making it "safe" to engage in such activities, or even larger conventional attacks, provided that certain redlines are not crossed. Each such incident between nuclear-armed states, however, would hold the potential for nuclear escalation.

The continued spread of nuclear capabilities in the greater Middle East, where several states will be facing succession challenges over the next 20 years, also will raise new concerns over the capacity of weak states to maintain control over their nuclear technologies and arsenals. If the number of nuclear-capable states increases, so will the number of countries potentially willing to provide nuclear assistance to other countries or to terrorists. The potential for theft or diversion of nuclear weapons, materials, and technology—and the potential for unauthorized nuclear use—also would rise. Finally, enough countries might decide to seek nuclear weapons capabilities in reaction to an Iranian capability that countries beyond the region would begin pursuing their own nuclear weapons programs.

New Conflicts Over Resources?

The rising energy demands of growing populations and economies may bring into question the availability, reliability, and affordability of energy supplies. Such a situation would heighten tensions between states competing for limited resources, especially if accompanied by increased political turbulence in the Middle East and a general loss of confidence in the ability of the marketplace to satisfy rising demands. National companies could control the lion's share of the world's hydrocarbon resources, leading to a further blending of energy-state relationships and geopolitical concerns.

Perceptions of energy scarcity will drive countries to take actions to assure their future access to energy supplies. In the worst case this could lead to interstate conflicts if government leaders deem assured access to energy resources to be essential to maintaining domestic stability and the survival of their regime. However, even actions short of war will have important geopolitical implications as states undertake strategies to hedge against the possibility that existing energy supplies will not meet rising demands. Energy security considerations are already driving countries such as China and India to purchase equity stakes in energy fields, and evolving competitions are increasingly being supported by military capabilities leading to the potential for heightened tensions and even conflict. Energy-deficient states may employ transfers of arms and sensitive technologies and the promise of a political and military alliance as inducements to establish strategic relationships with energy-producing states.

- Central Asia has become an area of intense international competition for access to energy. Although Russia and China currently are working cooperatively to reduce the leverage of outside powers, especially the United States, competition between the two in Central Asia could escalate if in the future Russia seeks to interfere with China's relations in the region or China becomes more aggressive in obtaining its access to energy supplies in parts of the former Soviet Union.
- The future development of novel drilling techniques may create new opportunities to find and exploit previously unexplored ultra-deep oil fields. Such fields, however, may be located in areas of contested ownership, such as Asia or the Arctic, creating the potential for conflict.

Middle East/North Africa: Economics Drives Change, but with Major Risk of Turmoil

The Middle East and North Africa (MENA) will remain a geopolitically significant region in 2025, based on the importance of oil to the world economy and the threat of instability. The region's future will depend on how leaders manage oil windfalls, demographic changes, pressure for political change, and regional conflicts.

In a positive scenario in which economic growth becomes increasingly rooted and sustained, regional leaders will choose to invest in the region; implement economic, educational, and social policies that encourage more growth; move forward with political reform that empowers moderate—and probably Islamic—political parties; work to settle regional conflicts; and implement security agreements that help prevent future instability.

- In a more negative scenario, leaders will fail to prepare their growing populations to participate productively in the global economy, authoritarian regimes will hold tightly to power and become more repressive, and regional conflicts will remain unresolved as population growth strains resources.

Demographically, a number of Middle Eastern and North African countries are positioned where Taiwan and South Korea were before their takeoff in the 1960s and 1970s. Over the next 15 or so years, the proportion of the economically active populations (ages 15–64) in countries like Egypt will exceed that of the economically dependent population by a much greater amount than in any other region. This differential provides an opportunity to accelerate economic growth if governments put appropriate economic and social policies in place. Prospects are best in the North African and Gulf states.

- Foreign investment—much of it originating from within the region—will increase integration between Arab economies and drive private-sector development. The most promising industries for job growth are likely to be in services, putting the region on a different developmental path than East Asia.
- To maximize growth potential, MENA governments will need to improve their educational systems to produce a more technically skilled work force and encourage citizens accustomed to public sector jobs to accept the demands and volatility of the private sector. (East Asian economies prospered because of sustained government efforts to improve rapidly the quality of the work force through universal education and by developing export industries.)

In other regions, integrating young adults into the work force—coupled with a declining birth rate and shrinking youth bulge—has provided an opening for democratization. Social scientists have found that, as an increasing proportion of the population had a stake in the system, formerly authoritarian states like

South Korea and Taiwan felt they could experiment with political liberalization. An important cluster of North African countries—Algeria, Libya, Morocco, Egypt, and Tunisia—has the potential to realize such a demographic-democratic nexus in the period to 2025, but it is unclear whether these authoritarian regimes will exploit these opportunities to liberalize.

A Two-Tier Muslim World? Although the Western paradigm separating religious and secular authority may still be less compelling to Muslim publics, a greater emphasis on economics and, most importantly, greater participation of women in the work force may spur new forms of progressive Islam. This does not mean that extremist strands will disappear; in the short term they might benefit from unease over the changing role of women and alternative family models. But over time, lower fertility promotes religious and political stability and, if secularization in southern Europe is a guide, modernized versions of Islam could take root by 2025.

The channeling of political dissent into Islamic discourse—a variant of the global revival of religious identity in the aftermath of the Cold War—and states' efforts to manipulate Islamic currents will reinforce the dominance of Islam in Middle Eastern politics and society in 2025. As a result, pressures for greater political pluralism are likely to produce a bigger role for Islamic political parties and a re-thinking of how Islam and politics should interact and influence each other, with considerable political and social turmoil generated in the process.

Even as some states may liberalize, others may fail: youth bulges, deeply rooted conflicts, and limited economic prospects are likely to keep Palestine, Yemen, Afghanistan, Pakistan, and others in the high-risk category. Spillover from turmoil in these states and potentially others increases the chance that moves elsewhere in the region toward greater prosperity and political stability will be rocky. The success of efforts to manage and resolve regional conflicts and to develop security architectures that help stabilize the region will be a major determinant of the ability of states to grow their economies and pursue political reform.

Resolution of the Syrian and Palestinian conflicts with Israel, in particular, would broaden the ideological and political discourse within secular and Islamic circles, undermine a traditional pretext for maintaining large militaries and curtailing freedoms, and help defuse sectarian and ethnic tensions in the region.

Iran's trajectory is also likely to have lasting regional impacts—for good or ill. Iran's fractious regime, nationalist identity, and ambivalence toward the United States will make any transition from regional dissenter toward stakeholder perilous and uneven. Although Iran's aims for regional leadership—including its nuclear ambitions—are unlikely to abate, its regional orientation will have difficulty discounting external and internal pressures for reform. An Iranian perception of greater shared interests with the West in Iraq and

Afghanistan, for example, and sustained progress on Arab-Israeli peace that weakens Iranian-Syrian ties and accommodates or sidelines Iran's sub-state allies would provide security incentives and pressures on Iran to adjust its regional role. A political consensus within Iran to develop further its significant economic potential—fueled potentially by a sustained popular backlash against corruption and economic mismanagement and a fall in energy rents—could provide an additional push to shift Iran's factional politics to the left and an incentive for Iran to adjust its policies with a view toward easing US and international sanctions.

Energy Security

Other possible examples of the militarization of energy security include:

States using their control of energy resources as weapons of political coercion and influence. Russia is seeking to position itself to control energy supply and related transportation networks from Europe to East Asia. This would enable Moscow to use its control over energy flows to promote Russian interests and influence.

Threats posed by terrorism and piracy to energy production and transit. Public statements by al-Qa'ida leaders indicate terrorists are interested in striking Persian Gulf oil facilities. The protection of energy pipelines, facilities, and shipping from terrorist attacks will be a key security concern and mission for military forces.

Domestic instability, insurgencies, and conflict within strategic energy-producing and exporting states. Ethnic and political violence and criminal activity currently threaten a large portion of Nigeria's oil production. State failure in a key energy producing country may require military intervention by outside powers to stabilize energy flows.

Concerns about assuring future access to energy supplies also are fostering increased naval competition. Despite the growing number of pipeline projects, in 2025 Asian countries will remain dependent on sea transfers of energy from suppliers in the Middle East. This is raising concerns about the future of maritime security in a zone extending from the Persian Gulf to East and Southeast Asia. Maritime security concerns are providing the rationale for a series of naval buildups and modernization efforts in the region, such as China's and India's development of "blue-water" naval capabilities, to protect critical economic assets and secure access to energy resources. Other national navies in the Middle East and Asia will not be able to replace the US Navy's role in protecting strategic sea lines of communication in 2025, but the buildup of regional naval capabilities could lead to increased tensions, rivalries, and counterbalancing.

- Growing concerns over maritime security may create opportunities for multinational cooperation in protecting critical sea lanes. Mutual suspicions regarding the intentions behind naval build-ups by potential regional rivals or the establishment of alliances that exclude key players would, however, undermine efforts for international cooperation.
- A naval arms race in Asia may emerge in response to China's further development of naval power projection. A naval arms race might also be spurred by "anti-access" capabilities—such as attack submarines and long-range antiship missiles—that become widely viewed as efforts by Beijing to extend its political influence in the region and to deter attempts to cut off China's seaborne energy supplies by threatening mutual disruption of sea trade.

Climate change is unlikely to trigger interstate war, but it could lead to increasingly heated interstate recriminations and possibly to low-level armed conflicts. With water becoming more scarce in several regions, cooperation over changing water resources is likely to be increasingly difficult within and between states, straining regional relations. Such regions include the Himalayan region, which feeds the major rivers of China, Pakistan, India, and Bangladesh; Israel-Palestinian Territories; along the Jordan River (Israel-Jordan) and the Fergana Valley of Central Asia. Such dire scenarios are not inevitable even with worse-than-anticipated climate change impacts, however. Economic development, the spread of new technologies, and robust new mechanisms for multilateral cooperation to deal with climate change may foster greater global collaboration.

Another Use of Nuclear Weapons?

The risk of nuclear weapon use over the next 20 years, although remaining very low, is likely to be greater than it is today as a result of several converging trends. The spread of nuclear technologies and expertise is generating concerns about the potential emergence of new nuclear weapon states and the acquisition of nuclear materials by terrorist groups. Ongoing low-intensity clashes between India and Pakistan continue to raise the specter that such events could escalate to a broader conflict between those nuclear powers. The possibility of a future disruptive regime change or collapse occurring in a nuclear weapon state such as North Korea also continues to raise questions regarding the ability of weak states to control and secure their nuclear arsenals.

In addition to these longstanding concerns, new political-military developments could further erode the nuclear "taboo." The prospect of a nuclear-armed Iran spawning a nuclear arms race in the greater Middle East will bring new security challenges to an already conflict-prone region, particularly in conjunction with the proliferation of long-range missile systems. Furthermore, future acquisition of nuclear weapons by states with weak command and control procedures and safeguards increases the probability of accidental or unauthorized nuclear use.

Future asymmetries in conventional military capabilities among potential rivals might tempt weak states to view nuclear weapons as a necessary and justifiable defense in response to the threat of overwhelming conventional attacks. In such cases, the defending power might try to limit the potential for escalation by employing a nuclear weapon test to signal resolve and deter aggression or by confining the use of nuclear weapons to the defense of its own territory. Options for limited physical destruction attacks such as those that use very low-yield weapons or high-altitude nuclear blasts designed to disrupt an enemy's information networks and systems via an electromagnetic pulse effect could further erode the taboo against nuclear weapon use and prompt reassessments of the vulnerabilities of modern conventional military forces.

If nuclear weapons are used destructively in the next 15–20 years, the international system will be shocked as it experiences immediate humanitarian, economic, and political-military repercussions. How the world would respond over the long-term to another use of nuclear weapons would, however, likely depend on the context in which such weapons were used. Prevailing perceptions regarding whether the use of a nuclear weapon was justified, the level of destructiveness it created, and the future utility of nuclear weapons would drive global reactions regarding counter-proliferation and nuclear disarmament.

- A terrorist use of a nuclear weapon or an escalating conflict between two nuclear powers, such as India and Pakistan, would graphically demonstrate the danger of nuclear weapons, prompting calls for global nuclear disarmament and energizing counter-proliferation and counterterrorism measures.

A successful nuclear weapon test or use of a nuclear weapon by a state to deter or halt a conventional attack might, on the other hand, enhance the perception of the utility of nuclear weapons in defending territorial sovereignty and increase pressures for proliferation in countries that do not possess a strong conventional military or security guarantees.

In either case, a future use of nuclear weapons probably would bring about significant geopolitical changes as some states would seek to establish or reinforce security alliances with existing nuclear powers and others would push for global nuclear disarmament. In Europe, for example, divisions could emerge between some countries in Western Europe that support nuclear disarmament and those of Eastern Europe that still might fear Russia's nuclear arsenal.

Terrorism: Good and Bad News

Terrorism is unlikely to disappear by 2025, but its appeal could diminish if economic growth continues and youth unemployment is mitigated in the Middle East. Economic opportunities for youth and greater political pluralism probably would dissuade some from joining terrorists' ranks, but others—motivated by a variety of factors, such as a desire for revenge or to become "martyrs"—will continue to turn to violence to pursue their objectives.

- In the absence of employment opportunities and legal means for political expression, conditions will be ripe for disaffection, growing radicalism, and possible recruitment of youths into terrorist groups.
- Terrorist and insurgent groups in 2025 will likely be a combination of descendants of long-established groups—that inherit organizational structures, command and control processes, and training procedures necessary to conduct sophisticated attacks—and newly emergent collections of the angry and disenfranchised that become self-radicalized.

As long as turmoil and societal disruptions, generated by resource scarcities, poor governance, ethnic rivalries, or environmental degradation, increase in the Middle East, conditions will remain conducive to the spread of radicalism and insurgencies. Future radicalism could be fueled by global communications and mass media. Increasing interconnectedness will enable individuals to coalesce around common causes across national boundaries, creating new cohorts of the angry, downtrodden, and disenfranchised. In some situations these new networks could act as forces for good by pressuring governments through non-violent means to address injustice, poverty, the impacts of climate change, and other social issues. Other groups, however, could use networks and global communications to recruit and train new members, proliferate radical ideologies, manage their finances, manipulate public opinion, and coordinate attacks.

Why al-Qa'ida's "Terrorist Wave" Might Be Breaking Up

As al-Qa'ida celebrates its 20th birthday, most experts assert that the struggle against it will continue indefinitely, the so called "long war." Other experts who have studied past "waves" of terrorism believe that al-Qa'ida is an "aging" group by terrorist standards and suffers from strategic weaknesses that could cause it to decay into marginality, perhaps shortening the lifespan of the Islamic terrorist wave.

A wave of terror is a cycle of activity—which can last up to 40 years—characterized by expansion and contraction phases: rise, floodtide of violence, and ebb. The wave of terror concept was developed by UCLA Professor David C. Rapoport and provides a basis for the comparative analysis of terrorist movements. In each wave, similar terrorist activities occur in many countries, driven by a common vision—such as anarchism, Marxism, nationalism, or Islamic extremism. ***Terrorist groups who form the crest of each wave usually dissolve before the entire wave does, and their decay contributes to the breaking of the wave.*** Al-Qa'ida's weaknesses—unachievable strategic objectives, inability to attract broad-based support, and self-destructive actions—might cause it to decay sooner than many people think.

Research indicates that terrorists' strategic objectives fail on two fronts. Objectives that pose a threat to the existing political order court tough counterterrorism measures, while objectives that are seen as neither achievable nor relevant to solving problems have little appeal to elites or the general populace. The two primary strategic aims of al-Qa'ida—the establishment of a global Islamic caliphate and the removal of US and Western influence so that "apostate" regimes can be toppled—are clearly threats to many existing Muslim governments and are resulting in stronger counterterrorism measures.

- There is little indication that the vast majority of Muslims believe that such objectives are realistic or that, if they could come to pass, would solve the practical problems of unemployment, poverty, poor educational systems, and dysfunctional governance.

Despite sympathy for some of its ideas and the rise of affiliated groups in places like the Mahgreb, al-Qa'ida has not achieved broad support in the Islamic World. Its harsh pan-Islamist ideology and policies appeal only to a tiny minority of Muslims.

- According to one study of public attitudes toward extremist violence, there is little support for al-Qa'ida in any of the countries surveyed—Algeria, Egypt, Jordan, Kuwait, Lebanon, Morocco, Qatar, Saudi Arabia, United Arab Emirates, and Yemen. The report also found that majorities in all Arab countries oppose jihadi violence, by any group, on their own soil.
- Al-Qa'ida is alienating former Muslim supporters by killing Muslims in its attacks. Recent scholarly research indicates that terrorist groups that

kill civilians seldom accomplish their strategic goals. Although determining precisely the number of Muslims worldwide who have died in al-Qa'ida attacks is difficult, examination of available evidence suggests that at least 40 percent of the victims have been Muslims.

The roughly 40-year cycle of terrorist waves suggests that the dreams that inspire terrorist group members' fathers to join particular groups are not attractive to succeeding generations. The prospect that al-Qa'ida will be among the small number of groups able to transcend the generational timeline is not high, given its harsh ideology, unachievable strategic objectives, and inability to become a mass movement.

In relying almost exclusively on terrorism as a means to achieve its strategic objectives, rather than transforming into a political movement like Hizbollah or Hamas, al-Qa'ida is using a stratagem that rarely is successful. Recent academic research indicates that only 6 percent of terrorist groups active in the last 40 years have achieved their proclaimed strategic objectives. Al-Qa'ida's lack of success in executing attacks against the "far enemy" could portend a period of operational futility leading to increased frustration, decreased organizational élan, and inability to attract new members.

Because history suggests that the global Islamic terrorist movement will outlast al-Qa'ida as a group, strategic counterterrorism efforts will need to focus on how and why a successor terrorist group might evolve during the remaining years of the "Islamic terrorist wave."

On a positive note, support for terrorist networks in the Muslim world appears to be declining. To succeed, terrorist groups need a large number of passive supporters who sympathize with terrorists' objectives. Reducing those numbers is key to lessening the appeal within societies. Analysis of terrorists' communications among themselves indicates they see themselves in a "losing" battle with Western materialistic values. Surveys and analysis of jihadist websites indicate growing popular dissatisfaction with civilian casualties—particularly of fellow Muslims—caused by terrorist actions.

For those terrorist groups active in 2025, the diffusion of technologies and scientific knowledge will place some of the world's most dangerous capabilities within their reach. The globalization of biotechnology industries is spreading expertise and capabilities and increasing the accessibility of biological pathogens suitable for disruptive attacks. Radiological and chemical weapons may also be used by terrorists or insurgents seeking an advantage against opposing security or military forces and to create mass casualties. The proliferation of advanced tactical weapons will increase the potential that they will be used by terrorists. Improved anti-tank guided missiles and other man-portable weapon systems, thermobaric and other advanced explosives, and the spread of cheap sensors and robotics that could be used to create more capable improvised explosive devices illustrate this danger.

Some governments will likely respond to increasing terrorism and internal threats by expanding domestic security forces, surveillance capabilities, and the employment of special operations-type forces. Counterterrorism and counterinsurgency missions increasingly will involve urban operations as a result of greater urbanization. Governments, citing the need for enhanced internal security and their desire to control the influx of unwanted refugees and immigrants, may increasingly erect barricades and fences around their territories to inhibit access. Gated communities will continue to spring up within many societies as elites seek to insulate themselves from domestic threats.

The Changing Character of Conflict

Conflict will continue to evolve over the next 20 years as potential combatants adapt to advances in science and technology, improving weapon capabilities, and changes in the security environment. Warfare in 2025 is likely to be characterized by the following strategic trends:

The Increasing Importance of Information. Advances in information technologies are enabling new warfighting synergies through combinations of advanced precision weaponry, improving target and surveillance capabilities, enhanced command and control, and the expanding use of artificial intelligence and robotics. Future proliferation of long-range precision weapons will permit a growing number of states to threaten rapid destruction of an adversary's critical economic, energy, political, and military and information infrastructures. The growing importance of information technologies as an enabler of modern warfighting capabilities will make information itself a primary target in future conflicts. By 2025 some states probably will deploy weapons designed to destroy or disable information, sensor, and communication networks and systems including anti-satellite, radiofrequency, and laser weapons.

The Evolution of Irregular Warfare Capabilities. The adoption of irregular warfare tactics by both state and nonstate actors as a primary warfighting approach in countering advanced militaries will be a key characteristic of conflicts in 2025. The spread of light weaponry, including precision tactical and man-portable weapon systems, and information and communication technologies will significantly increase the threat posed by irregular forms of warfare over the next 15–20 years. Modern communication technologies such as satellite and cellular phones, the Internet, and commercial encryption, combined with hand-held navigation devices and high-capacity information systems that can contain large amounts of text, maps, and digital images and videos will greatly enable future irregular forces to organize, coordinate, and execute dispersed operations.

The Prominence of the Non-military Aspects of Warfare. Non-military means of warfare, such as cyber, economic, resource, psychological, and information-based forms of conflict will become more prevalent in conflicts over the next two decades. In the future, states and nonstate adversaries will engage in "media warfare" to dominate the 24-hour news cycle and manipulate public opinion to advance their own agenda and gain popular support for their cause.

The Expansion and Escalation of Conflicts Beyond the Traditional Battlefield. Containing the expansion and escalation of conflicts will become more problematic in the future. The advancement of weapons capabilities such as long-range precision weapons, the continued proliferation of weapons of mass destruction, and the employment of new forms of warfare such as cyber and space warfare are providing state militaries and nonstate groups the means to escalate and expand future conflicts beyond the traditional battlefield.

Afghanistan, Pakistan, and Iraq: Local Trajectories and Outside Interests

Developments in Afghanistan, Pakistan, and Iraq will critically affect regional stability, if not the global order. By 2025, the trajectories of these three states probably will have diverged sharply.

In 2025, **Afghanistan** may still evince significant patterns of tribal interaction and conflict. With the exception of the Taliban interlude, Afghanistan has not experienced strong central authority; centrifugal forces are likely to remain strong even if Kabul increases its sway.

- Western-driven infrastructure, economic assistance, and construction are likely to provide new stakes for local rivalries rather than the basis for a cohesive Western-style economic and social unity.
- Globalization has made opium Afghanistan's major cash crop; the country will have difficulty developing alternatives, particularly as long as economic links for trade with Central Asia, Pakistan, and India are not further developed.

Tribal and sectarian disputes probably will continue to arise, be fought out, and shift constantly in Afghanistan as the various players realign themselves. Outsiders will choose between making temporary alliances to destroy terrorist enemies, gain access to local resources, and advance other immediate interests or more ambitious—and costly—goals.

The future of **Pakistan** is a wildcard in considering the trajectory of neighboring Afghanistan. Pakistan's Northwest Frontier Province and tribal areas probably will continue to be poorly governed and the source or supporter of cross-border instability. If Pakistan is unable to hold together until 2025, a broader coalescence of Pashtun tribes is likely to emerge and act together to erase the Durand Line,[8] maximizing Pashtun space at the expense of Punjabis in Pakistan and Tajiks and others in Afghanistan. Alternatively, the Taliban and other Islamist activists might prove able to overawe at least some tribal politics.

In **Iraq**, numerous ethnic, sectarian, tribal, and local notables will compete to establish and maximize areas of political and social authority, access to resources, and to control the distribution of those resources through their patronage networks.

- By 2025 the government in Baghdad could still be an object of competition among the various factions seeking foreign aid and pride of place, rather than a self-standing agent of political authority, legitimacy, and economic policy.

What happens in Iraq will affect neighbors as well as internal contestants. Iran, Syria, Turkey, and Saudi Arabia will have increasing difficulty staying aloof. An Iraq unable to maintain internal stability could continue to roil the region. If conflict there breaks into civil war, Iraq could continue to provide a strong demonstration of the adverse consequences of sectarianism to other countries in the region. Alternatively, a stable Iraq could provide a positive example of economic growth and political development.

End of Ideology?

We judge that ideological conflicts akin to the Cold War are unlikely to take root in a world where most states will be preoccupied with the pragmatic challenges of globalization and shifting global power alignments. The force of ideology is likely to be strongest in the Muslim world—particularly the Arab core where Islam's diverse expressions will continue to influence deeply social norms and politics as well as serve as a prism through which individuals will absorb the economic and cultural forces of globalization. Increasing religious observance and the failures of secular Arab nationalism will leave Islamic political and social movements best positioned to assert ideological influence over governments and publics in much of the Muslim world over the next 15–20 years.

[8] The Durand Line is the border between Pakistan and Afghanistan—an artificial division that the Afghan Government does not recognize.

The ensuing Islamic discourse will be increasingly fluid as the clerical leadership detaches from established seats of learning and traditions of jurisprudence and asserts its own interpretations of the Quran and the Hadith (oral tradition). The trend toward bypassing tradition, aided by the spread of media technologies, will encourage the spread of Salafism (reverence for the earliest period in Islam), including its most radical forms, which risks undermining Western allies in the Muslim world, especially in the Middle East. Nonetheless, the dispersal of religious authority into networks of like-minded thinkers also could set the stage for a revival of innovative perspectives on Islam's relationship to the modern world and provide a counterweight to the radical trend.

The direction of Islam's internal ideological struggle will be determined primarily by local conditions. In countries where economic and demographic trends are favorable and publics and governments opt for the benefits of globalization, there will be strong incentives to revive and broaden Islamic teachings that promote a culture of innovation, scientific learning, political experimentation, and respect for religious pluralism. In those countries that are likely to struggle with youth bulges and weak economic underpinnings—such as in Afghanistan, Nigeria, Pakistan, and Yemen—the radical Salafi trend is likely to gain traction.

- All players will look to the United States to guarantee stability, but Tehran will continue to fear US designs for Iran's own regime and sovereignty.
- Public opinion polls likely will continue to suggest popular adherence to being "Iraqi," but the persistence of competing security systems, social organizations, and economic subsistence networks will animate robust local and sectarian identities.

The **Sunnis** will have an interest in the central state only if it provides them with what they judge to be an adequate share of resources largely generated outside their areas of control. Absent this satisfaction, agitation by Sunni jihadists, tribal leaders, and other notables could remain a destabilizing factor. In addition, any significant increase in the number of Iraqi Sunnis emigrating to Jordan and Syria could jeopardize the stability of those countries.

Shi'a, flush with their newfound primacy, have historically been divided, and personal rivalries among the Sadrs, Hakims, and other Shi'a notables are likely to continue to color politics in this community. Tribes of mixed Sunni-Shi'a ethnicity could serve as an integrating intercommunal glue, but only if economic development leads to a more transparent and trustworthy central administration and national system for material production and distribution.

Potential Emergence of a Global Pandemic

The emergence of a novel, highly transmissible, and virulent human respiratory illness for which there are no adequate countermeasures could initiate a global pandemic. If a pandemic disease emerges by 2025, internal and cross-border tension and conflict will become more likely as nations struggle—with degraded capabilities—to control the movement of populations seeking to avoid infection or maintain access to resources.

The emergence of a pandemic disease depends upon the natural genetic mutation or reassortment of currently circulating disease strains or the emergence of a new pathogen into the human population. Experts consider highly pathogenic avian influenza (HPAI) strains, such as H5N1, to be likely candidates for such a transformation, but other pathogens—such as the SARS coronavirus or other influenza strains—also have this potential.

If a pandemic disease emerges, it probably will first occur in an area marked by high population density and close association between humans and animals, such as many areas of China and Southeast Asia, where human populations live in close proximity to livestock. Unregulated animal husbandry practices could allow a zoonotic disease such as H5N1 to circulate in livestock populations—increasing the opportunity for mutation into a strain with pandemic potential. To propagate effectively, a disease would have to be transmitted to areas of higher population density.

Under such a scenario, inadequate health-monitoring capability within the nation of origin probably would prevent early identification of the disease. Slow public health response would delay the realization that a highly transmissible pathogen had emerged. Weeks might pass before definitive laboratory results could be obtained confirming the existence of a disease with pandemic potential. In the interim, clusters of the disease would begin to appear in towns and cities within Southeast Asia. Despite limits imposed on international travel, travelers with mild symptoms or who were asymptomatic could carry the disease to other continents.

Waves of new cases would occur every few months. The absence of an effective vaccine and near universal lack of immunity would render populations vulnerable to infection.[a] In this worst-case, tens to hundreds of millions of Americans within the US Homeland would become ill and deaths would mount into the tens of millions.[b] Outside the US, critical infrastructure degradation and economic loss on a global scale would result as approximately a third of the worldwide population became ill and hundreds of millions died.

[a] US and global health organizations currently are working to develop vaccines that may prevent or mitigate influenza pandemics. A breakthrough in the next several years could reduce the risk posed by pandemic influenza during upcoming decades.

[b] How fast a disease spreads, how many people become sick, how long they stay sick, the mortality rate, and the symptoms and after-effects will vary according to the specific characteristics of whatever pathogen is responsible for a pandemic. This scenario posits plausible characteristics that fall within a range of possibilities for these variables.

Development of a well-integrated national army would be an important factor in maximizing prospects for a more functional Iraqi state. This would require replacing the current tribal and sectarian loyalties of officers and troops with a much more robust sense of corporate élan and national purpose.

Global Scenario III: *BRICs' Bust-Up*

In this fictionalized scenario, Chinese fears of disruption of China's energy supplies spark a clash with India. With increasing resource constraints likely out to 2025, disputes over resources appear to us to be a growing potential source of conflict. The sense of vulnerability is heightened by the dwindling number of energy producers and increasing concentration in unstable regions such as the Middle East. A world in which there are more confrontations over other issues—such as new trade barriers—is likely to increase the potential for any dispute to escalate into conflict. As outlined in this scenario, misperceptions—along with miscommunications—could play as important a role as any actual threats. Also illustrated by this scenario is the competition by rising powers for resources. Both China and India—though rich in coal—have limited and dwindling oil and gas reserves and must rely on foreign sources. In thinking about the increased potential for conflict in this multipolar world, we need to keep in mind the scope for the emerging powers to clash with one another.

Preconditions underpinning this scenario include:

- A steady period of growth has slowed as states struggle to cope with energy and resource shortages, which are particularly acute in the Asian economies.
- A rise in nationalist sentiments occurs with the intense energy competition in this zero-sum world.
- A balance of power emerges that resembles a 21st century replay of the years before 1914.

Simulated Document: ***NOT*** **AN ACTUAL DOCUMENT**

Brazil

Letter by current Foreign Minister to former Brazilian President

February 1, 2021

I once heard a story—though I don't know whether it is true—that Goldman Sachs added Brazil as an afterthought to the now-famous grouping of emerging powers or BRICs. Rumor has it that they needed a fourth country, preferably from the southern hemisphere since the others were in the north. It also helped that Brazil began with a B.

True or not, Brazil has pulled its weight over the past six months, performing feats of diplomacy that even the US could not equal in present circumstances.

Let me go back to the beginning even though a lot of this you probably know. In fact, to get to the root of the Sino-Indian clash one has to go back to before there was any news coverage of the events. A lot of little incidents led to the Chinese attack on two Indian warships near the Gulf of Oman, which in turn triggered the US attack disabling the Chinese ships as they tried to withdraw from the area.

For a couple years, the Chinese had been watching what from their standpoint was a dangerous confluence of events that could jeopardize their economic, and therefore political survival. First, the Japanese had been making considerable progress in increasing their sea control capabilities in contested ocean areas that looked promising for producing oil and gas.

Second, there had been a notable acceleration in Indian military modernization as well as Indian attempts to erode Chinese gains in influence in Southeast Asia, increasing India's sea denial capabilities in the areas through which oil and gas move to China from the Middle East. China responded, extending its naval presence in the region by establishing naval basing rights in Pakistan. It became clear that Beijing's strategy was to deter any attempts by India to cut off China's sea access to energy resources by creating a threat to India's sea lanes in return. Tensions between India and China increased sharply when a Chinese submarine disappeared without explanation while monitoring an Indian naval exercise.

Third, Sino-Russian ties were simultaneously taking a tumble despite earlier cooperation in the Shanghai Cooperation Organization. Beijing detected increasing signs of Russia undercutting Chinese relations with Central Asian energy producers. This stoked Chinese energy insecurity. The fact that emerging alternative energy technologies—clean coal, solar, wind, and geothermal—did not materialize after heavy Chinese and US investments did not help.

As you know, even before the Sino-Indian incident, there had been a skirmish or two last year between the Chinese and Russians in Russia's Far East. If the Chinese had feared Russian double-dealing in Central Asia, the Russians were just as paranoid about what the Chinese were up to in Russia's Far East. Russia's accusation of spying by a group of students from Beijing and their subsequent imprisonment in Vladivostok occasioned, as you well remember, the spectacular Chinese rescue effort which thoroughly humiliated the Russians. Some called it a second Port Arthur in reference to the Japanese sinking the Russian fleet in 1905.

Finally, the strategic competition for influence and access to energy that emerged in the Middle East provided a new backdrop for the increasing rivalry among

China, India, and Russia. As the United States reduced its military forces in the Middle East following its involvement in Iraq, the other great powers sought to fill the vacuum. The Gulf Arab states in particular sought to strengthen their relationships with other powers to compensate for what they perceived as a weakened US security commitment post Iraq.

Tensions in the Middle East meanwhile were building as Iran continued to exert its growing power. A crisis erupted after a series of naval incidents between Iranian and Arab naval forces in the Persian Gulf and the Iranian threat to close off access to the Persian Gulf to all naval forces from outside the region except those of "friendly" powers. In response the United States introduced new economic sanctions against Tehran and sought to conduct an embargo of arms shipments to Iran. Tehran countered by threatening to disrupt oil traffic through the Gulf if Washington did not back down.

US pressure on the Chinese, Indians, and others to reject Iranian blandishments and eschew trade with the Iranians was intense. Beijing, fearing a disruption of its energy supplies, sought to play both sides, maintaining good relations with the Saudis while also promising Iran its support. China had established years back a strategic reserve, but that would last only so long and the uncertainty about what happened after a couple months was putting political pressure on the government. New Delhi also sought to nuance its response noting its need for natural gas from Iran but also seeking to maintain its good relationships with the United States and the Arab states. As a result, India declined to participate in economic sanctions that were deemed to be most harmful to ordinary Iranian citizens but agreed to help the United States enforce an arms embargo of Iran.

You can see how this set the stage for the incident at sea. Chinese nerves were on edge, but the Chinese were feeling very confident after the Russian Far East affair. The Indian attempt to stop a Chinese vessel believed to be carrying new antiship cruise missiles to Iran was resisted by Chinese naval forces in the area. The Chinese saw the Indian warships as surrogates for the United States. The US attack confirmed it. The original crisis in the Middle East—which really pitted the US and Europe against Iran—was suddenly transformed into a serious global one.

Fortunately over the past few weeks, unlike 1914, all the powers drew back from the brink. But oil is now over $300 a barrel and stock markets are tanking everywhere. That gets me to the Brazilian angle. We were the only country of any stature that had the trust of all the others. Even the Europeans were discredited because of their links to the US in the Iranian crisis. China was desperate to find a way out of what could have been an even worse position if a full-scale conflict with the Indians and the United States had ensued. The US too wanted a face-saving way out of the impasse since it looked like the only victor would be the Iranians and to an extent the Russians who sat smugly on the sidelines, reaping a fortune from the spike in energy prices. Of course, our continued development of biofuels in a responsible way only added to our credibility.

In the negotiations, I have tried to do more than just get all sides to back off and pay compensation to one another for the damages to each others' fleets. China needs to be assured about energy flows from the Gulf—at least once they resume.

I'm not sure that I have succeeded in building up mutual confidence and trust. I sense that the militaries in all three places—the US, China, and India—will use the incident to push for greater militarization of energy security. We could experience a new naval arms race.

In China, the government still fears public retribution because of the humiliation suffered by the US attack. Of course, for the moment, the US is the target of the nationalistic outburst—the United States' new embassy is a charred ruin. The Iranians have let up some, particularly as the US and its European partners made some concessions to get the oil flowing again and defuse the crisis with China and India.

I've told the three—the US, India, and China—that the next round of talks has to be held here in Rio. I'm hoping a more convivial atmosphere will do the trick. Rio Carnival is around the corner. . .

Chapter 6
Will the International System be up to the Challenges?

The trend toward greater diffusion of authority and power occurring for a couple decades is likely to accelerate because of the emergence of new global players, increasingly ineffective institutions, growth in regional blocs, advanced communications technologies, and enhanced strength of nonstate actors and networks.

- By 2025, nation-states will no longer be the only—and often not the most important—actors on the world stage and the "international system" will have morphed to accommodate the new reality. But the transformation will be incomplete and uneven. Although states will not disappear from the international scene, the ***relative power*** of various nonstate actors—including businesses, tribes, religious organizations, and even criminal networks—will grow as these groups influence decisions on a widening range of social, economic, and political issues.

The growing multiplicity of actors could strengthen the international system by filling gaps left by aging post-World War II institutions, but it also has the potential to further fragment the existing system and to impede international cooperation. The diversity in both types and kinds of actor increases the likelihood of fragmentation over the next two decades given the apparently waning ability of legacy international institutions to address new transnational challenges.

Multipolarity without Multilateralism

In such a world, we are unlikely to see an overarching, comprehensive, unitary approach to global governance. Current trends suggest that global governance in 2025 will be a patchwork of overlapping, often ad hoc and fragmented efforts, with shifting coalitions of member nations, international organizations, social movements, NGOs, philanthropic foundations, and companies.

- This fragmentation of interests and actors will further erode prospects for the United Nations to strengthen consensus among its members for effective multilateral action—particularly within the current or an expanded Security Council—or for sustaining broader reforms of the UN system.
- This multipolarity is also unlikely to include a single dominant nation-state with the overwhelming power and legitimacy to act as the agent of institutional overhaul. (See below for discussion of the role of the US.)

Most of the pressing transnational problems—including climate change, regulation of globalized financial markets, migration, failing states, crime networks, etc.—are unlikely to be effectively resolved by the actions of individual nation-states. The need for effective global governance will increase faster than existing mechanisms can respond. Leaders will pursue alternative approaches to solving transnational problems—with new institutions, or more likely, many informal groupings. Recent trends suggest that existing multilateral institutions—which are large and cumbersome—will have difficulty adapting quickly enough to undertake new missions, accommodate changing memberships, and obtain necessary resources. NGOs and philanthropist foundations— concentrating on specific issues—increasingly will be a part of the landscape but are likely to be limited in their ability to effect change in the absence of concerted efforts by multilateral institutions or governments.

Quests for greater inclusiveness—to reflect the emergence of newer powers—may make it harder for international organizations to tackle transnational challenges. Respect for the dissenting views of member nations will continue to shape the agenda of organizations and limit the kinds of solutions possible. Large and enlarging organizations—from the UN General Assembly to NATO and the EU—may find the challenges to be particularly difficult. There is unlikely to be any effort to "zero base" the international organizational structure such that some organizations go away or are reinvented.

Effective action also may be impeded by the existence of too many institutions—many of which have declining purpose—with limited legitimacy and effectiveness. This is likely to apply across the board, from Western-driven institutions to those of the historic Third World.

We anticipate that arms races, territorial expansion, and military rivalries that characterized late 19th century multipolarity will be less significant in the emerging one, but we cannot rule out such possibilities. For most countries, strategic rivalries are likely to revolve around trade, investment, technology innovation, and acquisition. However, increasing worries about resources—such as energy or even water—could easily put the focus back on territorial disputes or unresolved border issues.

Asia is one region where the number of such border issues is particularly noteworthy or, in the case of Central Asia, where large deposits of energy resources increase the potential for a repeat of the 19th century's "Great Game" with outsiders contending for the exclusive right to control market access. The fact that a number of countries may experience a sharp fall in national power if alternatives for fossil fuel are developed quickly injects a potentially dangerous risk of instability. As the national power of China, India, and others grows, smaller countries in the neighborhood may seek outsiders' protection or intervention in a balancing effort.

How Many International Systems?

The emerging powers, particularly China and India, have a shared interest in maintaining a stable and open order, but they espouse different "means." Their spectacular economic success has been achieved with an economic model that is at odds with the West's traditional laissez faire recipe for economic development. As we have seen, climate change, energy, and other resource needs are likely to be more problematic for what many see as their primary goal of continued economic development. Given these differing perspectives, the question arises as to whether the new players—and their alternative approaches—can be melded with the traditional Western ones to form a cohesive international system able to tackle the increasing number of transnational issues.

While sharing a more state-centric view, the national interests of the emerging powers are diverse enough, and their dependence on globalization compelling enough, that there appears little chance of an alternative bloc forming among them to directly confront the more established Western order. The existing international organizations—such as the UN, WTO, IMF, and World Bank—may prove sufficiently responsive and adaptive to accommodate the views of emerging powers, but whether the emerging powers will be given—or will want—additional power and responsibilities is a separate question. Indeed some or all of the rising powers may be content to take advantage of the institutions without assuming leadership burdens commensurate with their status. At the same time, their membership does not necessarily have to involve heavy responsibilities or burden-sharing, allowing them to pursue their goals of economic development. For some, the fact that agreement on new permanent members of the Security Council appears remote even over the next 15–20 years provides an additional excuse to forego a global role which could come at the expense of domestic goals. One large uncertainty is whether the political will exists to reshape the international system to offer the emerging powers enough responsibility for them to shoulder more global burdens.

Greater Regionalism—Plus or Minus for Global Governance?

One exception to the trend toward greater multipolarity with less multilateralism may occur on a regional level in Asia. Greater Asian integration, if it occurs, could fill the vacuum left by a weakening multilaterally based international order but could also further undermine that order. In the aftermath of the 1997 Asian financial crisis, a remarkable series of pan-Asian ventures—the most significant being ASEAN + 3—began to take root. Although few would argue that an Asian counterpart to the EU is a likely outcome even by 2025, if 1997 is taken as a starting point, Asia arguably has evolved more rapidly over the last decade than the European integration did in its first decade(s). In the economic realm, extra-regional players such as the US will continue to be a significant part of the 2025 Asian economic equation. However, movement over the next 15 years toward an Asian basket of currencies—if not an Asian currency unit as a third reserve—is more than a theoretical possibility.

- Such a development would be in part an effort by Asians to insulate themselves from financial volatility outside their region, facilitate economic integration, and to achieve greater representation at the global table.
- Aspects of Asian regionalism that are difficult to quantify include the growing habits of cooperation, buoyant confidence, frequency of encounters by a host of high-level officials and the cultural diffusion that is bridging historical and political differences and is engendering a new sense of community.

Asian regionalism would have global implications, possibly sparking or reinforcing a trend toward three trade and financial clusters that could become quasi-blocs (North America, Europe, and East Asia).

Establishment of such quasi-blocs also would have implications for the ability to achieve future global World Trade Organization agreements and regional clusters could compete in the setting of trans-regional product standards for IT, biotech, nanotech, intellectual property rights, and other "new economy" products.

An Asian regional energy posture could set the terms for the rest of the world. Some two-thirds of Mideast oil exports go to Asia, and some 70 percent of Asian imports are from the Middle East. This pattern is likely to intensify. Whether this nexus is primarily commercial—complementary investments and military sales—or acquires an increasingly political/strategic character could determine the character of the international system.

- As stated, in the worst case—absent greater regional cooperation—concern over oil supply routes could lead to a China-Japan-India naval arms race.

Developments in the security realm—where Asian integration is currently weakest and where trends toward competition and hedging persist—could dilute regionalism. Whether and how Korea is reunified and the status of its nuclear program, and whether Taiwan's relationship to the Mainland moves toward conflict or is resolved peacefully, will be key factors shaping regional dynamics. Current trends suggest traditional security concerns are declining in importance but may be replaced by new issues, such as competition over resources. Managing and adjusting to a transition to a reunified Korea could expand the Six-Party talks into a mechanism that features new levels of cooperation among the US, Japan, and China.

Whether greater or lesser integration occurs also depends largely on the future character of Sino-Japanese ties. This is the first time in modern history that China and Japan have been major regional and global actors at the same time. A key question is whether they can transcend historical suspicions and compete peacefully. Peaceful resolution of the Korea and Taiwan disputes and a Franco-German type entente between China and Japan would sharply diminish the regional desire for a US "offshore" balancer role. However, US allies and security partners in the region will not trade in the US balancing role for any collective regional security arrangement until the political and economic consequences of China's rise become better known.

Most experts—US and foreign—we consulted do not expect the rising powers to challenge or radically alter the international system as did Germany and Japan in the 19th and early 20th centuries. The emerging powers will have a high degree of freedom to "customize" their political and economic policies rather than fully adopting Western norms. Because of their growing geopolitical clout, domestic markets, and roles in global resource extraction, manufacturing, finance, and technology, the rising powers are also likely to want to preserve their policy freedom to maneuver and will want others to carry the burden of dealing with global challenges such as terrorism, climate change, proliferation, and energy security. Russia's and China's resource nationalism and state capitalism underpin, for example, their elite-based politics and limit their willingness to compromise on major international economic issues such as trade, energy, finance, or climate change.

- Others, such as India, lack strategic economic and political visions and do not possess domestic grassroots support for deep economic liberalization. Many global issues require sacrifices or abrupt changes to these countries' development plans, another reason for them to prefer to be bystanders rather than leaders in a multilateral system.

A World of Networks

In response to likely deficits in global governance, networks will form among states and nonstate actors focused on specific issues. These networks will operate to pursue convergent goals and interests, including a genuine intent to solve problems, business self-interest, moral grounds, and the desire of international organizations and NGOs to be relevant to the problems facing a changing world. In some cases, the nucleus of an issue network will be a national or international commission or body of experts—unelected but with substantial clout—to report on or oversee some aspects of governance, trade, or other issues. Current examples of such networks include the Financial Stability Forum, the Carbon Sequestration Leadership Forum, and the International Partnership for the Hydrogen Economy.

Issue groups likely will help develop and diffuse standards and regulations for various realms, including information technology (IT), regulatory regimes, and management of the "new post-industrial economy." For some kinds of issues, the networks likely will provide the basis for agreement among nation-states. With the groundwork done in informal contexts, nation-states will be able to adopt problem-solving measures, gaining legitimacy and sometimes taking credit for initiatives, while avoiding the stigma of solutions being imposed by external international organizations. The numbers and types of NGOs could well explode by 2025. Low entry costs, low overhead, and the capacity of individuals and groups to affiliate with each other using the Internet will facilitate such collectives.

In addition to such issue groups, a new set of social actors—superempowered individuals and even criminal networks—increasingly will influence outcomes. These elites are empowered by their wealth and an array of national and transnational contacts—oftentimes spanning businesses, governments, international organizations, and NGOs. Using their broad contacts and multiple national identities, they help leverage "transnational" outcomes across national and organizational boundaries.

A Growing Role for Religion. Religion-based networks may be quintessential issue networks and overall may play a more powerful role than secular transnational groupings in exerting influence and shaping outcomes in the period out to 2025. Indeed, we could be entering a new age of clerical leadership in which religious leaders become major power brokers in resolving future international disputes and conflicts.

- Rich rewards in power and influence already fall to those religious entrepreneurs and televangelists who span the two hemispheres, the Global South and North—Amir Khalede for Muslims and Matthew Ashimolowo or Sunday Adelaja for Christians. Khalede's website is the third most popular Arabic website in the world (al-Jazeera's is number one).

Within the Christian tradition, the emergence of whole new patterns of authority and leadership across the Global South entails autonomous ministers and religious entrepreneurs, whose activities reap high status and great wealth. Before 2025, some evangelists and megachurch preachers probably will seek to become the leaders of nations, especially if those countries have been economically devastated during a global downturn.

Although religious groups have been a great beneficiary of globalization, religion also has the potential to be a primary vehicle for opposition to that same modernizing process. Religious structures can channel social and political protest, especially for those who lack the means of communication and influence available to social elites. This is relevant because many of the economic trends that will dominate the next two decades have the potential to drive social fragmentation and popular resentment, including the growing gaps between rich and poor, the urban and rural gulfs in India and China, the vast disparities between nations and regions advantaged or left behind by modernization, and between states able to manage the consequences of globalization and those with governments unable to do so. Religious activists can draw on sacred texts and long historical tradition to frame popular grievances in terms of social justice rhetoric and egalitarianism.

Proliferating Identities and Growing Intolerance?

One aspect of the growing complexity of the international system is that no single political identity—such as the conflation of citizenship and nationality—is likely to be dominant in most societies by 2025. Class struggles will matter as much as religion and ethnicity. The Internet and other multi-media will enable the revitalization of the reach of tribes, clans, and other fealty-driven communities. Explosive urbanization will facilitate the spread of these identities and increase the likelihood of clashes between groups. The increasing numbers of migrants moving to cities from rural areas will coalesce in neighborhoods settled by previous co-ethnics or will find themselves targeted for recruitment by gangs and more complex criminal structures. As these communities coalesce and become "self-governing" or sometimes co-opted by organized crime groups, state and local government will face "no-go" areas in many large cities as has already happened in cities like Sao Paulo and Rio de Janeiro.

Although inherited and chosen layers of identity will be as "authentic" as conventional categories of citizenship and nationality, one category possibly will continue to stand out. Islam will remain a robust identity. Sectarian and other differences within Islam will be a source of tension or worse. The challenge of Islamic activism could produce a more intense backlash of Christian activism. Nigeria, Ethiopia, and other places in Africa will remain battlegrounds in this sectarian struggle. In 2025, notions of multiethnic integration and the value of "diversity" could face a combination of challenges from nationalists, religious zealots, and perhaps some version of a revived Marxist and other class-based or secular ideology.

If global economic growth did suffer a severe reverse—akin to the Indonesian crisis of the late 1990s but on a worldwide scale—religiously based rural insurgencies and ethnic struggles probably would ensue in a number of countries including Brazil, India, China, and in much of Africa. If even the moderately severe projections of climate change are correct, the impacts could spur religious conflict through large sections of Africa and Asia. Among the countries at greatest risk of such conflict and scapegoating of minority communities are a number of predominantly Muslim countries with significant Christian minorities (Egypt, Indonesia, and Sudan); predominately Christian states with substantial Muslim minorities (e.g., DROC, Philippines, and Uganda) or finely balanced between Christian and Muslim (Ethiopia, Nigeria, and Tanzania).

If religious structures offer vehicles to resist globalization, they also help people cope with those same forces, enhancing social stability and economic development. Without religious safety nets, the degree of chaos and fragmentation in developing nations would be far worse. As predominantly rural societies have become more urban over the last 30 or 40 years, millions of migrants have been attracted to larger urban complexes without the resources or infrastructures to provide adequate healthcare, welfare, and education. The alternative social system provided by religious organizations has been a potent factor in winning mass support for religion. This holds across faiths.

The weaker the state and its mechanisms, the more critical the role of religious institutions and the stronger the appeal of religious ideologies, usually of a fundamentalist or theocratic nature.

Future of Democracy: Backsliding More Likely than Another Wave

We remain optimistic about the long-term prospects for greater democratization, but advances are likely to slow and globalization will subject many recently democratized countries to increasing social and economic pressures that could undermine liberal institutions.

- Ironically, economic setbacks could enhance prospects for movement toward pluralism and greater democratization in China and Russia. The Chinese Communist Party's legitimacy increasingly rests on its ability to ensure greater material wealth for Chinese society. Resentment of elite corruption is already on the rise but may overwhelm the regime in event of a serious economic crisis. The government's standing in Russia would be similarly challenged if living standards fell dramatically.
- Elsewhere surveys have shown democracy having taken root, particularly in Sub-Saharan Africa and Latin America, where opinion views it positively independent of any material benefits. Still, nascent democracies have historically been shown to be unstable to the extent that they lack strong liberal institutions—especially rule of law—which can help support democracy during economic downturns. Case studies suggest widespread corruption is especially threatening because it undermines faith in democratic institutions.
- As we have suggested elsewhere in the text, the better economic performance of many authoritarian governments could sow doubts among some about democracy as the best form of government. The surveys we consulted indicated that many East Asians put greater emphasis on good management, including increasing standards of livings, than democracy. Elsewhere even in many well-established democracies, surveys show growing frustration with the current workings of democratic government and questioning among elites over the ability of democratic governments to take the bold actions necessary to deal rapidly and effectively with the growing number of transnational challenges.

A "Shadow" International System by 2025? Further fragmenting the international system is the threat posed by growing transnational criminal networks in managing the world's resources—especially global energy, minerals, and other strategic markets—in addition to their traditional involvement in international narcotics trafficking. Increased demand for energy worldwide provides opportunities for criminals to expand their activities through direct ties to energy suppliers and leaders of countries where suppliers are located. With energy supplies increasingly concentrated in countries with poor governance, longstanding practices of corruption, and an absence of the rule of law, the potential for penetration by organized crime is high.

- The illicit activities of organized crime in the energy sector provide affiliated companies with an unfair competitive advantage in the global energy market.
- Over time, given their far-reaching tentacles into government offices and corporate board rooms, criminals may be in a position to control states and influence market actions, if not foreign policies. For many resource-rich countries, energy revenues provide the basis for the whole economy and energy policies are a key consideration in foreign policy decisions.
- The likelihood of penetration by criminal networks is probably greatest in Eurasian markets where organized crime has been an institutionalized part of the political and economic environment and where over time organized crime figures have evolved into influential businessmen and become valuable partners for corrupt officials.
- As Russian and Eurasian suppliers capture a larger and larger portion of the energy markets in Europe and Asia, we expect these organized crime networks to expand their operations, fostering greater corruption and manipulation of foreign policies to their advantage.

Global Scenario IV: Politics Is Not Always Local

In this fictionalized scenario, a new world emerges in which nation-states are not in charge of setting the international agenda. The dispersion of power and authority away from nation-states has fostered the growth of sub-national and transnational entities including social and political movements. Growing public concerns about environmental degradation and government inaction come together in this example to "empower" a network of political activists to wrest control of the issue out of country-level officials in capitals. Global communications technology enables individuals to affiliate directly with identity-driven groups and networks that transcend geographic boundaries. Environmentalism is an issue for which there is a widespread confluence of interests and desires.

Preconditions for this scenario include:

- National governments' relevance and power lessens in an increasingly decentralized world.
- Diasporas, labor unions, NGOs, ethnic groups, religious organizations, and others acquire significant power and establish formal and informal relationships with states.
- Communications technology permits ubiquitous and constant integration into identity networks.

Simulated Document: ***NOT*** **AN ACTUAL DOCUMENT**

Financial Times

Politics is Not Always Local

September 14, 2024

We are in a new era in which governments are no longer king. All of us commentators talked a lot about the end of the Westphalian era, but we never really believed it. Moreover it was harder to get our arms around nonstate actors than to report on government ministries with their solid granite foundations and columned porticos. Now we have to recognize the new force of these loose networks. Unlike governments, they actually got something done. They have shown they really matter. I'm talking about the new climate change treaty that was recently agreed upon—even before the previous one expired—that instituted stricter carbon emissions ceilings and established global programs for renewable energy and new technologies to deal with the increasing water supply problems.

Of course, there is no single network and maybe that is the secret. Not only were there various national groups, but many of the networks responsible for forcing the climate change negotiations collected together professional groups, NGOs, and religious groups, across national, class, and cultural divides. The wide deployment of the next-generation Internet (Ubiquitous computing), although done for commercial reasons, greatly facilitated the empowerment of these nonstate interest groups.

This probably would not have come about without a succession of environmental disasters. The New York hurricane was a trigger. Importantly the fact that it happened about the time of UNGA, which many of these networks and groups had been scheduled to attend, facilitated the initial coalescence. However, it would not have happened without other events like the cyclone a year earlier that devastated Bangladesh and the recent Intergovernmental Panel on Climate Change report showing much higher levels of $CO2$ despite efforts at cutbacks. A crisis atmosphere prevailed. Indeed it was one of those moments in history in which a new millennium or apocalyptic atmosphere was operating—as if the end of the world was nigh—and immediate action was needed.

In a sense, we have reached the Promised Land in which global cooperation is more than a "conspiracy" among elites but bubbles up from the grassroots across historic national and cultural divides. We had hoped for this with the European Union but never achieved it. Everyone maintained his narrow parochial viewpoint, speaking first as a Frenchman, or Pole, not as a European.

A lot of this can be ascribed to the rise of the middle classes in Russia, China, and India. Like their Western counterparts before them in the 19th and 20th centuries, they are wealthy enough now to decry the health hazards associated with pollution and rapid growth. They wanted their governments to take action, but they did not. The middle classes have been incensed by the shoddy construction and poor planning that led directly to large numbers of casualties when disasters struck. Anti-corruption and environmentalism merged. As the poor in Sub-Saharan Africa and elsewhere suffered more and more from climate change, religious activists also became mobilized. Migrants pushed off unproductive land, and unable to get access to clean water technologies, turned to churches for help.

Institutions were more savvy than governments in detecting the change. The annual Davos meeting was transformed several years ago. It brought in a host of activists from these networks and has since established virtual meetings where thousands more could participate. The pressure became too much for member-states to ignore. The UNGA set aside 20 seats for NGOs who yearly competed among themselves to take up a seat for a year and have the same voting rights as nation-states. International politics is forever changed even though I doubt these networks can be as effective on other issues. The environment was tailor-made because the widespread commonality of interest in avoiding Armageddon. At another time or on a different issue, my guess is national, religious, ethnic, and class differences will resurface. But the achievement stands and the precedent set will make it hard for governments to ignore NGOs. Maybe they can even begin to partner.

Chapter 7
Power-Sharing in a Multipolar World

The United States will have greater impact on how the international system evolves over the next 15–20 years than any other international actor, but it will have less power in a multipolar world than it has enjoyed for many decades. Owing to the relative decline of its economic, and to a lesser extent, military power, the US will no longer have the same flexibility in choosing among as many policy options. We believe that US interest and willingness to play a leadership role also may be more constrained as the economic, military, and opportunity costs of being the world's leader are reassessed by American voters. Economic and opportunity costs in particular may cause the US public to favor new tradeoffs.

Developments in the rest of the world, including internal developments in a number of key states—particularly China and Russia—are also likely to be crucial determinants of US policy. A world of relatively few conflicts with other major powers would smooth the way toward development of a multipolar system in which the US is "first" among equals. In the end, events will shape the parameters of US foreign policy. Contingencies—such as the use of nuclear weapons or WMD terrorism—could convulse the entire international system and refocus the US role.

Demand for US Leadership Likely to Remain Strong, Capacities will Shrink

Despite the rise in anti-Americanism over the past decade, the US is still likely to continue to be seen as a much-needed regional balancer in the Middle East and in Asia. A recent survey (see box on pages 111–112) indicates growing unease with China's rise among its neighbors and, in many regions, a leveling off of antagonism, if not some improvement in attitudes toward the United States. In addition to its increasing economic power, China's military modernization program is a growing source of concern to its neighbors. The level of concern may rise even if Asia's security improves, for example, with a PRC-Taiwan accommodation, though in such an eventuality the opposite reaction is also possible. In the Middle East, a nuclear Iran would increase pressure for extension of a US security umbrella to Israel and other states.

Other states will continue to seek US leadership on the newer "security" issues, such as climate change. For example, many countries view US leadership as critical to encouraging major developing countries like China and India that are emitters of greenhouse gasses to take on serious commitments to reduce carbon emissions in a post-2012 emissions control regime. Most G-77 countries realize they are absorbing environmental harm from polluters and are not averse to the US intervening with Beijing.

Further, others will seek US leadership on countering WMD proliferation by taking steps to dissuade interest in WMD, strengthening nonproliferation regimes, preventing acquisition of WMD and associated expertise and technology, rolling back or eliminating WMD in countries of concern, fostering deterrence in the use of WMD, and mitigating the consequences of WMD use.

New Relationships and Recalibrated Old Partnerships

An increasingly multipolar world suggests a greater number of actors—including influential nonstate ones—with whom the US and other powers will have to contend. Descent into a world in which mercantilism and resource nationalism become the overriding *modus operandi* for others probably would narrow the number of US partners, increasing the risks of tensions, if not confrontation among the powers in such a zero-sum world. On the other hand, a world of continuing prosperity would enhance prospects for greater burden-sharing and steps towards revitalization of multilateralism and global institutions.

During the period out to 2025, China and India are likely to remain *status quo* powers focused on their own development, drawing benefits from the current system and not too eager for the US or others to seek radical changes to the international order until Beijing and New Delhi judge that they are in a better position to help set the new rules of the road.

Although the emerging powers will want to preserve ample leeway and autonomy to exert regional influence independent of the United States, their relationships with the US are likely to deepen if their plans for greater economic development remain on track. Economic collapse, especially in China's case, could lead to a nationalistic upsurge and increased tensions with foreign powers, including the United States.

Europe will face difficult domestic challenges that *could* constrain its ability to play a larger global role, especially in the security realm. A sense of increased threat—whether from terrorism or a resurgent Russia—could change the European calculus on the need for more defense spending and greater capacity for unified action. Growing interest in Maghreb and Middle East economic and social developments increases the potential for Europe to play a stabilizing role similar to what it accomplished with enlargement to the East. Japan, to keep pace with China, may increase its political and security role in the region. We expect other countries, such as Brazil, to assume more expansive regional roles and to increase their involvement on certain key global issues such as trade and climate change.

Current trends suggest Russia has a more immediate interest in directly challenging what it sees as a US-dominated international system than do other rising powers. A more diversified economy, development of an independent middle class, and reliance on foreign technological expertise and investment for development of its energy resources could change that trajectory, however. An earlier-than-anticipated move away from fossil fuels also could undercut Russia's recent resurgence.

In the Middle East, where the US is likely to remain the dominant external actor, current trends suggest a greater role for Asian states which are reinforcing their growing economic links with stronger political ties. Asian powers—in addition to European ones—could seek or be drawn into roles in any future international security effort in the Middle East. The role of NGOs will grow commensurate with the increase of humanitarian needs owing to climate change. In turn, the international community, including the US, will become more dependent on NGOs to shoulder the burden of humanitarian relief.

Less Financial Margin of Error

The dollar is vulnerable to a major financial crisis and the dollar's international role is likely to decline from that of the unparalleled "global reserve currency," to something of a first among equals in a basket of currencies by 2025. This could occur suddenly in the wake of a crisis, or gradually with global rebalancing. This decline will entail real tradeoffs and force new, difficult choices in the conduct of American foreign policy.

Anti-Americanism on the Wane?

America's reputation abroad has fluctuated over the decades—from the *Ugly American* of the 1950s to the widespread international protests over Vietnam in the 1960s and 1970s to antinuclear activism in Europe in the 1980s. Anti-Americanism has experienced an upsurge during this decade. Between 2002 and 2007, the US image became less favorable in 27 of 33 countries polled. Attitudes critical of the United States can be parsed into two basic categories:

- "Transitory criticism" fueled by disagreements with specific aspects of the United States that can change with time, such as its foreign policies.
- "Anti-Americanism" reflecting deep and undifferentiated antipathy toward most aspects of the United States.

To the extent that certain aspects of American life—for example, its political system, people, culture, S&T, education, and business practices—are seen abroad as admirable, perceptions of the United States will be complex, keeping views flexible and open to revision. The downward trajectory of America's reputation suggested above may have bottomed out. Polling in 2008 by Pew's Global Attitudes Project found US favorability ratings up in 10 of the 21 countries for which trend data are available. Looking ahead, what regional drivers and dynamics might be pivotal for encouraging such a turnaround?

Europe/Eurasia. In contrast to regions more uniformly pro- or anti-American, Europe/Eurasia tends to hold more volatile views of the US. The views of Western Europeans appear to be buoyed to the extent that the United States, its key allies, NATO, and the EU deepen practical multilateral approaches to international problems. The views of Central and East Europeans, who are traditionally favorable toward the United States, probably will recede over time to the West European norm. No single set of US actions will reassure all states of the former Soviet Union, but avoiding a heavy movement of military assets into Moscow's perceived Near Abroad would stave off the tensest of relations with Russia.

Near East/South Asia. Societies most hostile to the United States are found in the Islamic Middle East, as well as Pakistan and North Africa. India is an important exception. Drivers for turning around the US image include a strong commitment to significant progress on Israel/Palestine, disentangling anti-terrorism from a perceived war on Islam, and seeking to provide aid to needy citizens in addition to military-security elites. To the extent Iran is perceived to be a dangerous revisionist power, people and states in the region will tend to view US military capability positively.

Sub-Saharan Africa. Africa continues to harbor goodwill toward the United States. Publics in Sub-Saharan Africa tend to find American lifestyles and standards of living enviable. If AFRICOM, the new US military command, does not present an overly militarized face to citizens in African countries, and humanitarian and economic developmental aid continues, the surveys suggest African opinion about the United States will remain favorable.

East/Southeast Asia: Views of the United States in this region are relatively positive. Despite China's economic growth, and nascent Asian integration, US "soft power" still eclipses China's. The United States will continue to be looked to as a reliable security partner in Northeast Asia, and to a lesser extent in Southeast Asia. Public perceptions are at risk of downward swings in China, depending on portrayals of the United States in the country's official media.

Latin America: On balance, views of the United States are fairly favorable and stable, much more so in Central America, but less so in the Andean region. Some level of migration to the United States for jobs and subsequent remittance of earnings back to Latin America will be a key. Also important will be the degree to which US and Latin interests are viewed as shared, especially on multilateral tasks such as interdicting illegal drug supplies and combating organized crime and gangs.

Aggregating across regions, what does the tally sheet of factors affecting anti-Americanism look like out to 2025? First, factors favorable to the United States:

- Many state leaders and publics are distrustful of vast ***power*** itself, independent of the owner. As China becomes more powerful, some wariness will be displaced onto Beijing, and the United States' own function as a counterweight will become more appreciated.
- The US is benefiting from a likely turn in the ***battle of ideas***. First, and foremost, support for terrorism has declined dramatically over the last few years in many Muslim countries. Fewer Muslims now consider suicide bombing justifiable, and confidence in Usama Bin Ladin has waned.
- As big emerging markets in Asia and elsewhere grow, ***globalization*** will less often be equated with *Americanization*. As traditional ways of life are upset around the globe, unwanted foreign ideas and customs will appear more the product of modernity than of American sprawl.

Potentially unfavorable would be perceived slowness in tackling pressing transnational problems such as global climate change, food security, and energy security. A currently indeterminate factor will be the effect of increasingly pervasive mobile telephony, Internet connectivity, and direct satellite media on how individuals around the world receive their images of the United States. On balance, however, major trends suggest that anti-Americanism is declining.

- The dollar's global reserve status confers privileges on the US including insulation from risk of currency shocks, which enables lower interest rates, while a steady source of outside demand for US dollars affords the US a unique ability to run large fiscal account deficits without reproach from the global economy.

Enjoyed by the US for more than 60 years, these privileges have perhaps so permeated US thinking as to go unnoticed. While total loss of reserve status is unlikely, the dollar's decline may force the US into difficult tradeoffs between achieving ambitious foreign policy goals and the high domestic costs of supporting those objectives. In the face of higher interest rates, higher taxes, and potential oil shocks, the US public would have to weigh the economic consequences of taking strong military action, for example. The impact on others desirous of a stronger US role could be equally great if the US would decline or be unwilling to take action. In addition, US financial dependence on external powers for fiscal stability may curtail US freedom of action in unanticipated ways.

More Limited Military Superiority

In 2025, the US will still retain unique military capabilities, especially its ability to project military power globally, that other nations will continue to envy and rely on to secure a safer world. The United States' ability to protect the "global commons" and ensure the free flow of energy could gain greater prominence as concerns over energy security grow. The US also will continue to be viewed as the security partner of choice by many states confronted with the rise of potential hostile nuclear powers. Although the emergence of new nuclear-weapon states may constrain US freedom of action, US military superiority in both conventional and nuclear weapons and missile defense capabilities will be a critical element in deterring openly aggressive behavior on the part of any new nuclear states. The US will also be expected to play a significant role in using its military power to counter global terrorism.

However, potential US adversaries will continue to try to level the playing field by pursuing asymmetrical strategies designed to exploit perceived US military and political vulnerabilities. In the future, advanced states might engage in counterspace strikes, network attacks, and information warfare to disrupt US military operations on the eve of a conflict. Cyber and sabotage attacks on critical US economic, energy, and transportation infrastructures might be viewed by some adversaries as a way to circumvent US strengths on the battlefield and attack directly US interests at home. In addition, the continued proliferation of long-range missile systems, anti-access capabilities, and nuclear weapons and other forms of WMD might be perceived by potential adversaries and US allies alike as increasingly constraining US freedom of action in time of crisis despite US conventional military superiority.

- Traditional US allies, particularly Israel and Japan, could come to feel less secure in 2025 than they do today as a result of emerging unfavorable demographic trends within their respective countries, resource scarcities, and more intensive military competitions in the Middle East and East Asia, especially if there is also doubt about the vitality of US security guarantees.

Surprises and Unintended Consequences

As we have made clear throughout this volume, the next 15–20 years contain more contingencies than certainties. All actors—not just the United States—will be affected by unforeseen "shocks." For various reasons the US appears better able than most to absorb those shocks, but US fortunes also ride on the strength and resiliency of the entire international system, which we judge to be more fragile and less prepared for the implications of obvious trends like energy security, climate change, and increased conflict, let alone surprises.

While, by their nature, surprises are not easily anticipated, we have tried through the scenarios to lay out possible alternative futures and each is suggestive of possible changes in the US role.

A World Without the West. In this scenario the US withdraws and its role is diminished. In dealing with unstable parts of the world in its neighborhood like Afghanistan, China, and India, the Central Asians must form or bolster other partnerships—in this case the Shanghai Cooperation Organization. The fragmentation and breakdown of the global order into regional and other blocs—while not on the scale of US-Soviet bipolar split—probably would usher in an era of slower economic growth and globalization, less effective action on transnational issues like climate change and energy security, and the potential for increased political instability.

October Surprise. The lack of effective management of the tradeoffs among globalization, economic growth, and environmental damage is shared widely among more players than the US. Implicit in the scenario is the need for better US leadership and stronger multilateral institutions if the world is to avoid even more devastating crises. The results of miscalculation on the part of others—such as the Chinese—have significant political costs, which probably would make it more difficult for the US and others to put together a plan for more sustainable economic development, including conflicts among the major powers.

BRICs' Bust-Up. In this scenario, growing great power rivalries and increasing energy insecurity lead to a military confrontation between India and

China. The US is perceived by Beijing as favoring India to China's detriment. Great power war is averted, but the protagonists must rely on a third party—in this case Brazil—to help reconstitute the international fabric. Given the BRICs' disarray, the United States' power is greatly enhanced, but the international system is in for a bumpy ride as the military clash leads to internal upheavals increasing nationalist fervor.

Politics Is Not Always Local. On some issues, such as the environment, a seismic shift in government versus nonstate actor authorities has occurred. For the first time, a coalition of nonstate actors is seen by a large number of electorates as better representing "planetary" interests and, in this scenario, governments must heed their advice or face serious political costs. This may not always be the case since on other more traditional national security issues, national, ethnic, class and other differences are likely to re-emerge, undercutting the clout of transnational political movements. The US, like other governments, must adapt to the changing political landscape.

Leadership Will Be Key

As we indicated at the beginning of the study, human actions are likely to be the crucial determinant of the outcomes. Historically, as we have pointed out, leaders and their ideas— positive and negative—were among the biggest game-changers during the last century. Individually and collectively over the next 15–20 years, leaders are likely to be crucial to how developments turn out, particularly in terms of ensuring a more positive outcome. As we have emphasized, today's trends appear to be heading toward a potentially more fragmented and conflicted world over the next 15–20 years, but bad outcomes are not inevitable. International leadership and cooperation will be necessary to solve the global challenges and to understand the complexities surrounding them. This study is meant as an aid in that process: by laying out some of the alternative possibilities we hope to help policymakers steer us toward positive solutions.

B. REGIONAL TRENDS IN TERRORISM

COMMENTARY

REGIONAL TRENDS IN TERRORISM

By
Douglas C. Lovelace Jr.

This section of the volume proceeds from the global trends assessment of the preceding section to assessments of terrorism developments in five areas of concern: Pakistan, Afghanistan, Latin America, China, and India. The section focuses in on key issues to apprise the reader of the most important terrorist and counterterrorism activities and to suggest trend vectors. *Combating Terrorism: The United States Lacks Comprehensive Plan to Destroy the Terrorist Threat and Close the Safe Haven in Pakistan's Federally Administered Tribal Areas,* is an April 2008 Government Accountability Office (GAO) report to the U.S. Congress. The report addresses a key issue in the war against terrorists in general and the war in Afghanistan in particular. The central concern is sanctuary for terrorists, their support base, and their training facilities. Such sanctuary is arguably the single most determinative factor in the success or defeat of terrorist organizations, especially al Qaeda.

With respect to actions against the Taliban and its al Qaeda supporters in Afghanistan, one should be cognizant of the fact that throughout history there have been few successful insurgencies that did not feature external sanctuary for the insurgents. China, Cuba, Vietnam, South Africa, Zimbabwe, and Uganda come readily to mind. Many noted national security strategists assert, with good reason, that al Qaeda will not be defeated so long as it is able to enjoy sanctuary in Pakistan, and Pakistan is either unwilling or unable to deny such sanctuary. In fact, some reports claim that Pakistan's Directorate for Inter-Services Intelligence (ISI) actually supports the terrorists. Why would the Pakistan government allow that? The simplest answer would be to maintain a modicum of stability in the Federally Administered Tribal Areas (FATA) and North West Frontier Province (NWFP) so the Pakistan government is less threatened by terrorist efforts to overthrow it. However, many in Pakistan's government recognize how pernicious and insidious the terrorists can be and are reluctant to offer additional concessions.

The situation seems to have devolved to one in which the ISI provides some targeting data to the United States and the government in Islamabad feigns opprobrium after the United States conducts an attack. At best, this approach to eliminating terrorists inside Pakistan is yielding indecisive results. In spite of this state of affairs, the GAO report notes that since 2002, the United States has provided Pakistan more than $10.5 billion to help make it a better partner in the war against terrorists. Nonetheless, the report notes, the FATAs and NWFP remain relatively unpoliced and ungoverned from Islamabad and continue to provide safe haven for terrorists. The report assesses U.S. progress in meeting its national security goal of eliminating the terrorist threat and closing the safe havens in the FATAs and NWFP. In short, it gives the United States government a failing grade.

Specifically, the report concludes that the U.S. government, in collaboration with the government of Pakistan, has not developed, let alone implemented, a comprehensive plan for eliminating the terrorist threat emanating from the FATAs and NWFP, although it has resolved to do so in several national level strategy documents and reports. The GAO report recommends that such a plan be developed and the U.S. Agency for International Development agreed. However, the Bush administration's Department of State rejected the contention that such a strategy does not exist, as did its Director of National Intelligence.

It appears the Obama administration is not as sanguine about the state of planning and plan implementation to reduce the terrorist threat from the FATAs and NWFP and seeks to increase cooperation with Pakistan's military. U.S. Under Secretary of Defense for Policy, Michele Flournoy, said the United States would like to train and advise the Pakistani army on counterinsurgency and support Pakistani efforts with intelligence and other assistance. The new approach must overcome at least two hurdles, however. Pakistan's army is reluctant to shift its focus to counterinsurgency and away from countering India's military power. Additionally, Pakistani leaders, including military officers, must be careful that visible cooperation with the United States does not fuel ever-present anti-American sentiment in the FATAs and NWFP.

In essence, the new administration would like to establish a new "strategic partnership" among the United States, Pakistan, and Afghanistan that will yield a unified strategy for both countries. To that end, Pakistan's and Afghanistan's presidents met with President Obama on May 6 and 7, 2009. While the Obama administration considers the partnership critical to success in Afghanistan and in the wider war against terrorists, Pakistan and Afghanistan lack a history of close cooperation. Additionally, criticism of the administration's policy, which some administration officials refer to as Af-Pak, is emerging. After visiting Pakistan recently, Senator Kerry said the Obama plan is not a real strategy, is inadequate to address the perils Pakistan faces, and use of the term "Af-Pak" is not only a disservice to each country but also is viewed negatively by both. Additionally, exposing the sensitivities involved, Pakistan strongly objects to any language in aid bills that would require the U.S. president to have Pakistan officially state it does not support terrorism.

The second document provided in this section on regional terrorism trends is a February 2009 GAO report to Congress on *Securing, Stabilizing, and Developing Pakistan's Border Area with Afghanistan: Key Issues for Congressional Oversight*. The report complements in many respects the April 2008 GAO report previously presented in this section. This report also concludes, almost a year later, that the United States still has failed to achieve its strategic objective of denying sanctuary to terrorists located along Pakistan's border with Afghanistan, notwithstanding the enormous amount of aid the United States has provided Pakistan. The report notes that al Qaeda finds safe haven in Pakistan and is once again capable of mounting attacks against the United States and other countries. The report repeats the April 2008 report's call for the United States to develop a comprehensive plan, employing all instruments of national power, to achieve its strategic objectives within the FATAs and NWFP.

The 2009 report states that the U.S. government's response to the 2008 report's recommendations varied among agencies. Most importantly, while the 2009 report acknowledges that individual agencies have plans for addressing the terrorist threat emanating from the FATAs and NWFP, the U.S. government still lacks a comprehensive overall plan that would bring to bear all the instruments of national power wielded synergistically by the various government agencies, and that such a comprehensive plan is requisite to achieving U.S. strategic objectives. The report also provides useful background information on Pakistan and an assessment of the mix of the instruments on national power presently being applied. It does not address the U.S. intelligence community's accomplishments and ongoing actions. The 2009 report is a very useful update to the 2008 report, if for no other reason, because it clearly points to an unacceptable lack of progress to address the FATA and NWFP sanctuary issue comprehensively and effectively.

The third document provided in this section on regional terrorism trends is a January 23, 2009 Congressional Research Service (CRS) report on *The War in Afghanistan: Strategy, Military Operations, and Issues for Congress*. It adds to the discussion provided by the preceding two documents. It pessimistically describes the war in Afghanistan as a "deteriorating situation" with no "comprehensive political outcome yet in sight." The report very astutely names the many stakeholders in the effort, domestically and internationally.

The report accurately describes the multifaceted nature of the struggle as a diffused counterinsurgency effort to provide sufficient security for effective governance and economic development—three interdependent areas. The report correctly concludes that the U.S. government must make several key decisions concerning the war. It must define and clarify current U.S. national interests in Afghanistan and the region, derive clear strategic objectives from those interests, determine the most appropriate combination of the instruments of national power for achieving the objectives, assess the costs of bringing such capabilities to bear in the capacities needed against other claimants of resources, and coordinate international efforts. The report concludes by suggesting what the U.S. Congress can do to assist. The report is replete with informative and useful data and assessments and likely helped provide the context for the Obama administration's new strategic direction for Afghanistan and Pakistan.

The fourth document provided in this regional trend section brings the reader up to date on the Afghanistan and Pakistan FATA and NWFP terrorist sanctuary issues. The *White Paper of the Interagency Policy Group's Report on U.S. Policy toward Afghanistan and Pakistan*, published by the White House on March 27, 2009, announces what is claimed to be a comprehensive new U.S. strategy for Afghanistan and Pakistan. The White House states that it was developed in consultation with the Afghan and Pakistani governments and other key stakeholders and potential contributors. The goal of the strategy is to disrupt, dismantle, and defeat al Qaeda and its safe havens by applying a new "flexible and adoptive" approach that features "frequent evaluations of the progress being made." The approach also is considered regional, viewing Afghanistan and Pakistan as partners facing a common threat. Notwithstanding the perceived inadequate return on past investment, the new strategy calls for even more increases in U.S. support to Pakistan. However, the strategy states that such increases will depend on Pakistan's performance against the terrorist threat in the FATAs and NWFP. The new strategy also envisions enhanced intelligence sharing and military cooperation.

Specifically. the strategy calls for building capacity in Afghanistan by deploying more U.S. forces and increasing the training provided to the Afghan National Security Forces to prepare them for assuming responsibility for securing Afghanistan's population. Other central themes of the strategy include use of all the elements of national power, forging a multilateral effort by all stakeholders, and providing increased resources for tasks to be performed by civilian entities. The strategy clearly incorporates the Obama administration's Special Representative for and Pakistan, Richard Holbrooke's view that the United States must deal with Afghanistan and Pakistan as a pair and not individually. Thus far, that approach appears to be working, although it has received some criticism. The ultimate effectiveness of the strategy will depend on the extent to which Congress adequately resources it and the intra- and intergovernmental cooperation and synergy that can be achieved in its implementation.

Since its drafting, a significant challenge to the new strategy has developed as it applies to Pakistan. Glenn Kessler of the *Washington Post* reports on congressional testimony in which Secretary of State Clinton stated that the Pakistani government "is basically abdicating to the Taliban and to the extremists." Her concerns are shared by many national security strategists and relate to the recent ceding of sovereignty of Pakistan's Swat Valley to the terrorist-supporting Taliban. The valley is located about 100 miles west of Islamabad and there are reports that 400 to 500 Talban insurgents have consolidated control of a strategic district called Buner, less than 70 miles from the capital. As of this writing, several senior U.S. officials seriously doubt the government of Pakistan's willingness and ability to defeat the Taliban insurgents. The officials also critically question the wisdom of the government's attempts to appease the Taliban and the Pakistani military's decision to remain focused on India, at least initially. The increased concern will greatly complicate ongoing congressional action to pass legislation that would provide Pakistan $7.5 billion in nonmilitary aid over five years. Recent reports suggest, however, that Pakistan's military may be willing and able to limit the Taliban's control over Pakistan territory.

Some make the argument that with Pakistan believed to be a nuclear-armed state, the overthrow of the government by the Taliban could result in nuclear weapons falling into the hands of terrorists. That Richard C. Holbrooke, the U.S. special envoy for the region, sends the U.S. secretary of state memos several times a day reporting the situation in Pakistan and that the Chairman of the Joint Chiefs of Staff, Admiral Mike Mullen, visited Pakistan on April 22, 2009 to meet with the chief of Pakistan's army evidence the great concern U.S. leadership has with the situation. Given recent developments, one could expect the Obama administration's new strategy to be implemented with increased firmness, especially regarding expectations of tangible results achieved by Pakistan's government.

The final three documents in this section on regional terrorism trends take us to Latin America, South Asia, and East Asia. The first, an August 27, 2008 CRS report on *Latin America: Terrorism Issues*, surveys in summary form the terrorist threat in Latin America, how it has evolved, and what regional counterterrorism measures are under way. Perhaps the first point the report makes is that terrorism in Latin America, for the most part, is not the work of radical Islamists. Except for Hamas' and Hezbollah's fundraising among the large Muslim populations in the tri-border area of Argentina, Brazil, and Paraguay, radical Islamists have virtually no operational capability in Latin America. Two bombings in Argentina in 1992 and 1994 targeting Israelis have been attributed to Hezbollah, but no other radical Islamist attacks have been reported since.

The terrorism Latin America suffers stems from Colombia's three terrorist groups: the leftist Revolutionary Armed Forces of Colombia (FARC), the leftist National Liberation Army (ELN), and the remnants of the rightist paramilitary United Self-Defense Forces of Colombia (AUC), as well as Peru's Shining Path (Sendero Luminoso or SL). All of these groups can be considered as much insurgents as terrorists. They use terrorist tactics to delegitimize governments for both political and profit motives, although of late, their primary concerns seem to have become economic. For all practical purposes, Colombia has defeated the AUC and the ELN has indicated a desire to reach an accommodation with the Colombian government. The Colombian military also has weakened the FARC, although it continues to commit all manner of crime for profit, including kidnapping, assassinations, and narcotrafficking. Likewise, the Peruvian government all but defeated SL in the 1990s and that organization also has now turned to committing crimes for profit.

The CRS report correctly notes that while terrorism has been present in Latin America for many decades, it has attracted increased attention since September 11, 2001. Cuba remains on the U.S. list of states sponsoring terrorism, along with Iran, North Korea, Sudan, and Syria. Venezuela is likely to join that nefarious club in the near future, absent a change in its policies, especially with regard to the FARC. Today, the United States is more concerned with terrorists using Latin America as a transit route to the United States than terrorist attacks on U.S. citizens or interests in Latin America. Nonetheless, the kidnapping of Americans for ransom remains a concern.

The key point that the report fails to address adequately is the rise of gangs in Latin America, the members of which are becoming accomplished 21st century bandits. The virulence of the gangs has become such that they threaten the viability of legitimate governments, even that of America's closest Latin American neighbor. The level of violence of the gangs continues to rise and may soon evoke a significant response from the United States, in concert with regional allies. One can expect to see more investigation and reporting on the gang phenomenon in the near future.

The next document in this section takes us to East Asia. The October 28, 2008 CRS report for Congress, *U.S.-China Counterterrorism Cooperation: Issues for U.S. Policy*, provides an update on United States-China counterterrorism cooperation. In the aftermath of the al Qaeda attacks on the United States on September 11, 2001, hopes of improved cooperation and collaboration between the two countries arose. Such hopes led to a superficial warming of relations, at least on the terrorism issue. From 2001 to 2005, the U.S. government commented favorably about diplomatic and other support for the war against terrorists. However, by 2005, many began to doubt whether there was any substance to China's public statements of support. For example, the CRS report notes that China's military has not participated in the counterterrorism coalition. The report correctly suggests that many question whether the limited support the United States was able to garner from China was worth the cost in terms of pursuing other U.S. interests vis-à-vis China.

The CRS report correctly notes that by 2005, senior U.S. officials began to question the genuineness and sincerity of China's promises of support. The doubts were well founded. U.S. adversaries in Afghanistan have been found armed with weapons produced by China. China also appears to have consciously cloaked its oppression of the Uighurs (Uyghurs) in western Xinjiang in apparent legitimacy by claiming them to be linked to terrorists. Importantly, China has provided not convincing evidence of the link. The CRS report leaves the reader with many doubts concerning the efficacy of United States-China counterterrorism cooperation.

The final document presented in this section on regional trends addresses one of the most widely reported terrorists attacks since September 11, 2001, not so much because of the resulting deaths, casualties, and physical damage, but because of the brazenness and sophisticated simplicity of the terrorists' operation. The December 19, 2008 CRS report on *Terrorist Attacks in Mumbai, India and Implications for U.S. Interests* examines the possible strategic ramifications of the attack. The report notes that the attackers are believed to have been from a terrorist group located in Pakistan, although there is no credible evidence of involvement of the Pakistani government. Nonetheless, wars and tensions between the two countries dating back to 1947 caused the attack to be viewed with great suspicion by the Indian population, if not the government, as well.

The United States and other responsible stakeholders in global security perforce view such a potential escalation in tension between two historical antagonists, both of whom have become nuclear powers, with great alarm. The CRS report suggests, somewhat naïvely, that the Obama administration should increase U.S. diplomatic efforts aimed at resolving conflict between these two countries. The attack was an important test for the Indian government. Although many Indians criticized their government's anti-terrorist and counterterrorist efforts, the government's response was measured and calculated to not increase tensions precipitously. The reasonableness of the government's response was remarkable, given the discord the attack engendered within the ruling elite. The restraint most likely reflects India's belief that with its expanding economy and ever-increasing international status, it has the upper hand over Pakistan in the long-term and was not willing to risk that position by overreaction to the Mumbai attacks. The CRS report concludes with interesting observations concerning the various impacts the attack had and will have on relations between and among India, Pakistan, and the United States.

DOCUMENT NO. 2

COMBATING TERRORISM: THE UNITED STATES LACKS COMPREHENSIVE PLAN TO DESTROY THE TERRORIST THREAT AND CLOSE THE SAFE HAVEN IN PAKISTAN'S FEDERALLY ADMINISTERED TRIBAL AREAS

GAO Report
GAO-08-622

April 2008

What GAO Found

The United States has not met its national security goals to destroy terrorist threats and close the safe haven in Pakistan's FATA. Since 2002, the United States relied principally on the Pakistan military to address U.S. national security goals. Of the approximately $5.8 billion the United States provided for efforts in the FATA and border region from 2002 through 2007, about 96 percent reimbursed Pakistan for military operations there. According to the Department of State, Pakistan deployed 120,000 military and paramilitary forces in the FATA and helped kill and capture hundreds of suspected al Qaeda operatives; these efforts cost the lives of approximately 1,400 members of Pakistan's security forces. However, GAO found broad agreement, as documented in the National Intelligence Estimate, State, and embassy documents, as well as Defense officials in Pakistan, that al Qaeda had regenerated its ability to attack the United States and had succeeded in establishing a safe haven in Pakistan's FATA.

No comprehensive plan for meeting U.S. national security goals in the FATA has been developed, as stipulated by the *National Strategy for Combating Terrorism* (2003), called for by an independent commission (2004), and mandated by congressional legislation (2007). Furthermore, Congress created the National Counterterrorism Center (NCTC) in 2004 specifically to develop comprehensive plans to combat terrorism. However, neither the National Security Council (NSC), NCTC, nor other executive branch departments have developed a comprehensive plan that includes all elements of national power—diplomatic, military, intelligence, development assistance, economic, and law enforcement support—called for by the various national security strategies and Congress. As a result, since 2002, the U.S. embassy in Pakistan has had no Washington-supported, comprehensive plan to combat terrorism and close the terrorist safe haven in the FATA. In 2006, the embassy, in conjunction with Defense, State, and U.S. Agency for International Development (USAID), and in cooperation with the government of Pakistan, began an effort to focus more attention on other key elements of national power, such as development assistance and public diplomacy, to address U.S. goals in the FATA. However, this does not yet constitute a comprehensive plan.

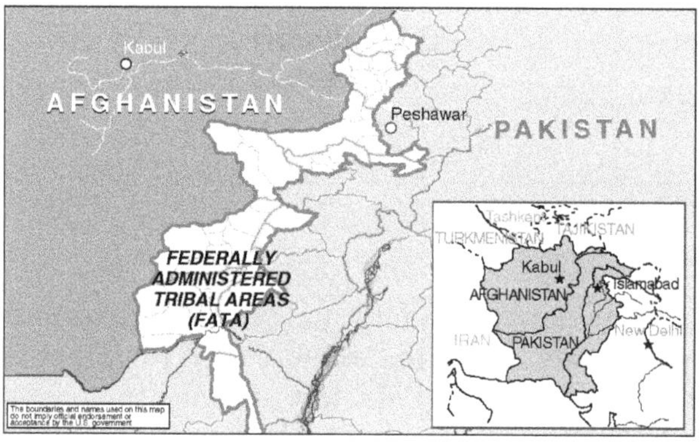

Sources: GAO; USAID and Map Resources (maps).

Abbreviations

CENTCOM	U.S. Central Command
CIA	Central Intelligence Agency
CSF	Coalition Support Funds
Defense	Department of Defense
DNI	Director of National Intelligence
FATA	Federally Administered Tribal Areas
FCR	Frontier Crimes Regulations
NIE	National Intelligence Estimate
NCTC	National Counterterrorism Center
NSC	National Security Council

ODNI	Office of the Director of National Intelligence
State	Department of State
USAID	U.S. Agency for International Development

United States Government Accountability Office
Washington, DC 20548

April 17, 2008

Congressional Requesters:

The terrorist attacks of 9/11 were planned from an Afghan safe haven, and many of the terrorists who attacked the United States used Pakistan as the main route to travel from Afghanistan to the United States. Since the 9/11 attacks in 2001, the administration and Congress have repeatedly stated that destroying terrorist threats and closing terrorist safe havens are the nation's critical national security goals.[1] As such, the United States has provided Pakistan, which has become a key U.S. ally in the global war on terror, with more than $10.5 billion for military, economic, and development activities in support of these goals. The 9/11 Commission, an independent, bipartisan commission created by congressional legislation in late 2002, concluded in 2004 that it is hard to overstate the importance of Pakistan in the struggle against Islamist terrorism. The commission found that the country's vast unpoliced regions have made it attractive to extremists seeking a safe haven and have reportedly provided a base for terrorist operations against U.S. and coalition forces in Afghanistan. Following the defeat of the Taliban in Afghanistan, al Qaeda and Taliban fighters are believed to have retreated across the Afghan border and into Pakistan's Federally Administered Tribal Areas (FATA) in an effort to re-establish a terrorist safe haven.

Because of the challenges the United States faces in Pakistan in meeting its goals to destroy the terrorist threats and close the terrorist safe haven, we were asked to assess (1) U.S. progress in meeting its national security goals in Pakistan's FATA region, and (2) the status of U.S. efforts to develop a comprehensive plan for the FATA.

This report is the first in a series of reports we plan to issue in response to your interest in U.S. support of the Pakistani government's efforts in the FATA region bordering Afghanistan. We plan to issue an interim product

[1] These goals have been set forth in the 2002 *National Security Strategy*, the 2003 *National Strategy for Combating Terrorism*, the 2004 *9/11 Commission Report*, and endorsed by the Intelligence Reform and Terrorism Prevention Act of 2004 (P.L. 108-458, sec 7102 (b)(3)) and the Implementing the Recommendations of the 9/11 Commission Act of 2007 (P.L. 110-53, sec. 2042(b)(2)).

on the use and oversight of Coalition Support Funds (CSF) in May 2008 and a report on CSF in the summer of 2008, followed by a broader report covering security, political, and development assistance activities undertaken by the United States to meet U.S. national security goals in the FATA.

To address our objectives, we reviewed relevant national security strategies, the *9/11 Commission Report*, key congressional legislation, and related documentation from the Departments of Defense (Defense) and State (State) and the U.S. Agency for International Development (USAID), and discussed these issues with relevant department officials in Washington, D.C. We also interviewed Defense officials operating out of the U.S. Central Command (CENTCOM) headquarters in Tampa, Florida. We requested meetings with the Central Intelligence Agency (CIA), the National Counterterrorism Center (NCTC), and the National Security Council (NSC); however, only the CIA agreed to meet with us. To determine progress in meeting national security objectives, we compared the national security goals stated in strategic documents with unclassified assessments conducted by the Director of National Intelligence (DNI), State, and U.S. officials operating in Pakistan. To determine if comprehensive plans were developed and contained the elements recommended by national security documents, legislation, and GAO, we requested all plans addressing U.S. efforts in the FATA from the CIA, Defense, NCTC, NSC, State, USAID, and the U.S. Embassy in Pakistan. CIA, NCTC, and NSC did not provide any plans. We reviewed all plans provided by Defense, State, and USAID, as of April 17, 2008. We also met with members of the International Crisis Group in Washington, including the director of their office in Pakistan.[2] In addition, we conducted field work in Pakistan, where we met with officials from the U.S. embassy and Pakistan's Ministries of Defense and Interior, as well as international donors from Canada, Japan, the Netherlands, and the United Kingdom. We visited Peshawar, near the FATA, to conduct discussions with the U.S. consulate, Pakistan's 11th Army Corps, the Frontier Corps, the FATA Secretariat and Development Authority, and a Pakistani nongovernmental organization with experience working in the FATA. We determined the amount of U.S. funding to Pakistan by analyzing Defense, State, and USAID budget documents covering the period from fiscal years 2002 through 2007 and by verifying the amounts used for the FATA and the border regions through discussions with agency officials. This analysis does not include funding for covert activities in Pakistan.

We conducted this performance audit from July 2007 through April 2008 in accordance with generally accepted government auditing standards. Those standards require that we plan and perform the audit to obtain sufficient,

[2] The International Crisis Group is an independent, nonpartisan source of analysis on the prevention and resolution of global conflicts.

appropriate evidence to provide a reasonable basis for our findings and conclusions based on our audit objectives. We believe that the evidence obtained provides a reasonable basis for our findings and conclusions based on our audit objectives.

Results in Brief

The United States has not met its national security goals to destroy the terrorist threat and close the safe haven in Pakistan's FATA region. Since 2002, the United States has relied principally on the Pakistani military to address its national security goals. There have been limited efforts, however, to address other underlying causes of terrorism in the FATA by providing development assistance or by addressing the FATA's political needs. Of the over $10.5 billion that the United States has provided to Pakistan from 2002 through 2007, we identified about $5.8 billion specifically for Pakistan's FATA and border region; about 96 percent of this funding reimbursed Pakistan for military operations in the FATA and the border region. According to Defense and State Department officials, Pakistan deployed up to 120,000 military and paramilitary forces in the FATA and killed and captured hundreds of suspected al Qaeda operatives. In October 2007, State reported that it had determined that Pakistan was making "significant" progress toward eliminating the safe haven in the FATA. However, we found broad agreement, as documented in the unclassified 2007 *National Intelligence Estimate* (NIE), State and embassy documents, as well as among Defense, State, and other officials, including those operating in Pakistan, that al Qaeda had regenerated its ability to attack the United States and had succeeded in establishing a safe haven in Pakistan's FATA.

No comprehensive plan for meeting U.S. national security goals in the FATA has been developed, as stipulated by the *National Strategy for Combating Terrorism*, recommended by the independent 9/11 Commission, and mandated by congressional legislation.[3] Since 2003, the administration's national security strategies and Congress have recognized that a comprehensive plan that includes all elements of national power—diplomatic, military, intelligence, development assistance, economic, and law enforcement support—was needed to address the terrorist threat emanating from the FATA. Furthermore, in 2004, a provision of the Intelligence Reform and Terrorism Prevention Act of 2004 (Intelligence Reform Act) established the

[3] The administration's 2003 *National Strategy for Combating Terrorism*, the independent *9/11 Commission Report*, and Congress's (1) Intelligence Reform Act and Terrorism Prevention Act of 2004 (P.L. 108-458, sec. 7120) and (2) the Implementing the Recommendations of the 9/11 Commission Act of 2007 (P.L. 110-53, sec. 2042 (c)) all support the development of a comprehensive plan that uses all elements of national power.

NCTC to develop comprehensive plans to combat terrorism that included clear objectives, the assignment of tasks among executive branch departments, and interagency coordination. We have previously reported on the need for these and other elements to enhance interagency cooperation and improve effectiveness.[4] The NCTC also was tasked with monitoring each department's efforts. However, neither the NCTC, the NSC, nor the other executive branch departments have developed a comprehensive plan that integrates the capabilities of the executive agencies and the intelligence community. As a result, since 2002, the embassy has had no Washington-supported, comprehensive plan to combat terrorists and close the terrorist safe haven in the FATA. In 2006, the U.S. government, in conjunction with the government of Pakistan, began an effort to focus more attention on other key elements of national power, such as development and public diplomacy, to address U.S. goals in the FATA. In support of this effort, Defense, State, and USAID began to develop department-specific plans and hold interagency meetings to address security and development issues in the FATA. However, this effort has not yet resulted in a comprehensive plan. As of April 2008, not all of these efforts have been approved in Washington, funding shortfalls exist, and support from the recently elected government of Pakistan is unknown.[5]

We are recommending that the National Security Advisor and the Director of the NCTC, in consultation with the Secretaries of Defense and State, the Administrator of USAID, the intelligence community, and other executive departments as deemed appropriate, work to develop a comprehensive plan using all elements of national power to combat the terrorist threat and close the associated safe haven in Pakistan's FATA region. The comprehensive plan should also include key components called for in the Intelligence Reform Act and components that we have previously reported as being needed to improve the effectiveness of plans involving multidepartmental efforts to combat terrorism.

State, the Office of the Director of National Intelligence (ODNI), Defense, and USAID provided written comments on a draft of this report, which are reproduced in appendixes I, II, III, and IV.

[4] We reported that strategic plans should clearly define objectives to be accomplished, identify the roles and responsibilities for meeting each objective, ensure that funding necessary to achieve the objectives is available, and employ monitoring mechanisms to determine progress and identify needed improvements. See GAO, *Combating Terrorism: Law Enforcement Agencies Lack Directives to Assist Foreign Nations to Identify, Disrupt, and Prosecute Terrorists*, GAO-07-697 (Washington, D.C.: May 25, 2007); GAO, *Results-Oriented Government: Practices That Can Help Enhance and Sustain Collaboration among Federal Agencies*, GAO-06-1 5 (Washington, D.C.: Oct. 21, 2005); and GAO, *Combating Terrorism: Observations on National Strategies Related to Terrorism*, GAO-03-519T (Washington, D.C.: Mar. 3, 2003).

[5] We will continue to monitor the status and progress of the U.S. government's effort in the FATA and report on the matter in a subsequent report.

State and ODNI did not comment on our recommendation, while Defense and USAID concurred. In general, they all commented on their individual planning efforts and interagency meetings to coordinate these efforts that began in 2006. This, however, was not the focus of our review; our report assessed whether a comprehensive plan had been developed that incorporated all elements of national power.

State's comments asserted that embassy and U.S. government efforts to date have resulted in a comprehensive strategy. We disagree, and note in our report that while the initiatives begun by Defense, State, and USAID are being coordinated by the embassy, they have not been fully approved or integrated into a formal, comprehensive plan.

ODNI's comments stated that they agreed with our finding that the United States had not met its national security goals in Pakistan's FATA; however, they disagreed that the United States lacks plans to combat terrorism. Our report does not state that the U.S. lacks agency-specific plans; rather, we found that there was no comprehensive plan that integrated the combined capabilities of Defense, State, USAID, the intelligence community, and others, as called for by the 2003 national security strategy, the 9/11 Commission report, and Congress.

We also received technical comments from Defense and USAID, which we have incorporated throughout the report where appropriate.

Background

The FATA is mountainous and shares a 373-mile border with Afghanistan known as the Durand Line (see fig. 1). The FATA, which has a population of 3.1 million people, is one of Pakistan's poorest regions, with high poverty, high unemployment, and an underdeveloped infrastructure. Most of the population depends on subsistence agriculture. The FATA's per capita income is $250 per year, which is half of the national per capita income; about 60 percent of the population lives below the national poverty line. Per capita public development expenditure is reportedly one-third of the national average. Social development indicators are also poor. The overall literacy rate is 17 percent, compared with 56 percent nationally, with male literacy at 29 percent and female literacy at 3 percent. The FATA has just 41 hospitals for its population of 3.1 million, and a doctor to population ratio of 1 to 6,762.

The FATA is governed by an administrative system and a judicial system different from the rest of Pakistan—the Frontier Crimes Regulations (FCR) of 1901, codified under British rule.[6] Because Pakistan retained the colonial

[6] The information on foreign law in this report does not reflect our independent legal analysis but is based on interviews and secondary sources.

Figure 1: Map of the Federally Administered Tribal Areas, Pakistan

Sources: GAO; USAID and Map Resources (maps).

administrative and legal structures of the British, as codified in the FCR, the FATA populations are legally separate from and unequal to other Pakistani citizens. Examples of these differences under the FCR follow:

- FATA residents do not have access to national political parties, and political parties are forbidden from extending their activities into the agencies of FATA.
- The FATA is under the direct executive authority of the President of Pakistan. Laws framed by the National Assembly of Pakistan do not apply in the FATA unless so ordered by the President, who is empowered to issue regulations for the tribal areas.
- FATA residents do not have the right to legal representation, to present material evidence, or to cross-examine witnesses in Pakistan's

judicial system. Those convicted are denied the right of appeal in Pakistan's courts.

- The President's representatives to the FATA, who are called political agents, can punish an entire tribe for crimes committed on the tribe's territory by issuing fines, making arrests, implementing property seizures, and establishing blockades.

In response to the draft, Defense noted that the FCR is a culturally acceptable recognition of the tribal structure of the FATA, where the population is ethnically different from the majority of Pakistan's citizens, and precludes forced assimilation. Further, Defense noted that removing the FCR without a replacement mechanism that is accepted by the indigenous population has the potential to create a vacuum that could result in negative consequences. A recent announcement by Pakistani Prime Minister Yousaf Raza Gillani regarding the repeal of the FCR drew mixed reactions from tribesmen and political leaders, some of whom called for amendments to the FCR, rather than its repeal.

The U.S. Government Has Not Met National Security Goals in Pakistan's FATA

The United States has not met its national security goals to destroy the terrorist threat and close the safe haven in the FATA, despite more than $10.5 billion in U.S. support to Pakistan since 2002. Various national security strategies have called for the use of all elements of national power, such as diplomatic, military, intelligence, development assistance, economic, and law enforcement support, to meet these goals; however, the United States has relied principally on supporting the Pakistani military to meet these goals. According to Defense and State, the Pakistani government deployed up to 120,000 military and paramilitary forces to combat terrorism in the FATA. Despite this effort, the 2007 NIE, State and embassy documents, and Defense and State officials, including those operating in Pakistan, have concluded that al Qaeda has regenerated its ability to attack the United States and succeeded in establishing a safe haven in Pakistan's FATA.

Although State Has Reported Some Progress in Pakistan's FATA, Other Sources Indicate Resurgence of an al Qaeda Threat and the Establishment of a Terrorist Safe Haven in the FATA

On October 1, 2007, State provided Congress with a report in response to a requirement in the Implementation of the 9/11 Commission Act of 2007 (9/11 Commission Act).[7] The report stated that it had determined that Pakistan was (1) committed to eliminating from Pakistani territory any

[7] P.L. 110-53, sec. 2042(d), Aug. 3, 2007.

organization, such as the Taliban, al Qaeda, or any successor engaged in military, insurgent, or terrorist activities in Afghanistan; (2) undertaking a comprehensive military, legal, economic, and political campaign to achieve the goal described; and (3) making demonstrated, significant, and sustained progress toward eliminating support or safe havens for terrorists. Notwithstanding State's report to Congress, we found broad agreement that al Qaeda had established a safe haven in the FATA and reconstituted its attack capability. In particular, the unclassified versions of the 2007 NIE and 2008 *Annual Threat Assessment* state that al Qaeda has regenerated its attack capability and secured a safe haven in Pakistan's FATA.[8] These conclusions are supported by a broad array of sources, including Defense, State, and senior U.S. embassy officials in Pakistan.

The NIE and other sources have found that al Qaeda has established a safe haven in Pakistan. The DNI's 2008 assessment stated that the safe haven in Pakistan provides al Qaeda with many of the same advantages it had when it was based across the border in Afghanistan. According to the assessment, the safe haven in the FATA serves as a staging area for al Qaeda's attacks in support of the Taliban in Afghanistan. Further, it serves as a location for training new terrorist operatives for attacks in Pakistan, the Middle East, Africa, Europe, and the United States. U.S. government officials in Washington and Pakistan also acknowledge that al Qaeda has established a safe haven near Pakistan's border with Afghanistan. For example, State's April 2007 *Country Reports on Terrorism* states that Pakistan remains a major source of Islamic extremism and a safe haven for some top terrorist leaders, including those of al Qaeda.

The NIE, *The Terrorist Threat to the U.S. Homeland,* also found that al Qaeda had effectively found replacements for many of its senior operational planners over the years. The NIE stated that, in the past 2 years, al Qaeda's central leadership regenerated the core operational capabilities needed to conduct attacks against the United States. It also found that al Qaeda's central leadership, based in the border area of Pakistan, is and will remain the most serious terrorist threat to the United States.

The 2008 DNI *Annual Threat Assessment* and other sources have concluded that the resurgence of al Qaeda terrorists on the border between Pakistan and Afghanistan now pose a preeminent threat to U.S. national security. The assessment also examines the impact of not meeting the national security goals. It states that al Qaeda is now using the Pakistani safe haven to put the last element necessary to launch another attack against America into place, including the identification, training, and positioning of Western

[8] The DNI's 2007 NIE and its 2008 *Annual Threat Assessment* are designed to help U.S. civilian and military leaders develop policies to protect U.S. national security interests and represent the combined judgments of 16 U.S. intelligence agencies, according to the NIE.

operatives for an attack. It stated that al Qaeda is most likely using the FATA to plot terrorist attacks against political, economic, and infrastructure targets in America "designed to produce mass casualties, visually dramatic destruction, significant economic aftershocks, and/or fear among the population."

DNI's 2008 assessment found that al Qaeda and other Pakistan-based militants now also pose a threat to Pakistan. The assessment found an unparalleled increase in suicide attacks against Pakistan's military and civilians over the past year, with total casualties in 2007 exceeding all such attacks in the preceding 5 years. These attacks were ordered by Pakistan-based militants, many of whom are allied with al Qaeda. It found that the terrorist assassination of former Prime Minister Benazir Bhutto could encourage terrorists to strike the Pakistani establishment anywhere in the country. The assessment concluded that radical elements now have the potential to undermine Pakistan itself.

The United States Has Relied Primarily on the Pakistani Military to Accomplish Its Goals in Pakistan's FATA, with Little Focus on Economic Development and Improving Governance

Since 2002, the United States has relied principally on the Pakistani military to address U.S. national security goals in the FATA. There have been limited efforts, however, to address other underlying causes of terrorism in the FATA, such as providing development assistance or addressing the FATA's political needs. For example, although the FATA has some of the worst development indicators in Pakistan and is ruled under colonial administrative and legal structures dating from 1901, the United States has devoted little funding to address these issues in the FATA.

From fiscal years 2002 to 2007, the United States has provided Pakistan with more than $10.5 billion in funds and assistance.[9] Approximately $5.8 billion of this amount has been directed at efforts to combat terrorism in Pakistan's FATA and the border region. As figure 2 shows, about 96 percent of this amount was used to reimburse the Pakistani government through CSF[10] for military operations in support of Operation Enduring Freedom in

[9] GAO arrived at this figure by analyzing Defense, State, and USAID documents. We identified major sources of U.S. funding to Pakistan, including $5.56 billion in CSF reimbursed through June 2007, $1.98 billion in development assistance (through December 2007), $1.6 billion in economic support fund cash transfers to support basic government operations, $1.22 billion for the purchase of military equipment, $9 million in international military training, and $202 million in border security assistance.

[10] CSF reimburses Pakistan for a variety of activities in support of the global war on terror, the majority of which consists of Army and Air Force operations against terrorists in Pakistan's FATA and the border region. However, some of the CSF also supports Pakistani Navy and Air Force activities outside of this area. Defense was unable to quantify what was reimbursed for activities outside the FATA and the border region at the time of our report, and therefore, we included all CSF funds in figure 2 as funds going toward the FATA and the border region.

Figure 2: Percentage of U.S. Funding Directed toward Military, Border Security, and Development Activities in Pakistan's FATA and Border Region from Fiscal Years 2002 to 2007

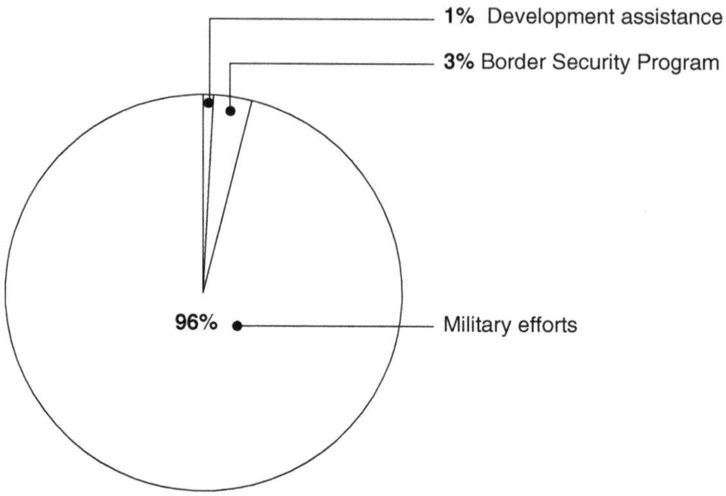

Source: GAO analysis of Defense, State, and USAID data.

Afghanistan, most significantly against terrorists in Pakistan's FATA and border region. We identified only two nonmilitary activities that occured in the FATA and border region: State's Border Security Program, which received about $187 million, and USAID development activities, which amounted to about $40 million.

According to a State Department report, Pakistan's military forces have had some tactical successes in the FATA. The Pakistani government stationed military and paramilitary forces along the border with Afghanistan, and security operations in the FATA disrupted terrorist activity by targeting and raiding al Qaeda and other militant safe havens.[11] According to State, Pakistan has helped kill or capture hundreds of suspected terrorists, including al Qaeda operatives and Taliban leaders. In addition, Pakistani military operations have resulted in the deaths of approximately 1,400 members of its security forces.

Key Government Stakeholders Recognize That a More Comprehensive Approach Is Needed

Defense, State, U.S. embassy, and Pakistani government officials recognize that relying primarily on the Pakistani military has not succeeded in

[11] Department of State report to Congress, pursuant to Section 2042 of the Implementing Recommendations of the 9/11 Commissions Act of 2007 (P.L. 110-53).

neutralizing al Qaeda and preventing the establishment of a safe haven in the FATA. State's April 2007 *Country Reports on Terrorism* states that, despite having Pakistani troops in the FATA and sustaining hundreds of casualties, the government of Pakistan has been unable to exert control over the area. The report concluded that Pakistan has now recognized that military operations alone will not restore security and stability to the FATA. Similarly, U.S. embassy officials in Pakistan stated that Taliban and al Qaeda elements have created a safe haven in the FATA and have used it to plan and launch attacks on Afghan, Pakistani, U.S., and coalition forces in Afghanistan and Pakistan. The embassy further noted that al Qaeda and the Taliban continue to recruit, train, and operate in the FATA.

According to senior embassy officials, U.S. reliance on Pakistan's military stemmed from the lack of a comprehensive plan to guide embassy efforts and the sense that the Pakistani military was the most capable institution in Pakistan to quickly undertake operations against al Qaeda immediately after the attacks of 9/11. Senior embassy officials stated that this may have led to an "over-reliance" on the Pakistani military to achieve U.S. national security objectives in Pakistan.

No Comprehensive Plan for Guiding U.S. Efforts in the FATA Has Been Developed, as Called for by the Administration and Congress

Despite the recognition of U.S. government officials, including the U.S. President and Congress, that a comprehensive plan employing all elements of national power—diplomatic, military, intelligence, development assistance, economic, and law enforcement support—was needed to combat terrorism and close the terrorist safe haven in Pakistan's FATA region, a comprehensive plan to meet U.S. national security goals in the region was never developed. Recognizing in 2006 that military efforts alone would not succeed in the FATA, the embassy, with Defense, State, and USAID support, and in conjunction with the Pakistani government in power at that time, began an effort to focus more attention on the other key elements of national power, such as development and public diplomacy, to address U.S. national security goals in the FATA. However, this effort has not been formally approved by U.S. government stakeholders who would play a key role in the funding and implementation of such an effort, and support from the recently elected Pakistani government is uncertain.

Presidential Powers for Implementing National Security Strategies and Developing a Comprehensive Plan

The President of the United States has primary responsibility to ensure that his national security strategy is carried out effectively. The President has the authority to task executive branch departments to develop comprehensive plans that use all elements of U.S. power—diplomatic, military, intelligence, development assistance, economic, and law enforcement support—toward meeting U.S. national security goals. As a result, the President can task key national security agencies, such as Defense, State, USAID, the Departments of Homeland Security, Justice, the Treasury, and intelligence agencies, to develop a comprehensive, integrated strategy and to use their combined capabilities to combat terrorism, as called for in the national security strategies. The President can also use the NSC[12] and the NCTC[13] to assist in developing, coordinating, and monitoring these plans.

Despite Executive, Congressional, and Independent Calls for Comprehensive Plans to Combat Terrorism and Close Terrorist Safe Havens, Such Plans Were Never Developed

As table 1 shows, the need for the development of comprehensive plans employing all elements of national power—diplomatic, military, intelligence, development assistance, economic, and law enforcement support—to combat terrorism and close terrorist safe havens has been recognized by the President's national security strategies (2003), the independent 9/11 Commission (2004), and by Congress in repeated legislation (2004 and 2007). As it became clearer that al Qaeda had retreated from Afghanistan into Pakistan and was creating a safe haven in the FATA, Congress increased its demands on the U.S. administration to develop comprehensive plans to help Pakistan combat terrorism and close the FATA safe haven.

Despite recommendations by the President's own national security strategy, by the independent 9/11 Commission, as well as legislative mandates from Congress, a comprehensive plan to destroy the terrorist threat or close the safe haven in the FATA was never developed. Even after the creation of the NCTC, an organization specifically intended to develop, implement, and monitor multidepartment plans to combat terrorism, the embassy has yet to receive any such plan to combat terrorism in Pakistan's FATA. In addition, the administration did not report to Congress on its plans for assisting Pakistan in (1) combating terrorism and (2) closing terrorist safe havens, as required by both the 2004 and 2007 legislation.

As a result, the embassy has lacked a Washington-approved, comprehensive plan that combines the capabilities of Defense, State, USAID, intelligence agencies, and other U.S. departments to combat terrorism in the FATA.

[12] The NSC is charged with more effectively coordinating the policies and functions of the departments and agencies related to national security. The NSC advises the President with respect to the integration of domestic, foreign, and military policies relating to national security to enable the departments and agencies to cooperate more effectively in matters involving national security.

[13] The NCTC is charged with conducting strategic operational planning for counterterrorism activities, integrating all instruments of national power—including diplomatic, military, intelligence, development assistance, economic, and law enforcement support—within and among agencies, with the ultimate goal of preventing future attacks against the United States and its interests worldwide. Both report directly to the President.

Table 1. Key Recommendations by Executive, Independent, and Congressional Sources to Combat Terrorism and Close Terrorist Safe Havens

Key Document	Source	Recommendation
National Strategy for Combating Terrorism, 2003	President Bush and the NSC	• Called for comprehensive plans employing all elements of national power—diplomatic, military, intelligence, development assistance, economic, and law enforcement support—to combat terrorism • Gave State lead to develop coordinated plans; all appropriate departments were to develop supporting strategies • Directed Defense, State, and intelligence agencies to annually assess and develop plans to close safe havens
9/11 Commission Report, 2004	9/11 Commission, an independent, bipartisan study group mandated by Congress in 2002	• Stated that long-term success demands coordinated, comprehensive, multidepartment efforts employing all elements of national power • Recommended that a single entity be responsible for comprehensive, multidepartment planning for U.S. efforts to combat terrorism • Recommended U.S. (1) make a long-term, comprehensive commitment to assist Pakistan to combat terrorism and (2) develop a strategy to close safe havens
Intelligence Reform Act, 2004	Congress	• Authorized creation of the NCTC to develop comprehensive, multidepartment plans to combat terrorism employing all elements of national power • Stipulated that such plans should include (1) the mission, (2) objectives, (3) tasks to be performed, (4) interagency coordination, and (5) roles and responsibilities. It also tasked the NCTC with monitoring each agency involved • Required a report within 180 days of passage of the act on the administration's strategies for (1) closing terrorist safe havens and (2) assisting Pakistan to combat terrorism
9/11 Commission Act, 2007	Congress	• Required the President to submit a report by November 2007 on the strategy, employing all elements of national power, to combat terrorism in the FATA

Source: GAO analysis of key documents.

According to senior embassy officials in Islamabad, the embassy had not received a comprehensive plan from the CIA, Defense, State, the NCTC, the NSC, the White House, or any other executive department. Further, these officials stated that they had not received any strategic guidance on designing, implementing, funding, and monitoring a comprehensive effort that would use all elements of national power to combat terrorism in Pakistan. According to senior embassy officials, given the strategic threat to America, the United States should have a comprehensive strategy to defeat terrorists that uses all elements of national power.

Defense, State, the DNI, USAID, and the government of Pakistan recognize that a comprehensive approach is needed to meet U.S. national security goals in Pakistan. For example, in its 2007 *Country Reports on Terrorism*, State indicated that Pakistan recognized that military operations alone would not restore stability to the FATA; instead, a comprehensive strategy was needed that also included economic, social development, political, and administrative efforts to enhance security in the region. The U.S. Embassy in Pakistan also concluded that, while force is a necessary component of an overall strategy to combat terrorism in the FATA, it is not sufficient as the sole component. Similarly, the DNI stated that Pakistan now recognizes it must take a more comprehensive approach to defeating terrorism and that an intensified and sustained effort that combines administrative, economic, educational, legal, and social reforms to defeat the terrorist threat is required.[14]

We have previously reported on the need for plans to combat terrorism to include elements that would enhance interagency cooperation and improve effectiveness. Specifically, in large-scale interagency efforts where collaboration is essential, we have found that agencies should (1) define and articulate a common outcome; (2) establish mutually reinforcing or joint strategies; (3) identify and address funding needs by leveraging resources; (4) agree on roles and responsibilities; (5) establish compatible policies, procedures, and other means to operate across agency boundaries; (6) develop mechanisms to monitor, evaluate, and report on results; (7) reinforce agency accountability for collaborative efforts through agency plans and reports; and (8) reinforce individual accountability for collaborative efforts through performance management systems.[15]

Pakistan and the U.S. Embassy are Encouraging More Focus on Other Key Elements of National Power to Achieve U.S. Goals in the FATA

In March 2006, the President of Pakistan requested that President Bush support Pakistan's effort to support a more comprehensive approach to combating

---

[14] Annual Threat Assessment of the Director of National Intelligence for the Senate Select Committee on Intelligence, Feb. 5, 2008.

[15] See GAO-07-697, GAO-06-1 5, and GAO-03-519T.

terrorism in the FATA. As a result, the U.S. Embassy in Pakistan began coordinating efforts by Defense, State, and USAID to develop department-specific efforts to support Pakistan's Sustainable Development Plan for the FATA. Pakistan's Sustainable Development Plan is a 9 year, $2 billion effort to provide economic development, extend the influence of the Pakistani government, and establish security in the FATA. To assist this effort, Defense undertook a counterinsurgency assessment in the FATA and began developing its Security Development Plan. At the same time, USAID provided technical assistance to the Pakistani government to help formalize its Sustainable Development Plan, as well as to plan USAID-development activities in the FATA.

This approach, if approved by the administration and key U.S. government agency stakeholders, would constitute the U.S. government's first attempt to focus more attention on other key elements of national power to address U.S. counterterrorism goals in the FATA. These elements include development assistance and public diplomacy, as well as counterinsurgency training, which have not been part of the previous military approach. This new approach also calls for greater levels of direct U.S. planning, implementation, coordination, and oversight. However, this new approach does not yet constitute a comprehensive plan, and all of the agencies' individual efforts have not been fully approved in Washington. Furthermore, funding shortfalls exist, and support by the recently elected government of Pakistan is uncertain.

If fully approved, the United States would provide an estimated $956 million between fiscal years 2008 through 2011 for development, security, capacity building, and infrastructure in support of the Pakistani government. This approach represents the first effort by the U.S. embassy to directly plan, implement, coordinate, and monitor a multidepartment effort to combat terrorism in the FATA. According to officials with the U.S. embassy, the Pakistani government, and international donors, this comprehensive approach is critical to addressing the terrorist threat in the FATA and represents a significant departure from the past.

As of September 2007, the embassy planned to spend $187.6 million on this initial effort using fiscal year 2007 funds. The funding has been directed to four areas:

- **Development:** The $99 million development effort would be led by USAID and would include capacity building for the FATA institutions needed to plan, manage, and monitor development projects; efforts to build community and government relations; funding for health and education services; and efforts to increase employment and economic growth.[16]

[16] In commenting on this report, USAID stated they received $88 million for these efforts in the Fiscal Year 2007 Supplemental Appropriation.

- **Security:** The $54.1 million Defense and State security effort would include training for military and paramilitary units in the FATA—including the Frontier Corps, special operations forces, and air crews—and for providing night vision goggles, radios, and other equipment.
- **Infrastructure:** The $32.5 million the U.S. embassy has designated for infrastructure improvements related to both its security and development efforts would be used for road construction, the Frontier Corps training center, and border surveillance outposts.
- **Public diplomacy:** $2 million in funding was allotted for public diplomacy programs.

According to the embassy, the success of this new effort in the FATA will depend on close coordination among an array of institutions within the U.S. and Pakistani governments. The new effort also will involve partner agencies and allies, including the United Kingdom, Japan, and Europe; the Asian Development Bank; nongovernmental organizations; and the Pakistani private sector, civil society, and the tribes of the FATA.

We plan to monitor the status and progress of the U.S. government in developing this effort and provide an assessment in a subsequent report covering security, political, and development activities undertaken by the United States to meet U.S. national security goals in the FATA.

Conclusion

Combating terrorism is the United States' top national security priority at home and abroad. Since 9/11, U.S. national security strategies have consistently called for using all elements of national power to combat terrorism, including diplomatic, military, intelligence, development assistance, economic, and law enforcement support. Because the use of the various elements of national power falls under the authority of numerous U.S. government agencies, the development of a comprehensive plan is needed to ensure that the full capacity of the U.S. government is focused on meeting U.S. national security goals.

We believe that such a plan would help to ensure coordination, integration, and implementation of U.S. efforts to close the terrorist safe haven in the FATA. A comprehensive plan to combat terrorism in the FATA that establishes goals, objectives, priorities, outcomes, and milestones, including specific performance measures, would allow an assessment of progress and help ensure accountability of U.S. efforts. As such, we believe that the administration should develop a comprehensive plan using the full capabilities provided by Defense, State, USAID, and other U.S. agencies and stakeholders to further assist Pakistan in combating terrorism.

Recommendations for Executive Action

We recommend that the National Security Advisor and the Director of the NCTC, in consultation with the Secretaries of Defense and State, and the Administrator of USAID, the intelligence community, and other executive departments as deemed appropriate, implement the congressional mandate to develop a comprehensive plan using all elements of national power to combat the terrorist threat and close their safe haven in Pakistan's FATA region.

The comprehensive plan should also include key components called for in the Intelligence Reform Act, the Implementing Recommendations of the 9/11 Commission Act of 2007, and components that we have previously reported as being needed to improve the effectiveness of plans involving multidepartmental efforts to combat terrorism.[17] The plan should (1) place someone directly in charge of this multidepartment effort to improve accountability; (2) articulate a clear strategy to implement the national security goal to destroy terrorists and close the safe haven in the FATA; (3) clarify roles and responsibilities of each department for implementing the goal; (4) provide guidance on setting funding priorities and providing resources to meet these national security goals; and (5) require a monitoring system and provide periodic reports to Congress on the progress and impediments to meeting national security goals in Pakistan.

Agency Comments and Our Evaluation

State, the Office of the Director of National Intelligence (ODNI), Defense, and USAID provided written comments on a draft of this report, which are reproduced in appendixes I, II, III, and IV.

State and ODNI did not comment on our recommendation, while Defense and USAID concurred with our recommendation. In general, they all commented on their individual planning efforts and interagency meetings to coordinate these efforts that began in 2006. This, however, was not the focus of our review; our report assessed whether a comprehensive plan had been developed that incorporated all elements of national power. We plan to conduct a detailed assessment of the individual agency efforts from 2002 to the present as part of our broader engagement efforts and look forward to working closely with ODNI, Defense, State, USAID, and other agencies in assessing their plans and efforts to meet national security goals in Pakistan.

State's comments assert that embassy and U.S. government efforts to date have resulted in a comprehensive strategy. We disagree and note in our report that, while the initiatives begun by Defense, State, and USAID are being coordinated by the embassy, they have not been fully approved or

[17] GAO-07-697, GAO-06-15, and GAO-03-519T.

integrated into a formal, comprehensive plan. While we acknowledge that this effort is a step in the right direction toward implementing the 2003 national security strategy, the recommendations by the 9/11 Commission, and Congress, it is unclear whether the new approach will include all of the key elements of national power, such as intelligence, economic, and law enforcement support.

ODNI's comments stated that they agreed with our finding that the United States had not met its national security goals in Pakistan's FATA and that countering the growth of terrorist safe havens requires all elements of national power. They disagreed, however, that the United States lacks plans to combat terrorism in the area. Our report does not state that the U.S. lacks individual plans; rather, we found that there was no comprehensive plan that integrated the combined capabilities of Defense, State, USAID, the intelligence community, and others to meet U.S. national security goals in Pakistan.

We also received technical comments from Defense and USAID, which we have incorporated throughout the report where appropriate.

As agreed with your offices, unless you publicly announce the contents of this report earlier, we plan no further distribution until 30 days from the report date. At that time, we will send copies of this report to interested congressional committees, to the National Security Advisor of the NSC, the Director of the NCTC, the Secretaries of State and Defense, and the Administrator of USAID. We will also make copies of this report available to others upon request. We will also make copies available at no charge on the GAO Web site at http://www.gao.gov.

If you or your staffs have any questions about this report, please contact me at (202) 512-7331 or johnsoncm@gao.gov. Contact points for our Offices of Congressional Relations and Public Affairs may be found on the last page of this report. GAO staff who made major contributions to this report are listed in appendix V.

Charles Michael Johnson Jr.
Director, International Affairs and Trade

Congressional Requesters

The Honorable Howard Berman
Chairman
The Honorable Ileana Ros-Lehtinen
Ranking Member
Committee on Foreign Affairs
House of Representatives

The Honorable Gary Ackerman
Chairman
The Honorable Mike Pence
Ranking Member
Subcommittee on the Middle East and South Asia
Committee on Foreign Affairs
House of Representatives

The Honorable John F. Tierney
Chairman
The Honorable Christopher Shays
Ranking Member
Subcommittee on National Security and Foreign Affairs
Committee on Oversight and Government Reform
House of Representatives

The Honorable Tom Harkin
The Honorable Robert Menendez
United States Senate

Appendix I: Comments from the Department of State

United States Department of State

Washington, D.C. 20520

APR 07 2008

Ms. Jacquelyn Williams-Bridgers
Managing Director
International Affairs and Trade
Government Accountability Office
441 G Street, N.W.
Washington, D.C. 20548-0001

Dear Ms. Williams-Bridgers:

We appreciate the opportunity to review your draft report, "COMBATING TERRORISM: U.S. Lacks Comprehensive Plan to Destroy Terrorist Threat and Close Safe Haven in Pakistan's Federally Administered Tribal Areas," GAO Job Code 320573.

The enclosed Department of State comments are provided for incorporation with this letter as an appendix to the final report.

If you have any questions concerning this response, please contact Tom West, Desk Officer, Bureau of South and Central Asian Affairs, at (202) 647-6710.

Sincerely,

Bradford R. Higgins

cc: GAO – Charles Michael Johnson
SCA – Richard Boucher
State/OIG – Mark Duda

Department of State Comments on GAO Draft Report

<u>Combating Terrorism: U.S. Lacks Comprehensive Plan to Destroy Terrorist Threat and Close Safe Haven in Pakistan's Federally Administered Tribal Areas</u>
(GAO-08-622; GAO Code 320573)

The Department of State appreciates the opportunity to review the Government Accountability Office (GAO) draft report titled: *Combating Terrorism: U.S. Lacks Comprehensive Plan to Destroy Terrorist Threat and Close Safe Haven in Pakistan's Federally Administered Tribal Areas.*

The study does not acknowledge that the United States had an overall plan for Pakistan, put together in the immediate aftermath of 9/11. That initial plan called for working closely with and supporting the Pakistani military to confront the extremists militarily and working to deny them their safe havens along the Pakistan-Afghan border. To a large extent, the plan worked. From 2001-2006, we – or the Pakistanis – arrested or killed hundreds of al-Qaeda and Taliban extremists, shattered terrorist networks, disrupted their training camps and short-circuited terrorist operations. U.S.-Pakistani cooperation made it more difficult for terrorists to operate in Pakistan. By the end of 2006, 120,000 Pakistani troops were involved in on-going operations against violent extremists along the Pakistan-Afghan border. The GAO draft report acknowledges this but fails to attribute it to a deliberate planning effort.

The immediate post-9/11 plan was, however, largely military and was therefore limited in its effect. Additionally, the plan was undercut by events following the 2006 North Waziristan agreement between the militants and the Government of Pakistan (also unaddressed in the report), during which time terrorists were able to rebuild and regroup.

We and the Pakistanis recognized that a new plan was needed to address the broader conditions that support terrorism; specifically, the abysmal social conditions in the Tribal Areas and the absence of central authority there. A series of interagency meetings in summer of 2006 (Deputies Committees meetings on July 16 and August 22, specifically) laid further groundwork for what became our current FATA strategy and our support for the Pakistani Sustainable Development Plan for the Tribal Areas. This strategy brought

2

together security assistance for the local Frontier Corps, economic and development assistance for the Tribal Region, private sector development programs, and our proposal for Reconstruction Opportunity Zones for job creation in border areas of both Pakistan and Afghanistan. Taken together with complementary military and intelligence participation, this became our comprehensive, integrated strategy and has been implemented since that time.

The GAO draft does acknowledge the difficult conditions in Pakistan, the vast un-policed territories, the abysmal social conditions in the tribal belt and our need to rely completely upon a Pakistani military under-equipped and under-trained to conduct counter-insurgency operations. It also acknowledges the decades when the Tribal Areas were used as a jihadist training area and jumping off point for the anti-Soviet war in Afghanistan. But the Report fails to acknowledge the continuing efforts that have gone into devising, funding and implementing a broad-based plan to address these conditions.

Appendix II: Comments from the Department of Defense

THE ASSISTANT SECRETARY OF DEFENSE
2700 DEFENSE PENTAGON
WASHINGTON, DC 20301-2700

APR 0 7 2008

Mr. Charles Johnson Jr.
Director, International Counterterrorism Issues,
International Affairs and Trade
Government Accountability Office
441 G Street, N.W.
Washington, D.C. 20548

Mr. Johnson:

This is the Department of Defense (DoD) response to the GAO Draft Report, GAO-08-622, "COMBATING TERRORISM: U.S. Lacks Comprehensive Plan to Destroy Terrorist Threat and Close Safe Haven in Pakistan's Federally Administered Tribal Areas," dated March 28, 2008 (GAO Code 320573).

We have enclosed comments addressing the report and its recommendations.

My point of contact is Mr. Eric Lebson, 703-697-3754, or e-mail: eric.lebson@osd.mil.

Sincerely,

James J. Shinn

GAO DRAFT REPORT DATED MARCH 28, 2008
GAO-08-622 (GAO CODE 320573)

"COMBATING TERRORISM: U.S. LACKS COMPREHENSIVE PLAN TO DESTROY TERRORIST THREAT AND CLOSE SAFE HAVEN IN PAKISTAN'S FEDERALLY ADMINISTERED TRIBAL AREAS"

DEPARTMENT OF DEFENSE COMMENTS
TO THE GAO RECOMMENDATION

RECOMMENDATION: The GAO recommends that the National Security Advisor and the Director of the National Counterterrorism Center, in consultation with the Secretaries of Defense and State, and the Administrator of United States Agency for International Development, the intelligence community, and other executive departments as deemed appropriate, implement the congressional mandate to develop a comprehensive plan using all elements of national power, to combat the terrorist threat and close their safe haven in Pakistan's Federally Administered Tribal Areas region. The comprehensive plan should also include key components called for in the Intelligence Reform Act and by GAO to improve the effectiveness of plans involving multi-departmental effort to combat terrorism. (p. 25/GAO Draft Report)

DOD RESPONSE: Concur. DoD supports the development of a comprehensive plan to close safe havens in Pakistan's Federally Administered Tribal Areas. In November 2007 and February 2008, DoD provided to the State Department inputs for a comprehensive strategy. DoD has participated in a wide variety of inter-agency meetings that have addressed the on-going development of this strategy. This includes Deputies Committee meetings on 14 and 20 March 2008 and long-standing weekly informal South/Central Asia inter-agency meetings hosted by the Assistant Secretary of State for South and Central Asia. DoD is continuing to play an active role in the inter-agency effort to develop and coordinate a comprehensive plan to close terrorist safe havens in Pakistan.

NOTE: DoD has forwarded technical comments (context, inaccuracies and additional background) about the report directly to GAO and recommended their consideration for the final version of the report.

Attachment
Page 1 of 1

Appendix III: Comments from the U.S. Agency for International Development

USAID
FROM THE AMERICAN PEOPLE

APR 9 2008

Mr. Charles Michael Johnson, Jr.
Director
International Affairs and Trade
Government Accountability Office
441 G Street, N.W.
Washington, DC 20548

Dear Mr. Johnson:

The U.S. Agency for International Development (USAID) appreciates the opportunity to review and respond to your draft audit report entitled "COMBATTING TERRORISM: U.S. Lacks Comprehensive Plan to Destroy Terrorist Threat and Close Safe Haven in Pakistan's Federally Administered Tribal Areas," GAO-08-622.

In general, we concur with your overall recommendation that the U.S. Government (USG) needs a comprehensive plan for work in the FATA. However, work in the FATA should be guided by the Government of Pakistan's own FATA Sustainable Development Plan, which was developed in consultation with the USG and was completed in 2006. The USAID plan for programs in the FATA was presented to the USG's interagency in December 2006. Prior to the formal presentation, this plan was vetted thoroughly with, and approved by, the country team in Islamabad, and also in the interagency in Washington.

Additionally, please note that:

- USAID is an instrument of "soft power" as opposed to the "hard power" programs with the Pakistani military described extensively in the draft report. Our programs focus on addressing the underlying causes of insurgencies and the development issues which allow for terrorist safe havens. Successful strategies in settings such as the FATA depend on mutually reinforcing hard and soft approaches conducted in tandem.
- The embassy's engagement on strategic development in FATA began in summer 2006 and included reopening a USAID office in Peshawar, launching a

U.S. Agency for International Development
1300 Pennsylvania Avenue, NW
Washington, DC 20523
www.usaid.gov

- 2 -

development strategy in tandem with the GOP and organizing a FATA donor's discussion at the fall 2006 World Bank/IMF meetings in Singapore.

- USAID initially started with small scale programs in education, health and microfinance as pilots which then determined the strategy for our larger programs currently being implemented.

In conclusion, we feel that the GAO should recognize the Government of Pakistan, USAID and the wider country team for advancing strategic thinking on the FATA development program.

Thanks very much for the opportunity to comment on this report and for the courtesies extended by your staff in the conduct of this review.

Sincerely,

Lisa Chiles
Deputy Assistant Administrator
Bureau for Asia

Appendix IV: Comments from the Office of the Director of National Intelligence

OFFICE OF THE DIRECTOR OF NATIONAL INTELLIGENCE
WASHINGTON, DC 20511

April 8, 2008

Ms. Janet St. Laurent
Managing Director, Defense Capabilities
and Management
United States Government Accountability Office
Washington, D.C. 20548

Dear Ms. St. Laurent:

(U) The Office of the Director of National Intelligence and the National Counterterrorism Center appreciate the opportunity to review the GAO report number 08-622 *Combating Terrorism: U.S. Lacks Comprehensive Plan to Destroy Terrorist Threat and Close Safe Haven in Pakistan's Federally Administered Tribal Areas.* Although we agree that the United States has not yet met its national security goals in Pakistan's Federally Administered Tribal Areas (FATA), we disagree that the United States lacks plans to combat terrorism in the area.

(U) Effectively countering the growth of extremism and the emergence of terrorist safehavens requires all elements of national power, to include diplomatic, military, development assistance, financial, law enforcement, and intelligence. The National Security Council, the Department of State, and the Department of Defense, have, therefore, been actively involved in the United States Government efforts to deny our terrorist enemies safehavens such as the FATA. The Office of the Director of National Intelligence, the National Counterterrorism Center, and the Intelligence Community have also been actively involved in such efforts.

(U) The National Counterterrorism Center, for example, produced the landmark National Implementation Plan for the War on Terror, which was signed by the President in June 2006, and was the first-ever United States Government-wide strategic plan for countering terrorism. This war plan does not stand alone. Rather, it complements two types of planning efforts that have long existed and continue to exist: (1) high-level national strategies directed by the President and the National Security and Homeland Security Councils, and (2) very granular and tactical department and agency-specific implementation plans.

(U) The National Counterterrorism Center (NCTC) has also been expanding its ongoing efforts to coordinate near-term department and agency activities at the strategic operational level in certain key regions of the world. NCTC combines regional and functional priorities to ensure its strategic operational planning initiatives, which by definition are interagency in nature, properly balance high-level and mission centric perspectives, and are comprehensive in drawing on all instruments of national power. NCTC has participated in a recently-completed interagency initiative to determine counterterrorism priorities, which, along with other efforts, provide a regional perspective to functional efforts and plans, such as the National Implementation Plan.

- 2 -

(U) I thank you again for the opportunity to review this report and look forward to working with your office in the future.

Sincerely,

Kathleen Turner

Kathleen Turner
Director of Legislative Affairs

Appendix V: GAO Contacts and Staff Acknowledgments

GAO Contact:

Charles Michael Johnson Jr., Director, International Affairs and Trade, (202) 512-7331 or johnsoncm@gao.gov

Staff Acknowledgments

In addition to the individual named above, Hynek Kalkus, Assistant Director; Edward J. George; Claude Adrien; David Hancock; Lynn Cothern; Karen Deans; Mark Dowling; and Jena Sinkfield made key contributions to this report.

GAO's Mission

The Government Accountability Office, the audit, evaluation, and investigative arm of Congress, exists to support Congress in meeting its constitutional responsibilities and to help improve the performance and accountability of the federal government for the American people. GAO examines the use of public funds; evaluates federal programs and policies; and provides analyses, recommendations, and other assistance to help Congress make informed oversight, policy, and funding decisions. GAO's commitment to good government is reflected in its core values of accountability, integrity, and reliability.

Obtaining Copies of GAO Reports and Testimony

The fastest and easiest way to obtain copies of GAO documents at no cost is through GAO's Web site (www.gao.gov). Each weekday, GAO posts newly released reports, testimony, and correspondence on its Web site. To have GAO e-mail you a list of newly posted products every afternoon, go to www.gao.gov and select "E-mail Updates."

Order by Mail or Phone

The first copy of each printed report is free. Additional copies are $2 each. A check or money order should be made out to the Superintendent of Documents. GAO also accepts VISA and Mastercard. Orders for 100 or more copies mailed to a single address are discounted 25 percent. Orders should be sent to:

U.S. Government Accountability Office
441 G Street NW, Room LM
Washington, DC 20548
To order by Phone: Voice: (202) 512-6000
TDD: (202) 512-2537
Fax: (202) 512-6061

To Report Fraud, Waste, and Abuse in Federal Programs

Contact:

Web site: www.gao.gov/fraudnet/fraudnet.htm
E-mail: fraudnet@gao.gov
Automated answering system: (800) 424-5454 or (202) 512-7470

Congressional Relations

Ralph Dawn, Managing Director, dawnr@gao.gov, (202) 512-4400
U.S. Government Accountability Office, 441 G Street NW, Room 7125
Washington, DC 20548

Public Affairs

Chuck Young, Managing Director, youngc1@gao.gov, (202) 512-4800
U.S. Government Accountability Office, 441 G Street NW, Room 7149
Washington, DC 20548

DOCUMENT NO. 3

SECURING, STABILIZING, AND DEVELOPING PAKISTAN'S BORDER AREA WITH AFGHANISTAN: KEY ISSUES FOR CONGRESSIONAL OVERSIGHT

GAO Report
GAO-09-263SP

February 2009

Abbreviations

ATA	Department of State's Antiterrorism Assistance
CENTCOM	U.S. Central Command
CSF	Coalition Support Funds
DEA	Drug Enforcement Administration
ESF	USAID's Economic Support Fund
FATA	Federally Administered Tribal Areas
FBI	Federal Bureau of Investigation
FCR	Frontier Crimes Regulations
FY	fiscal year
GDP	Gross Domestic Product
IMF	International Monetary Fund
INL	Department of State's Bureau of International Narcotics and Law Enforcement
NWFP	North West Frontier Province
OPDAT	Department of Justice's Office of Overseas Prosecutorial Development, Assistance and Training
USAID	U.S. Agency for International Development

United States Government Accountability Office
Washington, DC 20548

February 23, 2009

Congressional Requesters

Since 2002, destroying the terrorist threat and closing the terrorist safe haven along Pakistan's border with Afghanistan have been key national security goals. The United States has provided Pakistan, an important ally in the war on terror, with more than $12.3 billion for a variety of activities, in part to address these goals. About half of this amount has been to reimburse Pakistan for military-related support, including combat operations in and around the Federally Administered Tribal Areas (FATA). Despite 6 years of U.S. and Pakistani government efforts, al Qaeda has regenerated its ability to attack the United States and continues to maintain a safe haven in Pakistan's FATA. As the United States considers how it will go forward with efforts to assist Pakistan in securing, stabilizing, and developing its FATA and Western Frontier bordering Afghanistan, it is vital that efforts to develop a comprehensive plan using all elements of national power be completed and that continued oversight and accountability over funds used for these efforts are in place. As such, we have enclosed a series of issue papers for your consideration.[1] These papers focus on U.S. efforts in Pakistan's FATA and the Western Frontier and are largely based on GAO reports, briefings, and testimonies provided to Congress in 2008.

In 2008, we issued three products and delivered two testimonies before Congress on Pakistan covering various aspects of U.S. efforts to combat terrorism in the FATA.[2] In summary, we reported that:

- The United States had not met its national security goals to destroy terrorist threats and close the safe haven in Pakistan's FATA;
- The United States lacked a comprehensive plan to meet these goals that included all elements of national power—diplomatic, military, intelligence, development assistance, economic, and law enforcement support—called for by various national security strategies and Congress, as well as key components we have previously reported as

[1] GAO plans to issue similar issue papers on Iraq (March 2009) and Afghanistan (April 2009).

[2] GAO, *Combating Terrorism: Increased Oversight and Accountability Needed over Pakistan Reimbursement Claims for Coalition Support Funds*, GAO-08-806 (Washington, D.C.: June 24, 2008); *Combating Terrorism: U.S. Oversight of Pakistan Reimbursement Claims for Coalition Support Funds*, GAO-08-932T (Washington, D.C.: June 24, 2008); *Combating Terrorism: U.S. Efforts to Address the Terrorist Threat in Pakistan's Federally Administered Tribal Areas Require a Comprehensive Plan and Continued Oversight*, GAO-08-820T (Washington, D.C.: May 20, 2008); *Preliminary Observations on the Use and Oversight of U.S. Coalition Support Funds Provided to Pakistan*, GAO-08-735R (Washington, D.C.: May 6, 2008); *Combating Terrorism: The United States Lacks Comprehensive Plan to Destroy the Terrorist Threat and Close the Safe Haven in Pakistan's Federally Administered Tribal Areas*, GAO-08-622 (Washington, D.C.: Apr. 17, 2008).

being needed to improve the effectiveness of plans involving multiple departments; and

- Increased oversight and accountability was needed over Pakistan's reimbursement claims for Coalition Support Funds (CSF).

Based on our work, we made recommendations to the National Security Advisor and the Director of the National Counterterrorism Center relating to the development of a comprehensive plan to combat the terrorist threat in the FATA, and to the Department of Defense (Defense) on the improvement of oversight of CSF reimbursements to Pakistan.

Responsiveness to our recommendation to develop a comprehensive plan has varied. For example, officials from Defense and the U.S. Agency for International Development (USAID) generally concurred with our April 2008 recommendations on the need to develop a comprehensive plan using all elements of national power to combat the terrorist threat and close the terrorist safe haven. The Department of State (State) asserted that a comprehensive plan exists, while the Office of the Director of National Intelligence and the National Counterterrorism Center stated in their April 2008 comments, as well as in an August 2008 follow-up letter, that plans to combat terrorism exist.[3] We do not assert that the United States lacks individual agency plans to destroy the terrorist threat in the FATA; rather, we found that there was no comprehensive plan that integrated the combined capabilities of Defense, State, USAID, the intelligence community, and others, and included key components we called for in our report to meet U.S. national security goals in Pakistan. As of January 2009, neither the National Security Council, the National Counterterrorism Center, nor Defense, State, or USAID, has produced for our review a comprehensive plan as recommended in our April 2008 report. Defense concurred with the recommendations in our June 2008 CSF report on accountability over CSF reimbursements. In response, Defense issued new guidance and traveled to Pakistan to begin working with Pakistani and U.S. Defense officials to implement this guidance.

The enclosures that follow provide background information on Pakistan; the status of U.S. government efforts to develop a comprehensive plan; and information on the goals, funding, and current status of U.S. efforts to use various elements of national power (i.e., military, law enforcement, development and economic assistance, and diplomacy) to combat terrorism in Pakistan. The scope of this report does not include the plans, goals, operations, activities, and accomplishments of the intelligence community. Included in these enclosures are oversight issues for Congress and the new administration to consider. The final enclosure discusses oversight and

[3] The National Security Council provided no comments.

accountability issues relating to U.S. funds or assistance provided to Pakistan.

These enclosures incorporate updated information from agency program documents through February 2009 as well as budget information through fiscal year 2008. We discussed the updated status of our prior findings and recommendations with Departments of Defense, State, Justice, and USAID officials involved in efforts to meet national strategic goals in the FATA and Western Frontier, as well as the status of the U.S. effort to implement the various elements of national power. We conducted this performance audit from August 2008 through February 2009, in accordance with generally accepted government auditing standards. Those standards require that we plan and perform the audit to obtain sufficient, appropriate evidence to provide a reasonable basis for our findings and conclusions based on our audit objectives. We believe that the evidence obtained provides a reasonable basis for our findings and conclusions based on our audit objectives.

We requested comments from the National Security Council, the Office of the Director of National Intelligence, Defense, Justice, State, and USAID. The National Security Council and the Office of the Director of National Intelligence did not provide comments. We received technical comments from Defense, Justice, State, and USAID, which we incorporated throughout the report where appropriate.

We are sending copies of this report to Members of Congress, cognizant congressional committees, the President and Vice President of the United States, and executive branch agencies. The report also is available at no charge on the GAO Web site at http://www.gao.gov.

If you or your staff have any questions about this report, please contact Charles Michael Johnson at (202) 512-7331 orjohnsoncm@gao.gov. In addition to the contact named above, Steve Sebastian, Director; Hynek Kalkus, Assistant Director; Roger Stoltz, Assistant Director; Edward J. George; Claude Adrien; David W. Hancock; Cara Bauer; Janice Friedeborn; Karen Deans; and Mark Dowling made key contributions to this report. Contact points for our Office of Congressional Relations and Public Affairs can be found on the last page of this report.

Gene L. Dodaro
Acting Comptroller General of the United States

Enclosures

Congressional Requesters

The Honorable Howard Berman
Chairman
The Honorable Ileana Ros-Lehtinen
Ranking Member
Committee on Foreign Affairs
House of Representatives

The Honorable Gary Ackerman
Chairman
The Honorable Dan Burton
Ranking Member
Subcommittee on the Middle East and South Asia
Committee on Foreign Affairs
House of Representatives

The Honorable John F. Tierney
Chairman
The Honorable Jeff Flake
Ranking Member
Subcommittee on National Security and Foreign Affairs
Committee on Oversight and Government Reform
House of Representatives

The Honorable Tom Harkin
The Honorable Robert Menendez
United States Senate

The Honorable Mike Pence
House of Representatives

Enclosure I: Pakistan Facts and Figures

Located in southern Asia, bordering the Arabian Sea, between India on the east, Iran and Afghanistan on the west, and China on the north, Pakistan's area is about 300,600 square miles, which is slightly less than twice the size of California (see fig. 1). It is divided into four provinces, the North West Frontier Province (NWFP), Punjab, Sindh, and Balochistan, as well as the FATA. The entire Pakistani/Afghan border, known as the Durand Line, is 1,640 miles of difficult, widely differentiated terrain, from the southern deserts of Balochistan to the northern mountain peaks of the NWFP.

The FATA is a tribal belt administered by the Pakistani government consisting of seven tribal agencies (Khyber, Kurram, North and South Waziristan, Mohmand, Bajaur, and Orakzai). Its area is approximately 10,500 square miles, roughly the same size as the state of Maryland. The FATA shares a 373-mile border with Afghanistan.

Figure 1: Pakistan and the FATA

Sources: GAO; USAID and Map Resources (maps).

Demographics and Development Indicators

Pakistan's population is estimated at roughly 170 million. Pakistan's largest ethnic groups include Punjabi (45 percent), Pashtun (15 percent), Sindhi (14 percent), Siraiki (8 percent), Mohajirs (8 percent), and Balochi (4 percent). Some ethnic groups predominantly populate specific regions, such as the Pashtun along both sides of the border with Afghanistan. Several languages are spoken in Pakistan, the most common being Punjabi (48 percent). Urdu and English are the official languages spoken in Pakistan. About 38 percent of the population is under age 15, and Pakistanis have a life expectancy of about 64 years. Islam is the predominant religion—75 percent of the population are Sunni and 20 percent are Shi'a.

Economy

Pakistan's principal natural resources are arable land, water, and energy reserves. Agriculture accounts for about 21 percent of Pakistan's gross domestic product (GDP) and employs about 42 percent of the labor force. The most important crops are cotton, wheat, rice, sugarcane, fruits, and vegetables, which together account for more than 75 percent of the value of total crop output. Pakistan exports rice, fish, fruits, and vegetables and imports vegetable oil, wheat, and cotton. Pakistan is a net food importer and the economic prominence of agriculture has declined since independence, when its share of GDP was around 53 percent. Pakistan's manufacturing sector accounts for about 25 percent of GDP. Cotton textile production and apparel manufacturing are Pakistan's largest industries, accounting for about 70 percent of total exports. Pakistan has extensive energy resources, including natural gas, oil, coal, and hydroelectric power potential. According to State officials, however, these energy resources are not fully exploited. For instance, domestic gas and petroleum production totals only about half the country's energy needs.

The World Bank considers Pakistan a low-income country and it is among the largest recipients of World Bank financial assistance. In fiscal year 2007, World Bank support to Pakistan totaled $985 million, making it the seventh largest borrower in the world. Pakistan's economy also contends with structural problems and corruption.[4] Pakistan's macroeconomic situation deteriorated significantly because of large price increases in key commodities such as oil and food. In November 2008, the IMF's Executive Board approved a $7.6 billion loan for Pakistan to support its program to stabilize

[4] The Heritage Foundation's *2008 Index of Economic Freedom* ranked Pakistan's economy 93rd out of 157 countries. The index identified restrictive trade policies, a heavy fiscal burden, weak property ownership protections, and limited financial freedoms as issues. Corruption is another serious problem; in 2007, Berlin-based Transparency International placed Pakistan 138th out of 179 countries in its annual ranking of world corruption levels.

and rebuild the economy while expanding its social safety net to protect the poor. The loan is intended to enable the government to address economic concerns such as bringing down both the inflation rate and the budget deficit, while increasing expenditures on the poor through such measures as targeted electricity subsidies.

The FATA and the Pakistan-Afghan Border

The FATA, where al Qaeda and other militants have succeeded in establishing safe havens, has an estimated population of 3.1 million, and is characterized by harsh geography, poor education, and scarce infrastructure. The FATA is the poorest, least developed part of Pakistan. Literacy is only 17 percent, compared to the national average of 56 percent, and among women it is 3 percent. Annual per capita income is roughly $250—half the national average. About 60 percent of households live beneath the poverty line. There is little employment in the industrial sector. The FATA's forbidding terrain further serves to isolate tribal communities from markets, health and education services, and many outside influences.

Figure 2: Village in the FATA [Omitted]

The FATA is governed by an administrative system and a judicial system different from the rest of Pakistan—the Frontier Crimes Regulations (FCR) of 1901, codified under British rule. Because Pakistan retained the colonial administrative and legal structures of the British, the FATA populations are legally separate from and unequal to other Pakistani citizens. Examples of differences under the FCR include the following:

- FATA residents do not have access to national political parties, and political parties are forbidden from extending their activities into the FATA.
- The FATA is under the direct executive authority of the president of Pakistan. Laws framed by the National Assembly of Pakistan do not apply in the FATA unless so ordered by the president, who is empowered to issue regulations for the tribal areas.
- FATA residents do not have the right to legal representation, to present material evidence, or to cross-examine witnesses in Pakistan's judicial system. Those convicted of crimes are denied the right of appeal in Pakistan's courts.
- The president's representatives to the FATA, who are called political agents, can punish an entire tribe for crimes committed on the tribe's territory by issuing fines, making arrests, implementing property seizures, and establishing blockades.

Some believe that the FCR is a culturally acceptable recognition of the tribal structure of the FATA, where the population is ethnically different from the majority of Pakistan's citizens, and precludes forced assimilation and that removing the FCR without a replacement mechanism that is accepted by the indigenous population has the potential to create a vacuum that could result in negative consequences. An announcement by Pakistani Prime Minister Yousaf Raza Gillani proposing the repeal of the FCR drew mixed reactions from tribesmen and political leaders, some of whom called for amendments to the FCR, rather than its repeal.

U.S. Funding to Pakistan

Since fiscal year 2002, the United States has provided Pakistan with approximately $12.3 billion in assistance and reimbursements. Table 1 provides a breakdown of U.S. funds for Pakistan from fiscal year 2002 to 2008, broken out by elements of national power—military, law enforcement, diplomacy, development assistance, economic, and intelligence—that the administration's national security strategies and Congress have recognized are needed to address the terrorist threat emanating from the FATA.[5] Greater details for these elements of national power are provided in the following enclosures.

Enclosure II: The United States Needs to Develop a Comprehensive Plan

In our April 2008 report, we reported that the U.S. government had not met its national security goals to destroy terrorist threats and close the safe haven in the FATA and had not developed a comprehensive plan reflecting the integration of multiple U.S. government agencies' efforts for meeting U.S. national security goals in Pakistan's FATA,[6] as called for by the National Strategy for Combating Terrorism (2003), the independent 9/11 commission (2004), and as mandated by congressional legislation (2007).[7] We also reported that the U.S. embassy in Pakistan has had no Washington-supported, comprehensive plan to combat terrorism and close the terrorist safe haven in the FATA. We concluded that a comprehensive plan to combat terrorism was needed. We noted that this plan should include, among other things, the various elements of national power and clear goals, objectives, priorities, and milestones in order to help ensure the continuity of effort and allow Congress and the American public to assess progress and ensure accountability of U.S. efforts in Pakistan's FATA and Western Frontier.

[5] Intelligence funding is covert and was not included in this report.

[6] GAO, *Combating Terrorism: The United States Lacks Comprehensive Plan to Destroy the Terrorist Threat and Close the Safe Haven in Pakistan's Federally Administered Tribal Areas*, GAO-08-622 (Washington, D.C.: Apr. 17, 2008).

[7] Implementing the Recommendations of the 9/11 Commission Act of 2007 (P.L. 110-53, sec. 2042).

Table 1. U.S. Funding to Pakistan by Element of National Power, FY 2002–2008

Dollars in thousands

Element of National Power[a]	FY 2002	FY 2003	FY 2004	FY 2005	FY 2006	FY 2007	FY 2008	Total	Percentage
Military	$1,464,911	$1,473,183	$781,928	$1,273,037	$1,218,435	$1,095,315	$1,387,543	**$8,694,352**	70.4%
Law enforcement	100,725	31,700	36,400	40,200	46,220	31,327	31,547	**318,119**	2.6%
Development & Economic	662,899	258,262	303,538	404,733	677,477	542,277	445,194	**3,294,380**	26.7%
Diplomacy[b]	3,486	3,957	6,811	5,869	9,144	8,735	1,497[c]	**39,499**	0.3%
Total	**$2,232,021**	**$1,767,102**	**$1,128,677**	**$1,723,839**	**$1,951,276**	**$1,677,654**	**$1,865,781**	**$12,346,350**	

Source: GAO analysis of budget documents provided by State Director of Foreign Assistance.

[a] These elements of national power are based on National Strategies and other national security documentation. To classify the funding we relied on State budget documents and consultations with State Director of Foreign Assistance, and made judgments based on the nature of many of the programs funded. We combined the Development and Economic elements due to the similar nature of the programs funded. These figures do not include normal operating costs, such as salaries of U.S. government officials.

[b] To capture the diplomatic element of national power we combined programmatic State Public Diplomacy from the State Operations account with State Education and Cultural Exchange programs in Pakistan.

[c] State did not provide GAO with FY 2008 State Education and Cultural Exchange funding.

Prior Recommendations and Agency Responses

To address the lack of a comprehensive plan, we recommended that the National Security Advisor and the Director of the National Counterterrorism Center, in consultation with the Secretaries of Defense and State, and the Administrator of USAID, the intelligence community, and other executive departments as deemed appropriate, implement the congressional mandate to develop a comprehensive plan. We also recommended that the comprehensive plan include all elements of national power—diplomatic, military, intelligence, development assistance, economic, and law enforcement support—called for in the Intelligence Reform Act, the Implementing Recommendations of the 9/11 Commission Act of 2007, and components that we have previously reported as being needed to improve the effectiveness of plans involving multi-departmental efforts to combat terrorism. Specifically, we recommended that the plan should

- place someone directly in charge of this multi-department effort to improve accountability;
- articulate a clear strategy to implement the national security goal to destroy terrorists and close the safe haven in the FATA;
- clarify roles and responsibilities of each department;
- provide guidance on setting funding priorities and providing resources;
- require a monitoring system; and
- provide periodic reports to Congress on the progress and impediments.

In written responses to our report, Defense and USAID concurred with the recommendation that a comprehensive plan should be developed; State asserted that a comprehensive plan existed; the NSC provided no comments; while the Office of the Director of National Intelligence and the National Counterterrorism Center stated that plans to combat terrorism exist. During a May 20, 2008, hearing before the Senate Foreign Relations Committee, the Deputy Secretary of State also indicated plans exist for a variety of efforts underway to assist Pakistan in combating terrorism, but he acknowledged that more can be done to integrate plans to focus on the threat along the Afghanistan-Pakistan border. The Deputy Secretary of State also indicated that efforts were underway to revisit the U.S. plans to focus on the key components suggested in our April 2008 report. The Office of the Director of National Intelligence noted in an August 2008 response to our request for a status update on the development of a comprehensive plan that it continues to disagree that the United States lacks plans to combat terrorism in Pakistan's FATA. The Director also noted that the United States has a multi-faceted strategy, with short- and long-term elements to increase the capability of Pakistani security forces to confront terrorist groups. We do not assert that the United States lacks individual plans; rather, we did not find nor were we provided a comprehensive plan that integrated the combined capabilities of Defense, State, USAID, the intelligence community, and others, and included key components we called for in our report to meet U.S. national security goals in Pakistan. As of January 2009, neither the National Security Council, the National Counterterrorism Center, nor Defense, State, or USAID has produced for our review an integrated comprehensive plan as recommended in our April 2008 report.

Efforts Underway to Improve Interagency Coordination

Since the release of our report in April 2008, the U.S. embassy in Islamabad has taken steps to coordinate the various efforts of Defense, USAID, and State to implement their department-specific efforts focused on combating terrorism in the FATA and Western Frontier. In addition, the embassy, in conjunction with State headquarters, was working to build support in Washington, D.C., for the need for a more comprehensive approach to combating terrorism, including greater integration of U.S. and Pakistani efforts in the FATA. State also continued to collect information on Defense, USAID, and State activities in the FATA, and added new objectives under the diplomatic element of national power, including (1) increased cross-border dialogue with Afghanistan, and (2) a public diplomacy objective intended to undermine the ideological foundation of extremism and bolster the image of the Pakistan government in the FATA.

State has staffed three new coordinator positions—one at State in Washington, D.C., and one each for the U.S. embassies in Pakistan and Afghanistan—intended to improve coordination among U.S. programs on each side and across the Pakistan–Afghanistan frontier. Their goals include (1) increasing interagency communications at the working level and (2) integrating elements of U.S. strategy into a comprehensive effort along the border. In addition, an Afghan-Pakistan Border Working Group was convened in July 2008 and has met seven times as of December 18, 2008. It includes representatives from the National Security Council; the Departments of State, Defense, Treasury, and Commerce; USAID, and the U.S. Trade Representative.

Oversight Questions

As the United States moves forward in its efforts to address the terrorist threat and close the safe haven, the following oversight issues should be addressed:

- What progress has been made in developing a comprehensive plan, as called for by the Intelligence Reform and Terrorism Prevention Act of 2004 and the Implementing the Recommendations of the 9/11 Commission Act of 2007?

- What obstacles or impediments have prevented the completion of a comprehensive plan?
- Are there sufficient resources devoted by the various agencies toward completing the development of a comprehensive plan to address U.S. national security goals in the FATA?
- How well are the various agencies coordinating their efforts in developing a comprehensive plan and what interagency agreements, if any, have been reached?

Enclosure III: Use of Military Element of National Power

The United States has relied primarily on the use of the military element of national power to address national security-related priorities in Pakistan, providing about $8.7 billion in military-related reimbursements and assistance since 2002. As figure 3 shows, the military element of national power has accounted for about 70 percent of U.S. funds devoted to addressing the U.S. strategic goals in Pakistan. This enclosure provides information on the U.S. military-related funding and programs for Pakistan including status of the U.S. Security Development Plan for FATA and the Western Frontier. It also highlights several oversight issues for Congress and the new administration to consider.

Figure 3: Percentage of Funding Devoted to Military Activities

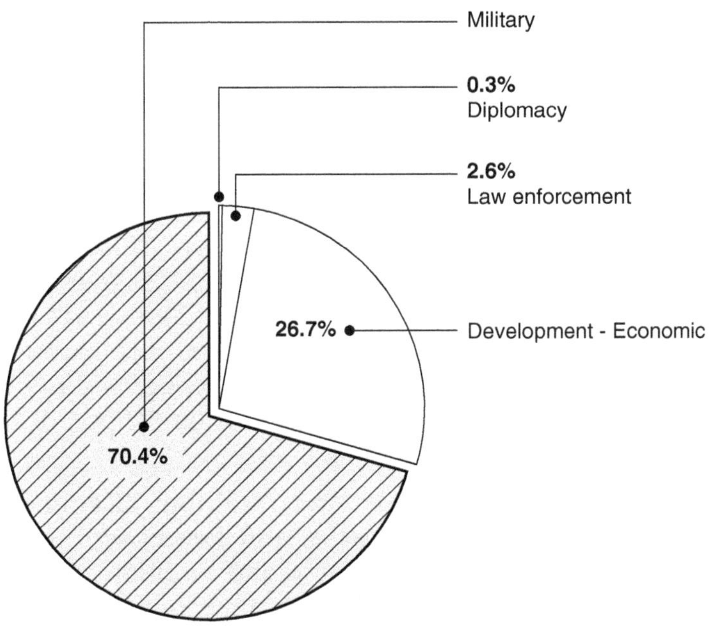

Source: GAO analysis of budget documents provided by State Director of Foreign Assistance.

Note: Funding figures do not include normal operating costs, such as salaries of U.S. government officials or funding for covert activities.

Table 2 indicates the amount and sources of U.S. military-related funding to Pakistan.

U.S. Military-Related Programs in Pakistan

Coalition Support Funds Used to Reimburse Pakistan for Military Operations: CSF payments have been used since fiscal year 2002 to reimburse the Pakistani government for incremental costs (i.e., costs above and beyond normal operating costs) incurred in direct support of U.S. military operations associated with the war on terror.[8] CSF has reimbursed a broad range of Pakistani military operations, including navy support for maritime patrols and interdiction operations; air force support for combat air patrols, reconnaissance and close air support missions, airlift support, and air traffic control; army military operations in the FATA; and increased management requirements at the Pakistan Joint Staff Headquarters. These activities include Operation Al Mizan, a major deployment of the Pakistani army to combat al Qaeda, Taliban, and other militants in the North West Frontier Province and the FATA that began in 2001 and has continued in various phases to date. The goal of this operation was to intercept militants attempting to escape the U.S. invasion of Afghanistan by fleeing into Pakistan. According to Defense, Pakistan has deployed over 100,000 army and paramilitary troops in support of this operation, incurred more than 1,400 casualties, and killed hundreds of al Qaeda, Taliban, and other terrorists. According to Defense, CSF is critical to ensure Pakistan's continued support of U.S. efforts to combat terrorism. Defense officials stated that without CSF or a similar mechanism to reimburse Pakistan for its support, Pakistan could not afford to deploy military forces along the Pakistan-Afghanistan border.

Foreign Military Financing Program: Foreign Military Financing is the second-largest source of military-related funding provided to Pakistan, superseded only by CSF reimbursements. Foreign Military Financing has been used to provide grants for the acquisition of U.S. defense equipment to enable key allies to improve their defense capabilities and to foster closer military relationships between the United States and recipient nations. Pakistan has used Foreign Military Financing to purchase military equipment, such as Cobra helicopters, Harris radios, and upgrades to its F-16 fighter aircraft.

International Military Education and Training, Regional Defense Counterterrorism Fellowship Program, and Peacekeeping Operations: Both the International Military Education and Training and the Regional Defense Counterterrorism Fellowship Program provide training to foreign military and related civilian personnel. The International Military Education

[8] CSF is used to reimburse 27 coalition allies, of which Pakistan is the largest recipient.

Table 2. U.S. Military-Related Funding to Pakistan, FY 2002–2008

Dollars in thousands

Funding Source		FY 2002	FY 2003	FY 2004	FY 2005	FY 2006	FY 2007	FY 2008	Total
State	Foreign Military Financing	$75,000	$224,500	$74,560	$298,800	$297,000	$297,000	$297,570	**$1,564,430**
	International Military Education and Training	894	990	1,384	1,885	2,037	1,992	2,325	**11,507**
	Peacekeeping Operations	220,000	0	0	0	850	700	750	**222,300**
Defense	CSF Reimbursements	1,169,017	1,246,571	705,278	963,925	861,604	731,772	900,600	**6,578,767**
	Counterterrorism Fellowship Funding	0	1,122	706	727	744	998	816	**5,113**
	Counternarcotics Funding	0	0	0	7,700	28,700	49,100	54,700	**140,200**
	Section 1206 Funding	0	0	0	0	27,500	13,753	55,782	**97,035**
	Frontier Corps Train and Equip Authority	0	0	0	0	0	0	75,000	**75,000**
Total		**$1,464,911**	**$1,473,183**	**$781,928**	**$1,273,037**	**$1,218,435**	**$1,095,315**	**$1,387,543**	**$8,694,352**

Source: GAO analysis of budget documents provided by the State Director of Foreign Assistance.

Note: Funding figures in this table do not include normal operating costs, such as salaries of U.S. government officials.

and Training program specifically allows these personnel to train at various U.S. military war colleges in the United States. The Regional Defense Counterterrorism Fellowship Program provides education and training to the same foreign personnel, but concentrates on counterterrorism activities intended to bolster the capacity of friendly foreign nations to detect, monitor, and interdict or disrupt the activities of terrorist networks. Additionally, Peacekeeping Operations funding is currently used by State to engage the Pakistan Ministries of Foreign Affairs and Defense to develop plans to increase Pakistan's capacity for conducting international peace support operations.

Security Development Plan: Defense's Security Development Plan, which seeks to enhance the counterinsurgency capacity of Pakistani security forces in FATA and the Western Frontier, has three objectives: (1) to secure Pakistan's border with Afghanistan, (2) to deny terrorists a safe haven in the FATA, and (3) to create a security environment that allows economic development and political reform to begin. The plan encompasses Defense's initiatives in the FATA and the Western Frontier to achieve these goals and is funded through several sources: Counternarcotics, Section 1206, and Frontier Corps Train and Equip Authority. According to Defense officials, Defense Counternarcotics funding can be used to support counterterrorism efforts in Pakistan due to the nexus between terrorism and drug trafficking along the Pakistan-Afghanistan border. Section 1206 funds are used to build the capacity of foreign military forces to conduct counterterrorism operations or support U.S. military operations. The Frontier Corps Train and Equip Authority is an authority created in the fiscal year 2008 National Defense Authorization Act that allows Defense to provide assistance to enhance the ability of the Frontier Corps to conduct counterterrorism operations along the Pakistan-Afghanistan border. The plan calls for annual investments of around $200 million through 2012. The centerpiece of the plan, according to Defense officials, is the expansion, training, and equipping of the Pakistan Frontier Corps, a paramilitary force that has previously experienced deficiencies in training and equipment.[9] The goal is to turn the Frontier Corps into a local security force capable of supporting Pakistan's counterinsurgency operations and providing sufficient security to allow for investments in local governance and economic development to yield results.

Training and Equipping of the Frontier Corps

The Security Development Plan seeks to assist the Pakistani government in establishing 16 new Frontier Corps units of about 650 personnel each

[9] Beginning in 2007, responsibilities for training the Frontier Corps in the FATA shifted from State to Defense as part of Defense's Security Development Plan.

capable of counterinsurgency operations. However, a deteriorating security environment has delayed the completion of a training center in the NWFP that was to be used to train Frontier Corps units. Defense expects that the facility will not be operational until early 2009.

As the additional Frontier Corps units proceed through training, Defense plans to supply each trainee with equipment needed to carry out their counterinsurgency efforts, such as helmets and protective vests. Defense is also currently supplying mobility equipment—pickup trucks, water trucks, ambulances, motorcycles—to existing Frontier Corps units already deployed to address existing mobility deficiencies.

Figure 4: Frontier Corps Checkpoint in the FATA [Omitted]

Enhancement of Pakistani Military's Helicopter Capability

The Security Development Plan is also intended to support the maintenance and re-servicing of Pakistani army helicopters used for counterinsurgency operations in the FATA and Western Frontier, including Bell 412s, Cobra gunships, and MI-17 troop transports. Bell 412s are utility helicopters used primarily for command and control functions in the border region where there is rough terrain. These helicopters are also used for administrative airlift and have been equipped with door guns to use in the provision of security for Pakistani army convoy movements. Cobra gunships are used in the FATA to support ground forces with missiles, rockets, and guns. MI-17s are heavy-lift helicopters used to move commando units in and out of combat operations, including for medical evacuation. According to Defense officials, these MI-17s are reaching their 1,500 flight hour marks, at which point they must go through mandatory re-servicing. Defense plans to enhance the operational readiness of all three helicopter types by providing initial maintenance and developing long-term sustainment programs. According to Defense officials, the MI-17s are particularly important for the air mobility of the Special Services Group Quick Reaction Squadron, a Pakistani army commando unit that conducts targeted counterterrorism missions in the FATA and elsewhere. Under the Security Development Plan the Special Services Group Quick Reaction Squadron is being provided with night vision equipment as well as air assault training and tactics.

Figure 5: MI-17 Troop Transport [Omitted]

Border Coordination Centers

Finally, the Security Development Plan includes the establishment of six Border Coordination Centers to integrate border security operations. Their mission is to coordinate friendly forces and coordinate the interdiction of terrorists and others. Each center is to be staffed with officers from Afghanistan, Pakistan, and coalition forces, and will possess communications and surveillance capabilities intended to provide tactical intelligence to military forces on both sides of the border. The first center in Torkham, Afghanistan, became operational in October 2008. A second center is under construction in Afghanistan. Defense plans for the third and fourth Border Coordination Centers to be located on the Pakistan side of the border. The locations for the centers, however, have not been finalized with the Pakistani government.

The Security Development Plan May Face Funding Shortfall in Fiscal Year 2009

Defense estimated that around $230 million would be required to fully support the Security Development Plan initiatives in fiscal year 2009. In fiscal year 2009, the plan received a total of $62.5 million ($37.5 million in Counternarcotics funding and $25 million in Frontier Corps Train and Equip Authority funding). As a result, Defense's Security Development Plan faces a shortfall of approximately $167.5 million, about 73 percent of its funding goal for fiscal year 2009. As of December 2008, no existing security assistance funds have been re-directed toward the Security Development Plan. Defense officials stated that without dedicated long-term funding, implementation of the Security Development Plan may be hampered, and the training and equipping of the Frontier Corps could slow down by March 2009.

Oversight Questions

- To what extent do the U.S.-funded Pakistani military efforts align with the U.S. national security goals in Pakistan's FATA and Western Frontier? What are future U.S. plans and strategies for this area?
- What have been the results of the U.S. investment of about $8.7 billion toward military efforts to address the terrorist threat and close the safe haven in Pakistan?
- To what extent do the U.S.-funded Pakistani military efforts assist in securing and stabilizing regions for development projects to be undertaken in the FATA and Western Frontier? How is Defense measuring the Pakistani military's adoption and success at implementing an effective counterinsurgency doctrine to accomplish military goals and to allow for economic development?

- What has the Security Development Plan accomplished to date and what are future objectives?
- How is the Security Development program coordinated with other U.S. efforts? For example, how has Defense's effort to train and equip the Frontier Corps built on prior State efforts under the Border Security Program to train and equip the Frontier Corps?
- Given the shortfall in funding noted by Defense officials to fully implement the Security Development Plan in fiscal year 2009, how does Defense envision funding the remainder of the Security Defense Plan? What effect does the current funding situation have on planning and implementation?
- What measures does the United States have in place to assess the readiness and capability of Frontier Corps units that have been trained and equipped under the U.S.-funded Security Development Plan?
- What is the level of oversight and accountability controls over equipment provided to the Frontier Corps?

Enclosure IV: Use of Law Enforcement Element of National Power

The United States has used the law enforcement element of national power to address national security-related priorities in Pakistan, providing about $318 million in law enforcement-related assistance since 2002. As figure 6 shows, the law enforcement element of national power has accounted for about 3 percent of U.S. funds devoted to addressing the U.S. national security goals in Pakistan. This enclosure provides information on U.S. government agency efforts to provide law enforcement-related assistance to Pakistan, including the efforts of the Departments of State, Justice, and Treasury that relate to the training and equipping of law enforcement entities, improving law enforcement access, and combating terrorist financing. It also highlights several oversight issues for Congress and new administration to consider.

Table 3 indicates the amount of U.S. law enforcement-related assistance to Pakistan. This funding is provided through the State Department's International Narcotics and Law Enforcement and Nonproliferation, Antiterrorism, Demining, and Related Programs accounts. According to State, it also provides a small amount of operational support for law enforcement agencies.

State's Border Security Program Focused on the FATA

State's Bureau of International Narcotics and Law Enforcement (INL) assists foreign nations in developing their law enforcement capacity.

Figure 6: Percentage of Funding Devoted to Law Enforcement Activities

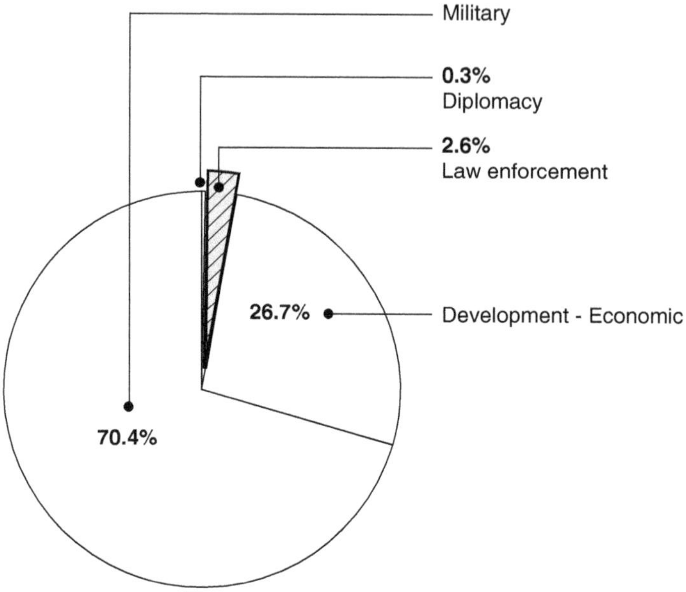

Source: GAO analysis of budget documents provided by State Director of Foreign Assistance.

Note: Funding figures do not include normal operating costs, such as salaries of U.S. government officials or funding for covert activities.

INL has three general assistance efforts in Pakistan: (1) the Border Security Program, (2) the Counternarcotics program, and (3) law enforcement reform, which includes training and capacity building focused on the judicial system and rule of law programs.[10] INL funding from fiscal year 2002 through 2008 totaled about $266 million. The Border Security Program and the Counternarcotics program are intended to support and expand Pakistan's law enforcement capacity to secure the Afghan border and frontier regions against terrorists, narcotics traffickers, and other criminal elements.

Figure 7: Village Spanning Both Sides of the Pakistan-Afghanistan Border [Omitted]

[10] The Counternarcotics program focuses on eliminating poppy cultivation, inhibiting further cultivation, interdicting smugglers, building Pakistan government capacity, providing infrastructure for alternative livelihood, and reducing domestic demand. The program relies on law enforcement, air support, and judicial reform, which are bolstered by complimentary INL programs: the Border Security Program and the Law Enforcement Program. INL initiated law enforcement reform in fiscal year 2003, working mainly through the Department of Justice to focus on training and leadership/management development.

Table 3. U.S. Law Enforcement-Related Funding to Pakistan, FY 2002–2008

Dollars in thousands								
Funding Source	**FY 2002**	**FY 2003**	**FY 2004**	**FY 2005**	**FY 2006**	**FY 2007**	**FY 2008**	**Total**
International Narcotics and Law Enforcement	$90,625	$31,000	$31,500	$32,200	$37,620	$21,350	$21,822	**$266,117**
Nonproliferation, Anti-terrorism, Demining, and Related Programs	10,100	700	4,900	8,000	8,600	9,977	9,725	**52,002**
Total	**$100,725**	**$31,700**	**$36,400**	**$40,200**	**$46,220**	**$31,327**	**$31,547**	**$318,119**

Source: GAO analysis of budget documents provided by State Director of Foreign Assistance.

Note: Funding figures in this table do not include normal operating costs, such as salaries of U.S. government officials.

The Border Security Program is State's primary law-enforcement effort to build the capacity of the Pakistani government to identify and arrest al Qaeda and Taliban terrorists and other criminals in Pakistan's border region with Afghanistan. State launched the Border Security Program shortly after the attacks of 9/11 to help the government of Pakistan better secure its western border and coast against exploitation by terrorists, drug traffickers, and other criminals and support bilateral cooperation with the government of Afghanistan. The Border Security Program's goals also include arresting criminals operating in the border region through combined use of ground forces and the Air Wing, expanding Pakistan's road and bridge network, constructing forts, outposts, and pickets for border security forces, and integrating modern law enforcement training techniques to enhance border security. The Border Security Program is a key law enforcement element of the U.S. embassy's strategy in the FATA, with efforts that include:

- improving law enforcement access within the FATA through road and outpost construction,
- providing training and equipment to law enforcement agencies operating in the FATA, and
- supplying technical and material support to law enforcement agencies operating on the western border.

Under the program, the United States has provided funding and assistance to Pakistan's Ministry of Interior; the Anti-Narcotics Force; the Frontier Corps in the FATA, NWFP, and Balochistan; and others.[11] It has also provided funds for the maintenance, support, and operating expenses of the Border Security Program-established Ministry of Interior Air Wing based in Quetta, Balochistan. The Air Wing, with three fixed-wing surveillance aircraft and nine Huey II helicopters, was intended to permit monitoring and interception of terrorists, drug traffickers, and other criminals operating in remote areas.[12]

Border Security Program Accomplishments

According to State, the Border Security Program has made progress toward many of its program goals. Program accomplishments cited by State include Pakistan's detaining roughly 600 suspected al Qaida and/or Taliban personnel, in part because of Border Security Program assistance. In addition, State indicates that the program helped Pakistan extend its authority into

[11] The Border Security Program also provided funding to the Frontier Constabulary; the Federal Investigation Agency; the coast guard; and the Customs Department.

[12] State indicates that the Air Wing has the best operational rate of any helicopter unit in Pakistan and is the country's only nighttime-capable air unit. According to Defense, the operational rate was supported by civilian contractors for some maintenance.

autonomous tribal border areas for the first time and substantially increased drug seizures. Reported progress on other efforts includes:

- construction of 137 of 176 planned outposts;
- construction of 113 of 370 planned kilometers of fully paved border security roads, and 2 of 18 bridges;
- provision of 2,496 vehicles and motorcycles, 1,012 night vision goggles and binoculars, 4,338 pieces of communications equipment, 1,824 bulletproof jackets, and 2,850 bulletproof helmets; and
- completion of 500 kilometers of gravel roads intended to extend the authority of the Pakistan government into previously inaccessible areas in the FATA and open these areas up to the mainstream economy.

Figure 8: State/INL-Funded Road in the FATA Next to a Highway [Omitted]

Border Security Program Faces Implementation and Monitoring Challenges

Program managers in Washington and Pakistan have raised concerns about the implementation and impact of this program. For example, since 2005 the pace of road and bridge construction, as well as monitoring efforts, has slowed because Pakistan cannot guarantee the security of the work crews or U.S. end-use monitors; the security situation has caused the roads, bridges, and outpost construction efforts to be shut down for months or even years, as in the Waziristans since 2005. Additionally, U.S. trainers increasingly face security restrictions on conducting training at locations in the NWFP according to State officials. As a result, some training scheduled for the NWFP has been either postponed or moved to secondary locations near Islamabad.

Monitoring of the Border Security Program has been hampered by the deteriorating security situation in FATA and the NWFP, which has restricted travel in the last 3 years. State officials told us that this limits their ability to monitor road construction progress in two of the seven FATA agencies, North and South Waziristan. According to State, in 2007, all monitoring visits to the FATA were cancelled for security reasons. In some instances, Pakistani officials were asked to bring the Border Security Program-supplied equipment to safer locations for inspection by embassy staff.

Other U.S. Government Law Enforcement Training Efforts in Pakistan

State also provides law enforcement training in Pakistan through its Antiterrorism Assistance (ATA) program. ATA's objectives are to provide partner nations with counterterrorism training and equipment, improve bilateral ties, and increase respect for human rights. ATA assistance generally consists of (1) training courses on tactical and strategic counterterrorism issues and (2) grants of counterterrorism equipment, such as small arms, bomb detection equipment, vehicles, and computers. ATA provides training primarily through contract employees and interagency agreements with other U.S. law enforcement agencies. According to our February 2008 report on ATA, Pakistan was the third largest recipient of ATA funding in the world.[13]

State has also funded law enforcement-related training activities carried out by Department of Justice agencies. In August 2002, the Department of Justice's International Criminal Investigative Training Assistance Program (ICITAP) initiated an assistance program to increase the capacity of the Pakistan law enforcement agencies to combat major internal criminal activities and terrorist threats. ICITAP training has primarily been targeted to address three specific needs: (1) building training capacity by training institutional staff and assisting in revision of core curricula, (2) improving investigative skills and capability through training in crime scene processing and basic criminal investigation, and (3) improving management and leadership ability through training in modern police management practices. The ICITAP program in Pakistan encompasses three major areas of responsibility: (1) border security, (2) law enforcement reform, and (3) the Automated Fingerprint Identification System. According to Justice, the program has developed and presented more than 150 training programs in both the border security and law enforcement reform areas.

In addition, Justice has one representative in Islamabad from the Criminal Division's Office of Overseas Prosecutorial Development, Assistance and Training (OPDAT). OPDAT's mission is to develop and administer technical and developmental assistance designed to enhance the capabilities of foreign justice sector institutions and their law enforcement personnel to combat terrorism and other types of crime. According to Justice, an OPDAT assessment led to the placement of a Justice Resident Legal Advisor at the U.S. Embassy in 2006 to assist Pakistan in legal reforms. Since than, the Advisor has worked to improve Pakistan's anti-money laundering legislation, and monitored terrorism prosecutions and the government's closure of Islamic charities linked to terrorist organizations. According to Justice, funding for OPDAT activities comes from State INL funds.

The Drug Enforcement Administration (DEA) and the Federal Bureau of Investigation (FBI) both have mandates to assist host nations, such as Pakistan, combat threats emanating from criminal activities, including

[13] See GAO, *Combating Terrorism: State Department's Antiterrorism Program Needs Improved Guidance and More Systematic Assessments of Outcomes*, GAO-08-336 (Washington, D.C.: Feb. 29, 2008).

those associated with illicit drugs and terrorist activities. DEA has offices in Islamabad and Peshawar intended to target drug-related threats to American citizens. Although it has not been given the specific goal to assist foreign nations to combat terrorism, in response to the 9/11 terrorist attacks, it has expanded its intelligence capabilities and information sharing, and instituted a formal procedure to query its in-country sources on terrorist-related information, which is then shared with the FBI and other agencies involved with efforts to fight terrorism. According to DEA officials, DEA cannot access the FATA; however, DEA can query its in-country sources on terrorist-related information when they leave the FATA. DEA training has been focused on improving the counter-narcotics capabilities of their Pakistani counterparts.

The FBI operates a Legal Attaché office in Islamabad, Pakistan. The office is intended to (1) coordinate international investigations with their foreign nation colleagues; (2) cover international leads for domestic U.S. investigations; (3) link U.S. and international resources in critical criminal and terrorist areas to protect Americans at home and abroad; and (4) coordinate FBI training, including counterterrorism classes, for police in their geographic regions. The FBI has also provided terrorist financing and money laundering training to Pakistan's law enforcement agencies. It also reported providing other types of training, including post-blast crime scene instruction and training related to the prevention, interdiction, and investigation of terrorist acts.

The U.S. embassy also coordinates efforts by State, Justice, Treasury, and Homeland Security to assist Pakistan identify and disrupt terrorist financing. For terrorist financing, the embassy, working with representatives from the FBI's Legal Attache office and the Department of Homeland Security, provided the Pakistani government technical assistance to develop an anti-money laundering law and helped create a financial intelligence unit to implement the law and reduce sources of terrorist financing. Treasury provided Pakistan assistance on its draft money laundering legislation to ensure it meets minimum international standards. Nonproliferation, Anti-terrorism, Demining, and Related Programs provides the bulk of the funding for interagency assistance for counterterrorism financing programs in Pakistan, with additional support provided by International Narcotics and Law Enforcement funds.

Oversight Questions

- What performance indicators are in place to measure progress toward the U.S. law enforcement goals in Pakistan's FATA and Western Frontier? What progress has been made through the various law enforcement efforts? What are the desired end states, and what are the expected time frames for completion?

- Given that several U.S. agencies are involved in various law enforcement activities in Pakistan, how well are law enforcement efforts in Pakistan coordinated among the various U.S. agencies?
- How effectively is the experience and expertise of the Department of Justice, its components, and others being used?
- To what extent are U.S. agencies working along the Afghanistan and Pakistan border sharing information on potential terrorists, drug traffickers, and other criminals?
- What are the anticipated costs of fully implementing the Border Security Program? What accountability measures are built into the Border Security Program to ensure U.S. funds are used as intended? How has State determined whether the Government of Pakistan deployed Border Security Program assets as intended?

Enclosure V: Use of Development and Economic Assistance Elements of National Power

The United States has used development and economic assistance to address national security-related priorities in Pakistan, providing about $3.3 billion in related activities since 2002. As figure 9 shows, the development and economic assistance elements of national power have accounted for about 27 percent of U.S. funds devoted to addressing the U.S. strategic goals in Pakistan. The development and economic needs of Pakistan are considerable. Pakistan is one of the world's poorest countries and ranks near the bottom of several development indicator categories, such as literacy; nutrition; and infant, child, and maternal mortality (see encl. I for additional information on Pakistan's development indicators). As such, development and economic assistance are two key elements of national power vital to U.S. efforts to address terrorism and close the safe haven in Pakistan. This enclosure provides information on U.S. development and economic policy assistance to Pakistan, including development assistance for Pakistan's underdeveloped areas, direct budget support to enhance Pakistan's macroeconomic stability, and use of economic policy to assist Pakistan to achieve economic prosperity. It also highlights several oversight issues for Congress and the new administration to consider.

Table 4 indicates the amount and sources of U.S. development and economic-related funding to Pakistan.

USAID activities in Pakistan have been funded from Child Survival and Health Assistance, Development Assistance, and ESF. These funds are intended to help improve the lives of ordinary Pakistanis; lay the groundwork for the country's sustained economic growth; and strengthen social, political, and economic institutions. A stated goal of these efforts in Pakistan

Figure 9: Percentage of Funding Devoted to Development and Economic Assistance Activities

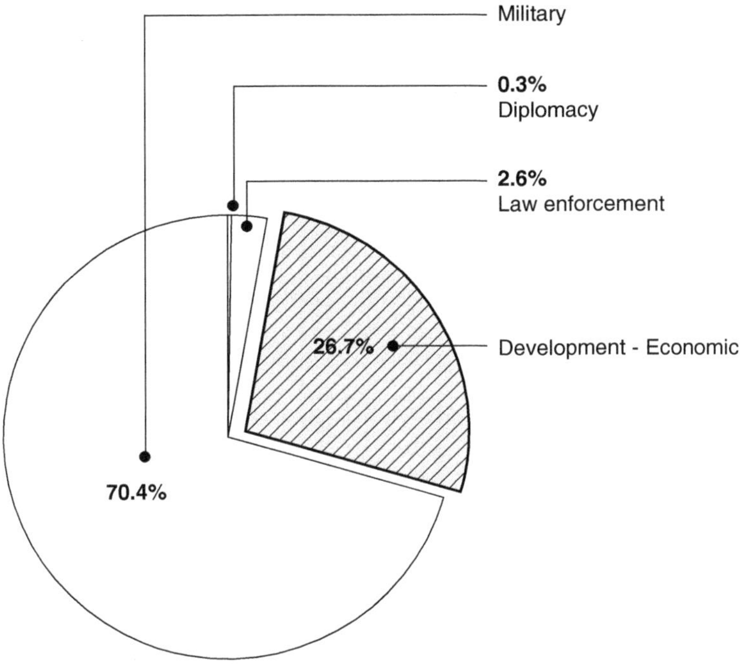

Source: GAO analysis of budget documents provided by State Director of Foreign Assistance.

Note: Funding figures do not include normal operating costs, such as salaries of U.S. government officials or funding for covert activities.

is also to alleviate the conditions that breed extremism while demonstrating that the United States' interest in Pakistan extends beyond the war on terror to concern for the Pakistani people as a whole. State is also supporting legislation for Reconstruction Opportunity Zones intended to promote trade and economic development. This legislation was not passed in the 110th Congress.

U.S. Development and Economic Assistance Programs

USAID's development programs have been organized into strategic objectives covering health, governance, education, and economic growth. In 2005, following the 7.6 magnitude earthquake in the northwestern part of Pakistan, USAID also began providing emergency relief and earthquake reconstruction assistance funded from the accounts detailed in table 4. In addition, the United States provides direct budget support through ESF, as well as economic policy assistance to Pakistan, including efforts to establish Reconstruction Opportunity Zones.

Table 4. USAID Development and Economic Funding to Pakistan, FY 2002–2008

Dollars in thousands

Funding Source	FY 2002	FY 2003	FY 2004	FY 2005	FY 2006	FY 2007	FY 2008	Total
Child Survival and Health Programs Fund	$14,000	$15,600	$25,600	$21,000	$28,100	$22,385	$29,816	**$156,501**
Development Assistance	10,000	34,500	49,400	29,000	37,500	95,327	29,757	**285,484**
Economic Support Fund (ESF)[a]	615,000	188,000	200,000	297,600	337,100	388,673	347,165	**2,373,538**
Other[b]	23,899	20,162	28,538	57,133	274,777	35,892	38,456	**478,857**
Total	**$662,899**	**$258,262**	**$303,538**	**$404,733**	**$677,477**	**$542,277**	**$445,194**	**$3,294,380**

Source: GAO analysis of budget documents provided by State Director of Foreign Assistance.

Note: Funding figures in this table do not include normal operating costs, such as salaries of U.S. government officials.

[a] About two-thirds of ESF was provided directly to the Pakistani government for debt relief, balance of payments, and direct budget support.

[b] Other categories of funding include International Disaster and Famine Assistance; Public Law 480, Title II (Emergency Food Aid); Migration and Refugee Assistance; Human Rights and Democracy Funding; Department of Agriculture's McGovern-Dole International Fund for Education and Child Nutrition Program; Department of Agriculture's Food for Progress; Overseas Humanitarian and Civic Aid; Foreign Assistance Act section 506(a)(2) drawdown; and Emergency Response Fund.

Health—USAID's Health Program has focused on improving maternal and newborn health services, enhancing the accessibility and availability of family planning products, preventing the spread of major infectious diseases, and increasing access to safe drinking water. For example, USAID's Pakistan Safe Drinking Water and Hygiene Promotion Project supports the Pakistani government's effort to install more than 6,000 water filtration plants, with the aim of providing clean drinking water.

Figure 10: Beneficiaries of a USAID Health Project [Omitted]

Governance—USAID's Democracy and Governance Program was intended to assist Pakistan's parliamentary institutions improve electoral processes and advance the decentralization process. For example, USAID's Pakistan Legislative Strengthening Project has trained hundreds of members of parliament on rules of procedure, the committee system, law drafting, and budget review.

Education—USAID's Education Program has supported projects to reform and revitalize Pakistan's education system, including educational assistance to young children. Education received the most development funding because the United States and Pakistan deemed it critical to improving the quality of life for the citizenry. For example, according to USAID, its Strengthening Teacher Education in Pakistan initiative is intended to improve teacher education through the development of national standards for teacher certification and accreditation.

Figure 11: Beneficiaries of a USAID/Pakistan Education Project [Omitted]

Economic growth—USAID's Economic Growth Program has sought to increase incomes and employment in Pakistan. The program focuses on expanding access to credit, improving the competitiveness of Pakistani small-and medium-sized enterprises through technical assistance, improving agricultural practices, and catalyzing development in energy. For example, according to USAID, its Developing Financial Services for Communities without Credit Program worked with the Khushhali Bank to disburse 356,361 micro-loans (average size approximately $200) in various districts, totaling more than $63 million and including 2,531 loans in FATA worth $429,450.

Earthquake reconstruction—On October 8, 2005, a 7.6 magnitude earthquake struck Pakistan, killing 74,000, injuring 70,000, and rendering more than

2.8 million people homeless. Focusing on immediate humanitarian needs, U.S. assistance provided emergency shelter, relief supplies, and medical help. Emergency relief efforts were followed by a USAID program to enable people to return home and rebuild their lives. In October 2006, USAID commenced a 4-year, $200 million Earthquake Reconstruction Program, through which it is constructing schools and healthcare facilities, improving education and health services, and enhancing economic well being by restoring livelihoods and expanding employment and enterprise opportunities.

Economic Support Funds Used for Emergency Economic Assistance to Pakistan—Although Economic Support Funds are used for a variety of U.S. programs in Pakistan, nearly $1.6 billion of these funds have been provided for direct budget support to the government of Pakistan via Emergency Economic Assistance, as shown in table 5. According to USAID, initially these funds provided balance of payments, budget support, and debt relief to the government of Pakistan during a time of economic hardship and political strain associated with Pakistan's participation in the Global War on Terror. Beginning in fiscal year 2005, these funds were direct grants for the government's health, education, clean drinking water and earthquake reconstruction initiatives. Following the announcement of a State of Emergency in Pakistan in November 2007, the fiscal year 2008 ESF committed for direct

Table 5. ESF-Funded Emergency Economic Assistance to Pakistan, FY 2002–2008

FY	ESF Level	Objective of Emergency Economic Assistance
2002	$600 million	Balance of payments and direct budget support grant
2003	188 million	Debt relief
2004	200 million	Debt relief
2005	200 million	Direct budget support grant to help Pakistan meet macroeconomic stability objectives and increase spending on human capital and private-sector development objectives
2006	200 million	Direct budget support grant to help Pakistan meet macroeconomic stability objectives and increase spending on human capital, specifically in education, health, and clean drinking water sectors
2007	200 million	Direct budget support grant to help Pakistan meet macroeconomic stability objectives and increase spending on human capital, specifically in education, health, clean drinking water, and earthquake reconstruction
2008	200 million	This funding was transferred into USAID development projects and was not used for Emergency Economic Assistance.

Source: USAID.

budget support to Pakistan was transferred into USAID-managed development programs. According to USAID officials, the fiscal year 2009 ESF commitment that would have gone to Emergency Economic Assistance will also be projectized.

Economic Policy Assistance—The embassy's objectives in economic policy includes encouraging the Pakistani government to promote structural reforms that further liberalize the economy and increase economic opportunities in underserved areas, such as the FATA. In addition, they include efforts to reduce the government's role in economic activity through privatization of state-owned enterprises, improve the efficiency of the financial sector, and increase the transparency of fiscal and monetary policies. In addition, the embassy planned to help Pakistan develop and strengthen its national export control system, expand trade, and eliminate trade barriers.

U.S. Efforts to Support Pakistan's Sustainable Development Plan for the FATA

The use of development assistance in the FATA was not prominent in the United States' efforts in Pakistan until March 2006, when the President of Pakistan requested that the United States adopt a more comprehensive approach to combating the terrorist threat in the FATA. Following these discussions, Pakistan proposed a Sustainable Development Plan that focuses on providing economic development and extending the influence of the Pakistani government in the FATA. USAID provided technical assistance to the Pakistani government's Sustainable Development Plan and has based its development activities in the FATA on this plan. The U.S. development activities include capacity building for the FATA institutions needed to plan, manage, and monitor development projects; efforts to build community and government relations; funding for health and education services; and efforts to increase employment and economic growth. The United States has pledged $750 million between 2007 and 2011 toward the Pakistani government's $2 billion, 9-year Sustainable Development Plan.

As of December 2008, according to USAID, its efforts in support of Pakistan's Sustainable Development Plan have led to numerous results, including the following:

- The $43 million FATA Capacity Building Program has provided administrative and management training for 340 staff from FATA development agencies, procured $1.7 million worth of computer and networking equipment, and started the development of a monitoring and evaluation system.
- The $300 million Livelihoods Program has benefited over 10,000 youth through short-term cash for work programs, enrolled over 800 youth

in vocational training and scholarship programs, and enrolled 350 youth in literacy and life skills programs.

- The $15.4 million education programs have trained over 360 education staff in areas such as school management, financial management, training of trainers, and educational planning. In addition, 58 primary, middle, and high schools have been constructed and furnished in the FATA.
- The $16.7 million health programs have conducted 1,824 Child Health Days that provided more than 207,821 children and 19,000 mothers with medical care and vaccinations. In addition, the programs provided training for 1,321 health providers in newborn and child health care.

U.S. Considering Establishment of Reconstruction Opportunity Zones in Pakistan

During the 110th Congress, bills were introduced in both the House and the Senate for Reconstruction Opportunity Zones in Afghanistan and Pakistan; neither bill was the subject of committee or floor action.[14] The proposed legislation was intended to provide economic incentives to address the widespread poverty and unemployment that, according to State, provide fertile ground for violent extremism in Afghanistan and the border region of Pakistan. By granting duty-free treatment to a wide array of goods produced in areas designated by the president as Reconstruction Opportunity Zones, the act was intended to promote investment and employment while giving local populations a stake in a more stable and prosperous future. The proposal included duty-free treatment for certain non-textile, textile, and apparel products for a period of 15 years. The Reconstruction Opportunity Zones eligible areas would be the entire territory of Afghanistan and the border region of Pakistan, which would include the FATA, the earthquake affected areas of Azad Jammu and Kashmir, parts of Balochistan, and the North West Frontier Province including Peshawar.

Oversight Questions

- To what extent is development and economic assistance to be included in future U.S. plans for addressing the terrorist threat and closing the terrorist safe haven in Pakistan's FATA and Western Frontier?
- How has USAID coordinated its plans to carry out development projects in Pakistan's FATA and Western Frontier with the Pakistani

[14] Afghanistan-Pakistan Security and Prosperity Enhancement Act, H.R. 6387, 110th Congress, and Afghanistan and Pakistan Reconstruction Opportunity Zones Act of 2008, S. 2776, 110th Congress.

government and what efforts are made to ensure that regions are secured before development projects are undertaken?

- How much of the development and economic assistance funding has been expended? How much of the development and economic assistance has Pakistan used to support health and education initiatives? What are the development and economic assistance priorities going forward and what are the projected future funding requirements?
- What are the cost and benefits to the United States of implementing Reconstruction Opportunity Zones?
- What performance indicators are in place to measure progress toward the U.S. development and economic assistance goals in Pakistan and its FATA and Western Frontier? What do the indicators show to date?
- How are USAID's activities in support of Pakistan's Sustainable Development Plan coordinated with State, Defense, Pakistan government, and other development activities to combat terrorism in the FATA?
- What challenges, if any, do USAID and others working on behalf of the U.S. face in implementing development projects in FATA and Western Frontier, and what are the United States' contingency plans for mitigating these challenges?

Enclosure VI: Use of the Diplomatic Element of National Power

The United States has used, to a limited extent, the diplomatic element of national power to address national security-related priorities in Pakistan, providing about $39 million in related activities since 2002. As figure 12 shows, the diplomatic element of national power has accounted for less than 1 percent of U.S. funds devoted to addressing the U.S. strategic goals in Pakistan. This enclosure provides information on U.S public diplomacy efforts in Pakistan and the FATA. It also highlights several oversight issues for the Congress and new administration to consider.

Table 6 indicates the amount of U.S. public diplomacy-related funding to Pakistan.

In November 2008, we identified public diplomacy as one of the key issues demanding urgent attention and continuing oversight by the new Congress and administration to ensure our nation's security and well-being.[15] State leads public diplomacy efforts overseas, but other agencies such as Defense

[15] See GAO, 2009 Congressional and Presidential Transition, http://www.gao.gov/transition_2009/index.php.

Figure 12: Percentage of Funding Devoted to Diplomatic Activities

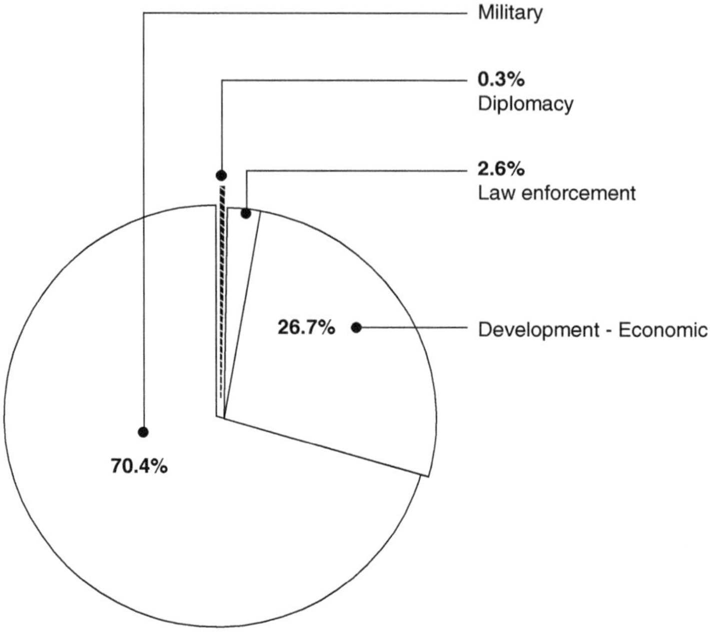

Source: GAO analysis of budget documents provided by State Director of Foreign Assistance.

Note: Funding figures do not include normal operating costs, such as salaries of U.S. government officials or funding for covert activities.

and USAID also seek to influence foreign public opinion through their public diplomacy and humanitarian relief efforts.

U.S. Embassy Plans for Diplomacy

According to the U.S. embassy in Pakistan, its public diplomacy efforts span a broad range of embassy objectives, including efforts to promote

Table 6. State Public Affairs Funding to Pakistan, FY 2002 to 2008

Dollars in thousands								
	FY 2002	**FY 2003**	**FY 2004**	**FY 2005**	**FY 2006**	**FY 2007**	**FY 2008**	**Total**
Funding to Pakistan	$3,486	$3,957	$6,811	$5,869	$9,144	$8,735	$1,497[a]	**$39,499**

Source: GAO analysis of budget documents provided by State Director of Foreign Assistance.

Notes: Funding figures in this table do not include normal operating costs, such as salaries of U.S. government officials. Data includes State Public Diplomacy program funding and State Education and Cultural Exchange programs in Pakistan, but does not include funding for the Fulbright exchange program, which is funded by USAID and included in our development and economic funding table.

[a]State did not provide FY 2008 Education and Cultural Exchange funding.

democracy and human rights, economic development, and regional security in Pakistan. The embassy uses its exchange and visitor programs in an effort to expose Pakistani opinion makers to the United States.

Figure 13: Pakistani Exchange Students' Pre-Departure Orientation [Omitted]

In addition, the embassy seeks to enhance its engagement with the public through the Lincoln Corner program. The program provides American books, Internet access, and other material, as well as space to conduct programs for education, seminars, round tables, and language training, with or without American involvement. It also utilizes a visiting speaker's program and enhanced public speaking engagements for mission personnel to educate the Pakistani public about U.S. policies and programs. State provided GAO numerous examples of public diplomacy efforts in Pakistan, such as student exchanges, press coverage, and training initiatives.

Figure 14: Lincoln Corner Children Gathering to Gain a Better Understanding of American Culture [Omitted]

Diplomacy Efforts for the FATA

According to State, the embassy plans to use public diplomacy to undermine the ideological underpinnings of extremism while bolstering the image of the Pakistani national government. The U.S. embassy included public diplomacy efforts toward its objective of preventing terrorist acts and denying a safehaven for terrorists. The embassy has used Pakistani government and local aid workers to implement and publicize U.S. supported projects in an effort to extend the authority of Pakistan's national government into the FATA, a key objective of the Pakistani and U.S. effort in the FATA. In addition, the embassy planned to deploy a variety of public diplomacy programs including speakers, scholarships, exchanges, and Lincoln Corner programs to reinforce other U.S. objectives in NWFP and Balochistan.

The U.S. government initiated a number of programs for the FATA for fiscal year 2008:

- **English Scholarship Program:** The State Department awarded multiple grants to higher education institutions in NWFP to conduct English language training for students from the FATA and surrounding areas for a period of 2 years.

- **Youth Radio Drama Program:** The State Department, through the Peshawar Consulate, awarded a grant to a U.S. institution to develop a radio drama program for broadcast in NWFP and FATA, the aim of which was to train and support moderate local voices. Through this grant, a team of trainers traveled to Peshawar to work with journalism and mass communications students from two area universities. The trainers provided training in script development and radio acting and helped the students to produce serial dramas highlighting real-life problems confronting residents in the FATA. This program was broadcast in Pashto on local radio stations.
- **Radio and Television Training Program:** The State Department provided a grant to a U.S. higher education institution to work with a higher education institution in the NWFP on television and radio broadcast training.
- **International Visitor Leadership Programs:** Two International Visitor Leadership Programs specifically targeted the FATA region. One was a program for tribal and community leaders from Pakistan's border region. A second program, with an emphasis on Advancing Peace through Community Problem Solving, targeted community leaders from both the Afghan and Pakistan border areas.
- **Small Grants Program for the FATA and NWFP:** Through the Peshawar Consulate, post provided small grants to support locally initiated civic education programs.
- **Sports Initiative:** The State Department awarded a grant to a local organization to encourage initiatives where sports can assist in creating a platform for post-conflict, peace-building and development by facilitating and equipping 150 youth sport teams with sports goods and establishing a sports network. The initiative directly involves 150 teams of cricket, football, and volleyball, more than 20,000 indirect beneficiaries (spectators), and provides recreational facilities for youth teams.
- **Social Awareness and Educational TV and Radio Programs:** The State Department awarded a grant to a higher education institution for the development of a series of radio and TV programs in Pashto, Urdu, and English designed to educate residents and promote tolerance through moderate messaging.
- **International Women of Courage Awards:** The State Department conferred an International Women of Courage Award on a community activist from the FATA for her work to empower the voice and role of women in traditional communities of the region.

State officials said that U.S. public diplomacy efforts in Pakistan have been historically hampered by a lack of funding, staffing, and the security environment. State officials characterized public diplomacy funding to Pakistan as "woefully under-funded" to counter Pakistani perceptions of U.S. policies in Pakistan. They also said that Pakistani public diplomacy efforts were "very understaffed" given the number of people in Pakistan (170 million), the number of media outlets, and the grave national security concerns that Pakistan represented. State officials said that there were eight officials with public diplomacy responsibilities for Pakistan, and two of these have other responsibilities. By contrast, they said, the U.S. mission in Afghanistan has seven full-time Americans engaged in public diplomacy efforts for a population of around 30 million people and a less complex media environment than Pakistan. State officials said that the lack of funding and staffing is one reason the United States has been unable to counter the public perception that terrorist attacks in Pakistan are caused by U.S. efforts to combat terrorism in the FATA. For example, a June 2008 Pakistan-wide public opinion poll released by the New America Foundation found negative views held by Pakistanis of the United States and its policies in Pakistan. According to the poll, more than half (52 percent) blamed the United States when asked who was most responsible for the violence that is occurring in Pakistan today, while 8 percent blamed al Qaeda fighters.

State public diplomacy officials said that there has been a recent increase in interest in expanding public diplomacy efforts in Pakistan. In August 2008, State's Office of the Under Secretary for Public Diplomacy and Public Affairs began to develop a list of potential public diplomacy activities intended to reaffirm the U.S. commitment to Pakistan as a key ally and counter the view that the United States is a threat to Islam. State officials estimated the potential cost of these proposed initiatives, still pending approval, at about $29 million.

Oversight Questions

- How do State's diplomacy priorities align with the overall U.S. strategy for combating terrorism emanating from Pakistan's border area?
- To what extent have diplomacy efforts been, or will they be, integrated with other efforts, such as development assistance, to combat terrorism in Pakistan's FATA and Western Frontier? What are the projected scope, priorities, and future funding requirements for diplomacy programs?
- What have been the results of U.S. diplomacy efforts in Pakistan? What performance measures are, or will be, included to assess progress?
- How have the worsening security situation and limited funding and resources devoted to U.S. diplomacy efforts impacted planning and implementation of State's public diplomacy efforts?

- What steps have been taken, among the U.S. government agencies, to coordinate public diplomacy and strategic communications activities in Pakistan?

Enclosure VII: Oversight and Accountability of CSF and Other Funds Provided to Pakistan

As noted earlier, the U.S. government has provided Pakistan more than $12.3 billion for military, law enforcement, development and economic assistance, and diplomacy efforts to secure, stabilize, and develop Pakistan, and particularly the FATA and Western Frontier. Where audits have been completed covering about $5.7 billion in military and development assistance, GAO and the Defense and USAID inspectors general have raised accountability and oversight concerns, such as the ability of the U.S. government to work with the Pakistani government to validate the use of U.S. funds.[16] Going forward, the U.S. government's plans for training and equipping Pakistan security forces in FATA and the Western Frontier call for annual investments of around $200 million per year from fiscal year 2009 through 2012. Additionally, the United States has committed $750 million for development efforts in the FATA over 5 years (fiscal years 2007 through 2011), and legislation currently under consideration, if passed, could provide billions more in development assistance to Pakistan over a 5-year period.[17] Given the oversight and accountability deficiencies that we and the inspectors general have previously identified, as well as the number of U.S. programs and activities that remain unaudited, continued congressional oversight and agency monitoring efforts are needed to help ensure U.S. funding is used as intended. This enclosure highlights our previous findings relating to the need for increased oversight and accountability of Pakistan's CSF reimbursement claims, prior recommendations for enhancing oversight, and efforts undertaken by Defense to improve the oversight and accountability of the CSF reimbursement process.

Previously Reported Deficiencies in Oversight and Accountability of CSF

We previously reported in June 2008 that Defense did not consistently apply its existing CSF oversight guidance. While Defense generally conducted macro-level analytical reviews called for in its guidance, such as determining whether the cost is less than that which would be incurred by

[16] Department of Defense Inspector General, *Financial Management: Coalition Support Funds,* D-2004-045 (Washington, D.C.: Jan. 16, 2004). This is a classified report. USAID, *Audit of Selected Activities under USAID/Pakistan's Basic Health Program,* Audit Report No. 5-391-07-005-P (May 23, 2007) and USAID, *Audit of USAID/Pakistan's Education Sector Reform Assistance Program,* Audit Report No. 5-391-08-004-P (Mar. 28, 2008). The office of the Chief Financial Officer for USAID has since issued a memorandum stating that final action is complete for all four of the recommendations to the 2007 Health Programs audit (5-391-07-005-P).

[17] Enhanced Partnership with Pakistan Act of 2008, S. 3263, 110th Congress.

the United States for the same service, for a large number of reimbursement claims, Defense did not obtain detailed documentation to verify that claimed costs were valid, actually incurred, or correctly calculated. For example, as of May 2008, Defense paid over $2 billion in Pakistani reimbursement claims for military activities covering January 2004 through June 2007 without obtaining sufficient information that would enable a third party to recalculate these costs.

We also found that Defense may have reimbursed costs that (1) were not incremental, (2) were not based on actual activity, or (3) were potentially duplicative. For example, Defense paid an average of more than $19,000 per vehicle per month for Pakistani navy reimbursement claims. These claims appeared to contain duplicative charges for a fleet of fewer than 20 passenger vehicles. We also found that additional oversight controls were needed. For example, Defense had no guidance to verify currency conversion rates used by Pakistan, which if performed would enhance Defense's ability to monitor for potential over-billings. In addition, Defense's 2003 guidance did not specifically task the Office of the Defense Representative (ODRP) in the U.S. embassy with attempting to verify Pakistani military support and expenses.

Prior Recommendations Regarding Oversight of CSF

To improve oversight of CSF payments to Pakistan, our June 2008 report made the following five recommendations to the Secretary of Defense:

- Consistently implement existing criteria to disallow or defer Pakistani claims that do not include the documentation needed to verify the claims.
- Define and formalize the roles and responsibilities of ODRP.
- Clarify guidance for Comptroller analysis of cost fluctuations.
- Develop and apply criteria to evaluate currency exchange rates to ensure that the U.S. government is not overpaying for Pakistan operations.
- Work with the government of Pakistan to develop procedures to allow ODRP or other U.S. representatives to conduct greater oversight of CSF use in Pakistan, including the potential use of onsite inspections.

Efforts Undertaken to Improve Oversight and Accountability of CSF

Defense concurred with our recommendations and has taken steps to address them. In June 2008, the Defense Comptroller issued formal guidance that, among other things, clarified the roles and responsibilities of Defense representatives at U.S. embassies. The guidance also added a requirement for the Defense Comptroller to analyze cost fluctuations that exceed 10 percent in each cost category and note changes in operational tempo, force strength, or cost elements that may have contributed to the change. The guidance also required that reimbursement requests provide costs in local currency, convert costs to the U.S. dollar equivalent, and indicate the effective date of and the exchange rate used.

To help ensure consistent implementation of its guidance, in the case of Pakistan, Defense staff from the Comptroller and U.S. Central Command (CENTCOM) visited Islamabad to conduct discussions on the administration and processing of CSF reimbursement claims with ODRP and Pakistani military representatives. The U.S. delegation spent several days in August 2008 discussing changes to the CSF claims approval process with Pakistani military officials, including a joint examination of the May 2008 claim.

As a result of these discussions, Defense agreed to: (1) provide Pakistan a set of revised guidelines on CSF administrative procedures; (2) provide Pakistan a revised format for the submission of Pakistan's June 2008 claim and all future CSF claims; and (3) return to Pakistan every 6 months beginning in February 2009 to discuss new CSF issues, provide training on CSF administrative processing requirements and revisit unresolved issues. Pakistani officials agreed to: (1) provide additional documentation and cost methodology information for the May 2008 claim; (2) provide a monthly operational summary of Pakistani army, air force, and navy actions in support of U.S. military operations; (3) provide feedback on the proposed submission format within 30 days of receipt; and (4) beginning with the May 2008 claim, provide additional information or documentation for all disputed claims within 90 days to substantiate claims deferred or disallowed by ODRP, CENTCOM, or the Defense Comptroller. However, the Pakistani military was reluctant to provide costs in rupees due to the long processing time on previous CSF reimbursements. According to Defense officials, the Pakistani officials worried that they would be significantly under-compensated due to inflationary pressure on their national currency. In addition, Defense would not agree to pay for certain Pakistani requests, such as equipment depreciation or injury compensation for Pakistani soldiers. As of December 2008, these remaining issues had not been fully resolved. Figure 15 provides an illustration of the revised CSF oversight process.

While we recognize Defense is taking various steps to strengthen oversight of CSF claims, the extent to which Defense is consistently implementing this new guidance cannot be determined until the more recent Pakistan reimbursement claims are fully processed. Furthermore, Defense's ability to improve oversight over the CSF program will depend upon the cooperation of the Pakistani government.

Oversight Questions

- Given that over $12 billion in U.S. assistance and reimbursements has been provided Pakistan, what oversight and accountability controls are now in place by the various U.S. agencies to oversee the use of U.S. funds? To what extent have the various agencies adequately implemented oversight and accountability controls?
- What are the challenges to ensuring funds are used towards U.S. national security goals in Pakistan? What steps have U.S. agencies taken, or do they plan to take, to address these challenges and to ensure that funds are used as intended?
- To what extent have the various U.S. agencies devoted sufficient resources for oversight of U.S. funds and efforts in Pakistan? How are resource requirements determined and to what extent do they include staff with appropriate skills (such as auditing, accounting, and program evaluation)?
- Given limited ability to collect first-hand data on the use of U.S. funds in Pakistan and the need, in some cases, to rely on the Pakistani government for sufficient documentation to support reimbursement claims, what has been the level of cooperation between U.S. agencies and their counterparts in the Pakistani government to ensure oversight and accountability over U.S. funds?

Related GAO Products

Combating Terrorism: Increased Oversight and Accountability Needed over Pakistan Reimbursement Claims for Coalition Support Funds. GAO-08-806. Washington, D.C.: June 24, 2008.

Combating Terrorism: U.S. Efforts to Address the Terrorist Threat in Pakistan's Federally Administered Tribal Areas Require a Comprehensive Plan and Continued Oversight. GAO-08-820T. Washington, D.C.: May 20, 2008.

Preliminary Observations on the Use and Oversight of U.S. Coalition Support Funds Provided to Pakistan. GAO-08-735R. Washington, D.C.: May 6, 2008.

Combating Terrorism: The United States Lacks Comprehensive Plan to Destroy the Terrorist Threat and Close the Safe Haven in Pakistan's Federally Administered Tribal Areas. GAO-08-622. Washington, D.C.: April 17, 2008.

Securing, Stabilizing, and Reconstructing Afghanistan: Key Issues for Congressional Oversight. GAO-07-801SP. Washington, D.C.: May 24, 2007.

Securing, Stabilizing, and Rebuilding Iraq: GAO Audits and Key Oversight Issues. GAO-08-231T. Washington, D.C.: May 24, 2007.

Figure 15: Revised CSF Oversight Process

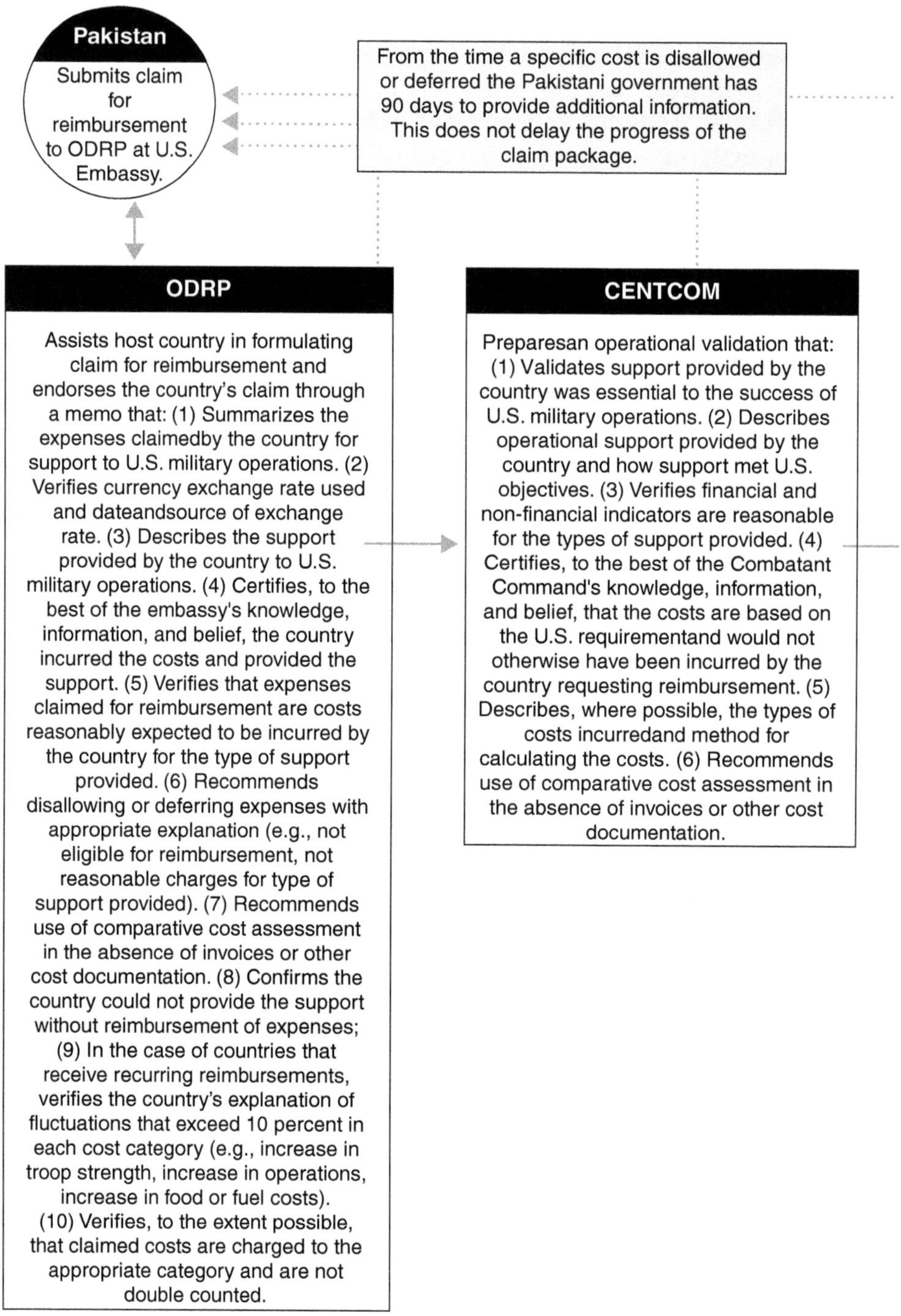

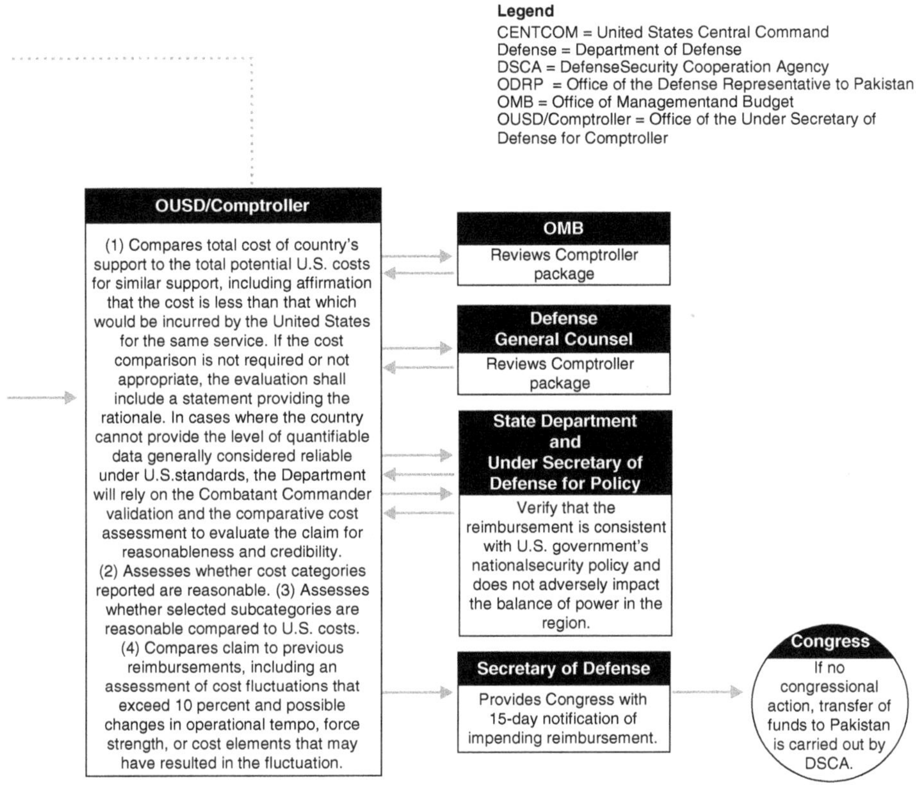

Source: GAO analysis of Defense documentation and discussions with Office of the Undersecretary of Defense for Comptroller.

GAO's Mission

The Government Accountability Office, the audit, evaluation, and investigative arm of Congress, exists to support Congress in meeting its constitutional responsibilities and to help improve the performance and accountability of the federal government for the American people. GAO examines the use of public funds; evaluates federal programs and policies; and provides analyses, recommendations, and other assistance to help Congress make informed oversight, policy, and funding decisions. GAO's commitment to good government is reflected in its core values of accountability, integrity, and reliability.

Obtaining Copies of GAO Reports and Testimony

The fastest and easiest way to obtain copies of GAO documents at no cost is through GAO's Web site (www.gao.gov). Each weekday afternoon, GAO posts on its Web site newly released reports, testimony, and correspondence. To have GAO e-mail you a list of newly posted products, go to www.gao.gov and select "E-mail Updates."

Order by Phone

The price of each GAO publication reflects GAO's actual cost of production and distribution and depends on the number of pages in the publication and whether the publication is printed in color or black and white. Pricing and ordering information is posted on GAO's Web site, http://www.gao.gov/ordering.htm.

Place orders by calling (202) 512-6000, toll free (866) 801-7077, or TDD (202) 512-2537.

Orders may be paid for using American Express, Discover Card, MasterCard, Visa, check, or money order. Call for additional information.

To Report Fraud, Waste, and Abuse in Federal Programs

Contact:

Web site: www.gao.gov/fraudnet/fraudnet.htm
E-mail: fraudnet@gao.gov
Automated answering system: (800) 424-5454 or (202) 512-7470

Congressional Relations

Ralph Dawn, Managing Director, dawnr@gao.gov, (202) 512-4400
U.S. Government Accountability Office, 441 G Street NW, Room 7125
Washington, DC 20548

Public Affairs

Chuck Young, Managing Director, youngc1@gao.gov, (202) 512-4800
U.S. Government Accountability Office, 441 G Street NW, Room 7149
Washington, DC 20548

DOCUMENT NO. 4

WAR IN AFGHANISTAN: STRATEGY, MILITARY OPERATIONS, AND ISSUES FOR CONGRESS

CRS Report
R40156

January 23, 2009

Catherine Dale

Summary

As the 111th Congress convenes and the Obama Administration assumes office, the war in Afghanistan has entered its eighth year. With a deteriorating security situation and no comprehensive political outcome yet in sight, most observers view the war in Afghanistan as open-ended. By early 2009, a growing number of Members of Congress, Administration officials, and outside experts had concluded that the effort—often called "America's other war"—required greater national attention. For the Government of the Islamic Republic of Afghanistan (GIRoA), the war is both a struggle for survival and an effort to establish sustainable security and stability. For the United States, the war in Afghanistan concerns the security of Afghanistan and the region, including denying safe haven to terrorists and helping ensure a stable regional security balance. For regional states, including India and Russia as well as Afghanistan's neighbors Pakistan and Iran, the war may have a powerful impact on the future balance of power and influence in the region. For individual members of the North Atlantic Treaty Organization (NATO), the war may be about defeating terrorist networks, ensuring regional stability, proving themselves as contributing NATO members, and/or demonstrating NATO's relevance in the 21st century.

Since 2001, the character of the war in Afghanistan has evolved from a violent struggle against al Qaeda and its Taliban supporters to a multi-faceted counterinsurgency (COIN) effort. In the aftermath of the terrorist attacks of

September 11, 2001, the United States launched Operation Enduring Freedom (OEF) in order to end the ability of the Taliban regime to provide safe haven to al Qaeda and to put a stop to al Qaeda's use of the territory of Afghanistan as a base of operations for terrorist activities. In that first phase, U.S. and coalition forces, working with Afghan opposition forces, quickly removed the Taliban regime.

After the fall of the Taliban, the character of the war shifted to a multifaceted COIN effort aimed at smothering the diffuse insurgency by shoring up GIRoA efforts to provide security, governance, and economic development. The three areas are generally viewed as interdependent and mutually-reinforcing—security is a prerequisite for some governance and development efforts, and longer-term, sustainable security requires both functional governance and economic opportunity. As one pillar of the COIN campaign in Afghanistan, the Afghan and international military effort aims broadly at defeating the remnants of the Taliban and other insurgents, securing the population, and helping extend the reach of the Afghan government. The international military effort includes both the NATO-led International Security Assistance Force (ISAF), to which the United States contributes troops, and the separate U.S.-led OEF mission.

The U.S. Government faces key strategic and operational decisions about its further engagement in the war in Afghanistan. These may include clarifying U.S. national interests in Afghanistan and the region; defining clear strategic objectives based on those interests; determining which diplomatic, economic, and military approaches to adopt, and what resources to commit to support those approaches; prioritizing "Afghanistan" versus other national security imperatives; and helping marshal a coordinated application of international efforts. Avenues available to Congress for exercising oversight include authorizing and appropriating funding for U.S. efforts in Afghanistan and the region; shaping policy through directive legislation; holding oversight hearings to assess policy execution; and adjusting Administration reporting requirements. This report provides analysis of current developments and future options concerning the war in Afghanistan. It will be updated as events warrant.

Overview

As the 111th Congress convenes and the Obama Administration assumes office, the war in Afghanistan has entered its eighth year. Unlike the war in Iraq, which, many argue, has entered its endstate, the war in Afghanistan—where the security situation has deteriorated and no comprehensive political outcome is yet in sight—appears to many observers to be open-ended. By early 2009, a growing number of Members of Congress, Administration officials, and outside experts had concluded that the effort—often called

America's "other war"—required greater national attention.[1] In his inaugural address, President Obama stated that the United States would "forge a hard-earned peace in Afghanistan."[2]

For the Government of Afghanistan, the war is first of all an existential struggle for survival against the Taliban and other insurgents, as well as a longer-term effort to establish sustainable security and stability. For the U.S. Government, the war in Afghanistan concerns the security of both Afghanistan and the region, including denying safe haven to terrorists and helping ensure a constructive and stable regional security balance.[3] For regional states, including India and Russia as well as Afghanistan's immediate neighbors Pakistan and Iran, the war is critical because it may have a powerful impact on the future security and balance of power and influence in the region. For individual member states of the NATO Alliance, the war may be about some combination of defeating terrorist networks, ensuring regional stability, proving themselves as contributing NATO members, and demonstrating the relevance of the Alliance to 21st century security challenges.

Looking ahead, the U.S. Government faces major strategic and operational decisions about its further engagement in the war in Afghanistan. Those decisions may include:

- Clarifying U.S. national interests in Afghanistan and the region;
- Defining clear strategic objectives based on those interests;
- Determining which diplomatic, economic, and military approaches to adopt, and what resources to commit to support those approaches;
- Prioritizing the Afghanistan war versus other national security imperatives including the war in Iraq and preparing to meet potential threats; and
- Helping marshal a coordinated application of international efforts.

[1] See for example the replies to questions for the record, submitted by Secretary of State nominee Hillary Clinton to the Senate Foreign Relations Committee (SFRC), for her January 13, 2009, confirmation hearing, available at http://www.foreignpolicy.com/files/KerryClintonQFRs.pdf; and replies to questions for the record, submitted by Under Secretary of Defense for Policy nominee Michèle Flournoy to the Senate Armed Services Committee (SASC), for her January 15, 2009, confirmation hearing, available at http://armed-services.senate.gov/statemnt/2009/January/Flournoy%2001-15-09.pdf. See also Joseph J. Collins, "Afghanistan: Faltered But Not Fallen," *Armed Forces Journal*, January 2009; Michael O'Hanlon, "Playing for Keeps," *USA Today*, January 7, 2009; Nathaniel C. Fick and John A. Nagl, "Counterinsurgency Field Manual: Afghanistan Edition," *Foreign Policy*, January/February 2009.

[2] President Barack Obama, Inaugural Address, January 20, 2009, text available at http://www.whitehouse.gov/blog/read_the_inaugural_address/.

[3] In her replies to questions for the record, submitted to the Senate Foreign Relations Committee (SFRC) for her January 13, 2009, confirmation hearing, Secretary of State nominee Hillary Clinton stated: "President-Elect Obama and I believe that Afghanistan and the Pakistani border are the central front in the war on terror." See text available at http://www.foreignpolicy.com/files/KerryClintonQFRs.pdf.

Avenues available to Congress for exercising oversight of these issues include authorizing and appropriating funding for U.S. efforts in Afghanistan and the region; shaping policy through directive legislation; confirming senior administration officials with responsibility for the Afghanistan effort; holding oversight hearings to assess policy formulation and execution; and extending or adjusting Administration reporting requirements.[4]

Character of the War in Afghanistan

While war is always about the organized use of violence to achieve political ends, the character of a given war may change dramatically over time. Since 2001, the character of the war in Afghanistan has evolved markedly, from a violent struggle against al Qaeda and its Taliban supporters, to a multi-faceted counterinsurgency (COIN) effort.

In the aftermath of the terrorist attacks of September 11, 2001, the United States launched Operation Enduring Freedom (OEF) in order to end the ability of the Taliban regime to provide safe haven to al Qaeda and to put a stop to al Qaeda's use of the territory of Afghanistan as a base of operations for terrorist activities. In that first phase, a primarily military effort, U.S. and other coalition forces, working closely with Afghan opposition forces, quickly removed the Taliban regime.

After the fall of the Taliban, the character of the war shifted to a multifaceted COIN effort aimed at smothering the diffuse insurgency by shoring up the efforts of the Government of the Islamic Republic of Afghanistan (GIRoA) to provide security, governance, and economic development. Leading practitioners view efforts in all three areas—and not just kinetic military operations—as essential to any successful counterinsurgency campaign. As U.S. Army General David Petraeus, now Commanding General of U.S. Central Command (CENTCOM), has frequently stated, "You can't kill your way out of an insurgency."[5] The three areas are generally viewed as interdependent and mutually-reinforcing—sufficient security is a prerequisite for some governance and development efforts, and longer-term, sustainable security requires both functional governance and economic opportunity. COIN theorists argue further that these areas require substantial civilian as

---

[4] For example, the *National Defense Authorization Act for Fiscal Year 2008*, P.L. 110-181, January 28, 2008, §1230 required a "report on progress toward security and stability in Afghanistan", no later than 90 days after enactment and every 180 days thereafter until the end of Fiscal Year 2010. That report is to include a "comprehensive strategy of the United States for security and stability in Afghanistan" that addresses NATO and its International Security Assistance Force (ISAF), the Afghan National Security Forces (ANSF), Provincial Reconstruction Teams (PRTs) and other development initiatives, counter-narcotics activities, the rule of law, and regional considerations. P.L. 110-181, §1231, required, no later than 90 days after enactment, and annually to the end of Fiscal Year 2010, a report on sustaining the Afghanistan National Security Forces.

[5] Babak Dehghanpisheh and Evan Thomas, "Scions of the Surge," *Newsweek*, March 24, 2008.

well as military efforts. As the U.S. Army and Marine Corps 2006 COIN Manual states: "Military efforts are necessary and important to counterinsurgency efforts, but they are only effective when integrated into a comprehensive strategy employing all instruments of national power."[6]

As a central pillar of the COIN campaign in Afghanistan, the Afghan and international military effort aims broadly at defeating the remnants of the Taliban and other insurgents, securing the population, and helping extend the reach of the Afghan government. The international military effort now includes the North Atlantic Treaty Organization-led (NATO) International Security Assistance Force (ISAF), to which the U.S. Government contributes troops, as well as the separate US-led OEF mission.

Prospects for the Outcome of the War

Afghanistan's results to date have been mixed, and no concrete end of the war is yet in sight. Despite the achievement of some major political milestones—including ratifying a new constitution and holding presidential and parliamentary elections—progress to date in extending the rule of law, establishing effective governance, and furthering economic development has been relatively limited. Presidential elections, scheduled for 2009, are expected to further test the fabric of society. Meanwhile, for several years, practitioners and observers have expressed concerns about a worsening security situation on the ground, including the greater frequency and sophistication of attacks, exacerbated by the ability of insurgents to find safe haven across the border in Pakistan.

Experts differ on the further prospects for the Afghanistan effort and the war's likely outcome, in part because they pose the question in different ways. One approach addresses the relatively short-term goal of defeating the insurgency—that is, ensuring that insurgents cannot directly challenge the authority of the Afghan state.

As of late 2008, few if any practitioners or observers expected the war to end in a clear Taliban victory, including Taliban control of the state of Afghanistan. Some suggested that a more likely worst-case scenario would be a reversion to the civil war and chaos of the early 1990's, including warlordism, a general lack of stability and opportunity for ordinary Afghans, and a proliferation of ungoverned spaces that might be used by terrorists as safe havens. To some extent, these conditions are currently manifested in parts of southern Afghanistan.

---

[6] Field Manual 3-24, *Counterinsurgency*, Headquarters, Department of the Army, December 2006, para. 2-1. Paragraph 2-2 of the COIN manual adds: "The integration of civilian and military efforts is crucial to successful COIN operations. All efforts focus on supporting the local populace and HN [host nation] government. Political, social, and economic programs are usually more valuable than conventional military operations in addressing the root causes of conflict and undermining an insurgency."

In late 2008, as a rule, U.S. and other international senior officials in Afghanistan expressed measured optimism regarding near-term results of the counterinsurgency effort. They pointed to some recent progress breaking down insurgent networks and expected further gains, particularly if more resources were made available and greater cooperation from all parties, including neighboring states, achieved. As a rule, international officials did not argue that without more resources, the COIN effort would fail, but rather, that without more resources, the effort would cost more money, more time, and more lives.[7] Some members of this school of thought offered the caveat that making timely progress was important, because a lingering stalemate with the insurgency would be likely to spur greater popular disaffection.

Another approach to the question of Afghanistan's prospects takes a broader and longer-term view. Observers from this school of thought point to thirty years of war, occupation, displacement and chaos that have destroyed Afghanistan's infrastructure, ravaged its human capital resources, and left most of its relatively youthful population with no memories of living in a society not disrupted by conflict. Some experts caution that even if the insurgency is defeated in the near-term, it is not hard to imagine that some remnants or some later generations might draw inspiration from the current fight, and resume the attack whenever the political and security constellation seems more conducive to their success—as Afghans say, "You have the watches; we have the time." Other observers note that in comparative and historical global perspective, it is quite rare for states to achieve "stability" and "good governance", and that Afghanistan, given its relative poverty of human and natural resources, faces steep challenges and unlikely odds in aiming at those objectives. Accordingly, some senior U.S. and other international officials have urged a tempering of expectations about Afghanistan's long-term prospects.

Purpose of the Report

This report provides:

- A concise summary of the war's background, context, and early execution;
- An analytical discussion of the COIN war to date, including strategy, organization, participation, and key facets of the effort including population security, advising the Afghan National Security Forces (ANSF), counter-narcotics, reconciliation, community outreach, and civil-military coordination; and

[7] In November 2008, International Security Assistance Force Commanding General, U.S. Army General David McKiernan noted that without additional resources, it would be "a longer fight with greater sacrifices." GEN David McKiernan, Interview, Kabul, Afghanistan, November 2008.

- An analysis of major strategic and operational issues and options that the 111th Congress may wish to consider.

Background: Context and Early History of the War

Current efforts to support security, governance and development in Afghanistan take place in the aftermath of thirty grueling years of conflict and unrest, followed by OEF military operations that removed the Taliban regime and the rapid creation of a new, post-Taliban political order.

Prelude to War[8]

In December 1979, the Soviet Union invaded Afghanistan to shore up a puppet communist regime. During the 1980's, armed Afghan resistance groups known as "mujahedin" waged war against Soviet forces and the Afghan security forces that supported them.[9] During that period, the U.S. Government, through the Central Intelligence Agency (CIA), provided covert assistance to mujahedin groups, working through Pakistan's Inter-Services Intelligence Directorate (ISI).

In 1989, Soviet forces withdrew from Afghanistan, and in April 1992, the Soviet-backed Afghan regime in Kabul fell to mujahedin forces, which established a form of rule including a rotating presidency. In November 1994, the ethnically Pashtun-dominated Taliban movement led by Mullah Omar seized the city of Kandahar, in southern Afghanistan.[10] In 1996, the Taliban captured Kabul and retained control over much of the country until ousted by OEF operations in 2001. However, throughout its tenure, the Taliban continued to face armed opposition, in particular from the Northern Alliance, a loose network dominated by ethnic Tajiks and Uzbeks, primarily from northern Afghanistan. Key legacies of Afghanistan's years of civil war, conflict, and oppressive rule included the deaths of over a million

---

[8] For background see Steve Coll, *Ghost Wars: The Secret History of the CIA, Afghanistan, and Bin Laden, from the Soviet Invasion to September 10, 2001* (New York: Penguin, 2004); George Crile, *Charlie Wilson's War: The Extraordinary Story of How the Wildest Man in Congress and a Rogue CIA Agent Changed the History of our Times* (New York: Grove Press, 2003); Robert D. Kaplan, *Soldiers of God: With Islamic Warriors in Afghanistan and Pakistan* (New York: Vintage Departures, 2001); and Ahmed Rashid, *Taliban: Militant Islam, Oil and Fundamentalism in Central Asia* (New Haven, CT: Yale University Press, 2001).

[9] The plural noun "mujahedin" (singular "mujahid"), borrowed from Arabic and now used in standard English, refers to a group of Muslims waging "jihad", or "a holy war waged on behalf of Islam as a religious duty." See "jihad", Merriam-Webster Online Dictionary 2008, Merriam-Webster online, available at http://www.merriam-webster.com/dictionary/jihad; and "mujahideen," *Merriam-Webster Online Dictionary 2008*, Merriam-Webster online, available at http://www.merriam-webster.com/dictionary/mujahideen>.

[10] The term "Taliban," in Pashto, is the plural of "talib" (student), which is derived from Arabic. See "Taliban," *Merriam-Webster Online Dictionary 2008*, Merriam-Webster online, available at http://www.merriam-webster.com/dictionary/Taliban.

people, the displacement of millions more, the proliferation of available weapons, and the destruction of key institutions and infrastructure.

The proximate cause of U.S. military operations in Afghanistan was the linkage of the September 11, 2001, terrorist attacks to al Qaeda, which trained and operated under Taliban protection in Afghanistan. In an address to a joint session of Congress on September 20, 2001, President George W. Bush stated U.S. demands on the Taliban, warning: "The Taliban must act, and act immediately. They will hand over the terrorists or they will share in their fate."[11]

Major Combat Operations

On October 7, 2001, following the refusal of the Taliban regime to cease harboring al Qaeda, the U.S. Government launched military operations in Afghanistan, with the stated purpose of disrupting the use of Afghanistan as a terrorist base of operations and attacking the military capability of the Taliban regime.[12]

In contrast to the lengthy, iterative preparations that preceded the launch of Operation Iraqi Freedom, the U.S. planning process for OEF was extremely condensed. The concept of operations was based on Secretary of Defense Donald Rumsfeld's vision of defense transformation, including the idea that a heavier reliance on cutting-edge technology and precision weaponry could make possible the deployment of smaller-sized conventional ground forces.

Military operations were preceded and complemented by work by the Central Intelligence Agency (CIA) with Afghan opposition groups on the ground. Initial U.S. operations relied on the use of special operations forces (SOF) on the ground, enabled by air assets, working by, with and through indigenous partners, in particular the Northern Alliance. Many U.S. defense experts regarded the operations as an important demonstration of operational "jointness"—the ability of Military Services to work together seamlessly. The United Kingdom and Australia also deployed forces to

[11] The full list of demands included: "Deliver to United States authorities all of the leaders of Al Qaeda who hide in your land. Release all foreign nationals, including American citizens you have unjustly imprisoned. Protect foreign journalists, diplomats and aid workers in your country. Close immediately and permanently every terrorist training camp in Afghanistan, and hand over every terrorist and every person and their support structure to appropriate authorities. Give the United States full access to terrorist training camps, so we can make sure they are no longer operating." See President George W. Bush, Address to Joint Session of Congress, September 20, 2001, available at http://www.whitehouse.gov/news/releases/2001/09/20010920-8.html.

[12] See Statement by President George W. Bush, October 7, 2001, available at http://www.whitehouse.gov/news/releases/2001/10/20011007-8.html. Many observers consider that at the launch of OEF, short-term U.S. objectives—including targeting al Qaeda—together with the means to achieve them, were much more clearly articulated than any longer-term U.S. vision for Afghanistan's future, together with the approaches necessary to achieve that vision.

support the major combat phase of operations, and dozens of other countries provided basing, access and overflight permission.[13]

Military victory, including the demise of the Taliban regime, came quickly. In November 2001, the Taliban fled Kabul, and in December they left their stronghold, the southern city of Kandahar. It is generally understood that in December 2001, key al Qaeda and Taliban leaders fled across the border into Pakistan.

To fill the political void, in December 2001, in Bonn, Germany, the United Nations hosted the so-called Bonn Conference. Participants included representatives of four Afghan opposition groupings, and observers included representatives of neighboring and other key countries including the United States. The resulting Bonn Agreement created an Afghan Interim Authority to serve as the "repository of Afghan sovereignty" and outlined a political process for producing a new constitution and choosing a new Afghan government. In contrast to the model pursued in Iraq from 2003 to 2004, in Afghanistan there was no period of formal occupation in which an international authority exercised sovereignty on behalf of the Afghans.[14] To help provide security to support the fledgling new regime, in December 2001 the United Nations authorized an international force—the International Security Assistance Force (ISAF)—with a mandate to help the Afghans maintain security in Kabul and surrounding areas. The United Kingdom agreed to lead the force initially.[15]

The major combat operations phase was regarded as a quick success by its Afghan protagonists and their U.S. and other international partners, but the challenges were far from over. The new Afghan leadership faced the profound political challenge of consolidating a fractious, scarred state, with very few resources. The new leaders also faced potential violent challenges,

---

[13] The United Kingdom's publicly stated campaign objectives included bringing Osama bin Laden and other al Qaeda leaders to justice; preventing them from posing a further terrorist threat; and ensuring that Afghanistan ceased to harbor terrorists; in pursuit of the broader objective to "do everything possible to eliminate the threat posed by international terrorism." See Ministry of Defence, United Kingdom, "Defeating International Terrorism: Campaign Objectives," October 16, 2001, available at http://www.mod.uk. For a detailed discussion of the March 2002 Operation Anaconda, which included SOF and conventional forces, coalition partners, and Afghan forces, see Sean Naylor, *Not a Good Day to Die: The Untold Story of Operation Anaconda* (New York: Berkley Books, 2005). For an analysis of the lessons of Afghanistan operations for future warfighting, see Stephen Biddle, Afghanistan and the Future of Warfare: Implications for Army and Defense Policy, Carlisle, PA: Strategic Studies Institute, November 2002.

[14] In accordance with the provisions of the Bonn Agreement, a large meeting—a "loya jirga"—was held in June 2002, at which Hamid Karzai was elected head of the new Afghan Transitional Authority. A new constitution was adopted in January 2004; presidential elections, in which Karzai was elected, were held in October 2004; and National Assembly elections were held in September 2005. See the *Agreement on Provisional Arrangements in Afghanistan Pending the Re-Establishment of Permanent Government Institutions,* Bonn, December 5, 2001, available at http://www.mfa.gov.af/Documents/ImportantDoc/The%20Bonn%20Agreement.pdf.

[15] See S/RES/1386 (2001), December 20, 2001. The UK was followed by Turkey, and then Germany, see S/RES/1413 (2002), May 23, 2002, and S/RES/1444 (2002), November 27, 2002.

both from resurgent al Qaeda and Taliban leaders who were defeated but not eliminated, and from Afghan local power-brokers, strengthened by years of battle-hardened autonomy and resistance, who were displeased by the emerging post-Taliban order.

Counterinsurgency War in Afghanistan to Date

Both the security climate—including the composition, strategy, and tactics of the insurgency—and the structure and focus of international efforts designed to support the Afghan government have changed substantially since the end of the major combat operations that ousted the Taliban regime. This section describes and analyzes key developments in the counterinsurgency war in Afghanistan with an emphasis on recent trends and initiatives.

Strategy

In 2008, as international interest in, and attention to, the war in Afghanistan grew, a number of observers stressed the need for clearer or more robust strategy to guide Afghan and international efforts. "Strategy" is commonly understood to include a statement of objectives, or desired ends; the ways and means designed to achieve those ends; and the roles and responsibilities of key players in executing those ways and means.[16]

Strategy-making for Afghanistan is particularly complicated, for two main reasons. First, the range of strategic objectives is quite broad, encompassing not only security progress but also, for example, civilian capacity-building, the rule of law, counternarcotics, and economic development. Those fields, in turn, are closely linked empirically—for example, long-term development requires a relatively stable environment, and successful counternarcotics efforts must be predicated on some form of rule of law. Second, strategy-making is complicated by the range of actors providing some support to GIRoA, including NATO, the United Nations, and other international organizations, as well as individual states, each of which may have its own—or even competing sets of—interests and priorities. Military strategy, in turn, is not easily separable from broader grand strategy for Afghanistan, since security is essential for progress in other areas, and since military forces play key supporting roles in the non-security lines of operation.

[16] It is a fundamental principle of military theory that war is driven by political goals of one kind or another. The Prussian writer Carl von Clausewitz argued that policy "...will permeate all military operations, and, in so far as their violent nature will admit, it will have a continuous influence on them." Carl von Clausewitz, *On War*, translated by Michael Howard and Peter Paret (Princeton, NJ: Princeton University Press, 1976.)

NATO Strategy

At its 20th Summit, held in Bucharest, Romania, in April 2008, NATO issued a streamlined but clear strategic vision for Afghanistan. That vision established four "guiding principles": a firm and shared long-term commitment; support for enhanced Afghan leadership and responsibility; a comprehensive approach by the international community, bringing together civilian and military efforts; and increased cooperation and engagement with Afghanistan's neighbors, especially Pakistan. The document also included a "vision of success", which is essentially a statement of objectives: "extremism and terrorism will no longer pose a threat to stability; Afghan National Security Forces will be in the lead and self-sufficient; and the Afghan Government will be able to extend the reach of good governance, reconstruction, and development throughout the country to the benefit of all its citizens."[17] What the "strategic vision" did not provide in any detail was a clear articulation of the specific ways and means ISAF would use to achieve those objectives.

Arguably closing the strategy gap substantially, ISAF, in October 2008, issued a classified Joint Campaign Plan (JCP). The JCP was GEN McKiernan's guidance to the force, and it specified key assumptions, objectives, and approaches to be used to achieve those objectives. It stated that the primary goal is the "transfer of lead security responsibility" to the Afghans, which includes planning as well as conducting operations. The JCP addressed all the lines of operation (LOO) discussed in the Afghanistan Compact but underscored that NATO has the lead only for the security LOO. Importantly, the JCP framed ISAF's mission in counterinsurgency (COIN) terms—the mission includes defeating an "insurgency" and the basic approach follows the COIN logic of "shape, clear, hold, build." ISAF officials considered the use of COIN terminology a breakthrough, following years of NATO preference for framing the effort in Afghanistan in terms of stability operations.[18]

U.S. Government Strategy

The U.S. Government plays a significant leadership role in both ISAF and NATO as a whole, and thus helps shape NATO and ISAF strategy and approaches. At the same time, the United States may have national interests in Afghanistan and the region that are not shared by all ISAF contributors, and the relative priority of various interests may differ among the Allies.

As of the start of 2009, the U.S. Government had not yet published a formal strategy for Afghanistan, along the lines of the November 2005 *National*

[17] "Strategic Vision", NATO, available at http://www.nato.int/docu/pr/2008/p08-052e.html.
[18] ISAF officials, Interviews, Kabul, Afghanistan, November 2008.

Strategy for Victory in Iraq.[19] However, in the context of January 2009 confirmation hearings, key Obama Administration officials gave indications about the likely content of future U.S. strategy. Nominated to the post of Under Secretary of Defense for Policy, Michèle Flournoy stated that "our strategic objective is a stable and secure Afghanistan in which al Qaeda and the network of insurgent groups, including the Taliban, are incapable of seriously threatening the Afghan state and resurrecting a safe haven for terrorism."[20] Secretary of State Hillary Clinton indicated that President Obama's Afghanistan strategy was likely to include these elements: sending additional troops to Afghanistan; providing a "major increase" in non-military aid to Afghanistan; confronting the drug trade; and developing a coherent Pakistan policy. Furthermore, based on a policy of "more for more," aid to GIRoA would be tied to better performance.[21]

Meanwhile, CENTCOM has been conducting a 100-day comprehensive strategic review of its entire area of responsibility, including Afghanistan. For his part, GEN McKiernan, noting that the views were his own, has suggested that U.S. interests might include ensuring that Afghanistan cannot harbor terrorists; establishing a controlled Afghanistan/Pakistan border; promoting a degree of regional stability; supporting a constructive role for Iran; and encouraging some form of freedom and democracy for the Afghan people.[22] These ideas and initiatives may contribute to a new articulation of U.S. strategic objectives regarding Afghanistan early in the Obama Administration.

International Efforts: Organization and Coordination

Afghanistan, which lacks sufficient institutional, material and human resources to make substantial progress on its own, relies deeply on the international community to support the three main pillars of the counter-insurgency effort: security, governance and development. However, most practitioners and observers contend that ever since the Bonn Conference, the multi-faceted international effort has suffered from a dearth of resources in each area, and from insufficient coordination among key players and their initiatives.

The "lead nation" model of international assistance to Afghanistan was agreed to at a donors' conference held in Tokyo in early 2002. Five countries

---

[19] National Security Council, *National Strategy for Victory in Iraq*, November 2005, available at http://www.whitehouse.gov/infocus/iraq/iraq_strategy_nov2005.html.

[20] See replies to questions for the record, submitted by Under Secretary of Defense for Policy nominee to the Senate Armed Services Committee (SASC), for her January 15, 2009, confirmation hearing, available at http://armed-services.senate.gov/statemnt/2009/January/Flournoy%2001-15-09.pdf.

[21] See the replies to questions for the record, submitted by Secretary of State nominee Hillary Clinton to the Senate Foreign Relations Committee (SFRC), for her January 13, 2009, confirmation hearing, available at http://www.foreignpolicy.com/files/KerryClintonQFRs.pdf.

[22] GEN David McKiernan, Interview, Kabul, Afghanistan, November 2008.

each agreed to assume lead coordination responsibility for assistance to a single area of security-related Afghan administration: the United States for the army, Germany for the police, Italy for the judiciary, the United Kingdom for counternarcotics, and Japan for the disarmament, demobilization and reintegration (DDR) of militias.

The Afghanistan Compact, a formal statement of commitment by the Government of the Islamic Republic of Afghanistan (GIRoA) and the international community, finalized in January 2006, shifted responsibility from lead nations to Afghanistan itself. The premise was a shared Afghan and international vision of Afghanistan's future, including the commitment of the international community to "provide resources and support" to realize that vision. The Compact established three broad pillars of activity for future efforts—security; governance, the rule of law and human rights; and economic and social development. To "ensure overall strategic coordination of the implementation of the Compact," the document established the Joint Coordination and Monitoring Board (JCMB), co-chaired by a GIRoA representative and the United Nations Special Representative of the Secretary-General (UN SRSG).[23]

The UN SRSG leads the United Nations Assistance Mission in Afghanistan (UNAMA), which was established by the UN Security Council in early 2002.[24] The current UNAMA mandate confirms the UN SRSG's lead coordination role, as described by the Afghanistan Compact, but clarifies that the UN plays a stronger coordination role vis-à-vis civilian assistance efforts, than for military ones. The mandate states that the UN SRSG will "lead the international civilian efforts" to promote "... more coherent support by the international community to the Afghan Government." Concerning military efforts, the UN SRSG will work to "strengthen cooperation with ISAF at all levels."[25]

According to UN SRSG Kai Eide, one challenge the UN faces in performing its coordination function in Afghanistan is that UNAMA is under-resourced and under-staffed to play that role well.[26] An additional and more subtle challenge may be an inherent tension between, on one hand, UNAMA's mandate to coordinate international assistance efforts and help ensure that the international community speaks to GIRoA with a unified voice; and on the other hand, the UN SRSG's role as an advocate for human rights, in which capacity the UN mission may need to preserve a measure of independence from, and the option of critiquing, international military activities.

[23] See *The Afghanistan Compact: Building on Success,* London Conference on Afghanistan, London, January 31–February 1, 2006, available at http://www.nato.int/isaf/docu/epub/pdf/afghanistan_compact.pdf.

[24] See S/RES/1401 (2002), March 28, 2002. The mandate is renewed annually.

[25] See S/RES/1806 (2008), March 20, 2008, which extended the mandate of UNAMA for one year.

[26] Kai Eide, Interview, Kabul, Afghanistan, November 2008.

In late 2008, UN SRSG Eide stressed the need to preserve the perception of UNAMA's role as an "honest broker."[27]

Security Line of Operation: Organization

International military forces in Afghanistan lead support to GIRoA in the field of security—one of the three pillars of the Afghanistan Compact—and support international civilian initiatives in the other two fields, governance and development. Over time, the mandates, structure and composition of the international force presence in Afghanistan have changed significantly, as the role of NATO has increased and the character of the fight has evolved. Today, NATO leads the International Security Assistance Force (ISAF), and the United States leads the OEF coalition effort. The U.S. government contributes troops to both missions.

NATO International Security Assistance Force (ISAF)[28]

ISAF represents NATO's first significant out-of-area deployment, and it is viewed by many observers as a key test for the Alliance—a measure of both its current capabilities and its possible future relevance. On September 12, 2001, in response to the 9/11 terrorist attacks, NATO for the first time invoked Article 5 of the North Atlantic Treaty, which confirms the commitment of the allies to collective self-defense in the event of armed attack on any party to the treaty.[29] That action helped clear the way for future NATO operations in Afghanistan. On August 9, 2003, NATO assumed responsibility for the ISAF mission, which had been established by UN mandate in December 2001 and led until mid-2003 by a series of lead nations.

ISAF Stages

ISAF, initially mandated to support Afghan efforts to secure Kabul and its immediate environs, expanded its geographical scope in four stages. During Stage 1, completed on October 1, 2004, ISAF expanded to the north of Kabul, assuming responsibility for a German-led Provincial Reconstruction Team (PRT) and establishing new PRTs. In Stage 2, completed in September 2005, ISAF expanded to the west. In Stage 3, completed on July 31, 2006, ISAF assumed responsibility for southern Afghanistan. In Stage 4, completed on October 5, 2006, ISAF assumed control of U.S.-led forces in eastern Afghanistan.[30]

[27] Interviews with UNAMA and ISAF officials, Kabul, Afghanistan, November 2008.
[28] For further background, including the perspectives of key ISAF troop contributors, see CRS Report RL33627, *NATO in Afghanistan: A Test of the Transatlantic Alliance*, by Vincent Morelli and Paul Belkin.
[29] See Article 5, *The North Atlantic Treaty*, signed April 4, 1949, Washington, DC, available at http://www.nato.int/docu/basictxt/treaty.htm.
[30] See International Security Assistance Force "Placemat", dated December 1, 2008, available at http://www.nato.int/isaf/docu/epub/pdf/isaf_placemat_081201.pdf.

ISAF Mandate

The focus of ISAF efforts has been a source of contention among the Allies, many of whom agreed to contribute troops on the premise that ISAF's focus would be post-conflict stability operations. That premise may have been valid at the time of ISAF's formation, but by several years later, the security climate had changed and an organized, capable insurgency had emerged. ISAF Commanding General, U.S. Army General David McKiernan, stated in November 2008: "The fact is that we are at war in Afghanistan. It's not peacekeeping. It's not stability operations. It's not humanitarian assistance. It's war."[31] ISAF's mission statement reflects the insurgency challenge: "ISAF conducts operations in partnership with GIRoA and in coordination with OEF, UNAMA, and the international community in order to assist GIRoA to defeat the insurgency, establish a secure environment, extend viable governance, and promote development throughout Afghanistan."[32]

ISAF Phases

From the outset, NATO planned that ISAF operations in Afghanistan would have four phases. The first phase was "assessment and preparation", including initial operations only in Kabul. The second phase was ISAF's geographic expansion throughout Afghanistan, completed in 2006. The final three phases would be stabilization; transition; and redeployment. At the start of 2009, ISAF was operating in Phase III, "stabilization", and NATO officials were reportedly discussing when to announce the commencement of Phase IV, the "transition" of lead security responsibility to the Afghan National Security Forces (ANSF). Some ISAF officials have expressed the concern that an announcement that ISAF has entered "transition" could trigger a rush by some troop-contributing countries to Phase V—"redeployment". They caution that in practice, the shift from stabilization to transition is likely to vary geographically across Afghanistan as the abilities of various ANSF to execute and then lead missions increase, and to take place in fits and starts, rather than at a clear single point in time.[33]

ISAF Organization

ISAF is led by a four-star combined headquarters, based in Kabul and headed by U.S. Army General David McKiernan. NATO's North Atlantic Council provides political direction for the mission. NATO's Supreme Headquarters Allied Powers in Europe (SHAPE), based in Mons, Belgium,

[31] General David McKiernan, Atlantic Council, Washington, DC, November 18, 2008, transcript available at http://www.acus.org/event_blog/general-david-d-mckiernan-speaks-councils-commanders-series/transcript.
[32] Interviews with ISAF officials, Kabul, Afghanistan, November 2008.
[33] Interviews with ISAF officials, Kabul, Afghanistan, November 2008.

and led by Supreme Allied Commander Europe (SACEUR), U.S. Army General John Craddock, provides strategic command and control. NATO's Joint Force Command Headquarters, which is based in Brunssum, The Netherlands, and reports to SHAPE, provides "overall operational control", including many administrative responsibilities. ISAF itself, which reports to SHAPE through Joint Forces Command, exercises "in-theater operational command". This arrangement, including two levels of operational headquarters, is somewhat unusual.

In Afghanistan, ISAF oversees five contiguous Regional Commands (RC), each led by a two-star general: RC-Center, led by France; RC-North, led by Germany; RC-West, led by Italy; RC-South, under rotating lead by Canada, the Netherlands, and the United Kingdom; and RC-East, led by the United States. Troop contingents from other Allies, and from some non-NATO partners, serve under these Regional Commands.

ISAF Troop Contributions

As of January 12, 2008, ISAF included 55,100 troops from 41 countries, including Allies and non-NATO partners.[34]

From the outset, NATO has struggled to secure sufficient troop contributions for ISAF. One consideration for potential troop contributors is cost—NATO's long-standing practice, "costs lie where they fall", typically means that countries pay their own costs when they contribute troops to a mission such as Afghanistan. Another consideration is the need for domestic political support. For some countries, this may require the ability to point to progress on the ground in Afghanistan to prove that the effort can yield results. As a senior Allied officer in ISAF explained, "right now it's all bad news about Afghanistan, so we need to show that something is possible."[35]

In 2008, and particularly during preparations for the April NATO Summit held in Bucharest, Romania, the U.S. Government actively sought pledges of additional troop contributions. While the Summit yielded pledges from Allies and partners for over 2,000 non-U.S. troops, not all of those pledges have been realized, and the pledge total fell short of the requests by ISAF commanders on the ground.[36] In December 2008, the United Kingdom announced the deployment—already accomplished—until August 2009,

[34] International Security Assistance Force "Placemat" dated January 12, 2009, available at http://www.nato.int/isaf/docu/epub/pdf/isaf_placemat_090112.pdf. The Placemat, which provides troop numbers for each troop-contributing country, shows two countries with "0" troops in Afghanistan; ISAF officials explained that these countries are still declared members of the coalition but had no troops on the ground on January 12th.

[35] Interview, ISAF senior official, November 2008.

[36] Pledges included 700 additional troops from France, 500 from Georgia, 400 from Poland, and 120 from the Czech Republic, as well as additional training teams from Italy, Romania and Greece. In the wake of the Russian invasion of Georgia in August 2008, Georgia has been unable to honor its pledge. See Richard Wolf, "Troop Pledges by Allies Fall Short," *USA Today*, April 23, 2008, and Steven Lee

of an additional 300 special operations forces to serve in restive Helmand province in southern Afghanistan.[37] At the start of 2009, the UK Government was reportedly considering the temporary deployment to Afghanistan of 3,000 additional British troops.[38] ISAF's planning assumption, in early 2009, was that NATO troop contributions were likely to remain steady for the next several years.

ISAF National Caveats

From the outset, ISAF operations have been constrained by "national caveats"—restrictions that individual troop-contributing countries impose on their own forces' activities. Caveats tend to be informed by domestic political constraints—a government may consider, for example, that only by limiting its troops' activities, and hedging against taking casualties, can it guard against strong popular domestic opposition to its troop contribution. As a rule, as a rule, troop-contributing countries state their caveats explicitly; but additional constraints may surface when unanticipated requirements arise and contingents seek additional guidance from their capitals.

The nature and extent of national caveats varies greatly among ISAF participants. Senior U.S. military officials point with concern, for example, to constraints on German forces in Afghanistan, which are imposed by Germany's parliament the Bundestag. These include restrictions on German training and advisory teams that do not allow them to conduct combined offensive operations with their Afghan counterparts, and on capable German Special Operations Forces (SOF) that are "FOB-locked", that is, effectively confined to their Forward Operating Base. Not all contingents are so constrained. U.S. officials praise, for example, the 700-strong French infantry battalion that works closely with U.S. SOF and Afghan counterparts in Kapisa province, at the "north gate" into Kabul, which witnessed growing insurgent infiltration in 2008.

National caveats frustrate commanders on the ground because they inhibit commanders' freedom to apportion forces across the battlespace—to move and utilize forces freely. With caveats, the "whole" of the international force, as some observers have suggested, is less than the sum of its parts. Even more damaging, ISAF officials note, is the impact caveats can have on ISAF's relationship with Afghan National Security Forces (ANSF) counterparts.

Myers and Thom Shanker, "Pentagon Considers Adding Forces in Afghanistan to Make Up for NATO Shortfall," *The New York Times*, May 3, 2008.

[37] Michael Evans, "SAS to take on Taliban 'decapitation' mission after leaving Iraq", *London Times*, December 13, 2008; and John F. Burns, "Britain Adds 300 Soldiers to Support Afghan Force," *The New York Times*, December 16, 2008.

[38] See Richard Norton-Taylor, "Hutton Attacks European Allies Over Lack of Support in Afghanistan," *The Guardian*, January 15, 2009; and Michael Smith, "Defence Chiefs Plan to Deploy 3,000 More Troops in Helmand," The Times, December 21, 2008.

For example, ISAF advisory teams that are unable to accompany ANSF counterparts on offensive operations quickly lose both the Afghans' respect, and their own ability to shape and mentor the Afghan forces. Afghan Minister of Defense Abdul Rahim Wardak stated that ISAF training teams "don't have the same quality" as their U.S. counterparts.[39] U.S. senior military officials in Afghanistan frequently note that the ANSF appreciate their U.S. counterparts because "we drink from the same canteen."[40]

At the 20th NATO Summit, held in Bucharest, Romania, April 2–4, 2008, the Bush Administration strengthened its efforts to urge ISAF troop contributors to drop or ease their national caveats, with some success.

Coordination within NATO/ISAF

ISAF officials note that both command and control, and coordination, within the NATO mission in Afghanistan leave some room for improvement.

One challenge is ensuring a full command relationship between ISAF headquarters and the Regional Commands. In RC-South, for example, the major troop contributors—the UK, Canada, the Netherlands—are strong partners relatively unconstrained by caveats. But ISAF officials note that RC-South effectively includes four provincially-based national campaigns—Dutch, British, Canadian, and U.S.—based on the provinces in which their respective troops are deployed. Each of these ISAF countries, in turn, tends to lobby the relevant Afghan Ministers in Kabul for assistance to "its" province. The RC-South commander, ISAF officials underscore, has never been empowered to give comprehensive guidance to the other nations in that RC command. In November 2008, the new RC-South Commanding General, Major General de Kruif from the Netherlands, indicated the relatively low standard of expectations, stating: "it's not about unity of command, but about unity of effort."[41] GEN McKiernan has stressed, however, that a more closely integrated effort is necessary, not least because insurgents and tribes do not define their efforts by provincial or district boundaries.[42]

An additional challenge is information flow among ISAF participants. Senior U.S. officials at the ISAF HQ in Kabul note that they have a much clearer operational picture of eastern and southern Afghanistan, where most U.S. forces operate, than of northern and western Afghanistan.

---

[39] Minister of Defense of Afghanistan Abdul Rahim Wardak, Interview, Kabul, Afghanistan, November 2008.

[40] GEN David McKiernan and other U.S. officials, Interviews, Kabul, Afghanistan, November 2008. One additional consequence of national caveats is a tendency for U.S. troops in Afghanistan to regard ISAF with a degree of humorous skepticism—"ISAF", the line goes, stands for "I Stop At Four", or alternatively, "I Saw Americans Fighting".

[41] Major General de Kruif, Interview, Kandahar, Afghanistan, November 2008.

[42] GEN David McKiernan, Interview, Kabul, Afghanistan, November 2008.

Constraints on information flow may include the use of different—national and NATO—communications channels, linguistic barriers, and some reluctance on the part of some countries to share information perceived to be especially sensitive.

Another major challenge is maintaining situational awareness of—let alone control over—the activities of the 26 nationally-sponsored Provincial Reconstruction Teams (PRTs), which foster the ability of Afghan provincial-level officials to provide and promote governance, development and security. Officially, the military component of each PRT falls under ISAF command.[43] In practice, despite an ISAF directive that the PRT military components must report to ISAF on their activities, information flow, as of late 2008, was spotty. One senior ISAF official speculated, in late 2008, that one reason for the historical failure to comply might have been the perception that such efforts were wasted—that is, that the ISAF HQ made little use of such data and provided nothing back to the PRTs in return. The lack of a clear, shared picture of PRT activities has frustrated not only the ISAF leadership, but also Afghan and UN officials, in their efforts to apply resources strategically and effectively.[44]

In November 2008, the ISAF HQ restructured PRT oversight, to include the capability to share lessons learned and provide analytical feedback to PRTs. And in December 2008, a long-moribund Executive Steering Committee, including senior leadership from ISAF, GIRoA, and UNAMA, was reconstituted. As a result, some officials are optimistic that information flow concerning PRTs may improve in 2009.

One further challenge to full ISAF unity of command is the distinct mandate and role of the NATO Senior Civilian Representative (SCR), a position held since July 2008 by Italian Ambassador Fernando Gentilini. The SCR is the representative in Afghanistan of the NATO Secretary-General and reports regularly to the North Atlantic Council. As described by Ambassador Gentilini, the purpose is to "show that NATO is not just a military organization but that it can contribute to the political process more broadly."[45] Some ISAF senior officials view the SCR position—not necessarily any specific incumbent—as a "free agent", since the SCR is not part of ISAF, and ISAF and the SCR are not required to speak to counterparts in Afghanistan with a single NATO voice.[46]

---

43 PRTs are variously civilian- or military-led, and may include any combination of civilian and military personnel, see below.

44 Interviews with ISAF officials, Kabul, Afghanistan, November 2008. The March 2008 Report of the UN Secretary-General stressed the role of UNAMA in addressing "how to harmonize the activities of the provincial reconstruction teams." See A/62/722-S/2008/159, *The situation in Afghanistan and its implications for international peace and security, Report of the Secretary-General*, March 6, 2008.

45 Ambassador Fernando Gentilini, Interview, Kabul, Afghanistan, November 2008.

46 ISAF officials, Interviews, Kabul, Afghanistan, November 2008.

U.S. Forces in Afghanistan

The U.S. footprint in Afghanistan, and command and control arrangements for U.S. forces deployed there, have evolved over time, partly in response to the expansion of ISAF's area of responsibility to include all of Afghanistan.

U.S. Command Structure

Since major combat operations in 2001, the U.S. military has maintained a distinct special operations forces (SOF) presence in Afghanistan, reporting to U.S. Special Operations Command (SOCOM). By early 2002, some U.S. conventional forces, including a two-star U.S. Army Division Headquarters, had flowed into Afghanistan, but the footprint remained light—only one brigade combat team (BCT)—until early 2007.

In October 2003, the U.S.-led three-star Combined Forces Command-Afghanistan (CFC-A) was established in Kabul. CFC-A oversaw two U.S.-led two-star commands that also included coalition partners—a training command for the ANSF, and a Combined Joint Task Force (CJTF) of conventional forces in eastern Afghanistan. CFC-A served until ISAF assumed security responsibility for all of Afghanistan, and was then deactivated, in February 2007. Following the deactivation of CFC-A, its subordinate ANSF training command, the Combined Security Transition Command-Afghanistan (CSTC-A), began reporting directly to U.S. Central Command (CENTCOM), and its subordinate CJTF assumed a dual U.S./NATO reporting chain, to CENTCOM for U.S. issues and to ISAF in its NATO capacity as RC-East. In October 2008, the Department of Defense activated United States Forces-Afghanistan (USFOR-A), a new four-star headquarters designed to streamline command and control for U.S. forces operating in Afghanistan. ISAF Commanding General GEN McKiernan was given the additional assignment of serving as the USFOR-A Commanding General. As the head of ISAF, GEN McKiernan reports up the NATO chain of command to SACEUR GEN John Craddock; as the head of USFOR-A, he reports to the Commanding General of CENTCOM, GEN David Petraeus.

U.S. Force Levels

As of December 10, 2008, the United States had 36,234 total forces deployed in Afghanistan, including 22,658 in ISAF, and 13,576 in USFOR-A. The USFOR-A forces included CSTC-A. The ISAF forces included the 101st Airborne Division Headquarters, serving as the RC-East HQ, plus two BCTs and an aviation brigade.

The December 2008 numbers marked a significant increase from two years earlier, in December 2006, when U.S. forces in Afghanistan included only one BCT. In early 2007, an additional BCT was added, by extending the tour of the 3rd BCT, 10th Mountain Division (3/10) by 120 days, flowing in its original replacement, 4th BCT, 82nd Airborne Division, on schedule, and later replacing 3/10 with the 173rd Airborne BCT.[47] In January 2008, the Department of Defense announced that President Bush had approved an "extraordinary, one-time" deployment of 3,200 additional Marines to Afghanistan.[48] Those forces included the 24th Marine Expeditionary Unit (MEU), which served as a combat force in southern Afghanistan, and the 2nd Battalion, 7th Marine Regiment (2/7) who served as advisors for the ANSF. Both units redeployed in November 2008, but a Marine Air Ground Task Force (MAGTF), including 3rd Battalion, 8th Marine Regiment, plus additional logistics and air support, deployed to southern Afghanistan in November 2008 to serve both as battlespace owners—responsible for security in a given area of operations—and as ANSF advisors.

In 2008, GEN McKiernan requested significant additional forces to serve in RC-East and RC-South. The first result was the deployment of the 3rd BCT, 10th Mountain Division, in January 2009. That brigade is serving in Wardak and Logar provinces, marking the southern entrances to Kabul, which witnessed growing insurgent infiltration and activity in 2008.

For RC-South, GEN McKiernan requested a U.S. force package similar to the one in RC-East—that is, three BCTs (or equivalents), an aviation brigade, and key enablers including engineers. He has argued that in southern Afghanistan, sufficient international and Afghan security forces are simply not available to "provide for adequate security for the people."[49] U.S. military officials in Afghanistan noted in late 2008 that some areas of southern Afghanistan contained known security challenges that still needed to be addressed—these included Kandahar city, and a part of Garmsir District in Helmand province known as the "fish hook" and long used by insurgents as a base of operations. Other areas, including Nimroz province, were "unknowns" given the lack of international and Afghan forces deployed there. Further areas simply had too few forces to fully clear and hold them—for example, when ISAF assumed responsibility for southern Afghanistan, Romanian forces replaced U.S. forces in Zabul province, but the Romanians had been prepared to conduct stability, not counterinsurgency, operations.[50]

The Department of Defense approved the request for some additional forces, pending their availability. On a visit to Afghanistan in December

[47] See Matthew Cox, "10th Mountain Brigade Extended in Afghanistan," *Army Times*, January 25, 2007.
[48] See Ann Scott Tyson, "3,200 Marines to Deploy to Afghanistan in Spring," *Washington Post*, January 16, 2008.
[49] GEN David McKiernan, Atlantic Council, Washington, DC, November 18, 2008, transcript available at http://www.acus.org/event_blog/general-david-d-mckiernan-speaks-councils-commanders-series/transcript.
[50] Interviews with ISAF officials, Kabul and Kandahar, Afghanistan, November 2008.

2008, Secretary of Defense Robert Gates stated that the Department of Defense (DoD) hopes to send an additional two BCTs by late spring 2009.[51] Those additional forces, according to U.S. commanders in Afghanistan, are expected to flow primarily into Kandahar, Helmand, and Zabul provinces.[52]

U.S. Leadership

In addition to the need for additional U.S. forces, GEN McKiernan and other U.S. commanders have stressed the need for additional U.S. leadership in southern Afghanistan, to help synchronize and strengthen ISAF efforts. "Without U.S. leadership," GEN McKiernan stated in late 2008, "we will not break out of the stalemate in the south."[53] In November 2008, a new billet—a Deputy Commanding General for Stability—was created at RC-South and filled by a U.S. Army Brigadier General. The United States is reportedly scheduled to take command of RC-South in 2010.[54]

Key Enablers

U.S. commanders and officials in Afghanistan stress the need for sufficient enablers to support the growing force. Engineers are critical, they underscore, to support both the construction of any additional defense infrastructure required by the deployment of additional forces, and to play a supporting role in reconstruction efforts.

Aviation is critical for both combat operations and also—especially—for air mobility in a country whose lack of infrastructure and forbidding terrain severely limit the utility of ground transportation. Helicopters, GEN McKiernan has stated, are ISAF's "trucks, our horses", for moving around the battlespace.[55] Ground vehicles, in turn, must be well-suited for their proposed use on Afghanistan's rugged terrain. Some U.S. troops have reportedly found that Mine-Resistant Ambush-Protected (MRAP) armored fighting vehicles, which have provided life-saving protection against improvised explosive devices (IEDs) in Iraq, are less well-suited to Afghanistan's unpaved roads and off-road requirements.[56]

Current Intelligence, Surveillance and Reconnaissance (ISR) assets are, according to one U.S. commander, "not even in the ballpark", and, according

---

[51] Secretary of Defense Robert Gates, Media Availability with Secretary Gates From Kandahar, Afghanistan, DoD News Transcript, December 11, 2008, available at http://www.defenselink.mil/transcripts/transcript.aspx?transcriptid=4331.

[52] ISAF officials, Interviews, Kabul and Kandahar, November 2008.

[53] GEN David McKiernan, Interview, Kabul, Afghanistan, November 2008.

[54] Gordon Lubold, "NATO Extends Afghanistan Tours," *Christian Science Monitor*, May 22, 2008.

[55] GEN David McKiernan, Interview, Kabul, Afghanistan, November 2008.

[56] See Nancy A. Youssef, "U.S. Marines Find Iraq Tactics Don't Work in Afghanistan," McClatchy Newspapers, January 11, 2009. For background on MRAPs, see CRS Report RS22707, *Mine-Resistant, Ambush-Protected (MRAP) Vehicles: Background and Issues for Congress*, by Andrew Feickert.

to a senior ISAF official, ground units "are screaming for more assets."[57] A former U.S. battalion commander in Afghanistan argued after his tour, "As a rule, each battalion-sized task force should have constant unmanned aerial vehicle and close-air-support coverage."[58] In 2008, Secretary Gates, recognizing a need to provide troops in the field with improved ISR assets, formed an ISR task force to assess requirements and speed the process of meeting warfighter needs.[59] A CENTCOM ISR Task Force is in the process of providing additional personnel and assets for U.S. forces in Afghanistan, but the impact may not become apparent until later in 2009.

Language capability is also essential, in order to support the ability of U.S. forces to follow the key counterinsurgency injunction to live with the population, and requirements will grow proportionally with increases in U.S. ground forces in Afghanistan. The need is complicated by the fact that Afghanistan's two official languages—Dari and Pashto—are not mutually intelligible, and many Afghans know one but not the other. One option is to utilize U.S. servicemembers with local language ability, but such troops may be in short supply. Dari and Pashto are regarded as difficult languages to learn, requiring time to develop the ability to communicate in either of them on substantive matters. Another option is to utilize Afghan interpreters. One challenge is that, in addition to the general challenge of sufficient supply, Afghan languages vary from region to region; in some situations, a non-local Afghan interpreter might be understood but nevertheless regarded with some suspicion as an outsider. Variations in regional dialect English-language instruction now available to members of the Afghan National Security Forces might also ease some mil-to-mil communication barriers, but will not directly help U.S. forces communicate with local populations.

Legal Basis for Presence of International Forces

Two separate sets of arrangements are in place, for ISAF and for U.S. forces deployed under U.S. command, to provide a legal basis for the presence of those forces in Afghanistan.

Legal Basis for U.S. Forces

In 2002 and 2003, U.S. Embassy Kabul and the Afghan Ministry for Foreign Affairs exchanged diplomatic notes, which together constituted

[57] TF Currahee and ISAF officials, Interviews, Khowst province and Kabul, Afghanistan, November 2008. Under GEN McKiernan's predecessor, ISAF went from two to four Predator lines.

[58] Christopher D. Kolenda, "How to Win in Afghanistan," *Weekly Standard*, October 13, 2008.

[59] See Secretary of Defense Robert Gates, Remarks, Air War College, Maxwell Air Force Base, Alabama, April 21, 2008, available at http://www.defenselink.mil/speeches/speech.aspx?speechid=1231. Secretary Gates said: "My concern is that our services are still not moving aggressively in wartime to provide resources needed now on the battlefield. I've been wrestling for months to get more intelligence, surveillance, and reconnaissance assets into the theatre. . . . While we've doubled this capability in recent months, it is still not good enough."

a formal agreement. The notes, which remain in force, confirmed that military and civilian personnel of the Department of Defense shall be accorded a status equivalent to that of Embassy administrative and technical staff under the 1961 Vienna Convention on Diplomatic Relations. The notes also addressed freedom of movement, licenses, the wearing of uniforms, the use of vehicles, exemption from taxation, and imports and exports. They confirmed U.S. criminal jurisdiction over U.S. personnel.[60]

Some of the basic provisions of that exchange of notes were reconfirmed by a joint declaration signed by President Karzai and President Bush, in May 2005, in which the two countries committed themselves to a strategic partnership with the goal of "strengthen[ing] U.S.-Afghan ties to help ensure Afghanistan's long-term security, democracy and prosperity." The Declaration confirmed the bilateral intent to work together closely on a range of activities including, in the security sector: ANSF training, security sector reform, counterterrorism operations, counternarcotics programs, intelligence-sharing, border security, and strengthening ties with NATO. The Declaration included the specific, practical commitment that U.S. military forces operating in Afghanistan would continue to have access to Bagram Air Base "and facilities at other locations as may be mutually determined," and that U.S. and coalition forces would continue to enjoy freedom of action to conduct military operations "based on consultations and pre-agreed procedures."[61]

Legal Basis for ISAF Forces

United Nations Security Council Resolutions (UNSCR) provide the legal basis for the presence of ISAF forces in Afghanistan. A December 2001 UNSCR authorized, under Chapter VII of the United Nations Charter, the establishment of ISAF to "assist . . . in the maintenance of security in Kabul and its surrounding areas."[62] That mandate was based on a specific appeal for such a force included in the December 2001 Bonn Agreement.[63]

---

[60] See "Diplomatic Note No.202," Embassy of the United States of America, Kabul, Afghanistan, September 26, 2002; "Note, Document No.791", Transitional Islamic State of Afghanistan, Ministry of Foreign Affairs, Fifth Political Department, December 12, 2002; and "Note, Document No.93", Transitional Islamic State of Afghanistan, Ministry of Foreign Affairs, American and Canada Political Affairs Department, May 28, 2003. See also Karen DeYoung, "Only a Two-Page 'Note' Governs U.S. Military in Afghanistan," *Washington Post*, August 28, 2008.

[61] See Joint Declaration of the United States-Afghanistan Strategic Partnership, May 23, 2005, available at available at http://www.whitehouse.gov/news/releases/2005/05/20050523-2.html.

[62] S/RES/1386 (2001), December 20, 2001.

[63] See Annex I, "International Security Force," *Agreement on Provisional Arrangements in Afghanistan Pending the Re-Establishment of Permanent Government Institutions*, Bonn, Germany, December 5, 2001, available at http://www.mfa.gov.af/Documents/ImportantDoc/The%20Bonn%20Agreement.pdf. The Agreement states: "This force will assist in the maintenance of security for Kabul and its surrounding areas. Such a force could, as appropriate, be progressively expanded to other urban centers and areas."

In January 2002, the Interim Authority of Afghanistan signed a Military Technical Agreement with the newly formed ISAF.

In October 2003, the UN Security Council authorized an expansion of the ISAF mandate to include supporting GIRoA in maintaining security outside Kabul and its environs, and providing security to support the accomplishment of other objectives outlined in the Bonn Agreement.[64] The current UN mandate extends the authorization of ISAF for a period of 12 months beyond October 13, 2008.[65]

GIRoA Concerns

Over time, the Afghan leadership has expressed interest in making sure that ISAF- and U.S.-led forces coordinate their operations with the ANSF and with each other. For example, the 2006 Afghanistan Compact, the basic framework for international community engagement in Afghanistan in all sectors, states that all "OEF counter-terrorism operations will be conducted in close coordination with the Afghan Government and ISAF."[66]

In August 2008, President Karzai called for a review of the presence of all foreign forces in Afghanistan and the conclusion of formal status of forces agreements.[67] He issued the call during the heated U.S.-Iraqi negotiation process aimed at achieving a status of forces-like agreement, and just after U.S. airstrikes in Azizabad, Afghanistan, had apparently produced a number of civilian casualties. In January 2009, GIRoA reportedly sent a proposed draft agreement to NATO, which outlined terms and conditions for the presence of NATO forces in Afghanistan.[68]

Security Situation

The year 2008 witnessed an increase in security incidents that led some observers to argue that the insurgency was gaining ground—that the Taliban was "winning"—while others argued instead that insurgent tactics were evolving. The insurgency remained a loose and sometimes internally fractious network of Afghans, supported by some outside help including the availability of safe haven across the border in Pakistan.

64 S/RES/1510 (2003), October 13, 2003.
65 UNSCR 1833 (2008), Sept 22, 2008.
66 *The Afghanistan Compact: Building on Success*, London Conference on Afghanistan, London, UK, February 1, 2006, available at http://www.nato.int/isaf/docu/epub/pdf/afghanistan_compact.pdf.
67 See Karen DeYoung, "Only a Two-Page 'Note' Governs U.S. Military in Afghanistan," *Washington Post*, August 28, 2008.
68 See Associated Press, "Afghanistan Seeks More Control of NATO Troops," *Los Angeles Times*, January 21, 2009.

Security Trends: Characterization

In general, the security climate in Afghanistan has tended to follow cyclical patterns, based on the seasons. The spring poppy harvest season draws some workers-for-hire away from the insurgency; insurgent leaders, who profit from the poppy crop, support this pattern. The forbidding winter cold makes movement and many activities harder, and usually finds some insurgents recuperating across the border in Pakistan. The warmer spring weather provides an opportunity for insurgents to attempt operations. Given the cyclical patterns, changes in security trends are best evaluated by year-to-year rather than month-to-month comparisons.

Recent years, by all accounts, have witnessed an upswing in security incidents. Many practitioners date the growing violence from mid-2006, when NATO assumed security responsibility first for southern, and then for eastern Afghanistan. Minister of Defense Wardak, for example, noted that in 2006 the insurgents "came on in a big way," and suggested that their intent had been to weaken political will in NATO capitals.[69]

ISAF officials note that from 2007 to 2008, there was a 33% increase in the overall number of kinetic events. ISAF defines "kinetic" events to include attacks against Afghan or international forces, whether by improvised explosive device (IED), indirect fire, or direct fire; but not, for example, kidnappings or intimidation. IED events, the single largest cause of casualties, increased by 27%. In addition, attacks on GIRoA officials and facilities increased by 119%. Afghan civilian deaths, in turn, increased by between 40 and 46%.[70]

Anecdotally, mid-2008 witnessed several insurgent attacks that prompted significant international attention. On July 13, 2008, in Konar province, nine U.S. soldiers were killed when their temporary outpost was attacked by 150 or more insurgents. On August 18, 2008, Forward Operating Base (FOB) Salerno in Khowst province was attacked by suicide bombers, killing Afghan civilians. Also on August 18, a large organized group of insurgents ambushed French forces in Kabul province, killing ten.[71]

Security Trends: Evaluation

These developments led some observers to conclude that the balance had tipped in favor of the insurgency. A study by the Paris-based International

69 Minister of Defense of Afghanistan Abdul Rahim Wardak, Interview, Kabul, Afghanistan, November 2008.

70 "Metrics Brief 2007–2008," International Security Assistance Force, January 2009. The range for Afghan civilian deaths reflects differences between ISAF and UNAMA data collection. UNAMA figures reflect a lower percentage increase, but higher absolute numbers of deaths. ISAF explains that UNAMA's capacity to investigate and verify reports, *inter alia* to prevent duplication, is more limited than ISAF's, ISAF official, personal communication, January 2009.

71 See James Kitfield, "Progress in Afghanistan Gets Rockier," *National Journal*, September 15, 2008.

Council on Security and Development, released in December 2008, concluded that ". . . the Taliban has been experiencing a renaissance that has gained momentum since 2005. The West is in genuine danger of losing Afghanistan."[72] In a December 2008 Op-Ed, former head of UNAMA Lakhdar Brahimi wrote: "The [Afghan] government is losing ground every day to insurgents and other outlaws who now control at least a third of the country."[73] After embedding with Taliban fighters, journalist Nir Rosen concluded that the Taliban was winning.[74]

ISAF officials explain the increased number of security incidents somewhat differently. They point out that the growing presence of "friendly" forces, including international troops and Afghan forces—including 11 new Afghan National Army battalions and 10,000 more ISAF troops, from November 2007 to November 2008—allowed the conduct of more operations, and thus more contact with the enemy. They add that deteriorating control of the border areas of Pakistan provided insurgents with additional safe haven opportunities.[75]

ISAF commanders also stress the importance of evaluating insurgent attacks qualitatively, as well as quantitatively. By late summer 2008, under pressure from international and ANSF operations, insurgents abandoned large-scale, relatively conventional-style attacks, because they were suffering heavy losses. Insurgent groups moved instead toward small-unit operations, applying more asymmetrical and more sophisticated tactics. These included attacks on key lines of communication (LOCs) including roads and bridges, more use of IEDs, assassination attempts against Afghan civilian and military officials, and attacks against government facilities such as district centers and schools. Insurgents, officials suggest, are "getting more effective" at these asymmetric activities. The specific impact of insurgent targeting of LOCs is hard to measure, ISAF officials note, since no systematic measure is made of highway traffic.[76]

---

[72] See Yochi Dreazen, "Taliban Expanding Foothold in Afghanistan, Report Finds," *Wall Street Journal*, December 8, 2008.

[73] Lakhdar Brahimi, "A New Path for Afghanistan," *Washington Post*, December 7, 2008.

[74] Nir Rosen, "How We Lost the War We Won," *Rolling Stone*, October 30, 2008. Rosen appeared to reach the conclusion that the Taliban was winning in part because they told him so; for example, one of his hosts noted, "From now on, it's all Taliban territory—the Americans and police don't come here at night." Of course, the same methodological questions, concerning reliance on the statements of one's informants, could also be applied to field interviews with "friendly" forces. Rosen's article also prompted some debate concerning the ethics of embedding with insurgent forces. See also Paul Watson, "Behind the Lines with the Taliban," *Los Angeles Times*, January 11, 2009. Watson, who briefly embedded with Taliban fighters in Ghazni province south of Kabul, concluded that the area was "Taliban country" where the Taliban were in charge. He quotes one fighter as saying, "Police and soldiers can never come to our territory. If they do, they won't go back safe and sound."

[75] GEN David McKiernan and other ISAF officials, Interviews, Kabul, Afghanistan, November 2008.

[76] See GEN David McKiernan, Atlantic Council, Washington, DC, November 18, 2008, transcript available at http://www.acus.org/event_blog/general-david-d-mckiernan-speaks-councils-commanders-series/transcript; and MG Robert Cone, DoD Press Briefing, November 12, 2008, available at http://www.defenselink.mil/transcripts/transcript.aspx?transcriptid=4314. Also, U.S. commanders, Interviews, November 2008.

At the same time, ISAF officials assess that the Taliban and other insurgents, while gaining some greater tactical facility, are not guided by a single, coherent strategy—the leadership does not appear to be formulating and directing an overall master plan.[77]

At the end of 2008, senior officials in Afghanistan tended to hedge their bets when describing the security climate. UN SRSG Kai Eide noted: "We haven't lost . . . but we haven't won . . ."[78] A senior U.S. military official described it this way: "We're winning the fight, but not the war".[79] Some COIN theorists argue, in turn, that such uncertainty is not neutral—that in a COIN fight, "not winning" is tantamount to losing.

Characterizing the Insurgency[80]

While many observers use the term "Taliban" as a short-hand for the insurgency in Afghanistan, senior western officials in Afghanistan stress that the insurgency is not unified. ISAF prefers the term "insurgent syndicate" to refer collectively to all its various strands. Further, insurgent activities are closely linked with criminality, always a potent force in ungoverned spaces, and in particular with drug cultivation and sales.

Taliban

The Taliban itself, Afghan and ISAF officials note, is more a network than a single organization.[81] The Taliban emerged from the Afghan civil war of the early and mid-1990's, and the organization ruled Afghanistan from its capture of Kabul in 1996 until its defeat in 2001. Mullah Mohammed Omar, the *de facto* head of state during Taliban rule, is generally assumed to be alive and leading the organization from Pakistan. In December 2008, for example, he reportedly issued new threats over the Internet against international forces in Afghanistan.[82] The Taliban leadership includes two main "shuras" (councils)—a leadership council in Quetta, Pakistan, under Mullah Omar's watch, and another shura based in Peshawar, Pakistan.[83] The Taliban reportedly receives support from some current and/or former

[77] ISAF officials, Interviews, Kabul, Afghanistan, November 2008. GEN McKiernan added that overall, the Taliban is "less than the sum of its parts."

[78] UN SRSG Kai Eide, Interview, Kabul, Afghanistan, November 2008.

[79] U.S. military official, Interview, Kabul, Afghanistan, November 2008.

[80] For background about insurgent groups in Afghanistan, see Seth G. Jones, *Counterinsurgency in Afghanistan*, (Santa Monica, CA: RAND Corporation, 2008).

[81] On the Taliban in general, see Major Shahid Afsar, Pakistan Army, Major Chris Samples, U.S. Army, and Major Thomas Wood, U.S. Army, "The Taliban: An Organizational Analysis," *Military Review*, vo. 88, no. 3 (May–June 2008).

[82] Reuters, "Taliban's Murderous Mullah Threatens West", *New York Post*, December 8, 2008.

[83] See Mohammad Masoom Stanekzai, "Thwarting Afghanistan's Insurgency: A Pragmatic Approach toward Peace and Reconciliation", United States Institute of Peace, September 2008. Stanekzai, who held a fellowship at the U.S. Institute of Peace, was previously a senior GIRoA official.

Pakistani officials, including members of the Inter-Services Intelligence Directorate (ISI), in the form of logistics, medical, and training assistance.[84]

Haqqani Network

The Haqqani network is closely associated with the Taliban and one of its strongest factions. Reportedly, the network is also particularly closely linked to al Qaeda. Jalaluddin Haqqani fought as a mujahedin leader against Soviet forces, receiving substantial assistance from the CIA by way of Pakistan's ISI.[85] When the Taliban came to power, he joined the government as a Minister but retained a separate power base in his home Zadran district and tribe, east of Kabul. His son Sirajudin has reportedly ascended to a key leadership role, and has reportedly called for changes in the leadership of the Quetta shura. U.S. officials in Afghanistan note that Sirajudin, like his father, has focused on his home Zadran district but has also expanded his activities into the areas south of Kabul.

Hezb-i-Islami Gulbuddin (HiG)

Gulbuddin Hekmatyar was a key mujahedin leader against Soviet forces. His organization, then known as the Hezb-e-Islami, received substantial aid from the U.S. Government, which reportedly considered him a key ally. He twice held the title of Prime Minister during the early 1990's civil war period, before seeking refuge in Iran when the Taliban came to power. He has reemerged in Afghanistan as the leader of the insurgent group, Hezb-i-Islami Gulbuddin (HiG), which is affiliated with both the Taliban and al Qaeda. In 2008, Hekmatyar apparently opened the door to talks with GIRoA, in part through a spring 2008 letter addressed to President Karzai. Some practitioners and observers suggest that there may be good potential for drawing Hekmatyar away from the insurgent fight and into a constructive role.[86] Others caution that his reputation for Islamic extremism and human rights abuses call into question the likelihood and advisability of any reconciliation with him.

Foreign Groups

Foreign groups play critical roles in the insurgency by variously supporting and enabling Afghan insurgents.[87]

---

[84] See Seth G. Jones, *Counterinsurgency in Afghanistan,* (Santa Monica, CA: RAND Corporation, 2008).

[85] For background about Haqqani, see Jay Solomon, "Troubled Border: Failed Courtship of Warlord Trips up U.S. in Afghanistan," *The Wall Street Journal,* November 8, 2007.

[86] ISAF senior officials, Interviews, Kabul, Afghanistan, November 2008. See Anna Mulrine, "Afghan Warlords, Formerly Backed by the CIA, Now Turn their Guns on U.S. Troops," *U.S. News and World Report,* July 11, 2008.

[87] For a concise discussion of Afghan insurgent groups and foreign groups supporting the insurgency, see Mohammad Masoom Stanekzai, "Thwarting Afghanistan's Insurgency: A Pragmatic Approach toward Peace and Reconciliation", United States Institute of Peace, September 2008.

Al Qaeda, which both enabled and leveraged the Taliban during its years in power, reportedly mobilizes foreign fighters from the Arab world, Chechnya, Uzbekistan, and other locations, to join the fight in Afghanistan.

Tehrik Taliban-i Pakistan (TTiP) is an umbrella organization for indigenous Pakistani Taliban commanders, based in Pakistan, in the Federally Administered Tribal Areas (FATA) along the border with Afghanistan. TTiP is led by Baitullah Mahsud, who is from South Waziristan in the FATA, and who has reportedly built up strongholds in North and South Waziristan by recruiting and training young men, and "killing uncooperative tribal leaders."[88]

Lashkar-e-Tayba, a Pakistani insurgent group originally focused on the disputed Kashmir region, reportedly cuts its insurgent teeth along the border with Afghanistan by training insurgents to fight there.

Tehrik Nefaz-e Shariat Mohammadi (TNSM) is a Pakistani insurgent group based primarily in the Northwest Frontier Province next to the FATA. Focused primarily on deepening its local control, the TNSM has also supported some Taliban operations in Afghanistan.[89]

Popular Support for the Insurgency?

The population is the center of gravity—the primary focus—in counterinsurgency operations. Evaluating a population's support, tacit as well as active, for an insurgency, as well as its perceptions of the fight, is one helpful tool for assessing the strength of that insurgency.

In general, it is common for insurgents to try to shape popular perceptions. Some experts argue that in 2008 in Afghanistan, the Taliban and other insurgents used high-profile attacks in and near Kabul to sow fear, or create a "sense of siege."[90] Those attacks included, among others, a strike against the opulent and popular Serena Hotel in January, an assassination attempt against President Karzai in April, a bombing at the Indian Embassy in July, and the kidnapping of International Rescue Committee workers in August.

Meanwhile, in late 2008, ISAF officials assessed that active Afghan popular support for the Taliban and other insurgents was not increasing—not least because the Taliban's ideology had little appeal for most Afghans. At the

[88] See Jane Perlez, "Taliban Leader Flaunts Power Inside Pakistan," *The New York Times*, June 2, 2008; "Tribal tribulations: The Pakistani Taliban in Waziristan," *Jane's Intelligence Review*, January 13, 2009; and "Tehrik-e-Taliban Pakistan", *Jane's Terrorism and Insurgency Centre*, January 13, 2009.

[89] See Rahimullah Yusufzai, "The emergence of the Pakistani Taliban," *Jane's Terrorism and Insurgency Centre*, December 11, 2007.

[90] James Kitfield, "Progress in Afghanistan gets rockier," *National Journal*, September 15, 2008. See also Sami Yousafzai and Ron Moreau, "The Taliban's Baghdad Strategy," *Newsweek*, August 4, 2008. The article cites a "senior Taliban intelligence operative in Pakistan" as stating that by focusing on Kabul "we can create panic and undermine the last vestiges of support for the regime."

same time, ISAF assessed that popular support was shifting away from the Government of Afghanistan toward "fence-sitting", driven by frustrations with poor governance, lack of economic progress, corruption, and lack of security. COIN theory underscores the importance of at least tacit popular support for the government—that popular neutrality is insufficient to defeat an insurgency.

COIN Operations

At least as important to the success of the counterinsurgency as the number of Afghan and international security forces, experts argue, is what those forces actually do. As a rule, counterinsurgencies share an emphasis on "population security", but circumstances, and therefore the most effective approaches, may vary widely from one COIN campaign to another, or even geographically or temporally within a given COIN campaign.[91] In Afghanistan, COIN efforts have been challenged by especially rugged terrain, by limited forces and resources, and by the need to gain sufficient understanding of local areas to develop situation-specific approaches.

Shape, Clear, Hold, Build

In Afghanistan, COIN terminology, if not yet practice, has become a lingua franca shared by Afghan and international practitioners. The basic tenet of COIN operations in Afghanistan, borrowed and adapted from Vietnam and more recently Iraq, is "shape, clear, hold, build." In general, that approach includes working closely with Afghan counterparts to target insurgents, kinetically if so required; using Afghan or if necessary international security forces to hold an area once it is cleared; and applying coordinated civil-military efforts to begin building institutions and services once the security landscape in an area so permits.

COIN efforts in Konar province in eastern Afghanistan, along the border with Pakistan, are frequently presented as an instructive model of coordinated civil-military action. There, a U.S. Army battalion working with a very capable Afghan National Army (ANA) unit first cleared the area, and then established outposts to provide presence. U.S. forces, supported by a Provincial Reconstruction Team, then negotiated deals with local tribal shuras—if the shuras would provide security, they would receive economic development "in the form of roads, bridges, schools and health clinics." Central to the approach was the construction of a paved road—a rarity outside big cities in Afghanistan—in which local residents had a vested interest.

[91] GEN David Petraeus, U.S. CENTCOM Commanding General, recently stated, "Every case is unique.... While general concepts that proved important in Iraq may be applicable to Afghanistan.... the application of those 'big ideas ' has to be adapted to Afghanistan." GEN David Petraeus, Interview, *Foreign Policy*, (January/ February 2009), available at http://www.foreignpolicy.com/story/cms.php?story_id=4587.

The road gave forces the access they needed to secure village populations, it made it harder for insurgents to emplace IEDs, it gave civilian assistance agencies freedom of movement, and it gave local residents a critical tool to support economic development. The U.S. Commanders Emergency Response Program (CERP) funded payments to locals to provide security for the road.[92]

Practitioners stress, however, that there is no cookie-cutter model for COIN in Afghanistan—roads, for example, cannot always play the role they did in Konar province. In mid-2008, insurgents stepped up their attacks against Afghanistan's major road arteries, include Highway 1 that connects Kabul with Kandahar. Officials speculated that the insurgents attacking the highway in Zabul wanted to tie up the ANA and other forces, forcing them to build check points and leaving them fewer resources to focus on insurgent strongholds. In southern Zabul province, along the Highway 1 artery, military and civilian officials wondered if the "Konar model" approach to roads might be applicable. What they discovered, however, is that roads served a different function in Zabul—the highway was used primarily by inter-state truck drivers and the insurgents themselves, while local residents required only some passable means for getting to and from local markets. In other words, local residents did not perceive that they had the same, strong vested interest in the security of the main highway as residents of Konar province had in their own road.

Operations by the U.S. Marines in 2008, in the town of Garmsir, in southern Helmand Province, also reflected some key COIN approaches including an emphasis on population security, close cooperation with local security forces, the use of both kinetic and soft tools, and the incorporation of civilian resources. By the time operations commenced in April 2008, Garmsir had become a key insurgent transit and logistics hub, and much of the local population had withdrawn. The action began with a large-scale aerial insertion, followed by a month of clearing and fighting against small but tenacious and well dug-in insurgent groups. As the insurgents were defeated in a given area, the local population began to return, and the Marines increased their focus on population security, including the use of "gated communities" for population control, and reaching out to community leaders. As the fighting wound down, the ANSF joined the Marines on patrols to provide presence and "hold" the area. In fall 2008, the Marines handed security responsibility for the Garmsir area over to UK counterparts and the ANA, to continue the "hold" mission. From the planning stages onward, the Marines worked with the U.S. Agency for International

[92] See David Kilcullen, "Road-Building in Afghanistan: Part 1 of a Series on Political Maneuver in Counterinsurgency," *Small Wars Journal*, April 24, 2008, available at http://smallwarsjournal.com/blog/2008/04/political-maneuver-in-counteri/; and David Ignatius, "Building Bridges in the Back of Beyond," *Washington Post*, May 1, 2008.

Development, asking, "What do we want this to look like, afterwards?" The AID representative working with the 24th MEU was ready to initiate projects as soon as the security situation so allowed.[93]

ISAF commanders stress that through 2008, insufficient international and Afghan forces were available to shape, clear, hold, and build effectively throughout Afghanistan. The ISAF 2009 winter campaign, for example, conducted in selected districts chosen to include the majority of the Afghan population, aimed to "hold" ground and deepen security there, without significantly expanding GIRoA's control geographically.

Living Among the Population

As a rule, the center of any counterinsurgency is the population, and living among the population is a central tenet of COIN. As CENTCOM Commanding General, General David Petraeus, and many others have stressed, "You don't commute to work."[94] Senior officials at U.S.-led RC-East noted that as of November 2008, RC-East had between 130 and 140 combat outposts (COPs) in their area of responsibility (AOR)— "We're really out with the people." Most of those COPs were co-located with ANA counterparts or supported nearby Afghan observation posts, although a few were U.S.-only.[95]

For some Allies, constrained by national caveats, the premise of living among the population is a challenge. The idea is generally understood to mean getting outside the wire and interacting with the population as much as possible, not merely living adjacent to it. Allied forces that are largely confined to forward operating bases (FOBs) cannot follow the approach.

For ISAF in general, a major constraint on living with the population has been insufficient international forces. As one commander argued, "The strategy doesn't work when you don't have enough forces to do it."[96] Writing about U.S. efforts in both Afghanistan and Iraq, leading defense expert Colonel H.R. McMaster noted: "Decisions against deploying coalition forces in numbers sufficient to secure populations left many commanders with no other option than to adopt a raiding approach to counterinsurgency operations—an approach that tended to reinforce the perception of coalition forces as aggressors and conflated tactical successes with actual measures of strategic effectiveness."[97]

It might seem that by scaling back the size of the force presence at each outpost, the number of outposts could be increased and the overall

---

[93] 24th MEU officials, Interviews, Kandahar, Afghanistan, November 2008.
[94] See for example GEN David Petraeus, COIN Guidance, Multi-National Force Iraq, 2008.
[95] RC-East officials, Interviews, Bagram, Afghanistan, November 2008.
[96] RC-East official, Interview, Bagram, Afghanistan, November 2008.
[97] H.R. McMaster, "The Human Element: When Gadgetry Becomes Strategy," *World Affairs*, Winter 2009.

footprint of forces "living with the population" could be extended. The problem is that, according to commanders on the ground, it takes one platoon to secure an outpost, so getting forces outside the wire to interact with the population requires two platoons at each location. As of November 2008, RC-East noted that about 40 of its COPs were single platoon-sized, with 30 Soldiers or fewer.

Afghanistan itself presents some particular challenges to living among the population—the Afghan population is much more rural and dispersed than that of Iraq, and many Afghans live in remote, isolated, and barely accessible valleys. Determining how best to live among the population may also sometimes require some discretion. Some practitioners and experts content that in many long-isolated valleys, the local population is generally hostile to all outsiders, whether "friendly" or otherwise. Insisting on living among them create new tensions, without necessarily strengthening that population's resistance to outside insurgents.

Borders

In general, successful counterinsurgency requires a closed system, so that COIN can gradually smother the insurgency. As discussed below, Afghanistan's open border with Pakistan significantly complicates the COIN effort. The border marks the boundary of the system for Afghan and international security forces, constrained by international law, but not for insurgents who make ample use of safe haven and resupply in Pakistan.

Role of Special Operations Forces in COIN

Special operations forces (SOF) play an essential role in COIN in Afghanistan, through direct action against insurgent leaders. One senior U.S. commander underscored SOF's "continuous disruptive effect on leadership." SOF efforts in Afghanistan include significant Allied as well as U.S. participation, as well as a growing role for elite Afghan "commando" forces.

The partnership between U.S. SOF and conventional forces in Afghanistan may differ somewhat from the analogous partnership in Iraq, due to the disparity in the size of the conventional force presence. In Iraq, especially in 2007 and 2008, a large conventional ground forces presence with a widely distributed footprint was able to gain substantial, detailed situational awareness about local conditions, and to provide that insight to SOF for use in targeting, and in planning operations. Further, the much larger conventional presence in Iraq made forces readily available to "hold" a given area once SOF cleared it. The significantly smaller conventional forces presence in Afghanistan may not yet have allowed the development such a robust SOF/conventional synergy.

Role of Air Power in COIN

The major combat phase of operations in Afghanistan relied heavily on ground SOF calling in airstrikes on al Qaeda and Taliban targets, and many experts pointed to those operations as a model of jointness—the ability of Military Services to work together seamlessly. Since then, due to Afghanistan's forbidding, mountainous geography, and to the relative dearth of Afghan and international ground forces, the COIN campaign has continued to rely greatly on the use of kinetic air power. A larger ground forces presence may reduce some of that reliance, but the terrain alone is likely to make air strikes a necessary counterpart to ground-based fires.[98]

Civilian casualties resulting from air strikes in Afghanistan have prompted strong expressions of concern from Afghan and international audiences. President Karzai strongly condemned a coalition air strike conducted on August 22, 2008, against the village of Azizabad, in Herat Province in western Afghanistan, which he said killed 95 Afghan civilians. Further complicating the incident were initial reports from the coalition that apparently conflicted with the numbers claimed by Afghan government officials and local residents.[99]

UNAMA further raised the stakes by issuing an early statement claiming "convincing evidence" that at least 90 civilians, most of them children, had been killed.[100] UN SRSG Kai Eide later asserted that he had been correct to strongly underscore the UN's grave concern with civilian casualties.[101] In a December 2008 interview, Eide warned again of the need to conduct military operations with care, and to guard against civilian casualties, stating, "I am not convinced that we are" listening to the concerns of President Karzai and the Afghan people.[102]

In September 2008, GEN McKiernan issued an ISAF Tactical Directive, which replaced a directive issued by his predecessor General Dan McNeill in June 2007. The new Directive stressed "proportionality, restraint, and utmost discrimination in the use of firepower." It provided specific conditions for the use of air-to-ground munitions, and underscored the need to minimize the risk to civilians.[103]

---

[98] For a recent analysis of the kinetic use of air in Afghanistan, which argues against "excessive restraint in the use of airstrikes", see Lara M. Dadkhah, "Close Air Support and Civilian Casualties in Afghanistan," *Small Wars Journal,* December 30, 2008, available at http://smallwarsjournal.com/blog/2008/12/close-air-support-and-civilian/.

[99] See James Kitfield, "Progress in Afghanistan Gets Rockier," *National Journal,* September 15, 2008; and Carlotta Gall, "Afghan Leader Assails Airstrike He Says Killed 95," *The New York Times,* August 23, 2008.

[100] Candace Rondeaux and Karen DeYoung, "U.N. Finds Airstrike Killed 90 Afghans," *Washington Post,* August 27, 2008.

[101] Kai Eide, Interview, Kabul, Afghanistan, November 2008.

[102] Kirk Semple, "Official Calls for Sensitivity to Afghan Demands," *The New York Times*, December 8, 2008.

[103] ISAF slide, 'Tactical Directive", October 2, 2008.

Regional Context

Afghan officials, and international practitioners and observers, generally agree that Afghanistan's security is intimately linked to its relationships with its neighbors, first of all Pakistan, and to relations among those neighbors. GEN McKiernan stated in late 2008, "This is a regional insurgency and it requires regional solutions."[104] GEN Petraeus added in early 2009, "In fact, those seeking to help Afghanistan and Pakistan need to widen the aperture even farther, to encompass at least the Central Asian states, India, Iran and even China and Russia."[105] By the end of 2008, most U.S. strategists had concluded that to be successful, a strategy for "Afghanistan" would need to address the broader region.

Pakistan[106]

A major challenge to the counterinsurgency effort in Afghanistan is the fact that the Afghanistan-Pakistan border is largely porous, and insurgents fighting in Afghanistan have long relied on safe haven and other forms of support in Pakistan. As a rule, counterinsurgency efforts assume a "closed system", in which persistent COIN efforts, and growing popular support, can gradually smother an insurgency, but Pakistan's open border disrupts that premise by giving Afghanistan's insurgents a ready escape hatch.

The insurgency problem is complicated by the fact that the Government of Pakistan (GoP) has traditionally enjoyed only limited control over the Federally Administered Tribal Areas (FATA) that border Afghanistan.[107] The FATA is a legacy of British rule. To boost the border defenses of British India, the British gave semiautonomous status to tribes in that area by creating tribal "agencies," largely responsible for their own security. The area became the "FATA" after independence. Regional experts Barnett Rubin and Ahmed Rashid have argued that today, the area is used as a "staging area" for militants preparing to fight in both Kashmir and in Afghanistan.[108]

Pakistan's turbulent recent history may further complicate the GoP's efforts to achieve control. That history has included the assassination of politician and former Prime Minister Benazir Bhutto in December 2007, just ahead of scheduled general elections. In February 2008, parliamentary elections brought to power a coalition of former opposition parties including Bhutto's

[104] GEN David McKiernan, Interview, Kabul, Afghanistan, November 2008.

[105] GEN David Petraeus, Interview, Foreign Policy, January/ February 2009, available at http://www.foreignpolicy.com/story/cms.php?story_id=4587.

[106] For a detailed discussion, see CRS Report RL33498, *Pakistan-U.S. Relations*, by K. Alan Kronstadt.

[107] For background and analysis of the FATA, see Daniel Markey, "Securing Pakistan's Tribal Belt," Council on Foreign Relations, *Council Special Report* no. 36, August 2008.

[108] See Barnett R. Rubin and Ahmed Rashid, "From Great Game to Grand Bargain: Ending Chaos in Afghanistan and Pakistan," *Foreign Affairs*, vol. 87, no. 6 (November/ December 2008). The authors add, "The area is kept underdeveloped and over-armed as a barrier against invaders".

Pakistan People's Party, led by her widower Asif Zardari. In August 2008, General Pervez Musharraf, who had come to power in a military coup in 1999, resigned as President of Pakistan. In September 2008, Zardari was elected president, completing a transition to civilian-led rule. The ability and will of that civilian-led government to exercise authority over Pakistan's security forces, and to take steps to stop insurgent activities, is not yet completely clear.

Throughout its short history, Pakistan has had deeply vested interests in Afghanistan. The international border—the British-drawn Durand Line—cuts through territory inhabited, on both sides, by ethnic Pashtuns, with significantly more Pashtuns living in Pakistan than in Afghanistan.[109] The Pashtun population of southern Afghanistan provided the primary base of support for the Taliban during it rise. Further, most observers underscore that the Government of Pakistan has a general interest in ensuring that Afghanistan is a regional ally, in part as a balance against Pakistan's long-simmering conflict with neighboring India. That broad interest was reflected in Pakistani support for the Afghan mujahedin fighting the Soviet occupiers in the 1980's, and later, for the Taliban regime—relationships that have created difficulties in post-Taliban bilateral relations.

In recent years, the GoP attempted to achieve a measure of stability along the border with Afghanistan by following the example of the British Raj and striking a series "truces" with local power brokers, in 2004, 2005, and 2006. In February 2005, for example, the Pakistani military reportedly reached a peace deal with Baitullah Mahsud, leader of the umbrella organization Tehrik Taliban-i Pakistan (TTiP), and withdrew its forces from check points in the region. In mid2006, Islamabad struck a major peace deal with insurgents in North Waziristan, agreeing to end military operations and remove local checkpoints, in return for an end to insurgent attacks on government officials.[110] In early- and mid-2008, Pakistani forces, tried a similar approach, pulling back from TTiP's stronghold in Waziristan in the FATA.[111] By all credible accounts, these "deals" did not lead to greater stability.

In July 2008, the U.S. Government reportedly confronted Pakistani authorities with evidence of ties between members of ISI and the Haqqani network in the FATA. At that time, President Bush authorized U.S. military

---

[109] According to unclassified CIA estimates from July 2008, ethnic Pashtuns comprise 15.42% of Pakistan's population of 172,800,048; and about 42% of Afghanistan's population of 32,738,376. See "Pakistan" and "Afghanistan", The World Fact Book, Central Intelligence Agency, available at https://www.cia.gov/library/publications/the-world-factbook/geos/pk.html and https://www.cia.gov/library/publications/the-world-factbook/geos/af.html.

[110] Text of agreement available at http://www.pbs.org/wgbh/pages/frontline/taliban/etc/nwdeal.html.

[111] See Jane Perlez, "Taliban Leader Flaunts Power Inside Pakistan," *The New York Times*, June 2, 2008, and Jon Hemming, "NATO Beefs Up Forces Along Afghan-Pakistan Border," *Reuters*, May 19, 2008. See also Daniel Markey, "Securing Pakistan's Tribal Belt," Council on Foreign Relations, *Council Special Report* no. 36, August 2008, p. 11.

cross-border operations into Pakistan, by ground or Predator unmanned aerial vehicles (UAV). Observers counted at least 11 attacks by Predator UAV in August and September 2008, in addition to a ground attack in early September.[112]

ISAF officials have noted that cross-border attacks have yielded big operational and tactical benefits—by causing the insurgent networks to feel disconnected, and prompting local residents in Pakistan to want al Qaeda and other outsiders to leave their communities.[113] At the same time, U.S. civilian and military officials acknowledge that such cross-border strikes have the potential to spark local protest and to destabilize the fragile Government of Pakistan, still struggling to consolidate civilian rule.

To be clear, NATO's policy for ISAF does not include cross-border strikes. Asked in July 2008 whether the Alliance would go after militants in Pakistan, Secretary-General Jaap de Hoop Scheffer said, "My answer is an unqualified 'no'. We have a United Nations mandate for Afghanistan and that's it. If NATO forces are shot at from the other side of the border, there is always the right to self-defense but you will not see NATO forces crossing into Pakistani territory."[114]

By mid- to late-2008, efforts by the Pakistani military to tackle the insurgency problem had increased noticeably; senior U.S. officials and tactical-level military commanders in Afghanistan attributed the changes to the pressure from U.S. cross-border attacks. In August 2008, the Pakistani military stepped up operations in Bajaur, the northernmost of the seven agencies in the FATA, across from Afghanistan's Konar province. ISAF officials with access to imagery noted that after the operations, Bajaur resembled Fallujah, Iraq, after kinetic coalition operations in November 2004—that is, with some allowances for the more rural setting in Pakistan, destruction from the relatively heavy-handed Bajaur operations was considerable. According to ISAF officials, while the Pakistani operations suggested some room for improvement in the "soft" skills of COIN, they had an impact by disrupting insurgent networks.[115]

In 2008, Pakistan's counterinsurgency approaches in the FATA also included arming "lashkars"—militias—of tens of thousands of local residents, to help maintain security.[116] The lashkars, which draw on the strength and

112 See Karen DeYoung, "Pakistan Will Give Arms to Tribal Militias," *Washington Post*, October 23, 2008, and Saeed Shah, "Pakistan Rejects 'America's War' on Extremists, *The Guardian*, October 24, 2008.

113 ISAF, Interviews, Kabul, Afghanistan, November 2008.

114 Hamid Shalizi, "NATO Chief Says Will Not Hunt Taliban in Pakistan," *Reuters*, July 24, 2008.

115 U.S. military officials, Interviews, Kabul and Bagram, Afghanistan, November 2008. More than one official cited in this context the phrase from Roman historian Tacitus: "They make a desert and call it peace."

116 See Karen DeYoung, "Pakistan Will Give Arms to Tribal Militias," *Washington Post*, October 23, 2008. Such approaches are not new. Just before independence, in 1946, the British government issued a statement noting a reconsideration of its frontier policy. They would now "enlist cooperative tribesmen themselves", rather than simply bombing the area. See "British End Bombing of Indian Tribesmen," *The New York Times*, September 13, 1946.

local authority of traditional tribal structures, were intended to help "hold" areas after they were cleared by military operations.

Late 2008 also witnessed an improvement in cross-border coordination. GEN McKiernan noted that the Tripartite Commission, a senior-level U.S.-Afghan-Pakistani coordination body, had resumed its functions and convened three times between June and November 2008.[117] RC-East reported that cooperation among Pakistani, Afghan, and U.S. forces continued to grow at the trilateral Border Coordination Center (BCC) at the Torkham Gate, one of six planned BCCs. That collaboration benefited from Predator feeds that provided a common picture of the battlespace. ISAF and their Afghan counterparts planned to establish 6 BCCs by Fiscal Year 2010.[118]

At the tactical level, U.S. ground forces in eastern Afghanistan reported that in late 2008, the tenor of their regular tactical-level border coordination sessions grew more constructive. Tactical-level coordination improved—including, by November 2008, 13 cases of direct cross-border coordination with Pakistani forces, to "fix and defeat the enemy at the border," particularly along the border with Afghanistan's Paktika province.[119]

Overall, senior U.S. officials in Afghanistan, and outside observers, suggest that substantial improvement of the Afghanistan-Pakistan border situation will require from Pakistan both political will and appropriate capabilities. GEN McKiernan stated in November 2008 that he has seen "a shift in thinking at the senior levels in Pakistan that this insurgency is a problem that threatens the very existence of Pakistan."[120] Other U.S. commanders in Afghanistan noted, in late 2008, that they have observed a "sea change" in the views of Pakistani military officials, who increasingly view insurgents as existential threats, and who are attempting to improve the COIN capabilities of Pakistani forces to counter the insurgents. Remaining differences, U.S. military officials suggest, tend to include different perceptions of various insurgent groups and the threats they represent.[121] Other observers suggest that the extent of the commitment of senior Pakistani civilian officials to defeat the insurgent challenge is less clear.

Observers suggest that a key strategic question concerns the fragility of the Pakistani polity, and the extent to which the GoP can be encouraged or pushed to cooperate in counterinsurgency efforts without significant domestic political blowback. For example, in October 2008, the Pakistani parliament unanimously passed a resolution calling for an end to military action against extremist groups, and its replacement with dialogue. The resolution stressed

[117] GEN David McKiernan, Interview, Kabul, Afghanistan, November 2008.
[118] Major General Jeffrey Schloesser, Interview, Bagram, Afghanistan, November 2008.
[119] Task Force Currahee officials, Interviews, Khowst Province, Afghanistan, November 2008.
[120] GEN David McKiernan, Atlantic Council, Washington, DC, November 18, 2008, transcript available at http://www.acus.org/event_blog/general-david-d-mckiernan-speaks-councils-commanders-series/transcript.
[121] U.S. military officials, Interviews, Kabul and Bagram, Afghanistan, November 2008

the need for an "independent foreign policy" for Pakistan, and stated that "the nation stands united against any incursions and invasions of the homeland."[122]

Iran

ISAF officials note that the role of Afghanistan's large neighbor to the west, Iran, is also critical to its future, and they describe Iran's approach as a "dual-track strategy." On one hand, Iran enjoys close, long-standing cultural, linguistic, and religious ties with significant portions of Afghanistan's population. ISAF officials estimate that Iran is the second-largest contributor of reconstruction assistance to Afghanistan, after the United States—its efforts are most evident in Herat Province in western Afghanistan. And since Iran is a major destination for Afghan heroin, with all of its attendant concerns about crime and drug addition, Iranian officials share with their Afghan counterparts a vested interest in effective counternarcotics approaches. Some officials also point to the generally positive role Iran played at the 2001 Bonn Conference, to help forge consensus among Afghan factions about the creation of a post-Taliban government, as evidence that Iran can play a constructive role on Afghan matters.[123]

At the same time, ISAF officials state that Iran has provided some weapons and training to Afghan insurgents. Some add that Tehran may be concerned about a growing U.S. military footprint along both its eastern and western borders, as additional U.S. military forces flow into southern Afghanistan, and U.S. forces assume battlespaces in southern Iraq that were formerly manned by coalition partners. One official argued that Iran's interest is to "keep it simmering" in Afghanistan.[124] Most practitioners and observers suggest that, in some capacity, a comprehensive solution for Afghanistan must take Iran into account.

Afghan National Security Forces (ANSF)[125]

A fundamental premise of counterinsurgency operations is the central importance of host-nation forces—including establishing and improving those forces should their quantity or quality be insufficient. Decades of

---

[122] Saeed Shah, "Pakistan Rejects 'America's War' on Extremists," *The Guardian*, October 24, 2008. This resolution was passed before the late November 2008 terrorist attacks in Mumbai.

[123] On Iran's behavior at the Bonn Conference, see Ambassador James F. Dobbins, *After the Taliban: Nation-Building in Afghanistan*, (Washington, DC: Potomac Books, 2008).

[124] ISAF and U.S. officials, Interviews, Kabul, Bagram, and Kandahar, Afghanistan, November 2008.

[125] *The National Defense Authorization Act for Fiscal Year 2008*, P.L. 110-181, January 28, 2008, §1230, required the Department of Defense to submit a "report on progress toward security and stability in Afghanistan", and §1231 required a report on sustaining the Afghanistan National Security Forces. DoD submitted the first edition of both reports in June 2008. See Department of Defense, *Report on Progress Toward Security and Stability in Afghanistan*, June 2008, available at http://www.defenselink.mil/pubs/Report_on_Progress_toward_Security_and_Stability_in_Afghanistan_1230.pdf; and Department of Defense, *United States Plan for Sustaining the Afghanistan National Security*

war, displacement, and mismanagement, followed by the defeat of the Taliban regime, left Afghanistan without organized, functioning security forces or equipment, so rebuilding the Afghan National Security Forces (ANSF) has been a high priority of the post-war international assistance effort. ISAF's broad goal is to transition "lead security responsibility" to the ANSF who are focused, as a rule, on the current fight, not Afghanistan's long-term security requirements. From a security perspective, one positive legacy of the years of conflict may be the fighting spirit so common among many Afghans, acknowledged by the common refrain of international military officials: "They will fight!"

Afghan National Army (ANA)

All of the Afghan security forces are still developing, but the Afghan National Army (ANA), under the Ministry of Defense, is currently, by a wide margin, the most capable force.

ANA Numbers

As of December 2008, approximately 68,000 soldiers were assigned to the ANA, of around 150,000 total assigned ANSF.[126] That marks an increase from 29,366 in July 2006, 39,081 in July 2007, and 65,547 in July 2008.[127]

The Bonn Agreement established an endstrength target of 70,000 for the ANA. A decision was made in early 2008 to stretch that goal to 86,000. In September 2008, the Joint Coordination Monitoring Board (JCMB)—the body co-led by GIRoA and UNAMA, and charged to oversee implementation of the Afghanistan Compact—endorsed GIRoA's plan to increase that target figure to 134,000. The new total would include a base of 122,000, plus a personnel "float" of 12,000, on the model of the U.S. and other militaries, to support ongoing training and education.

U.S. military officials training the ANA note that the target date for reaching the 134,000 total is the end of 2011, based on a growth rate, as of late 2008, of 28,800 per year, with an estimated attrition rate of 8 to 9%. In theory, one option for accelerating the training of new Afghan soldiers might be boosting the monthly intake of new recruits. One challenge would be the constraints of the training process, including the capacity of the Kabul Military Training Center (KMTC), and the numbers and capabilities of Afghan trainers.[128]

Forces, June 2008, available at http://www.defenselink.mil/pubs/united_states_plan_for_sustaining_the_afghanistan_national_security_forces_1231.pdf.

[126] "Command Changes Hands for Afghan Security Forces Training," *American Forces Press Service*, December 22, 2008; and information from ISAF, December 2008.

[127] CSTC-A officials, Interviews, Kabul, Afghanistan, November 2008.

[128] As of the end of 2008, most ANA recruits received most of their initial training at the KMTC. Significant construction was underway to improve the KMTC physical plant, but doubling the size of each class of recruits, for example, would require significantly more space in buildings and

Senior U.S. practitioners in Afghanistan almost universally question whether the ANA target of 134,000 is sufficient to meet the security challenges Afghanistan faces. In November 2008, GEN McKiernan noted that 134,000 is "probably not the right number," and the outgoing head of the Combined Security Transition Command-Afghanistan, Major General Robert Cone, said that "134,000 probably isn't enough." Another U.S. commander in Afghanistan called the 134,000 target a "blip in the road", and still another estimated that altogether, the ANSF would need to grow to 300,000.[129]

For their part, many Afghan officials share the view that "134,000" will prove insufficient. Minister of Defense Wardak stated that Afghanistan had never yet had the proper proportion of troops to the area to be secured and to the population to be protected. Current force sizing, he noted, assumes the presence of a large international force—which will not always be there, and whose capabilities, he argued, are roughly double that of their Afghan counterparts. He concluded that "between 200,000 and 250,000 would be the proper size for the ANA."[130] In a September 2008 analytical report, a former civilian advisor to President Karzai argued that the ANA end-strength should be "at least 220,000."[131]

Some outside experts have also strongly advocated programming for a larger ANA. COIN theorist John Nagl, who has helped train U.S. personnel to train the ANSF, argued in November 2008 that the ANA should grow to 250,000.[132]

Force Modernization

In 2008, the focus of the ANA itself, and of the coalition ANSF training and advisory effort, was counterinsurgency, with an emphasis on the equipment that could be most readily fielded, and the skills that could most readily be developed and applied to the fight.

---

on ranges. The Basic Warrior Training course was 10 weeks long, and a new class of 1,200—the size of an ANA "kandak" (battalion)—was admitted every two weeks. As of November 2008, the KMTC had 3,000 Afghan personnel, of whom 1,200 were trainers, and the near-term goal was to increase the number of Afghan trainers by 300. The "122 plus 12" target number for the ANA does not include additional Afghan trainers, and Afghan trainers are one of the few groups in the ANA that does not receive additional combat or incentive pay of some kind. KMTC senior officials, and U.S. and Afghan staff, Interviews, Kabul, Afghanistan, November 2008.

129 GEN David McKiernan, MG Robert Cone, U.S. military officials, Interviews, Kabul, Kandahar, and Bagram, Afghanistan, November 2008.

130 Minister of Defense of Afghanistan Abdul Rahim Wardak, Interview, Kabul, Afghanistan, November 2008.

131 Mohammad Masoom Stanekzai, "Thwarting Afghanistan's Insurgency: A Pragmatic Approach toward Peace and Reconciliation", United States Institute of Peace, September 2008.

132 "All Things Considered," National Public Radio, November 18, 2008, interview with John Nagl, transcript available at http://www.npr.org/templates/story/story.php?storyId=97170621: ANA should grow to 250,000.

One shift, in late 2008, was initial "NATO-ization" of some ANA weapons, first of all a shift from the AK-47 assault rifle of Soviet origins, to the M-16 rifle of U.S. origin, widely used by many NATO countries. The AK-47 was a natural choice, as a starting point—years of Soviet sponsorship and then occupation had made the weapons widely available throughout Afghanistan. In November 2008, the first shipment of M-16's arrived in Kabul, and U.S. trainers began training Afghan army trainers. Some critics have noted that the M-16 is more temperamental to use and maintain than the AK-47, and that it will require an adjustment for Afghan forces. Supporters underscore the operational importance of Afghan interoperability with NATO counterparts.

As of late 2008, warfighting ANA Corps commanders were focused exclusively on the current fight—making sure that their soldiers had the equipment and training necessary for counterinsurgency.[133] Minister of Defense Wardak, however, had taken a longer-term look at possible future requirements, including the traditional military role of providing external defense. That outward-looking perspective was reflected in his suggestion to size the ANA by comparing it with the armies of Afghanistan's neighbors—Pakistan, Iran, and "the bear to the north". To balance between current and future requirements, he urged equipping the ANA "with a mix, right from the beginning, so it works for COIN and later on". Afghanistan needs a force that is "light but as effective as heavy forces", he added, and should include tanks, and an infantry combat vehicle—protected mobility with some firepower.[134]

ANA Structure and Organization

In contrast to the post-war Iraqi army, which was built from the ground up starting with small units, the ANA has been built from the top down, starting with headquarters leadership and staff, and then gradually fielding units under those headquarters.

As of the end of 2008, the ANA had five ground forces Corps Headquarters—the 201st Corps in Kabul, the 203rd Corps in Gardez in the east, the 205th Corps in Kandahar in the south, the 207th Corps in Herat in the west, and the 209th Corps in Mazar-e Sharif in the north. Under those Corps headquarters, the ANA had 19 brigade headquarters, and 71 "kandak" (battalion) headquarters.[135] As of January 2009, according to ISAF officials, the ANA had 46 kandaks capable of battalion-level operations.[136]

---

[133] ANA Corps Commanding Generals, Interviews, Kandahar and Mazar-e-Sharif, Afghanistan, November 2008.

[134] Minister of Defense of Afghanistan Abdul Rahim Wardak, Interview, Kabul, Afghanistan, November 2008.

[135] See http://www.mod.gov.af, which calls itself the "website of the Afghan National Army."

[136] "Metrics Brief 2007–2008," International Security Assistance Force, January 2009.

ANA "Corps" follow the European model, in which a Corps is a two-star headquarters, whose subordinate units are brigades—much like a U.S. Army Division. The five ANA Corps areas of responsibility (AOR), like the ISAF Regional Commands, are situated in the center, east, south, west, and north, but the ISAF and ANA boundaries do not completely correspond.

ANA Operations and Capabilities

By the end of 2008, all ANA Corps were engaging regularly in combined operations with ISAF counterparts. The overall percentage of deliberate combined operations that were ANA-led had increased from 49%, in the period from October to December 2007, to 62% in the period from July to September 2008. The extent of ANA leadership of such operations varied significantly, however, among ISAF Regional Commands, from ANA leadership of 23% of combined deliberate operations in RC-South, to 43% in RC-North, to 79% in RC-East, and 86% in RC-West. U.S. officials responsible for training estimated that the disparities might have more to do with variations in the coalition-Afghan partnerships, from region to region, than with variations in the capabilities of the ANA Corps or security conditions in the various AORs.[137]

In qualitative terms, ISAF officials note that ANA operational capabilities grew markedly during 2008. For example, in June 2008, following a prison break in Kandahar, initiated by a suicide bomber, the ANA deployed more than 1,000 soldiers south from Kabul, providing over half of the air lift required to transport them, within 24 hours. RC-East officials noted in November 2008 that in the previous month, they had participated in 35 combined "air assault" missions with the ANA, most of them ANA-led. In one mid-November action in eastern Afghanistan, for example, a combined ANA, ISAF and Afghan police force air assaulted into an area to be cleared. There, the Afghan police knocked on the doors, the ANA provided the inner cordon, and ISAF forces provided an outer cordon.[138]

Meanwhile, coalition special operations forces are helping the ANA develop elite "commando" kandaks. In theory, the commando forces would be capable of working with coalition counterparts on high-value targeting lists, and also of playing key roles in broader ANSF COIN operations.[139]

ANA as a National Institution

A number of observers have suggested that the ANA may be Afghanistan's only truly "national" institution. The outgoing head of CSTC-A noted in

[137] CSTC-A officials, Interviews, Kabul, Afghanistan, November 2008.
[138] ISAF officials, Interviews, Kabul, Bagram, and Khowst Province, Afghanistan, November 2008.
[139] CSTC-A officials, Interviews, Kabul, Afghanistan, November 2008; and see Gordon Lubold, "Americans Build Elite Afghan Commando Force," *Christian Science Monitor*, May 1, 2008.

late 2008 that the ANA was "very integrated". In the immediate post-Taliban years, ethnic Tajiks and Uzbeks—strongly represented in the Northern Alliance—predominated in Afghanistan's fledgling army, at the expense of ethnic Pashtuns. But as of the end of 2008, the ANA ethnic balance more closely corresponded to that of the population of Afghanistan—Tajiks, about 27% of the population, accounted for between 30 and 40% of the ANA, while Pashtuns, 42% of the population, made up 41% of the ANA. One caveat is that ethnic balance may not always correspond to geographic balance—for example, instead of recruiting Pashtuns from former Taliban stronghold areas in southern Afghanistan, the ANA may look to Pashtun communities in other parts of the country to achieve balance.[140]

Meanwhile, Minister of Defense Wardak underscores that the ANA is well-regarded by the Afghan population.[141] This claim was supported by the results of a major survey of popular opinion conducted in 2008, under the auspices of the Asia Foundation, which identified the ANA as the public institution enjoying the highest level of public confidence in Afghanistan.[142]

Key Challenges to ANA Development

While ANA operational capabilities, by all accounts, continue to grow, the Army continues to contend with critical gaps and challenges. Like the Iraqi Army, the ANA lacks sufficient enablers, including logistics; intelligence, surveillance and reconnaissance (ISR); and air capabilities such as close air support (CAS). It continues to rely on U.S. and coalition forces for such support. In addition, the ANA faces a significant demographic gap, of personnel between the ages of 35 and 55, the legacy of Afghanistan's recent history of warfare. While the ANA can draw on its "older" personnel now to serve in leadership capacities, it will effectively take a generation to fully train and prepare the next contingent of ANA senior leaders. Further, the ANA—like Afghan society as a whole—suffers from a ravaged supply of Afghan human capital. Since a significant majority of new recruits are illiterate, ANA training relies on methodologies that do not utilize written language; and a number of literacy instruction opportunities are available.

---

140 MG Robert Cone, other CSTC-A officials, Interviews, Kabul, Afghanistan, November 2008.

141 Minister of Defense of Afghanistan Abdul Rahim Wardak, Interview, Kabul, Afghanistan, November 2008.

142 *Afghanistan in 2008: A Survey of the Afghan People*, The Asia Foundation, 2008, p.25, available at http://asiafoundation.org/country/afghanistan/2008-poll.php. Other public institutions considered included the media, NGOs, national, provincial and local governing bodies, and community organizations. In the survey, 89% of respondents agreed that the ANA is "honest and fair with the Afghan people" (48% strongly agreed, 41% somewhat agreed), and 89% of respondents agreed that the "ANA helps improve security" (51% strongly agreed, and 35% somewhat agreed). This apparent high regard was not unqualified; 55% of respondents agreed that the "ANA is unprofessional and poorly trained" (18% strongly agreed, and 37% somewhat agreed), see p.35.

Afghan National Army Air Corps (ANAAC)

The Afghan National Army Air Corps (ANAAC), effectively Afghanistan's air force, is organizationally part of the ANA and is considered its 6th Corps. Afghanistan has an independent air force tradition dating back to 1924—by the 1980's, after several periods of substantial Soviet assistance, Afghanistan had built a rather formidable air force. During the Taliban era, Pakistan assumed the foreign patronage role. During the war in 2001 that ousted the Taliban, Afghanistan's fleet was largely destroyed. Years of flying experience left the Afghans some human capital to draw on, in building a post-Taliban air force—although the current average age of its pilots, 44.7 years, is approximately the average life expectancy for Afghan males.

The ANAAC is trained and mentored by the Combined Air Power Transition Force (CAPTF), part of the CSTC-A. The CAPTF describes its ambitious goals for the ANAAC this way: "The ANAAC will be focused on the unique demands of Afghanistan but will also be modern, interoperable and sustainable, and integrated with the ANSF, capable of joint and combined operations. . . ."[143]

CAPTF officials note that ANAAC development is proceeding in stages, based on agreements with ANSF leadership, with an initial emphasis on contributing to the COIN fight, first of all through air mobility. Afghanistan's unforgiving terrain and dearth of sufficient highway and rail transportation make the ability to move troops and supplies absolutely critical. Later—in the period between Fiscal Year 2011 and Fiscal Year 2015—it is expected that the ANAAC will begin to acquire limited attack and ISR capabilities. Sometime thereafter, CAPTF officials note, the ANAAC might begin to build external defense capabilities, including air interdiction, but that is not a current focus. That timeline reportedly sits uneasily with some "legacy" Afghan fighter pilots, eager to rebuild the air force they once knew.[144]

As of November 2008, the ANAAC included 301 pilots, and the Afghan fleet included 31 tails: 18 Mi-17 and 3 Mi-35 helicopters; 6 AN-32 and 2 AN-26 transport fixed wing aircraft; and 2 L39 "Albatros" jet trainer aircraft. The ANAAC expected to receive additional aircraft by donation: 6 more Mi-35's, 3 in November 2008 and 3 in January 2009, from the Czech Republic; and 3 more Mi-17's from the United Arab Emirates in April 2009. The current fleet, and the donations expected in the near term, are all of Soviet-bloc origin—CAPTF officials note that the first priority was to acquire early capability by capitalizing on aircraft familiar to the Afghans.

143 CAPTF officials, Interviews, Kabul, Afghanistan, November 2008.
144 CAPTF officials, Interviews, Kabul, Afghanistan, November 2008.

Plans call for shifting the fleet's orientation away from former Soviet technology in future acquisitions, including fixed-wing cargo aircraft.[145]

By the end of 2008, the ANAAC was making substantial contributions to Afghan and coalition COIN efforts. In October 2008, the ANAAC set new records by transporting 9,000 passengers and 51 tons of cargo, and by flying 908 sorties. At the beginning of 2008, according to CAPTF officials, ISAF met 90% of ANA transport requirements for cargo and passengers, but by November, the ANAAC was meeting 90% of the requirement.[146]

Afghan National Police

The Afghan National Police (ANP) are Afghanistan's civilian security forces, which fall under the Ministry of the Interior. The ANP includes several distinct forces: the Afghan Uniform Police (AUP), responsible for general policing; the Afghan National Civil Order Police (ANCOP), a specialized police force that provides quick reaction forces; the Afghan Border Police (ABP), which provides law enforcement at Afghanistan's borders and entry points; and the Counternarcotics Police of Afghanistan (CNPA), which provides law enforcement support for reducing narcotics production and distribution.[147]

According to ANP officials, the ANP are being developed as a paramilitary force to contribute to the counterinsurgency effort by joining the ANA in COIN operations, and by protecting the population after the ANA "clears." As of late December 2008, the ANP included approximately 68,000 assigned personnel.[148] The Bonn Agreement established a target ANP endstrength of 62,000; the current target endstrength is 82,000.

Police Corruption

The most commonly expressed concern of Afghan and international senior officials about the ANP is that they are not merely incompetent but also corrupt—they have, GEN McKiernan has stated, "a lack of basic policing values."[149] Some observers charge that such corruption is more than an obstacle to a job well done, in that it also alienates the population—the center of gravity in COIN—who may grow to see the Taliban as no worse

---

145 CAPTF officials, Interviews, Kabul, Afghanistan, November 2008.

146 CAPTF officials, Interviews, Kabul, Afghanistan, November 2008.

147 See Department of Defense, United States Plan for Sustaining the Afghanistan National Security Forces, June 2008, p.21, available at http://www.defenselink.mil/pubs/united_states_plan_for_sustaining_the_afghanistan_national_security_forces_1231.pdf.

148 "Command Changes Hands for Afghan Security Forces Training," *American Forces Press Service*, December 22, 2008.

149 GEN David McKiernan, Atlantic Council, Washington, DC, November 18, 2008, transcript available athttp://www.acus.org/event_blog/general-david-d-mckiernan-speaks-councils-commanders-series/transcript. ISAF officials, Interviews, Kabul, Kandahar, Bagram, Afghanistan, November 2008.

than equally abusive civilian authorities.[150] Curiously, a major recent survey of Afghan popular opinion indicated that the ANP is the second most highly regarded public institution, after the ANA.[151]

Focused District Development

To address the problem, GIRoA and coalition forces launched the Focused District Development (FDD) initiative to retrain and reform local AUP forces, district-by-district. In the FDD program, the AUP are pulled out of a given district and sent to an intensive training course. Highly skilled ANCOP forces fill in, during their absence. After the AUP return, in order to reinforce their new skills, they operate under the tactical overwatch of, and then with mentoring by, coalition forces. As of January 2009, the AUP in 52 districts were undergoing the FDD process.[152] Coalition officials assess that FDD is generally successful, in that fewer violations by the AUP are reported after the training.

Some observers, including senior officials from international organizations, have charged that the program is not comprehensive enough to be effective. "Taking thugs away for a few weeks," one official observed, "just gives you better-trained thugs."[153]

Some outside observers, in turn, noting the urgent need for more and better policing on the streets of Afghanistan, have pushed for accelerated recruitment and fielding of weapons and equipment to the Afghan police. Coalition officials caution, however, that the reform process will take time, since the aim is a fundamental cultural shift. Providing gear, they argue, especially weapons, to "unreformed" districts, without proper accountability, would likely prove counterproductive.[154]

Afghan Border Police

By many accounts, the Afghan Border Police (ABP) may be beset by even greater incompetence and corruption than their AUP counterparts. To counteract these trends, GIRoA, working with coalition counterparts,

---

[150] See Sarah Chayes, "Clean Up the Afghan Government, and the Taliban Will Fade Away," *Washington Post*, December 14, 2008. The author lives in Kandahar and runs an Afghan cooperative. She argues: "Now, Afghans are suffering so acutely that they hardly feel the difference between Taliban depredations and those of their own government." She quotes one local resident of Kandahar as saying: "The Taliban shake us down at night, and the government shakes us down in the daytime."

[151] *Afghanistan in 2008— A Survey of the Afghan People*, The Asia Foundation, 2008, p.25, available at http://asiafoundation.org/country/afghanistan/2008-poll.php. In the survey, 80% of respondents agreed that the "ANP is honest and fair with the Afghan people," (40% strongly, 40% somewhat); while 80% agreed that the "ANP helps improve security" (40% strongly, 40% somewhat). At the same time, 60% agreed that the "ANP is unprofessional and poorly trained" (22% strongly, 38% somewhat).

[152] "Metrics Brief 2007–2008," International Security Assistance Force, January 2009.

[153] International organization official, Interview, Kabul, Afghanistan, November 2008.

[154] Coalition officials, Interviews, Kabul, Afghanistan, November 2008.

launched the Focused Border Development (FBD) program, similar to the AUP's FDD. Between October 2008 and September 2009, FBD is scheduled to train 52 company-sized units of ABP, at four training sites. The courses are conducted by U.S. private security contractors—Blackwater and DynCorp. The retraining also includes arming the ABP with heavier weapons, including Soviet-origin DShK heavy machine guns.[155]

The FBD initiative, like FDD, relies on follow-up mentoring by coalition forces, after the completion of the formal training sessions. Those mentorship responsibilities are assigned to ISAF battlespace owners. As the outgoing head of CSTC-A observed, FBD is possible "because the 101st is helping me and giving me assets."[156]

Coalition and Afghan officials readily acknowledge the great challenge of securing Afghanistan's borders. Afghanistan has nearly 3,500 miles of borders, primarily in difficult, remote, mountainous terrain. Minister of Defense Wardak flatly observed, "We will never be able to secure the whole border."[157] Protecting the borders, some officials suggest, may require not only trained and professional ABP personnel stationed along the border, but also additional aerial reconnaissance and quick response forces.

Command and Control

Command and control arrangements for the ANSF have been adapted to current COIN efforts, which require "joint" action by multiple Afghan forces together with coalition counterparts. The Ministry of Defense and the Ministry of the Interior maintain formal command authority over their own forces—the ANA and the ANP, respectively.

To facilitate coordination, GIRoA created, in 2008, a series of Operations Coordination Commands, at the regional (OCC-R) and provincial (OCC-P) levels. There are 6 OCC-R's, one in each of the five ISAF Regional Commands, and one for Kabul city; and 34 OCC-P's are being established. OCC's at both levels are physical (not virtual) facilities that facilitate monitoring and coordination of operational and tactical-level operations.

OCC's include representatives from the ANA; the ANP; and the National Directorate of Security (NDS), Afghanistan's intelligence service. ISAF and CSTC-A provide mentoring. The command relationships among the participating organizations are purely "coordination", not "command". For example, as contingencies arise, OCC members provide direct conduits of information with their respective organizations—OCC-P members reach out to ANA brigades and ANP provincial command centers; while OCC-R

155 "CJTF-101 Campaign Update" slides, November 2008.
156 MG Robert Cone, Interview, Kabul, Afghanistan, November 2008.
157 Minister of Defense of Afghanistan Abdul Rahim Wardak, Interview, Kabul, Afghanistan, November 2008.

members reach out to ANA Corps and ANP regional command centers. OCC-P's do not report to OCC-R's, and there is no national-level analogue. The ANA serves as the "lead agency" for OCC's, although OCC's may be physically located in police facilities.

Looking to the future, some observers have wondered how appropriate the OCC construct will prove to be for a "post-COIN" context when, for example, the focus of the ANA shifts from domestic to external concerns. A future transition might not prove especially difficult, since the OCC coordination relationships complement but do not replace the formal service command relationships.[158]

Training the ANSF

Since its inception, the international ANSF training effort has been characterized by multiple initiatives adopting sometimes divergent approaches, with a general trend toward greater unity of effort, and a stronger U.S. leadership role, over time.[159] Secretary of State Clinton has underscored President Obama's statement "that we must focus more attention and resources on training the Afghan Security Forces."[160]

Background and Organization of the Training Effort

The December 2001 Bonn Conference recognized the need for the international community to help the fledgling Afghan authorities with "the establishment and training of new Afghan security and armed forces." In early 2002, broad agreement was reach on a model in which individual "lead

---

158 The inter-service coordination arrangements in Afghanistan differ from those in Iraq, also designed for the exigencies of a counterinsurgency effort, where provincially-based "Operations Commands" bring together multiple Iraqi security forces under the formal command of the head of each Operations Command. Those arrangements may prove more difficult to rationalize, for a future post-COIN environment, than the OCC's in Afghanistan.

159 U.S. Government funding support to the ANSF has not followed a smooth trajectory to date. In Fiscal Year 2006, Congress appropriated approximately $1.9 billion for the Afghan Security Forces Fund, and in Fiscal Year 2007—meeting DoD's request based on the need to accelerate Afghan ground forces training and equipping—$7.4 billion. In Fiscal Year 2008, Congress appropriated approximately $2.7 billion for the Fund, again meeting DoD's request, which was based on the premise of building on the ANSF acceleration enabled by the FY 2007 appropriations. For Fiscal Year 2009, DoD requested an increase—$3.7 billion—in its Global War on Terror bridge request, submitted in May 2008, of which Congress provided $2 billion. See CRS Report RL33110, *The Cost of Iraq, Afghanistan, and Other Global War on Terror Operations Since 9/11*, by Amy Belasco, p.22. See also Department of Defense, "FY 2007 Emergency Supplemental Request for the Global War on Terror," February 2007, available at http://www.defenselink.mil/comptroller/Docs/FY2007_Emergency_Supplemental_Request_for_the_GWOT.pdf; Department of Defense, "FY 2008 Global War on Terror Request," February 2007, available at http://www.defenselink.mil/comptroller/Docs/FY2008_February_Global_War_On_Terror_Request.pdf; and Department of Defense, "Fiscal Year 2009 Global War on Terror Bridge Request," May 2008, available at http://www.defenselink.mil/comptroller/defbudget/fy2009/Supplemental/FY2009_Global_War_On_Terror_Bridge_Re quest.pdf.

160 See the replies to questions for the record, submitted by Secretary of State nominee Hillary Clinton to the Senate Foreign Relations Committee (SFRC), for her January 13, 2009, confirmation hearing, available at http://www.foreignpolicy.com/files/KerryClintonQFRs.pdf.

nations" would assume primary responsibility to coordinate international assistance in five different areas of security—these included placing ANA development under U.S. leadership, and police sector development under German leadership. The 2006 Afghanistan Compact transferred formal "lead" responsibility to GIRoA.

In 2002, to execute its "lead nation" role, the United States created the Office of Military Cooperation-Afghanistan (OMC-A) to train the ANA. In 2002, to supplement German efforts, the U.S. Government launched a police training initiative, led by the Department of State's Bureau of International Narcotics and Law Enforcement Affairs (INL), through U.S. Embassy Kabul, with contractor support. In 2005, the U.S. Government restructured its ANSF training efforts, shifting responsibility for supporting Afghan police development to the Department of Defense, and renaming the OMC-A the Office of Security Cooperation-Afghanistan (OSC-A).[161] Early in 2007, when the U.S. three-star military headquarters, the Combined Forces Command-Afghanistan (CFC-A) was deactivated, OSC-A was re-designated the Combined Security Transition Command-Afghanistan (CSTC-A), and assigned directly to US CENTCOM; CSTC-A was assigned to USFOR-A when that headquarters was established in 2008.

Training Teams

CSTC-A's primary mechanism for training and advising the ANSF is the use small teams that typically live and work with ANSF units. U.S. advisory teams working with the ANA—Embedded Training Teams (ETTs)—include between 12 and 20 personnel. ETTs work for CSTCA but are under the operational command of U.S. battlespace owners during combined operations with the ANSF. Non-U.S. NATO advisory teams are known as Operational Mentor and Liaison Teams (OMLT). In theory, their functions are similar to those of the ETTs, but due to national caveats, there are great variations in the degree to which OMLTs participate in operations with their Afghan counterparts. Advisory teams working with the ANP are known as Police Mentoring Teams (PMTs).

Some officials in battlespace-owning units have argued that the quality of ETT and PMT personnel varies and that, as one official put it, "the ETTs are better suited to planning than execution."[162] In October 2006, the U.S. Army consolidated, at Fort Riley, Kansas, the pre-deployment training and

[161] In a 2008 report, regarding the establishment of the OSC-A, DoD noted: "Efforts prior to this time were not comprehensive and lacked both resources and unity of effort within the international community". See Department of Defense, *United States Plan for Sustaining the Afghanistan National Security Forces*, June 2008, p.21, available at http://www.defenselink.mil/pubs/united_states_plan_for_sustaining_the_afghanistan_national_security_forces_1231.pdf. The OSC-A, like the OMC-A, reported to the U.S. military command in Afghanistan, but received policy guidance from the U.S. Chief of Mission, while contract management authority remained with State INL.

[162] ISAF and CSTC-A officials, Interviews, Kabul, Kandahar, Bagram, Afghanistan, November 2008.

preparation of U.S. Army, Navy and Air Force personnel for assignments as advisors to Afghan and Iraqi security forces; in October 2008, the Army announced that the program would shift to the Joint Readiness Training Center at Fort Polk, Louisiana.[163] One reason for some reported variation in the quality of U.S. advisors may be that they are selected on an individual basis and come from a wide variety of backgrounds that may or may not include extensive operational experience.

Since its inception, officials argue, the training and advisory effort has been undermanned. According to CSTC-A, as of November 2008, advisory teams were manned, overall, at 64%. That marked an increase from 54% earlier in the year, before the 2nd Battalion, 7th Marines arrived and assumed police training responsibilities in addition to battlespace ownership. ANA teams were more fully staffed, at 78%, than ANP teams, at 33%. Those November 2008 figures reflected a re-balancing from earlier in the year, when ANA teams were resourced at 93% but ANP teams were only resourced at 12%. They also reflected some breaking down of available advisory teams into smaller pieces, in order to extend coverage to more Afghan units.[164]

As of late 2008, CSTC-A had requested 2,300 additional police advisors, and 60 additional ANA advisory teams.[165] Those ANA teams could come either from the U.S. military or from NATO—although NATO, despite repeated requests, has been reluctant to provide ANA advisory teams in sufficient numbers, or to provide embedded police trainers. To be clear, the requirement is not static—as ANSF units improve their capabilities, their partner advisory teams can be "harvested" and assigned to new ANSF units.

Mentoring the ANSF Leadership

In addition to tactical- and operational-level training, the coalition ANSF advisory effort also includes mentoring Afghan senior leaders—Ministers, senior ministry officials, and senior ANA and ANP commanders. ISAF and CSTC-A senior leaders invest considerable time in working closely with the senior leadership of the Defense and Interior Ministers, and of their regionally-based commands. President Karzai replaced the Minister of Interior in October 2008, a step favored by a number of senior U.S. and other international officials in Afghanistan, and widely viewed as an effort to curb corruption.[166] The coalition "advisory" role is strong—Afghan

[163] John Milburn, "Adviser Mission to Leave Fort Riley," *Army Times*, October 1, 2008. The U.S. Marine Corps has its own program for preparing Marines for advisory roles.
[164] MG Robert Cone, Interview, Kabul, Afghanistan, November 2008.
[165] MG Robert Cone, DoD Press Briefing, November 12, 2008, available at http://www.defenselink.mil/transcripts/transcript.aspx?transcriptid=4314.
[166] John F. Burns, "Afghan President, Pressured, Reshuffles Cabinet," *The New York Times*, October 11, 2008.

regional commanders regularly seek coalition support, and advocacy with their respective ministries, for identified requirements. The fundamental challenge is building institutional capacity—including leadership ability, physical infrastructure, effective systems, and trained and competent human resources.

Unit Partnering

In 2008 in Iraq, the Iraqi security forces (ISF) training and advisory effort relied on two complementary approaches, embedded teams and "unit partnering". Unit partnering involved matching a full coalition unit with an Iraqi counterpart of equal or greater seniority in a mentoring relationship. Multi-National Corps-Iraq directed the use of such partnerships where appropriate. Those relationships, in the words of U.S. commanders in Iraq, provided the opportunity to "show, rather than tell"—to provide visible examples of a competent unit and staff in action.

In Afghanistan in late 2008, the use of unit partnering was more ad hoc, and more contentious. Overall, unit partnering was less widespread than in Iraq, a natural consequence of a far lighter coalition footprint, since unit partnering requires available, locally-based units of appropriate size. Nevertheless, battlespace-owning U.S. units underscored the importance of such partnerships—as one commander noted, "ANSF capacity-building is our main effort, and we accept some risk in our operational capabilities to focus on this." For example, one U.S. brigade-sized Task Force sends its tactical command post including key brigade staff, for two weeks every month, to co-locate and partner with the nearest ANA Corps headquarters. Its Military Police (MP) battalion headquarters staff, in turn, work closely with the ANP Regional Command Center.

Further, the ANP re-training effort, for both AUP and ABP, requires substantial follow-up in the form of mentoring. Battlespace-owning units were tasked to establish and maintain those mentoring partnerships—a form of unit partnering—with the "reformed" ANP.[167]

At the same time, in late 2008, senior Afghan and CSTC-A officials evinced an antipathy toward the concept of unit partnering. Minister of Defense Wardak argued forcefully: "There is some talk that we should do partnering, but I am against it—our units are standing on their own feet. I will try very hard to push against this partnering. If they have partner units, they would lose their ability to learn and operate independently."[168] CSTC-A officials argued, similarly, that ANSF units tended to perform less well

[167] Task Force Currahee, Interviews, Khowst Province, Afghanistan, November 2008.
[168] Minister of Defense of Afghanistan Abdul Rahim Wardak, Interview, Kabul, Afghanistan, November 2008.

when partnered with coalition units, and that advisory teams were more effective than "partners" in encouraging the ANSF to take initiative.[169]

European Union Police Mission in Afghanistan (EUPOL)

In June 2007, the European Union (EU), recognizing a still-urgent need for competent Afghan police, established a police training mission in Afghanistan (EUPOL). As of December 5, 2008, EUPOL's strength stood at 177 international and 91 local staff, from 18 EU member countries plus Canada, Croatia, and Norway.

In general, EUPOL has a longer-term, more institutional focus than CSTC-A. Its mission statement declares: "The mission aims at contributing to the establishment of sustainable and effective civilian policing arrangements under Afghan ownership and in accordance with international standards."[170]

Some senior ISAF and Afghan officials criticize EUPOL for taking too long-term a perspective, for failing to work at the local level, and for focusing on steady-state, peacetime policing skills rather than on the paramilitary capabilities that, they argue, are urgently needed for the counterinsurgency effort.[171] UN SRSG Kai Eide, in turn, has noted that EUPOL staffing should increase significantly and has urged the EU to provide more—and more appropriate—personnel.[172]

Community and Tribal Outreach

In early 2009, Afghan and ISAF officials were finalizing plans for a new community outreach program, sometimes called the "community guard program", designed to take what GEN McKiernan has called a "bottom-up, community-based approach to security."[173] The premise is that neither international forces nor the ANSF have sufficient numbers to provide full population security, and are not likely to have them in the near future, even with expected increases in ISAF and ANSF troop strength. Minister of

---

169 CSTC-A officials, Interviews, Kabul, Afghanistan, November 2008.

170 Available at http://consilium.europa.eu/cms3_fo/showPage.asp?id=1268&lang=EN. See also Council Joint Action 2007/369/CFSP, May 30, 2007, on the establishment of the European Union Police Mission in Afghanistan, available at http://eurlex.europa.eu/LexUriServ/site/en/oj/2007/l_139/l_13920070531en00330038.pdf. EUPOL objectives, listed in Article 3, include contributing to "sustainable and effective civilian policing arrangements" and supporting "the reform process towards a trusted and efficient police service."

171 Minister of Defense of Afghanistan Abdul Rahim Wardak, MG Robert Cone, Interviews, Kabul, Afghanistan, November 2008.

172 Kai Eide, Interview, Kabul, Afghanistan, November 2008.

173 GEN David McKiernan, Atlantic Council, Washington, DC, November 18, 2008, transcript available at http://www.acus.org/event_blog/general-david-d-mckiernan-speaks-councils-commanders-series/transcript; and "U.S. Backs Plan for Engaging Afghan Tribes," *Radio Free Europe Radio Liberty*, December 30, 2008.

Defense Wardak stated in late 2008, "There is still a big gap between forces available, and the space to secure, so we need help."[174]

In Afghanistan, local community leaders are often tribal leaders, and local community structure is intimately linked with tribal structure, though not necessarily clearly or consistently. Observers describe tribal bonds as "pragmatic, localized allegiances," which may have been shaped over time by migration, competition for resources, reallocation of land rights as rewards for services, and links to the narcotics trade. While residents of several isolated valleys may all belong to the same tribe, their fiercest rivalries may be with fellow tribesmen in an adjacent valley. Fostering local community support for security initiatives generally involves working with tribal leaders, among others, but given Afghanistan's complex tribal affiliations, the risk of "getting it wrong" is relatively high.[175]

The community guard program attempts to avoid "getting it wrong" by focusing on the concept of "community outreach," rather than "tribal outreach". The initiative began with the recognition of the need to protect Highway 1, the key artery running south from Kabul to Kandahar and the site of escalating insurgent attacks in mid-to-late 2008. The program was expected to begin with a pilot project in Wardak and Logar provinces, just south of Kabul. Muhammad Halim Fidai, Governor of Wardak province, was quoted as saying: "We don't have enough police to keep the Taliban out of these villages and we don't have time to train more police—we have to fill the gap now."[176]

In the program, each local "community"—including all relevant tribes—would select representatives to a shura; the shura, in turn, would select project participants to help provide security, for example through neighborhood watch efforts and guarding fixed sites. One goal, U.S. officials noted, is that local residents adopt a "not in my village" attitude toward insurgents and criminals.[177]

Funding for the program would be provided by U.S. CERP funds; this funding would not cover arming participants. U.S. accountability requirements mandate formal U.S. oversight, but additional Afghan oversight would be provided by both on-site ANSF representatives, and the moral authority of the community shura. The goal—as U.S. Ambassador William Wood stated—is "to empower locals, both local governance and tribal structures, to make them work for themselves."[178] "The idea," as Minister

---

[174] Minister of Defense of Afghanistan Abdul Rahim Wardak, Interview, Kabul, Afghanistan, November 2008.

[175] ISAF, RC-South officials, and western diplomats, Interviews, Kabul, Afghanistan, November 2008.

[176] Jon Boone, "Afghans Fear U.S. Plan to Rearm Villages," *Financial Times*, January 12, 2009.

[177] ISAF officials, Interviews, Kabul, Afghanistan, November 2008.

[178] Ambassador William Wood, Interview, Kabul, Afghanistan, November 2008.

of Defense Wardak expressed it, "is to bridge the gap between the government and the people, and to make the people feel responsible."[179]

The initiative draws to some extent on the model of "arbakai"—a traditional Pashtun institution, in which a tribally-based auxiliary force is formed to defend a village and its surrounding area on a temporary basis. That familiar association may help smooth the introduction of community outreach, but it also raises concerns in some quarters that the program might reignite and facilitate local warlordism. One U.S. senior official stated in late 2008, "I worry about arbakai."[180]

Minister of Defense Wardak is reportedly particularly concerned about the danger of a return to the chaos of the early 1990's civil war. He stated in late 2008 that the new program must not rearm anyone—"we should not create new warlords or reinforce old ones."[181] U.S. officials quoted a senior ANA commander as saying, reflecting cautiously on the initiative, "The army and police serve a nation, but a militia serves a man."[182]

The program must also overcome the legacy of similar and more recent initiatives to generate security at the local level. The Afghan National Auxiliary Police program was created in 2006, amidst some controversy, as a stop-gap measure in southern Afghanistan. The locally-recruited force, including many who previously worked for warlords, had an approved size of 11,271. Recruits were given ten days of training, and members received the same salaries as regular ANP street cops—$70 per month.[183] A number of practitioners and observers argued that the training was insufficient to produce a credible security force. At the time, the head of CSTC-A called the program "an attempt to take short-cuts," and its participants "a bunch of thugs," and more recently, an RC-East senior official concluded that they "went brigand."[184] By late 2008, the program had been completely dismantled.

Reconciliation

Military theorists and practitioners contend that war is a contest over the terms of an ultimate political settlement. In Afghanistan, both GIRoA and

---

179 Minister of Defense of Afghanistan Abdul Rahim Wardak, Interview, Kabul, Afghanistan, November 2008. He added, "If you make a community responsible, and you given them the feeling that they are sharing in that responsibility, then they will die for it."

180 RC-East official, Interview, Bagram, Afghanistan, November 2008.

181 Minister of Defense of Afghanistan Abdul Rahim Wardak, Interview, Kabul, Afghanistan, November 2008.

182 RC-East official, Interview, Bagram, Afghanistan, November 2008.

183 See Andrew Wilder, "Cops or Robbers? The Struggle to Reform the Afghan National Police", *Afghanistan Research and Evaluation Unit*, July 2007.

184 See Jerome Starkey, "US attacks UK plan to arm Afghan militias", *The Independent*, January 14, 2008; and Murray Brewster, "NATO Disbands Afghan Auxiliary Police," *Edmonton Sun*, May 15, 2008; MG Robert Cone, Interview, Kabul, Afghanistan, November 2008; RC-East official, Interview, Bagram, Afghanistan, November 2008.

the various insurgent groups are contending to set the conditions for a final settlement.

In an early preview of a possible end game for the war in Afghanistan, in late 2008 a rhetoric of "reconciliation" with the Taliban and other insurgents gained momentum. Practitioners and observers have used the word "reconciliation" to refer to two different kinds of efforts in Afghanistan—lower-level efforts to co-opt the fence-sitters and hired guns, and higher-level negotiations aimed at bringing senior leaders in from the cold.

GEN McKiernan refers to the first group as "small-t taliban", those driven by poverty, lack of jobs and other prospects, and general disaffection, who provide their services to insurgent leaders for some price.[185] The purpose of reconciliation efforts would be to "peel them off" from the hardcore insurgency, perhaps through some combination of economic incentives, opportunities for political participation, and removal from targeting lists. In late 2008, GIRoA was reportedly elaborating a new draft program for small-t taliban reconciliation.[186] To be clear, while GEN McKiernan supports such "reconciliation", he stresses that any such initiatives would be GIRoA—not ISAF or U.S.—efforts.

The second category of reconciliation includes outreach to, and possibly negotiations with, senior leaders of the Taliban and other insurgent groups. The Kingdom of Saudi Arabia has reportedly brokered preliminary talks between representatives of President Karzai—including one of his brothers—and former members of the Taliban who might have access to Mullah Omar and other current senior leaders. President Karzai has stated publicly that efforts to encourage the Saudis to broker contacts have been ongoing for several years, but so far without results.[187] The Saudis have also reportedly facilitated contact with representatives of Gulbuddin Hekmatyar and his HiG organization.[188]

For its part, the Taliban has reportedly named conditions that must be met before it would agree to enter any direct talks. These include the withdrawal of all international forces from Afghanistan, immunity of Taliban leaders from targeting by the ANSF, and the ability to retain their weapons. According to U.S. senior officials, such demands would contradict GIRoA

[185] GEN David McKiernan, Interview, Kabul, Afghanistan, November 2008. See also General David McKiernan, Atlantic Council, Washington, DC, November 18, 2008, transcript available at http://www.acus.org/event_blog/general-david-d-mckiernan-speaks-councils-commanders-series/transcript.

[186] See for example Anand Gopal, "Bid to Split Taliban, Al Qaeda," *The Christian Science Monitor*, December 16, 2008.

[187] See John F. Burns, "Karzai Sought Saudi Help With Taliban," *The New York Times*, October 1, 2008; and Anand Gopal, "No Afghan-Taliban Peace Talks for Now," *Christian Science Monitor*, October 9, 2008.

[188] Kim Sengupta, "Secret Saudi Dinner, Karzai's Brother and the Taliban," *The Independent*, October 8, 2008.

principles—for example, that all Afghan citizens must renounce violence and accept the Constitution—and U.S. Government views.[189] GEN McKiernan has noted that he would have great concern about any measures that would let them remain "the Taliban."[190] For his part, UN SRSG Kai Eide has stressed that the outcome of any talks must be based on the Afghan Constitution—"what is achieved cannot be a compromise," he said, and there should be no "rush to peace."[191]

One further challenge, according to many practitioners and observers, is that despite suffering some tactical-level set-backs, the Taliban leadership appears to feel confident, free to approach any talks from a position of strength. One senior UK official stressed that if negotiations took place today, the Taliban would make unrealistic demands, and he estimated that we are "many months if not years from the end game." He added, "there's no 'quick fix' through reconciliation."[192] Some ISAF officials add that Taliban leaders may be under some pressure from al Qaeda not to participate in negotiations.[193]

Counternarcotics[194]

The Narcotics Problem

One of the things that make the conflict in Afghanistan so intractable is the close linkage between the Afghan insurgency and narcotics. The United Nations Office on Drugs and Crime reported that "warlords, drug lords, and insurgents" collect a tax on the cultivation, transportation and processing of opium poppy—taxes that amounted to "almost $500 million in 2008."[195] The twin counternarcotics (CN) and counterinsurgency challenge is most evident in Helmand province in southern Afghanistan, which is responsible for about two-thirds of Afghan opium production and provides a base of operations for some Taliban insurgents.

Narcotics are big business in Afghanistan—with a climate conducive to cultivation, an absence of readily available economic alternatives such as the infrastructure for bringing legitimate crops to market, and permeable borders with neighboring states. Senior U.S. officials note the reluctance of many Afghan officials to challenge the narcotics industry because its tentacles are so deeply entwined with Afghan governing structures at all

189 Senior U.S. officials, Interviews, Kabul, Afghanistan, November 2008; and see John F. Burns, "Karzai Sought Saudi Help With Taliban," *The New York Times*, October 1, 2008.
190 GEN David McKiernan, Interview, Kabul, Afghanistan, November 2008.
191 Kai Eide, Interview, Kabul, Afghanistan, November 2008.
192 UK official, Interview, Kabul, Afghanistan, November 2008.
193 ISAF officials, Interviews, Kabul, Afghanistan, November 2008.
194 For a detailed discussion, see CRS Report RL32686, *Afghanistan: Narcotics and U.S. Policy*, by Christopher M. Blanchard.
195 *Afghanistan Opium Survey 2008*, United Nations Office on Drugs and Crime, November 2008.

levels. Furthermore, Afghanistan still lacks the robust judicial system that would be necessary to prosecute offenders.

Counternarcotics Approaches

The Government of Afghanistan and its international partners have produced no shortage of strategies designed to address Afghanistan's narcotics problem. The current GIRoA plan is the Afghan National Drug Control Strategy, issued in January 2006; a previous version was issued in May 2003.[196] In early 2002, as a follow-on to the Bonn Agreement, the United Kingdom assumed "lead nation" responsibility for coordinating international counternarcotics (CN) efforts; that lead responsibility shifted to GIRoA under the 2006 Afghanistan Compact.

The first premise of the CN effort is the illegality of narcotics. On January 17, 2002, President Karzai issued a decree banning the cultivation, production, abuse, and trafficking of narcotic drugs. Key Afghan CN organizations include: the Afghan Special Narcotics Force (or "Task Force 333"), a paramilitary force created in late 2003 to conduct raids; the Counternarcotics Police of Afghanistan, which investigates and helps target networks; an eradication force that physically carries out eradication; and a CN Criminal Justice Task Force created in early 2005 to expedite CN cases through the fledgling criminal justice system. GIRoA has sought the close cooperation of provincial Governors in its CN efforts. "Governor-led eradication" (GLE) efforts encourage Governors to cooperate by offering them control over the eradication process, and providing them rewards in the form of resources from the central government. Critics have suggested that GLE efforts may selectively target political rivals or small-scale cultivators, while avoiding confrontation with powerful larger-scale producers. In 2006, GIRoA launched the Good Performers Initiative to reward provinces for reducing poppy cultivation.

To support the Afghan CN strategy, and also in an attempt to shape it, the U.S. Government issued its own U.S. Counternarcotics Strategy for Afghanistan, in August 2007. While GIRoA has tended to favor negotiated eradication—including its collaboration with provincial Governors—the U.S. Government has supported the more forceful approach of centralized and enforced GIRoA-led "non-negotiated forced eradication."[197]

Since assuming command of ISAF, GEN McKiernan has lobbied for a more active NATO role in counternarcotics, including the ability for ISAF forces

[196] Government of Afghanistan, *Afghan National Drug Control Strategy: An Updated Five-Year Strategy for Tackling the Illicit Drug Problem,* Islamic Republic of Afghanistan Ministry of Counter-Narcotics, Kabul, January 2006.

[197] Ambassador Thomas A. Schweich, Coordinator for Counternarcotics and Justice Reform in Afghanistan, *U.S. Counternarcotics Strategy for Afghanistan,* August 2007, see especially pp.5–6, and 48.

to target narcotics labs. At an informal meeting of NATO Ministers of Defense, held in Budapest in October 2008, the Allies agreed to stretch the CN role that ISAF can play without changing its formal mandate. After the meeting, NATO Secretary-General Jaap de Hoop Scheffer announced that "under the existing operational plan, ISAF can act in concert with the Afghans against facilities and facilitators supporting the insurgency, in the context of counternarcotics, subject to authorization of respective nations."[198] The following month, GEN McKiernan explained that there was no change to the rules of engagement—just a decision "to be more aggressive." He added, "Where I can make the connection between narcotics, personalities, or facilities, and the insurgency, then I can treat that as a military objective."[199] In December 2008, a senior ISAF official noted that GIRoA had already asked for ISAF's assistance several times, on the basis of October policy update.[200]

Counternarcotics Results

In terms of results to date, according to the United Nations, the Afghan eradication force eliminated 210 hectares of poppy in 2005, 2,250 hectares in 2006, 3,149 hectares in 2007, and 1,174 hectares in 2008. UN data indicates that through Governor-led eradication, 4,000 hectares were eradicated in 2005; 13,050 hectares in 2006; 15,898 hectares in 2007; and 4,306 hectares in 2008.[201] UN data also indicated that the extent of cultivation, and the "farm gate" (pre-processing) value of opium cultivation, both declined in 2008.[202] The U.S. Government reported that in 2008, 18 provinces earned a total of $28 million through the Good Performers Initiative, including $10 million for Nangarhar province, now considered "poppy-free".[203]

Practitioners and outside experts differ concerning how best to evaluate these results. Some simply point to poppy-free provinces—in particular Nangarhar in eastern Afghanistan along the Pakistani border—as successes, and credit a combination of various GIRoA eradication efforts. They suggest in particular the importance of local authorities in discouraging

[198] NATO press release, October 10, 2008, available at http://www.nato.int/docu/update/2008/10-october/e1010b.html.

[199] GEN David McKiernan, Atlantic Council, Washington, DC, November 18, 2008, transcript available at http://www.acus.org/event_blog/general-david-d-mckiernan-speaks-councils-commanders-series/transcript.

[200] Dave Pugliese, "ISAF Commander Says Afghan Drug Lords to Be on 'Kill or Capture' Target List," *Ottawa Citizen*, December 23, 2008.

[201] *Afghanistan Opium Survey 2008*, United Nations Office on Drugs and Crime, November 2008, p.25.

[202] "Farm gate" cultivation was valued at $1 billion in 2007, and $730 million in 2008. 193,000 hectares of poppy were cultivated in 2007, and 157,000 hectares were cultivated in 2008, a decline of 19%. 2.5% of arable land was cultivated in 2007, while 2.1% was cultivated in 2008. In 2007, 13 provinces were considered "poppy-free", while 18 were so characterized in 2008. *Afghanistan Opium Survey 2008*, United Nations Office on Drugs and Crime, November 2008, pp.2, 5, 7.

[203] Bureau of International Narcotics and Law Enforcement Affairs, "Update on Counternarcotics in Afghanistan," U.S. Department of State, August 2008.

poppy planting. Other observers argue that global food prices may be a more important explanatory variable—in 2008, opium prices were down, while wheat prices, due to a widespread drought, were up, possibly affecting the decision calculus of many planters. They underscore the importance of cultivation trends over time, rather than one-time developments, as better indicators of program effectiveness. Two analysts from this school of thought have argued: "Sustainable reductions in opium poppy cultivation will only be achieved by a wider process of improved security, economic growth and governance."[204]

Capacity-Building as Part of COIN in Afghanistan

According to civilian and military practitioners, the three pillars of the counterinsurgency effort in Afghanistan—security, governance, and development—are inseparably linked. As former advisor to both GIRoA and ISAF Clare Lockhart asserts, "A country is not stable until it has a functioning state that performs key functions for its citizens."[205] International military forces in Afghanistan lead the security line of operation, and also play strong supporting roles in the other two fields, governance and development, particularly at the provincial and local levels where their footprint is much greater than that of civilian counterparts.[206]

The Need for Capacity-Building

Practitioners and observers generally agree that improving the capacity of Afghan institutions is essential for making progress in all three lines of operation—security, governance and development. Many further stress that a critical component of capacity-building in Afghanistan is connecting the center to the regions. Popular support—active or passive—is essential to counterinsurgency, and local-level institutions, whether political officials or the ANSF, are often the most readily-available "face" of government. Local capacity, it is argued, should be competent, and should help connect the local population to a larger "Afghanistan".

One fundamental challenge to capacity-building in general is that Afghanistan's would-be work force was decimated by years of violence and repression, and generally lacks the skills, the professionalism, and often the literacy, to work in a post-Taliban polity or economy.

---

204 David Mansfield and Adam Pain, "Counter-Narcotics in Afghanistan: The Failure of Success?" *Afghanistan Research and Evaluation Unit Briefing Paper Series*, December 2008, p.3.

205 Clare Lockhart, "Learning from Experience," *Slate*, November 5, 2008.

206 The 2006 COIN field manual states: "Political, social and economic programs are most commonly and appropriately associated with civilian organizations and expertise; however, effective implementation of these programs is more important than who performs the tasks. If adequate civilian capacity is not available, military forces fill the gap." Field Manual 3-24, *Counterinsurgency*, Headquarters, Department of the Army, December 2006, para. 2-5.

Some observers argue that the human capital problem was exacerbated by bad choices by the international community in the immediate aftermath of Taliban rule. Eager to place responsibility for leading Afghanistan in Afghan hands—and eager in some cases to focus primarily on the counter-terrorist mission—the international community, it is charged, failed to insist on high standards of experience or integrity in the selection of Afghan leaders at all levels. One ISAF official argued in late 2008, "We need a major housecleaning of GIRoA."[207]

Other observers have stressed that the international community, and particularly the U.S. Government, further aggravates the human capital problem by supporting specific individuals, rather than impartially supporting the Afghan political process as a whole. Such approaches, it is argued, make it difficult to hold such officials accountable. Noting another ramification, NATO SCR Gentilini described such approaches by the U.S. Government as "good but colonialist", because the U.S.-supported officials may be seen as U.S. pawns.[208]

A significant challenge to local-level capacity-building is that provincial Governors and district Administrators have very little formal authority, and they receive no budgets of their own from the central government. As one diplomat described it, in the absence of resources, Governors have to negotiate their authority with *de facto* local power-brokers, which compromises their efforts.[209]

Capacity-Building Initiatives by the Afghan Government

The Government of Afghanistan has launched initiatives of its own aimed at building capacity, particularly at the local level.

In August 2007, GIRoA established the Social Outreach Program (ASOP), under the leadership of the GIRoA-sponsored Independent Directorate of Local Governance (IDLG), led by Director-General Ghulam Jelani Popal.[210] The ASOP is an attempt to harness the power of traditional community organizations to address some local-level governance needs, and to build linkages from the district up to the provincial and national levels. It aims to create temporary community councils at the district level, including between 30 and 40 community leaders, local officials, religious scholars, and tribal heads. The councils are intended to "channel" public needs and grievances, and to provide a forum for conflict resolution, with national-level oversight provided by the IDLG and ministries. District council

---

207 ISAF official, Interview, Kabul, Afghanistan, November 2008.

208 Ambassador Ferrnando Gentilini, Interview, Kabul, Afghanistan, November 2008.

209 ISAF official, Interview, Kandahar, Afghanistan, November 2008.

210 See Independent Directorate of Local Governance (IDLG), "Afghanistan Social Outreach Programme: Programme Document," Islamic Republic of Afghanistan, April 2008.

elections, scheduled for 2010, are expected to replace the temporary councils.

One fundamental challenge is that GIRoA has budgeted no funding to support the effort. As of December 2008, the United States, the United Kingdom, and Canada had agreed to support the program in specific provinces, and talks were underway with other potential sponsors.

In related efforts, in 2008 the IDLG sponsored a series of regional "Governors Meetings", each bringing together a group of provincial Governors, GIRoA ministry officials, and senior officials from ISAF, UNAMA, and Embassies with forces deployed in those provinces. According to some participants, the initial meetings, if they did not produce significant concrete results, underscored the linkages among security, governance, and development, and helped build bridges between the center and the regions.[211]

UN SRSG Kai Eide, in an extension of his role as co-chair of the JCMB, responsible for overseeing implementation of the Afghanistan Compact, actively supports the ASOP initiative. He has said that, of UNAMA's various efforts, he is particularly proud of this program, designed to draw communities closer to the government.[212]

An earlier GIRoA initiative, the National Solidarity Program (NSP), had a somewhat similar focus. The NSP created community development councils (CDC) that received some money from the central government to spend on priorities they identified. ASOP recognizes this earlier work, particularly the success of some CDCs in identifying local needs, but argues that the CDCs did "not always have the same support and authority within communities as that enjoyed by traditional shuras." ASOP aims to build stronger credibility by basing its efforts more closely on traditional local authority structures.[213]

In addition, some international practitioners have noted that while the CDCs provided some opportunities for local-level innovation, funding streams were inconsistent and then gradually dried up, and some of the councils were "perfectly corrupt."[214]

Military Role and Perspectives on Capacity-Building

ISAF and U.S. military officials in Afghanistan acknowledge that their role in civilian capacity-building is a "supporting" one, but they stress the importance of their role in helping link together the various levels of government.

---

211 The IDLG convened a Governors Meeting for the southern region of Afghanistan in Kandahar in August 2008, and in Oruzgan in November 2008.

212 Kai Eide, Interview, Kabul, Afghanistan, November 2008.

213 See Independent Directorate of Local Governance (IDLG), "Afghanistan Social Outreach Programme: Programme Document," Islamic Republic of Afghanistan, April 2008.

214 ISAF officials, Interviews, Kabul and Bagram, Afghanistan, November 2008.

With a footprint that extends through most of the country, and that includes a presence at the local as well as the national and regional levels, the military is well-placed to make such contributions.

The mission statement of the 101st Airborne Division, the nucleus of ISAF's RC-East, underscored the military's role in all three pillars of efforts. It stated that RC-East, in conjunction with GIRoA, ISAF and U.S. civilian agencies, "conducts full spectrum operations to develop Afghan national capability to secure its people, exercise capable governance, and develop a sustainable economy, while defeating terrorists and insurgents, in order to extend GIRoA authority and influence as the legitimate government of the Afghan people."[215]

In 2008, a former U.S. brigade commander in eastern Afghanistan noted that his company commanders worked regularly with district-level officials, monitoring their efforts, and that this focus was important because "the cause of instability in Afghanistan is poor governance."[216]

In late 2008, a senior ISAF official explained that the military's role is to "facilitate" governance, which is "the long pole in the tent," and harder than either security or development. He added that squad and platoon leaders on the ground "regularly liaise with local Afghan officials." Their guidance is to work "bottom-up," to get information, to facilitate shuras, to connect district officials with representatives of Kabul-based ministries . . . and to follow up assiduously.[217]

Provincial Reconstruction Teams

Provincial Reconstructions Teams (PRT) in Afghanistan grew out of a U.S. military initiative in late 2002. In general, PRTs help Afghan provincial governments develop the capacity and capabilities to govern, provide security, ensure the rule of law, promote development, and meet the needs of the population.[218] The U.S.-led PRT in Zabul province, for example, succinctly states that its mandate is "to conduct civil-military operations in Zabul to extend the reach and legitimacy of GIRoA."[219] As ISAF's area of responsibility expanded geographically, it assumed responsibility for PRTs in each new area. As of early 2009, ISAF maintained 26 PRTs, each led by a single nation. PRT staff may include any combination of civilian and military personnel; the military components formally report to ISAF.

215 "CJTF-101 Campaign Update" slides, November 2008.
216 Ann Marlowe, "A Counterinsurgency Grows in Khowst," *Weekly Standard*, May 19, 2008. Colonel Marty Schweitzer led the 4th BCT, 82nd Airborne Division, in 6 provinces of RC-East.
217 ISAF official, Interview, Kabul, Afghanistan, November 2008.
218 For a current U.S. PRT mission statement, see "Fact Sheet: Making Afghanistan More Secure with Economic and Reconstruction Assistance," White House, September 26, 2008, available at http://www.whitehouse.gov/news/releases/2008/09/20080926-16.html.
219 Zabul PRT officials, Interviews, Zabul province, Afghanistan, November 2008.

The U.S. Government leads 12 of ISAF's 26 PRTs, 10 of them in RC-East, one in RC-South, and one in RC-West. PRTs do not currently cover all of Afghanistan's 34 provinces. In late 2008, some U.S. officials were considering possible future expansions, including creating two separate PRTs from the single entity currently responsible for Kapisa and Parwan provinces; establishing a PRT-like entity for Kabul city; and creating new PRTs in Dai Kundi and Nimroz provinces in RC-South.

U.S. PRTs are primarily military organizations, each led by a military officer—either an Air Force Lieutenant Colonel or a Navy Commander—who reports to the nearest U.S. battlespace owner. Typically, a PRT includes between 80 and 150 staff members, including one representative each from the Department of State, the Agency for International Development (AID), and the Department of Agriculture (USDA).

Practitioners and observers variously evaluate the successes of PRTs to date. Some argue that while PRTs have carried out useful work, they have not been resourced sufficiently to meet requirements. This may be particularly true for some Allies, for example Lithuania, that have fewer resources available in general for international assistance efforts.[220]

Others, including senior GIRoA officials, have argued that PRTs do not coordinate their efforts sufficiently with Afghan authorities. In November 2008, during a visit to Kabul by a U.N. Security Council delegation, President Karzai claimed that PRTs were setting up "parallel governments" in the countryside.[221] Other GIRoA officials reportedly express that many international resources channeled through PRTs are effectively "lost" amidst multiple layers of contractors and subcontractors, before they reach the Afghan people.[222]

Other U.S. Civilian Field Presence

In addition to the U.S. Government civilian agency presence at PRTs, civilian representatives from the State Department, AID, and USDA also serve at U.S. "Task Forces"—division and brigade headquarters under ISAF. Typically, these civilians provide advisory support, in their respective fields of expertise, helping inform military decision-making and operations. U.S. commanders typically express strong enthusiasm for these partnerships.[223]

---

220 The constraint of limited resources may also apply to U.S.-led PRTs. In late 2008, the Zabul PRT introduced a new ionizer-based water purification initiative—a scheme developed and proposed by an American Eagle Scout. While that Eagle Scout's contributions may be laudable, some suggest that PRTs ought to be able to draw on more readily available expertise.

221 Associated Press, "Afghan President Complains U.S., NATO Aren't Succeeding," Foxnews.com, November 26, 2008.

222 ISAF officials, and Minister of Defense of Afghanistan Abdul Rahim Wardak, Interviews, Kabul, Afghanistan, November 2008.

223 RC-East, TF Currahee officials, Interviews, Bagram and Khowst province, Afghanistan, November 2008.

In November 2008, a total of 60 U.S. civilians were serving in "field positions"—at PRTs and Task Forces.[224]

U.S. civilian experts work with battlespace-owning military units in another capacity, on Human Terrain Teams (HTT), established in Afghanistan in February 2007.[225] HTTs, recruited and employed by the U.S. Army, are small teams of social scientists, from various academic disciplines, who conduct deep anthropological fieldwork in order to understand and "map" demographic, social and economic dynamics. Their analysis, like the advice of the State, AID and USDA civilian advisors, helps inform military decision-making and operations. U.S. commanders praise the work of the HTTs as contributing directly to their understanding of the battlespace and some have noted that more HTTs—as much as one per district—would be welcome.[226] Their work, like that of servicemembers, entails risk—one member of the HTT in Khowst province, Afghanistan, was killed in May 2008 when his vehicle was struck by an improvised explosive device (IED).

At the same time, the deployment of HTTs has met with both criticism and complications. HTTs have been criticized, most frequently by the academic community, for "compromising" social science ethical standards.[227] In November 2008, an HTT member, Don Ayala, was charged with murder in connection with the killing of an Afghan man who had set a female HTT member on fire, in Kandahar province.[228]

Commanders Emergency Response Program (CERP)

Particularly in the absence of dedicated provincial or district budgets, U.S. commanders have made use of the Commanders Emergency Response Program (CERP), sponsored by the Department of Defense, to fund governance-and development-related projects. One U.S. commander recently called CERP "a surrogate for the government's failure to provide," and another stated, "If we didn't have CERP, we wouldn't be able to do anything."[229]

Since its inception, CERP has provided relatively unconstrained discretionary funds to military commanders on the ground, to meet relatively

[224] Zabul PRT officials, Interviews, Zabul province, Afghanistan, November 2008.

[225] For information, see the Human Terrain System website, http://humanterrainsystem.army.mil/default.htm.

[226] RC-East and TF Currahee officials and HTT members, Interviews, Bagram and Khowst province, Afghanistan, November 2008. To be clear, HTT members state that they "do not do targeting."

[227] See for example, Network of Concerned Anthropologists, "Anthropologists Up in Arms Over Pentagon's 'Human Terrain System' to Recruit Graduate Students to Serve in Iraq, Afghanistan: an interview with David Price," *Democracy Now*, December 13, 2007, available at http://www.democracynow.org/2007/12/13/anthropologists_up_in_arms_over_pentagons.

[228] See Jeff Schogol, "DoD Contractor Charged in Death of Afghan Man," *Stars and Stripes*, November 22, 2008; and Jerry Markon, "Contractor Charged," *Washington Post*, November 20, 2008.

[229] RC-East and TF Currahee officials, Interviews, Bagram and Khowst province, Afghanistan, November 2008.

near-term needs. With far fewer U.S. forces—and thus fewer senior U.S. commanders entitled to spend CERP funds—Afghanistan has received less CERP funding to date than Iraq.

According to U.S. civilian and military officials, and some Afghan provincial officials, decisions about CERP funding allocation are typically based on Afghan priorities and informed by both U.S. civilian and military expertise. The top expenditure to date, by a significant margin, has been road-construction, viewed by Afghans and U.S. officials as critical to security, governance and development.

CERP appropriations for Afghanistan have increased, though not steadily, over time, from $39.7 million in 2004, to $135 million in 2005, to $215 million in 2006, to $206 million in 2007, to $479.9 million in 2008.[230] U.S.-led RC-East noted that $690 million had been requested for Fiscal Year 2009.[231] As additional U.S. forces flow into both eastern and southern Afghanistan in 2009, including a number of additional command positions entitled to spend CERP money, Department of Defense requests for CERP funding may increase.

Agribusiness Development Teams

Supplementing the work of battlespace owners, their civilian advisors, and PRTs in eastern Afghanistan are Agribusiness Development Teams (ADT). ADTs are state-based Army National Guard (ARNG) teams that include "farmer soldiers" who have backgrounds in various facets of agribusiness. The ADTs draw on several decades of similar ARNG experience in Central America, and typically they leverage agricultural expertise from land grant universities in their home states. The teams include organic enablers that allow them to operate independently, including vehicles and force protection.

In 2008, the first ADT, from Missouri, deployed to newly poppy-free Nangarhar province, and the second ADT, from Texas, deployed to Ghazni province. Guardsmen and women from Indiana, Kansas, Kentucky, Nebraska, Oklahoma, and Tennessee have also been involved in the program.[232]

A Civilian Surge?

Many practitioners and observers have suggested that the capacity-building challenges in Afghanistan may require additional international civilian

[230] See Special Inspector General for Afghanistan Reconstruction, *Quarterly Report to the United States Congress*, October 2008, p.39

[231] "CJTF-101 Campaign Update," slides, November 2008.

[232] RC-East and TF Currahee officials, Interviews, Bagram and Khowst provinces, Afghanistan, November 2008. See also Tom Vanden Brook, "Harvesting Ties with Afghanistan," *Army Times*, December 31, 2008.

expertise, as well as the effective integration of such expertise with military efforts.

ISAF commanders argue that a stronger commitment to build capacity is required, because it is governance, more than security or development, that is lagging in Afghanistan. RC-East Commanding General MG Schloesser has argued, "We need an interagency surge!"[233] Senior officials from other Allies within ISAF echo this argument—in November 2008, RC-North Commanding General, German Major General Weigt, argued that he needed "civilian advisory teams", as complements to the OMLTs and ETTs. "The main problem for me," he stated," is not security, but deficits in governance."[234]

Outside observers have also argued that the civilian capacity-building effort should be as robust as security capacity-building initiatives. State-building expert Sarah Chayes wrote in December 2008 that the problem of governance in Afghanistan is particularly acute. She argued, "Western governments should send experienced former mayors, district commissioners and water and health department officials to mentor Afghans in those roles."[235]

Some observers have suggested that Afghanistan might be a useful test case for an integrated, balanced application of all instruments of U.S. national power.[236]

In late 2008, U.S. Embassy Kabul outlined a proposal for a "civilian surge" to support provincial-and local-level capacity-building in Afghanistan. The effort would expand the U.S. Government civilian field presence at U.S.-led PRTs and Task Forces, by more than 200 billets. Experts would come from the State Department, AID, and USDA. The additional personnel would augment existing civilian staff functions, and might also establish a presence at the district level to help mentor sub-provincial-level GIRoA officials. In addition, U.S. Embassy Kabul proposed, civilian officials might be given their own "ready funds", to support projects in the field of governance. U.S. officials noted that the availability of resources might prove a constraint on the implementation of these proposals, and that even if approved, there was likely to be a time lag before implementation could begin.[237]

---

[233] MG Jeffrey Schloesser, Interview, Bagram, Afghanistan, November 2008.

[234] MG Weigt, Interview, Mazar-e-Sharif, Afghanistan, November 2008.

[235] Sarah Chayes, "Clean up the Afghan Government, and the Taliban will Fade Away," *Washington Post*, December 14, 2008.

[236] See for example "Afghanistan: Winning the War. Problems, Solutions, and Critical Decisions for the Next Administration," Foundation for the Defense of Democracies, Washington DC, December 4, 2008, panel discussion video transcript available at http://www.defenddemocracy.org/index.php?option=com_content&view=article&id=11784099&Itemid=385.

[237] U.S. Embassy and Department of State officials, Interviews, Kabul, Afghanistan and Washington, DC, November and December 2008.

Future Options for the War in Afghanistan

This section outlines and assesses a number of key strategic and operational options for Afghanistan that the U.S. Government, including the U.S. Congress in its oversight capacities, may choose to consider.

Integrating the Overall Approach: Strategy and Implementation

Most Afghanistan observers have pointed to weaknesses in the coordination of the many disparate efforts to support Afghan security, governance or development, including ensuring that those three lines of operation complement one another. Some observers note that leaders of the primary international assistance efforts rarely speak with a unified voice, although their influence might be much stronger were they to do so. The scale of Afghanistan's needs, and the number and variety of entities offering help, make coordination a particularly great challenge.

To address the coordination challenge, some observers advocate crafting a new, overarching strategy for Afghanistan, which would state objectives for security, governance, and development; specify approaches; and assign roles and responsibilities for implementation. A new single set of guidelines, it is argued, would help focus cooperation and coordination.

Many practitioners and observers argue, however, that the basic contours of strategy are already in place. Importantly, GIRoA officials tend to agree with this view. The Afghanistan Compact, an agreement between the Government of Afghanistan (GIRoA) and the international community, identified basic objectives in each of the lines of operation. The 2008 Afghanistan National Development Strategy articulated a strategic vision and key objectives in security, governance, and development; provided multiple individual sector strategies under each of those headings; and stated guidelines for coordinating and monitoring implementation.[238] In the security arena, ISAF's 2008 Joint Campaign Plan (JCP) clearly stated objectives and approaches.

Experts have suggested two alternatives to writing a new strategy, in both of which the U.S. Government could play a leadership role. One school of thought suggests that the specific language of a strategy document may be less important than the "buy-in" to its principles and approaches by all relevant players. In the case of Afghanistan, as former head of UNAMA Lakhdar Brahimi argued, those actors would include all of Afghanistan's neighbors, other regional leaders "including India, Iran, and Saudi Arabia," all permanent members of the UN Security Council, and all major donors

[238] *Afghanistan National Development Strategy 1387–1391 (2008–2013): A Strategy for Security, Governance, Economic Growth and Poverty Reduction*, Islamic Republic of Afghanistan, 2008, available at http://www.ands.gov.af/ands/ands_docs/index.asp.

including Japan.[239] What is needed, this school suggests, are intensified diplomatic efforts to forge a broad consensus on the basic contours of existing strategy.

Other experts have suggested a second option—accepting the basic tenets of existing strategy documents and focusing on strengthening monitoring and implementation. Diplomatic efforts might urge contributing countries to more rigorously tailor their assistance efforts to Afghan national priorities, or they might attempt to curb the "national-first" approach of those contributing countries that regularly lobby GIRoA ministers for attention to "their" provinces. New efforts might also support strengthening UNAMA so that it might more effectively play its critical coordination role as co-chair of the Joint Coordination and Monitoring Board (JCMB), tasked to oversee coordinate implementation of the Afghanistan Compact.

Updating U.S. Grand Strategy for Afghanistan

As a leading protagonist of international support for Afghanistan, the U.S. Government has played a strong role in shaping the Afghanistan Compact, NATO's strategic vision, and ISAF's Joint Campaign Plan, all of which articulate strategic objectives and approaches for Afghanistan. Nevertheless, as a normal manifestation of international relations, specific U.S. national interests in Afghanistan and the region, and prioritized U.S. objectives designed to support those interests, may differ somewhat from broadly agreed international goals. Therefore, some experts suggest the utility of a rigorous internal review of strategic objectives and approaches, and a new articulation of national strategy, by the U.S. Government.

As of early 2009, several such reviews were underway or had recently been completed, including a review of strategy for Afghanistan and Pakistan by the George W. Bush White House, a study by the Joint Staff, and a 100-day strategic assessment of its entire area of responsibility by CENTCOM. Options for the Obama Administration might include publishing a formal, public, unclassified Afghanistan strategy document, or issuing internal guidance concerning the premises of U.S. strategy for Afghanistan for U.S. Government practitioners. Congress has required reports articulating Administration strategy in the past, and could do so again.

[239] Lakhdar Brahimi, "A New Path for Afghanistan," Washington Post, December 7, 2008. The Afghanistan Study Group, which released its results in January 2008, called for developing not only "a long-term, coherent international strategy" but also "a strategic communications plan to garner strong public support for that strategy" among NATO countries and regional leaders. If "strategic communications" is regarded as two-way dialogue, then the Group's proposal is similar to Brahimi's. See General James L. Jones, USMC (ret), Ambassador Thomas R. Pickering, Co-Chairs, Afghanistan Study Group Report, "Revitalizing our Efforts, Rethinking our Strategies," Center for the Study of the Presidency, January 30, 2008, Page 11.

Many experts suggest that U.S. Government strategic reviews and conclusions would benefit from a sober assessment of Afghanistan's starting point, including its poverty, dearth of human capital, lack of resources and development, and lack of tradition and experience as a functioning, effective government. That starting point, it is argued, might usefully help temper the expectations and assumptions underlying U.S. strategy.

Adjusting U.S. and Other International Forces

In 2008, NATO and U.S. commanders on the ground in Afghanistan requested additional international forces—requests echoed by GIRoA officials. Key policy questions include the scope of the requirement, the likely duration of the requirement, and the options, including possible combinations of U.S. and other NATO forces, for meeting the requirement.

For those who advocate troop level increases, the duration of the need for higher international troop levels in Afghanistan is hard to determine in advance. Future requirements might depend on changes in the strength of the insurgency, growth in the capacity and capabilities of the ANSF, adaptations in the approaches used by international forces, and concurrent progress in the areas of governance and development. GEN McKiernan has argued that international troop levels need to be increased until the "tipping point" is reached when the ANSF assume lead security responsibility—"three or four more years away."[240] To be clear, Afghan and U.S. officials do not use the term "surge", arguing that "surge" refers to a temporary increase in troop strength, while the requirement in Afghanistan is likely to last for some time.[241]

Requirement for Additional Forces?

A first premise of counterinsurgency is conducting operations "by, with and through" indigenous forces. Where such forces are not available, international forces may substitute, support, and/or help build additional indigenous forces. The military effort in Afghanistan was, from the start, an "economy of force" mission, in terms of both international troop strength, and early target endstrength goals for the Afghan National Security Forces (ANSF). That approach provided only limited geographical coverage of Afghanistan. Commanders on the ground argue that significant additional forces are needed to meet the full scope of requirements.

240 Tom Vanden Brook, "A 'Tough Fight' Seem for Afghan War in '09", *USA Today*, December 8, 2009.

241 Tom Vanden Brook, "A 'Tough Fight' Seem for Afghan War in '09", *USA Today*, December 8, 2009. Vanden Brook interviews GEN McKiernan, whom he quotes as saying: "I don't like to use the word surge here because if we put these additional forces in here, it's going to be for the next few years. It's not a temporary increase of combat strength."

At the same time, some key observers caution against additional U.S. or other international force deployments, on the grounds of general Afghan antipathy to the presence of foreign forces on their soil, exacerbated by any episodes of heavy-handedness by those forces. Thus, they suggest additional deployments could actually prove counterproductive to the COIN effort. Regional expert Rory Stewart has argued flatly, "the West should not increase troop numbers," because doing so would inflame Afghan nationalism and lend support to the insurgency. "The Taliban," he adds, "which was a largely discredited and backward movement, gains support by portraying itself as fighting for Islam and Afghanistan against a foreign military occupation."[242] Noted regional scholar Barnett Rubin has argued, similarly, that the "Afghans don't like their country being occupied by foreign soldiers any more than did their ancestors," and that reaching a political solution to the insurgency "may require decreasing the U.S. and other foreign military presence rather than increasing it."[243]

NATO Forces

One option for meeting any identified requirements for additional forces is through contributions from NATO Allies. Secretary of State Clinton has indicated the intention of the Obama Administration to use the opportunity of NATO's 60th anniversary, in April 2009, to seek additional contributions from Allies.[244] Key considerations include both the likelihood and the utility of additional NATO contributions.

Some experts have raised questions about the utility of possible contributions from some NATO Allies, given the national caveats that tightly constrain the activities of many contingents. One option for the U.S. Government would be to continue to press Allies to relax or eliminate such caveats—Secretary of State Clinton has indicated that the Obama Administration intends to pursue this approach.[245] One alternative in some cases would be to focus on contributions less likely to create domestic political opposition. Some contributors, for example, might provide so-called "niche" capabilities such as explosive ordnance disposal (EOD) expertise and medical facilities, while others might choose to "sponsor"—that is, pay for and run—branch schools used for training the Afghan National Army.

[242] See Rory Stewart, "How to Save Afghanistan," *Time*, July 17, 2008. Stewart, the author of *The Places in Between*, is a former British diplomat and the head of the Turquoise Mountain project in Kabul.

[243] Barnett R. Rubin, "Afghan Dilemmas: Defining Commitments," *The American Interest*, vol. 3, no.5 (May/June 2008), pp.45–46.

[244] See the replies to questions for the record, submitted by Secretary of State nominee Hillary Clinton to the Senate Foreign Relations Committee (SFRC), for her January 13, 2009, confirmation hearing, available at http://www.foreignpolicy.com/files/KerryClintonQFRs.pdf.

[245] See the replies to questions for the record, submitted by Secretary of State nominee Hillary Clinton to the Senate Foreign Relations Committee (SFRC), for her January 13, 2009, confirmation hearing, available at http://www.foreignpolicy.com/files/KerryClintonQFRs.pdf.

U.S. Forces

The most likely avenue for meeting any requirements for additional international forces is an increase in U.S. troop strength in Afghanistan. As of the beginning of 2009, an additional brigade combat team (BCT)—3rd BCT, 10th Mountain Division—was flowing into Regional Command-East, and GEN McKiernan had requested three additional BCTs or equivalents, plus an aviation brigade and all the necessary enablers. The Combined Security Transition Command-Afghanistan (CSTC-A), in turn, had repeatedly stressed a requirement for additional trainers—2,300 for the Afghan police, and 60 teams for the ANA. Key questions include how much U.S. force presence is enough, what balance of forces is needed, and for how long.

One factor that might have an impact on required U.S. troop numbers, and how those requirements are described, is force employment. GEN McKiernan notes that the plan for many additional U.S. forces expected to flow into Afghanistan in 2009 is "dual-missioning," in which a given unit owns geographical battlespace and also plays a training and advisory role with the ANSF. For example, a BCT might be "plussed up" with additional Military Police (MP) structure, to help advise the Afghan National Police (ANP).[246] The U.S. Marine Corps Task Force that includes 3rd Battalion, 8th Marine Regiment, that arrived to serve in southern Afghanistan in late 2008, performs such a dual mission. Such arrangements might affect the ways that requirements are described—deploying a BCT "plussed up" with additional MPs, for example, might meet part of the requirements for both combat brigades and police trainers.

Observers have raised several different concerns about the ramifications of substantially increasing the U.S. share of the total ISAF force, as well as strengthening the U.S. role in ISAF command and control arrangements. The more prominent the U.S. role, some argue, the less likely that Allies will increase or perhaps even sustain their own contributions, since it will be easier for them to argue that the United States is meeting the requirement. Other skeptics point to a potential operational challenge—the possibility of a *de facto* bifurcation of Afghanistan into two distinct sets of approaches, robust COIN by the United States and a few Allies in eastern and southern Afghanistan, and softer stability operations by all other Allies and partners in northern and western Afghanistan. Such visible disparity, if it emerged, would make it much harder for ISAF to speak with a unified voice to GIRoA. Many civilian and military senior ISAF officials from non-U.S. Allies gently caution that, at the very least, the United States should avoid suggesting that the increased U.S. role was made necessary by inadequacies in the performance of their Allies.

[246] GEN David McKiernan, Interview, Kabul, Afghanistan, November 2008.

Logistics

The deployment of additional U.S. forces is likely to raise significant logistics challenges. U.S. forces based in eastern and southern Afghanistan have relied heavily to date on lines of communication (LOC) running across Afghanistan's mountainous eastern border into Pakistan, and down to the port city of Karachi. According to ISAF officials, with increased force flow, the demand on those LOCs is likely to increase by 500%, posing challenges in terms of both capacity and security. In late 2008, a series of insurgent attacks on those LOCs, on the Pakistani side of the border, underscored their vulnerability. In addition, the Government of Pakistan (GoP) has occasionally closed the primary border crossing, at the Khyber Pass, ostensibly to support GoP military operations in border regions. "Our biggest vulnerability," said one ISAF senior official, "is our LOCs."[247]

One alternative is the use of northern supply routes through former Soviet republics north of Afghanistan. On January 20, 2009, GEN Petraeus, CENTCOM Commanding General, announced that new agreements had been reached with Russia and Central Asian states regarding the transit of goods and supplies to Afghanistan. These arrangements are intended to complement the Pakistani supply routes—GEN Petraeus commented, "It is very important as we increase the effort in Afghanistan that we have multiple routes that go into the country."[248] Some experts have raised a concern about this option—the uncertainty about Russia's future orientation, its support for the international effort in Afghanistan, and the influence it might choose to exercise over any Central Asian support to that effort.

One additional practical consideration is the additional requirement for contractors resulting from increased U.S. troop deployments. ISAF officials noted in late 2008 that the U.S. Army had insufficient engineering assets available to support the construction in southern Afghanistan required by the arrival of large numbers of additional U.S. troops. They added that the availability of local contractors in southern Afghanistan was already scarce, given that the limited pool of qualified personnel was already occupied with work for ISAF and other organizations.

---

[247] ISAF official, Interview, Kabul, Afghanistan, November 2008. Recent attacks on the supply line from Karachi, Pakistan, to the Afghanistan border included the December 7, 2008, insurgent attacks on two truck stops in Peshawar, Pakistan, destroying over 100 vehicles with supplies bound for Afghanistan, and the November 10, 2008, insurgent hijacking of a convoy of vehicles on the road to the Khyber pass, bound for Afghanistan. See Laura King, "Suspected Taliban Militants Destroy Supply Trucks," *Los Angeles Times*, December 8, 2008.

[248] Chris Brummitt, "U.S. Reaches Deal on Afghan Supply Routes," *Army Times*, January 20, 2009.

Sourcing U.S. Deployments

With concurrent wars in Afghanistan and Iraq, the Department of Defense (DoD) could find it a challenge to source and then sustain larger troop deployments to Afghanistan.

One ramification could be delays in the arrival of additional forces in theater. Department of Defense (DoD) leaders indicated in late 2008 that DoD was working to send additional military forces to Afghanistan but that it would take some time—perhaps half a year—for them to become available. Senior U.S. military officials have indicated that additional force flow into Afghanistan is connected to U.S. force drawdowns in Iraq. Some observers note that such a delay may not prove neutral—that even if the insurgency is held to what some practitioners call its current "stalemate", Afghan popular opinion, the center of gravity in COIN, may well slide toward greater disaffection.

A second implication could be a continuation of stress on parts of the force. Numerous defense strategists have commented on the stress that simultaneous wars in Afghanistan and Iraq have placed on U.S. military forces, and particularly on the Army and Marine Corps. That pressure has manifested itself in repeated and extended deployments for both units and individual servicemembers, and has affected the personal lives of individual servicemembers through medical conditions and stress on families.

One key decision concerning additional U.S. force flow to Afghanistan will be the mix of Military Services and in particular, the Army and Marine Corps. The Marine Corps has long advocated a transition of its primary focus from Iraq to Afghanistan, arguing that improved security conditions in Anbar province, its area of responsibility in Iraq, allow a drawdown, and that Marine warfighting capabilities are especially well-suited for the growing security challenges in southern Afghanistan.[249]

A further decision concerns the type of Army combat forces that would deploy. To date, the U.S. Army has deployed "light" combat units to Afghanistan. If the Army continues to provide the majority of U.S. forces in Afghanistan, and if the decision is to continue to deploy exclusively light combat units, then stress on the infantry could become acute. One option

[249] See Otto Kreisher, "Marine Commandant Expects Troop Surge in Afghanistan," *National Journal*, January 15, 2009. See also Gordon Lubold, "A 'Surge' for Afghanistan?, The Christian Science Monitor, November 29, 2007; Lubold cited General James Conway, Commandant of the Marine Corps, as saying: "The trend lines tell us that it may be time to increase the force posture in Afghanistan. . . .If it requires additional US forces, then it goes back to our suggestion that maybe we need more Marines in there with a more kinetic bent." Gen Conway has also expressed concern that the Marines have "become, in some ways, a second land army," and may be losing their "expeditionary flavor," a danger that deployment to Afghanistan might help to avert. See Remarks by General James T. Conway, Commandant of the Marine Corps, Center for a New American Security, Washington DC, October 15, 2007, Available at http://www.marines.mil/units/hqmc/cmc/Documents/Speeches20071015CNAS.pdf.

might be the introduction of heavy BCTs, but their capabilities might be less well-suited for Afghanistan's terrain.

Updating Counterinsurgency (COIN) Approaches

Counterinsurgency approaches, by definition, require continual adaptation to the local environment.

One set of COIN military strategy questions in Afghanistan concerns population security, and in particular, how best to balance the need to maintain a dispersed footprint, living among the population, given the antipathy of some parts of that population toward any foreign presence. In Afghanistan, this dilemma has been particularly evident in some isolated mountain valleys. One option is to sustain an international troop presence, coupled with development and governance assistance, aiming to win over the local population eventually. An alternative—diametrically opposed both theoretically and practically—is to accept that "population security" may not work identically in every context, to withdraw the antagonizing foreign force presence in some locations, and to sacrifice some measure of security against insurgents for a different kind of stability—an absence of discord between foreign forces and the local population.

Another set of options concerns possible adjustments to the use of kinetic air operations in Afghanistan. The year 2008 witnessed sharp criticism from GIRoA and UNAMA of civilian casualties caused by air strikes. Such incidents have the potential to sharply discourage popular support for the government, essential to the success of any counterinsurgency. In late 2008, ISAF updated its Tactical Directive, carefully articulating rules for the use of fires. The year 2009 may prove a good test of the impact on civilian casualties of the 2008 Directive, and of a larger international forces presence that may allow some reduction in the use of kinetic air power.

A further set of options concerns the balance of effort between Special Operations Forces (SOF) and conventional forces. Some experts have argued that the military effort in Afghanistan would benefit from boosting the role of SOF vis-à-vis conventional forces. In Afghanistan, SOF play the lead role in targeting insurgent leaders, and proponents argue that increasing SOF troop strength might lead to more targeting successes. Other experts counter that successful SOF efforts rely on international conventional forces and the ANSF, both to provide information about a battlespace in advance, and to "hold" that battlespace after kinetic operations. That collaborative partnership, they argue, is essential to the success of overall COIN efforts, and therefore, the utility of unilateral increases in SOF deployments for the overall COIN mission would be limited.

Developing the Afghan National Security Forces (ANSF)

Experts generally agree that the development of the Afghan National Security Forces is essential to the future security and stability of Afghanistan.[250] In late 2008, GIRoA, backed by the support of the international community, decided to increase the target endstrength of the Afghan National Army (ANA). Further major policy issues include the size of the total ANSF, the mix of forces within it, the focus of effort of those forces, the timeline for developing those forces, and funding further ANSF development.

Practitioners underscore that ANSF development is highly dynamic. As Afghan National Police (ANP) capabilities grow, the ANP may increasingly assume responsibility for some domestic missions now performed by the Afghan National Army (ANA). As total ANSF numbers and capabilities grow, Afghan forces may increasingly assume responsibility from international security forces. And when—as expected—the security challenges from the insurgency diminish, the ANSF may shift from COIN to more traditional peacetime foci, including external defense for the ANA, and civilian law enforcement for the ANP.

One critical issue is funding the development and sustainment of the ANSF. Senior Afghan and international officials estimate that it will cost approximately $3.5 billion per year to increase ANSF force structure, and then $2.2 billion per year to sustain it. Unlike Iraq, whose oil revenues have funded an increasing share of the costs of growing and sustaining the Iraqi Security Forces in recent years, Afghanistan has few natural resources and little economic activity, other than poppy production, that could generate significant revenue in the near future. GIRoA, which contributed $320 million to the ANSF in 2008, is not a realistic source of ANSF funding in the near term.[251] International support, and particularly U.S. support, is expected to bear the near-term burden of developing the ANSF, until it reaches its current endstrength targets.

Growing the ANA to 134,000—or more—raises the twin questions of funding and sustainability. It is expected that the currently planned ANA growth will be funded by the international community; the United States is currently the leading contributor. If GIRoA wanted to sustain the force beyond that time frame, theoretical options would include continued U.S. and international support, or Afghan assumption of some level of financial

[250] See General James L. Jones, USMC (ret), Ambassador Thomas R. Pickering, *Afghanistan Study Group Report: Revitalizing our Efforts, Rethinking our Strategies,* Center for the Study of the Presidency, January 30, 2008, p.23. The authors argued for an enhanced international effort: "The U.S. and its NATO partners also need to focus more efforts and resources on training and standing up the Afghan National Army and recruiting, training, and providing adequate pay and equipment to the Afghan National Police so they can maintain security in an area once coalition forces depart."

[251] MG Robert Cone, Interview, Kabul, Afghanistan, November 2008.

responsibility. Alternatives could include demobilizing some part of the force—if GIRoA had the ability to do so—or, hypothetically, making part of the force available to serve in multi-lateral peace operations, in which case the international community might bear some of its costs.

For the future, one option, in the absence of GIRoA ability to shoulder the burden, would be sustained international support, a responsibility likely to fall to the U.S. Government, based on current patterns. The policy question for the U.S. Government, in turn, would concern whether national interests support sustaining that sizable commitment—and if so, at what levels, and for how long.

In the absence of either Afghan or international funding sources, one option would be demobilizing some part of the Afghan forces. A conclusive defeat of insurgent forces might increase the plausibility of such an approach, by reducing the requirement for ANSF numbers for the COIN fight. One challenge could prove to be limited ability on the part of the Afghan civilian leadership to direct the security ministries to decrease their forces.

One additional option, with some cost implications, would be a future role for Afghanistan as net exporter of security, providing trained, interoperable ANSF to serve in UN peace operations or other multi-national coalition efforts around the world. Minister of Defense Wardak suggested this possibility by noting, "One day we will pay our debt by fighting shoulder to shoulder with you," words that might apply abroad as well as at home.[252] Playing such roles might help GIRoA secure some international support for maintaining its force.

A further policy issue concerning the ANSF is force modernization—including the likely future requirements the ANSF will face, and the steps the ANSF might begin taking now, in terms of training and procurement, to prepare to meet those future requirements. While army and police commanders on the ground are fully focused on the current fight, Minister of Defense Wardak has argued in favor of beginning to build a mix of forces that would also be appropriate to the post-COIN environment. One implication for the U.S. Government is the impact GIRoA force modernization decisions may have on foreign military sales requests.

One final consideration concerning the development of the ANSF, is the nature of emerging civil-military relationships within the Government of Afghanistan. Some civil-military experts caution that there is an inherent danger, when a state's army is by far its most competent, effective organization, that civilian control of the military may erode. In late 2008, some Afghan officials, including Minister of Defense Wardak, have pointed to a

[252] Minister of Defense of Afghanistan Abdul Rahim Wardak, Interview, Kabul, Afghanistan, November 2008.

tendency on the part of President Karzai to ask the ANA to play non-military roles—for example, guarding civilian prisons—when civilian personnel are unavailable. U.S. military officials have noted that they spend significant time with senior Afghan security officials, mentoring them on the role of security forces in a democracy.[253]

Addressing Regional Issues

By the end of 2008, a near-consensus had emerged among practitioners and observers that the challenges Afghanistan faces could not be successfully addressed without a "regional" approach. Policy options might include various avenues for influencing the behavior of neighboring states, particularly Pakistan and Iran, in order to shape the security climate in Afghanistan. Some but not all commentators argue, in addition, that because Pakistan and India tend to make use of Afghanistan as a pawn in their own long-simmering conflict, successful "regional" initiatives concerning Afghanistan must also take into account the Pakistan-India relationship. Some commentators also suggest that Iraq is germane as a major security preoccupation for Iran, whose behavior in Afghanistan may be affected by developments across its opposite border. While the exhortation to consider the broader region has widespread support, no consensus on regional strategy has emerged—to date, experts have put forward a very wide range of specific policy prescriptions, some of them mutually contradictory.

Pakistan

The U.S. Government may wish to address both strategic and operational policy options concerning Pakistan's role vis-à-vis Afghanistan.

At the strategic level, a central question concerns the most effective ways to encourage Pakistani action against those supporting and fomenting the Afghanistan insurgency. One group of experts urges assistance efforts to support governance and development in "the impoverished areas that have become breeding grounds for militants", in particular along the border, in order to diminish the generation of, and support for, insurgents.[254]

Several other groups of experts particularly emphasize the importance of the U.S.-Pakistani mil-to-mil relationship, as a tool for shaping Pakistani actions. Some argue that the key is to continue to build Pakistani capabilities and to shape their orientation by strengthening current initiatives—for example, by boosting U.S. efforts to train the Pakistan Army Special Forces

[253] MG Robert Cone, Interview, Kabul, Afghanistan, November 2008.

[254] Christopher D. Kolenda, "How to Win in Afghanistan," *Weekly Standard*, October 13, 2008. Colonel Christopher Kolenda recently commanded a U.S. Army battalion in Afghanistan along the border with Pakistan.

for counterterrorism operations, expanding Pakistani participation in military exchange programs, and fostering closer mil-to-mil coordination along the Afghanistan-Pakistan border.[255] Others agree that mil-to-mil initiatives are key but urge making the provision of the benefits they offer conditional on stronger Pakistani support along the border with Afghanistan.[256] Some experts, in contrast, argue that the close U.S.-Pakistan mil-to-mil relationship is part of the problem, as it may tend to diminish Pakistani civilian control over its military. Therefore, one regional expert writes, "the United States must relinquish, not strengthen, the privileged relationship between the United States and the Pakistani military."[257]

Another set of experts argues that efforts to shape Pakistani actions vis-à-vis Afghanistan are likely to be successful only as part of a broader approach to Pakistan's concerns and its role in the region. Key issues, in this broader perspective, might include Pakistan's role as a nuclear power, and its tendentious relationship with nuclear-armed neighbor India—in particular their rival claims to the disputed territory of Kashmir. Policy options might include, for example, more robust U.S. unilateral, or multilateral, diplomatic efforts to help India and Pakistan forge a stable, sustainable relationship.

The Obama Administration has indicated initial support for a Pakistan policy that includes both increasing non-military aid, and conditioning the provision of mil-to-mil assistance on Pakistani actions such as "... clos[ing] down training camps, evict[ing] foreign fighters, and prevent[ing] the Taliban and al Qaeda from using Pakistan as a sanctuary."[258]

Meanwhile, at the operational level, a key question is whether to continue U.S. cross-border attacks while strategic-level dialogue and other attempts to exercise leverage are underway. Continued cross-border attacks might lead to political blow-back in Pakistan, but they might also persuade Pakistani officials to take more decisive steps to end support to insurgents.

[255] See Thomas Lynch, "Afghan Dilemmas: Staying Power," *The American Interest*, vol. 3, no.5 (May/June 2008), p.36. U.S. Army Colonel Thomas Lynch has served in Afghanistan.

[256] See Vikram J. Singh and Nathaniel C. Fick, "Surging Statecraft to Save Afghanistan", *Small Wars Journal*, October 2, 2008.

[257] Barnett R. Rubin, "Afghan Dilemmas: Defining Commitments," *The American Interest*, vol. 3, no.5 (May/June 2008), p.49. He adds that the United States "must instead support civilian control over the government and military alike, even by parties that oppose U.S. objectives openly (rather than covertly, like the military)."

[258] See the replies to questions for the record, submitted by Secretary of State nominee Hillary Clinton to the Senate Foreign Relations Committee (SFRC), for her January 13, 2009, confirmation hearing, available at http://www.foreignpolicy.com/files/KerryClintonQFRs.pdf. Under Secretary of Defense for Policy Michèle Flournoy, in replies to questions for the record submitted for her own confirmation hearing, with the Senate Armed Services Committee on January 15, 2009, echoed the same premise, stating: "The U.S. must have an integrated strategy to promote development and prevent terrorism across the Afghanistan-Pakistan border region." See replies to questions for the record, submitted by Under Secretary of Defense for Policy nominee to the Senate Armed Services Committee (SASC), for her January 15, 2009, confirmation hearing, available at http://armed-services.senate.gov/statemnt/2009/January/Flournoy%2001-15-09.pdf.

Options, therefore, might include either accelerating or decreasing the use of cross-border attacks. Options might also include seeking additional avenues for strengthening tactical-level cross-border coordination, including increasing the frequency or scope of regular coordination meetings, establishing further border coordination centers, and improving the ease of tactical-level coordination in actions against insurgent targets.

Iran

Practitioners and observers recognize Iran's dual track role in Afghanistan—providing both humanitarian and lethal aid. The key issue in U.S. Afghanistan policy debates is how best to leverage concerns that Iran shares with the rest of the international community—including regional security and the impact of the narcotics trade—to shape Iranian choices.

Options include a more concerted diplomatic outreach to Tehran, by the United States and/or other members of the international community, designed to build on shared regional concerns. Some experts suggest that Tehran may be more likely to respond positively to outreach efforts by the Obama Administration, than to those by its predecessor. Another option—not mutually exclusive—is robust countering of any Iranian efforts to provide lethal aid to insurgents in Afghanistan.

Strengthening Counternarcotics Efforts

Despite the existence of broadly agreed counternarcotics (CN) strategies, and some recent declines in cultivation, many practitioners see little likelihood of significant further CN progress until GIRoA takes major further strides in establishing the rule of law, including both building a formal judicial system and encouraging a pervasive law-based culture. Some observers have further suggested that there may be inherent contradictions between CN and COIN efforts, since a key premise of COIN is fostering popular support for the government, while some CN initiatives may alienate parts of the population, at least temporarily.

One near term option is for GIRoA and ISAF to take full advantage of the October 2008 NATO decision expanding the interpretation of the CN role ISAF may play, to include targeting drug facilities when a connection with the insurgency can be shown. Focused diplomatic efforts might prove useful in persuading some Allies to fully embrace this broader interpretation.

A further option might be more assiduously cultivating the cooperation of community as well as provincial leaders in CN efforts, including strengthening the system of incentives available to those who lend their support. The Afghanistan Social Outreach Program, designed to foster and focus ground-up capacity-building, might naturally complement any such outreach efforts.

Achieving a NATO Success in Afghanistan?

Most NATO observers suggest that "Afghanistan" is a critical test for the Alliance, including its ability to conduct major out-of-area missions, and its relevance to 21st century security challenges, and many have argued that failure in Afghanistan could spell the end of the Alliance. The issue of the role of NATO in Afghanistan is likely to gain prominence on the world stage in early 2009, amidst preparations for NATO's 60th anniversary summit, scheduled for April 2009. In January 2008, the Afghanistan Study Group argued, "A failure of the NATO mission in Afghanistan would also damage the future prospects of the organization itself."[259] For a number of practitioners, that line of thinking implies an imperative to make sure that the Alliance is successful in Afghanistan—which is not quite the same thing, logically, as making sure that Afghanistan itself succeeds. Key policy considerations include what it would take for the outcome in Afghanistan to be considered a "NATO success", and what if any differences that might entail from a strict pursuit of security, good governance and development for Afghanistan. In some circumstances, U.S. policy-makers might wish to weigh the imperative of accomplishing the mission against the imperative to support NATO as an institution.

Some observers suggest that the growing presence of U.S. forces, and possibly a stronger U.S. role in ISAF command and control, may lead to the perception that any progress in Afghanistan is due to U.S. rather than NATO efforts. In that vein, the Afghanistan Study Group argued, "Burden-sharing among NATO allies is critical to the mission in terms of both available resources and public perceptions—an increasingly unilateral mission will be politically vulnerable in Afghanistan, the U.S., and NATO."[260] Options for countering such perceptions, if so desired, might include maintaining U.S. battlespace-owning units under ISAF command; using diplomatic channels to forge stronger consensus on the nature and stakes of the fight in Afghanistan; and soliciting non-military forms of assistance from those countries unwilling or unable to provide large ground force contingents for the counterinsurgency fight.

Supporting Reconciliation

A number of key practitioners and observers have supported "reconciliation" outreach initiatives, to insurgent leaders and/or their foot soldiers,

---

[259] See for example General James L. Jones, USMC (ret), Ambassador Thomas R. Pickering, *Afghanistan Study Group Report: Revitalizing our Efforts, Rethinking our Strategies,* Center for the Study of the Presidency, January 30, 2008, Page 17.

[260] General James L. Jones, USMC (ret), Ambassador Thomas R. Pickering, *Afghanistan Study Group Report: Revitalizing our Efforts, Rethinking our Strategies,* Center for the Study of the Presidency, January 30, 2008, Page 17.

as one avenue toward final settlement of the conflict in Afghanistan. Senior U.S. military officials in Afghanistan underscore that questions concerning to whom to reach out, at what time, with what offers, and with what endstate in view, are policy matters for GIRoA decision. Any "reconciliation" efforts would likely have a direct bearing on security efforts in Afghanistan, because they concern the formal adversary—the insurgents—in the fight.

Some experts have argued that leadership-level reconciliation initiatives risk institutionalizing formal political roles in the future Government of Afghanistan for known "bad guys". Such inclusion, they suggest, might alienate parts of the Afghan population who suffered repression under the Taliban regime. Worse, such alienated constituencies might take up arms to protest such brokered deals. Institutionalizing leading roles for former Taliban or other insurgent leaders might also, it is suggested, push the orientation of the Government of Afghanistan in more repressive directions.

U.S. Government policy considerations might include determining the U.S. preferred outcome of any such talks, and exercising diplomacy to influence the form and content of any such initiatives. From an operational perspective, U.S. deliberations might include assessing how different military strategies might contribute to bringing Taliban leaders to the negotiations table in a frame of mind conducive to agreeing to conditions acceptable to GIRoA. For example, Taliban leaders might be compelled to come to terms by even more aggressive targeting, or by more strident efforts to cut off the funding support they receive from the narcotics trade.

Applying the Lessons of Afghanistan for the Future Force Development

For the longer term, defense practitioners and analysts are likely to continue to seek lessons from U.S. military prosecution of the wars in Afghanistan and Iraq to apply to future U.S. force shaping and sizing. Such conclusions, and they way they are applied, are likely to have a profound impact on how the Military Services fulfill their responsibilities, in accordance with Title 10, U.S. Code, to organize, man, train and equip military forces. Critical policy considerations for DoD are likely to include the capabilities required to successfully prosecute complex contingency operations like those in Afghanistan and Iraq, the likelihood that the United States will engage in similar complex contingencies in the future, and the relative importance of such skills compared to more traditional military capabilities.

The publication of Department of Defense Directive 3000.07 on "Irregular Warfare", in December 2008, which stated that "IW is as strategically important as traditional warfare," reflected and helped institutionalize a growing DoD emphasis on complex contingency capabilities.[261]

Should this school of thought continue to hold sway, options might include further increasing the endstrength of the ground forces, and raising the profile of the mission to train and advise foreign security forces. In a resource-constrained environment, any such choices would like entail trade-offs with other DoD capability areas.

Balancing and Integrating Civilian and Military Efforts

Years of operational experience in Afghanistan, like those in Iraq, have helped fuel debates about appropriately balancing military and civilian capabilities in the U.S. Government, and effectively integrating those capabilities with each other.

A key short-term policy consideration is the U.S. Government response to the appeal from U.S. Embassy Kabul for further civilian resources—personnel and ready funds—to support capacity-building efforts in Afghanistan. One constraint may be the availability of trained civilian personnel with the appropriate expertise, ready to deploy. Another constraint may be the availability of funds—in particular, civilian funding streams relatively free of bureaucratic red tape that allow quick execution.

Some U.S. commanders on the ground, while generally welcoming the prospect of civilian expertise, caution that such an initiative would be most valuable if it carefully recruits people with relevant expertise. Simply "throwing bodies at the problem," they caution, would not be helpful. Some add that it would also be important to ensure that additional civilian personnel are included in clear civilian chains of command, to ensure unity of effort among their various activities.

Some outside experts, in turn, caution against any infusion of civilian personnel that might detract from GIRoA efforts to govern their own country. One regional expert, arguing that the U.S. Government should not increase its involvement in the Afghan government or economy, has written: "The more responsibility we take in Afghanistan, the more we undermine the credibility and responsibility of the Afghan government and encourage it to act irresponsibly."[262] Another expert has urged, "Rather than sending in

---

[261] Department of Defense, "Irregular Warfare (IW)", DoDD 3000.07, December 1, 2008. The Directive defined IW this way: "A violent struggle among state and non-state actors for legitimacy and influence over the relevant population(s). Irregular warfare favors indirect and asymmetric approaches, though it may employ the full range of military and other capacities, in order to erode an adversary's power, influence, and will." It noted that "IW can include a variety of steady-state and surge DoD activities and operations: counter-terrorism, unconventional warfare; foreign internal defense; counterinsurgency; and stability operations that, in the context of IW, involve establishing or reestablishing order in a fragile state."

[262] Rory Stewart, "How to Save Afghanistan," *Time*, July 17, 2008.

thousands of civilians, the shift in emphasis could be to training Afghans to do the jobs themselves."[263] U.S. Embassy appeals for a "civilian surge" are predicated on precisely that advisory approach.

Key policy considerations for the longer-term, suggested by U.S. experience in Afghanistan, might include whether the U.S. government requires increased civilian capacity to meet possible future complex contingency requirements, and if so, what capabilities would be required, and how might they best be cultivated and organized. A related consideration concerns the implications of any enhancement of U.S. government civilian capacity for military requirements—whether, for example, increased civilian capacity might decrease the missions military forces should be prepared to accomplish. And finally, regardless of the balance in numbers and capabilities between military and civilian personnel, a further policy consideration is how best to effectively integrate military and civilian complex contingency efforts, in both planning and execution.

Additional Reports

CRS Report RL33110, *The Cost of Iraq, Afghanistan, and Other Global War on Terror Operations Since 9/11*, by Amy Belasco.

CRS Report RL32686, *Afghanistan: Narcotics and U.S. Policy*, by Christopher M. Blanchard.

CRS Report RL33627, *NATO in Afghanistan: A Test of the Transatlantic Alliance*, by Vincent Morelli and Paul Belkin.

CRS Report RL30588, *Afghanistan: Post-War Governance, Security, and U.S. Policy*, by Kenneth Katzman.

CRS Report RL33498, *Pakistan-U.S. Relations*, by K. Alan Kronstadt.

[263] Clare Lockhart, "Learning from Experience," *Slate*, November 5, 2008.

Figure 1: Map of Afghanistan

Source: The University of Texas at Austin, Perry-Castaneda Library Map Collection, Afghanistan Political Map 2003.

Author Contact Information

Catherine Dale
Specialist in International Security
cdale@crs.loc.gov, 7-8983

DOCUMENT NO. 5

WHITE PAPER OF THE INTERAGENCY POLICY GROUP'S REPORT ON U.S. POLICY TOWARD AFGHANISTAN AND PAKISTAN

The U.S. Department of Defense

March 2009

Introduction

The United States has a vital national security interest in addressing the current and potential security threats posed by extremists in Afghanistan and Pakistan. In Pakistan, al Qaeda and other groups of jihadist terrorists are planning new terror attacks. Their targets remain the U.S. homeland, Pakistan, Afghanistan, India, Europe, Australia, our allies in the Middle East, and other targets of opportunity. The growing size of the space in which they are operating is a direct result of the terrorist/insurgent activities of the Taliban and related organizations. At the same time, this group seeks to reestablish their old sanctuaries in Afghanistan.

Therefore, the core goal of the U.S. must be to disrupt, dismantle, and defeat al Qaeda and its safe havens in Pakistan, and to prevent their return to Pakistan or Afghanistan.

The ability of extremists in Pakistan to undermine Afghanistan is proven, while insurgency in Afghanistan feeds instability in Pakistan. The threat that al Qaeda poses to the United States and our allies in Pakistan—including the possibility of extremists obtaining fissile material—is all too real. Without more effective action against these groups in Pakistan, Afghanistan will face continuing instability.

Objectives

Achieving our core goal is vital to U.S. national security. It requires, first of all, realistic and achievable objectives. These include:

- Disrupting terrorist networks in Afghanistan and especially Pakistan to degrade any ability they have to plan and launch international terrorist attacks.

- Promoting a more capable, accountable, and effective government in Afghanistan that serves the Afghan people and can eventually function, especially regarding internal security, with limited international support.
- Developing increasingly self-reliant Afghan security forces that can lead the counterinsurgency and counterterrorism fight with reduced U.S. assistance.
- Assisting efforts to enhance civilian control and stable constitutional government in Pakistan and a vibrant economy that provides opportunity for the people of Pakistan.
- Involving the international community to actively assist in addressing these objectives for Afghanistan and Pakistan, with an important leadership role for the UN.

A New Way Forward

These are daunting tasks. They require a new way of thinking about the challenges, a wide ranging diplomatic strategy to build support for our efforts, enhanced engagement with the publics in the region and at home, and a realization that all elements of international power—diplomatic, informational, military and economic—must be brought to bear. They will also require a significant change in the management, resources, and focus of our foreign assistance.

Our diplomatic effort should be based on building a clear consensus behind the common core goal and supporting objectives. To this end, we will explore creating new diplomatic mechanisms, including establishing a "Contact Group" and a regional security and economic cooperation forum. The trilateral U.S.-Pakistan-Afghanistan effort of February 24–26, 2009 will be continued and broadened, into the next meeting planned for early May, in Washington.

The United States must overcome the 'trust deficit' it faces in Afghanistan and Pakistan, where many believe that we are not a reliable long-term partner. We must engage the Afghan people in ways that demonstrate our commitment to promoting a legitimate and capable Afghan government with economic progress. We must engage the Pakistani people based on our long-term commitment to helping them build a stable economy, a stronger democracy, and a vibrant civil society.

A strategic communications program must be created, made more effective, and resourced. This new strategy will have no chance of success without better civil-military coordination by U.S. agencies, a significant increase of civilian resources, and a new model of how we allocate and use these resources. For too long, U.S. and international assistance efforts in

Afghanistan and Pakistan have suffered from being ill-organized and significantly under-resourced in some areas. A large portion of development assistance ends up being spent on international consultants and overhead, and virtually no impact assessments have yet been done on our assistance programs.

We must ensure that our assistance to both Afghanistan and Pakistan is aligned with our core goals and objectives. This will involve assistance that is geared to strengthening government capacity and the message that assistance will be limited without the achievement of results. Additional assistance to Afghanistan must be accompanied by concrete mechanisms to ensure greater government accountability. In a country that is 70 percent rural, and where the Taliban recruiting base is primarily among underemployed youths, a complete overhaul of our civilian assistance strategy is necessary; agricultural sector job creation is an essential first step to undercutting the appeal of al Qaeda and its allies. Increased assistance to Pakistan will be limited without a greater willingness to cooperate with us to eliminate the sanctuary enjoyed by al Qaeda and other extremist groups, as well as a greater commitment to economic reforms that will raise the living standard of ordinary Pakistanis, including in the border regions of the Federally Administered Tribal Areas, the North West Frontier Province, and Baluchistan.

Summary of Recommendations for Afghanistan and Pakistan

The following steps must be done in concert to produce the desired end state: the removal of al-Qaeda's sanctuary, effective democratic government control in Pakistan, and a self-reliant Afghanistan that will enable a withdrawal of combat forces while sustaining our commitment to political and economic development.

- *Executing and resourcing an integrated civilian-military counterinsurgency strategy in Afghanistan.*

Our military forces in Afghanistan, including those recently approved by the President, should be utilized for two priority missions: 1) securing Afghanistan's south and east against a return of al Qaeda and its allies, to provide a space for the Afghan government to establish effective government control and 2) providing the Afghan security forces with the mentoring needed to expand rapidly, take the lead in effective counterinsurgency operations, and allow us and our partners to wind down our combat operations.

Our counter-insurgency strategy must integrate population security with building effective local governance and economic development. We will establish the security needed to provide space and time for stabilization and reconstruction activities.

To prevent future attacks on the U.S. and its allies—including the local populace—the development of a strategic communications strategy to counter the terror information campaign is urgent. This has proved successful in Iraq (where the U.S. military has made a significant effort in this area) and should be developed in Afghanistan as a top priority to improve the image of the United States and its allies. The strategic communications plan—including electronic media, telecom, and radio—shall include options on how best to counter the propaganda that is key to the enemy's terror campaign.

- *Resourcing and prioritizing civilian assistance in Afghanistan*

By increasing civilian capacity we will strengthen the relationship between the Afghan people and their government. A dramatic increase in Afghan civilian expertise is needed to facilitate the development of systems and institutions particularly at the provincial and local levels, provide basic infrastructure, and create economic alternatives to the insurgency at all levels of Afghan society, particularly in agriculture. The United States should play an important part in providing that expertise, but responding effectively to Afghanistan's needs will require that allies, partners, the UN and other international organizations, and non-governmental organizations significantly increase their involvement in Afghanistan.

- *Expanding the Afghan National Security Forces: Army and Police*

To be capable of assuming the security mission from U.S. forces in Afghanistan's south and east, the Afghan National Security Forces must substantially increase its size and capability. Initially this will require a more rapid build-up of the Afghan Army and police up to 134,000 and 82,000 over the next two years, with additional enlargements as circumstances and resources warrant.

The international community must assume responsibility for funding this significantly enhanced Afghan security force for an extended period. We will also have to provide support for other Afghan security forces such as the Afghan Public Protection Force. Salaries paid to Afghan National Army and Afghan National Police must become more competitive with those paid by the insurgents.

Over time, as security conditions change, we should continue to reassess Afghan National Security Forces size, as it will be affected by such factors as: the overall security situation, the capabilities of the Afghan National Security Forces, and the rate at which we can grow local security forces and integrate them into the overall ANSF structure.

- *Engaging the Afghan government and bolstering its legitimacy*

International support for the election will be necessary for a successful outcome. We should do everything necessary to ensure the security and legitimacy of voter registration, elections, and vote counting. The international military presence should help the Afghan security forces provide security before, during and after the election. International monitoring will also be required to ensure legitimacy and oversee Afghanistan's polling sites.

The overall legitimacy of the Afghan government is also undermined by rampant corruption and a failure to provide basic services to much of the population over the past 7 years. Where Afghan systems and institutions have benefited from high quality technical assistance and mentoring, they have made great progress. Making such support more consistent with qualified mentors to advise and monitor officials, pushing such efforts to the provincial and district levels, and channeling more assistance through Afghan institutions benefiting from this high quality support will help restore and maintain the legitimacy of the Afghan government.

- *Encouraging Afghan government efforts to integrate reconcilable insurgents*

While Mullah Omar and the Taliban's hard core that have aligned themselves with al Qaeda are not reconcilable and we cannot make a deal that includes them, the war in Afghanistan cannot be won without convincing non-ideologically committed insurgents to lay down their arms, reject al Qaeda, and accept the Afghan Constitution.

Practical integration must not become a mechanism for instituting medieval social policies that give up the quest for gender equality and human rights. We can help this process along by exploiting differences among the insurgents to divide the Taliban's true believers from less committed fighters.

Integration must be Afghan-led. An office should be created in every province and we should support efforts by the Independent Directorate of Local Governance to develop a reconciliation effort targeting mid-to-low level insurgents to be led by provincial governors. We should also explore ways to rehabilitate captured insurgents drawing on lessons learned from similar programs in Iraq and other countries.

- *Including provincial and local governments in our capacity building efforts*

We need to work with the Afghan government to refocus civilian assistance and capacity-building programs on building up competent provincial and local governments where they can more directly serve the people and connect them to their government.

- *Breaking the link between narcotics and the insurgency*

Besides the global consequences of the drug trade, the Afghan narcotics problem causes great concern due to its ties to the insurgency, the fact that it is the major driver of corruption in Afghanistan, and distorts the legal economy. The NATO/International Security Assistance Forces and U.S. forces should use their authorities to directly support Afghan counternarcotics units during the interdiction of narco-traffickers. The new authorities permit the destruction of labs, drug storage facilities, drug processing equipment, and drug caches and should contribute to breaking the drug-insurgency funding nexus and the corruption associated with the opium/heroin trade. Crop substitution and alternative livelihood programs that are a key pillar of effectively countering narcotics have been disastrously underdeveloped and under-resourced, however, and the narcotics trade will persist until such programs allow Afghans to reclaim their land for licit agriculture. Targeting those who grow the poppy will continue, but the focus will shift to higher level drug lords.

- *Mobilizing greater international political support of our objectives in Afghanistan*

We need to do more to build a shared understanding of what is at stake in Afghanistan, while engaging other actors and offering them the opportunity to advance our mutual interests by cooperating with us.

- *Bolstering Afghanistan-Pakistan cooperation*

We need to institutionalize stronger mechanisms for bilateral and trilateral cooperation. During the process of this review, inter-agency teams from Afghanistan and Pakistan came to Washington, DC for trilateral meetings. This new forum should continue and serve as the basis for enhanced bilateral and trilateral cooperation.

- *Engaging and focusing Islamabad on the common threat*

Successfully shutting down the Pakistani safe haven for extremists will also require consistent and intensive strategic engagement with Pakistani leadership in both the civilian and military spheres. The engagement must be conducted in a way that respects, and indeed enhances, democratic civilian authority.

- *Assisting Pakistan's capability to fight extremists*

It is vital to strengthen our efforts to both develop and operationally enable Pakistani security forces so they are capable of succeeding in sustained counterterrorism and counterinsurgency operations. In part this will include increased U.S. military assistance for helicopters to provide air mobility, night vision equipment, and training and equipment specifically for Pakistani Special Operation Forces and their Frontier Corps.

- *Increasing and broadening assistance in Pakistan*

Increasing economic assistance to Pakistan—to include direct budget support, development assistance, infrastructure investment, and technical advice on making sound economic policy adjustments—and strengthening trade relations will maximize support for our policy aims; it should also help to provide longer-term economic stability. Our assistance should focus on long-term capacity building, on agricultural sector job creation, education and training, and on infrastructure requirements. Assistance should also support Pakistani efforts to 'hold and build' in western Pakistan as a part of its counterinsurgency efforts.

- *Exploring other areas of economic cooperation with Pakistan*

We need to enhance bilateral and regional trade possibilities, in part through implementing Reconstruction Opportunity Zones (which were recently re-introduced in Congress) and encouraging foreign investment in key sectors, such as energy. In addition, assisting Islamabad with developing a concrete strategy for utilizing donor aid would increase Islamabad's chances for garnering additional support from the international community.

- *Strengthening Pakistani government capacity*

Strengthening the civilian, democratic government must be a centerpiece of our overall effort. Key efforts should include fostering the reform of provincial and local governance in the Federally Administered Tribal Areas and the North West Frontier Province. We need to help Islamabad enhance the services and support in areas cleared of insurgents so that they have a real chance in preventing insurgents from returning to those areas.

With international partners, we should also promote the development of regional organizations that focus on economic and security cooperation, as well as fostering productive political dialogue.

- *Asking for assistance from allies for Afghanistan and Pakistan*

Our efforts are a struggle against forces that pose a direct threat to the entire international community. While reaching out to allies and partners for their political support, we should also ask them to provide the necessary resources to accomplish our shared objectives. They have the same interest in denying terrorists and extremists sanctuaries in Pakistan and Afghanistan that we do. In approaching allies we should emphasize that our new approach is integrated between civilian and military elements and in looking at Afghanistan and Pakistan as one theater for diplomacy.

For the mission in Afghanistan, we should continue to seek contributions for combat forces, trainers and mentors, strategic lift, and equipment from our friends and allies. The U.S. will also pursue major international funding and experts for civilian reconstruction and Afghan government capacity building at the national and especially the provincial and local levels.

The United Nations Assistance Mission in Afghanistan should take the lead in exploring ways that donors could systematically share the burden of building Afghan capacity and providing civilian expertise. As part of its coordination role for civilian assistance, the UN should consolidate requests and identify gaps.

In Pakistan, the U.S. will urge allies to work closely with us both bilaterally and through the 'Friends of Democratic Pakistan' to coordinate economic and development assistance, including additional direct budget support, development assistance, infrastructure investment and technical advice on making sound economic policy adjustments. Similarly, we should ask them to provide technical advice and assistance in strengthening government capacity, such as improving Pakistani institutions.

Conclusion

There are no quick fixes to achieve U.S. national security interests in Afghanistan and Pakistan. The danger of failure is real and the implications are grave. In 2009–2010 the Taliban's momentum must be reversed in Afghanistan and the international community must work with Pakistan to disrupt the threats to security along Pakistan's western border.

This new strategy of focusing on our core goal—to disrupt, dismantle, and eventually destroy extremists and their safe havens within both nations, although with different tactics—will require immediate action, sustained commitment, and substantial resources. The United States is committed to working with our partners in the region and the international community to address this challenging but essential security goal.

DOCUMENT NO. 6

LATIN AMERICA: TERRORISM ISSUES

CRS Report
RS21049

August 27, 2008

Mark P. Sullivan

Summary

Since the September 2001 terrorist attacks on New York and Washington, U.S. attention to terrorism in Latin America has intensified, with an increase in bilateral and regional cooperation. In its April 2008 Country Reports on Terrorism, the State Department highlighted threats in Colombia and the tri-border area of Argentina, Brazil, and Paraguay. Cuba has remained on the State Department's list of state sponsors of terrorism since 1982, which triggers a number of economic sanctions. In May 2008, for the third year in a row, the Department of State, pursuant to Arms Export Control Act, included Venezuela on the annual list of countries not cooperating on antiterrorism efforts. In the 110th Congress, the House approved H.Con.Res. 188 and H.Con.Res. 385, both condemning the 1994 bombing of the Argentine-Israeli Mutual Association in Buenos Aires, and H.Res. 435, expressing concern over the emerging national security implications of Iran's efforts to expand its influence in Latin America, and emphasizing the importance of eliminating Hezbollah's financial network in the tri-border area. The Senate approved S.Con.Res. 53, condemning the hostage-taking of three U.S. citizens for over four years by the Revolutionary Armed Forces of Colombia (FARC). In the second session, two resolutions have been introduced: H.Res. 1049 calls for Venezuela to be designated a state sponsor of terrorism because of its alleged support for the FARC, while H.Res. 965, among other provisions, calls for Venezuela to implement measures to deny the use of Venezuelan territory and weapons from being used by terrorist organizations.

Terrorism in Latin America: U.S. Concerns

Over the years, the United States has been concerned about threats to Latin American and Caribbean nations from various terrorist or insurgent groups that have attempted to influence or overthrow elected governments. Although Latin America has not been the focal point in the war on terrorism, countries in the region have struggled with domestic terrorism for decades and international terrorist groups have at times used the region as a battleground to advance their causes. The State Department's annual *Country Reports on Terrorism* highlights U.S. concerns about terrorist threats around the world, including in Latin America. The April 2008 report states that terrorism in the region was primarily perpetrated by terrorist organizations in Colombia and by the remnants of radical leftist Andean groups. According to the report, "there were no known operational cells of Islamic terrorists" in the region, but it maintained that "pockets of ideological supporters and facilitators in South America and the Caribbean lent financial, logistical, and moral support to terrorist groups in the Middle East." Overall, however, the report maintained that the threat of a transnational terrorist attack remained low for most countries in the hemisphere. The report also stated that regional governments "took modest steps to improve their counterterrorism capabilities and tighten border security" but that progress was limited by "corruption, weak government institutions, ineffective or lack of interagency cooperation, weak or non-existent legislation, and reluctance to allocate sufficient resources." The report lauded counterterrorism efforts in Argentina, Panama, Paraguay, Mexico, and El Salvador, and noted that Caribbean and Central American countries took steps to improve their border controls and to secure key infrastructure. It also noted that most hemispheric nations had solid cooperation with the United States on terrorism issues, especially at the operational level, with excellent intelligence, law enforcement, and legal assistance relations.

Colombia. Colombia has three terrorist groups that have been designated by the Secretary of State as Foreign Terrorist Organizations (FTOs): the leftist Revolutionary Armed Forces of Colombia (FARC), the leftist National Liberation Army (ELN), and remaining elements of the rightist paramilitary United Self-Defense Forces of Colombia (AUC). With more than 32,000 members demobilized, the AUC remained inactive as a formal organization, but some AUC renegades continued to engage in criminal activities, mostly drug trafficking, according to the terrorism report. The ELN, which had dwindling memberships and reduced offensive capability, has participated in peace talks with the Colombian government, but no agreements have been reached. The FARC has been weakened by the government's military campaign against it, including the killings of several FARC commanders in 2007 and the group's second in command, Raúl Reyes, during a Colombian government raid on a FARC camp in Ecuador on March 1, 2008.

Moreover, in May 2008, the FARC admitted that its long-time leader, Manuel Marulanda, had died of a heart attack in March. Nevertheless, the group has continued terrorist, kidnapping for profit, and narcotrafficking activities, including murders of elected officials and attacks against military and civilian targets in urban and rural areas. According to the terrorism report, both the FARC and the ELN often crossed into Venezuelan territory for rest and resupply, and the FARC regularly used Ecuadorian territory for rest, recuperation, resupply, and training. On December 19, 2007, the Senate approved S.Con.Res. 53 (Nelson, Bill) condemning the holding of three U.S. citizens by the FARC since February 2003—Thomas Howes, Keith Stansell, and Marc Gonsalves—and calling for their immediate and unconditional release. A similar resolution, H.Con.Res. 260 (Diaz-Balart, Mario), was introduced in the House on November 15, 2007. (Also see CRS Report RL32250, *Colombia: Issues for Congress.*)

Venezuela. The State Department's terrorism report stated that "it remained unclear to what extent the Venezuelan government provided support to Colombian terrorist organizations," but information on captured computer files from Colombia's March 2008 raid of a FARC camp in Ecuador has raised questions about alleged support of the FARC by the Venezuelan government of Hugo Chávez. Since May 2006, the Secretary of State has made an annual determination that Venezuela was not "cooperating fully with United States antiterrorism efforts" pursuant to Section 40A of the Arms Export Control Act (AECA). As a result, the United States imposed an arms embargo on Venezuela, which ended all U.S. commercial arms sales and re-transfers to Venezuela. (Other countries on the Section 40A list include Cuba, Iran, North Korea, and Syria, not to be confused with the "state sponsors of terrorism" list under Section 6(j) of the Export Administration Act of 1979.) According to the terrorism report, President Chávez continued public criticism of U.S. counterterrorism efforts and deepened Venezuelan relationships with Iran and Cuba, and his ideological sympathy for the FARC and ELN, along with high levels of corruption among Venezuelan officials, limited Venezuelan cooperation with Colombia in combating terrorism. In addition, according to the report, Venezuelan citizenship, identity, and travel documents remained easy to obtain, making the country a potentially attractive waystation for terrorists. In light of information on captured FARC computer files, H.Res. 1049 (Mack), introduced March 13, 2008, would call on the Administration to designate Venezuela as a state sponsor of terrorism. Another initiative, H.Res. 965 (Issa), introduced February 7, 2008, would call upon the Chávez government to implement measures to deny the use of Venezuelan territory and weapons from being used by terrorist organizations and to resume full cooperation with the United States on counterterrorism measures.

U.S. officials and Members of Congress also have expressed concerns about Venezuela's growing relations with Iran, especially because of Iran's links with Hezbollah. In November 2007, the House approved H.Res. 435 (Klein), expressing concern about Iran's efforts to expand its influence in Latin America, and noting Venezuela's increasing cooperation with Iran. On June 18, 2008, the U.S. Treasury Department's Office of Foreign Assets Control announced that it was freezing the U.S. assets of two Venezuelans for providing financial and other support to Hezbollah. (Also see CRS Report RL32488, *Venezuela: Political Conditions and U.S. Policy*.)

Peru. The brutal Shining Path (Sendero Luminoso or SL) insurgency, which the Department of State has designated as an FTO, was significantly weakened in the 1990s with the capture of its leader Abimael Guzman, who, after a new trial in 2006, was sentenced to life in prison. According to the State Department terrorism report, SL has several hundred armed combatants, and the group is now involved in drug trafficking. The SL killed 20 civilians, 11 police officers, and one military member in 2007, and conducted 80 terrorist acts in remote coca-growing areas this year. According to the terrorism report, the FARC continued to use remote areas along the Colombian-Peruvian border for rest and to make arms purchases.

Tri-Border Area. In recent years, U.S. concerns have increased over activities of the radical Lebanon-based Islamic group Hezbollah (Party of God) and the Sunni Muslim Palestinian group Hamas (Islamic Resistance Movement) in the tri-border area (TBA) of Argentina, Brazil, and Paraguay, which has a large Muslim population. The TBA has long been used for arms and drug trafficking, contraband smuggling, document and currency fraud, money laundering, and the manufacture and movement of pirated goods. The terrorism report maintains that the United States remains concerned that Hezbollah and Hamas sympathizers are raising funds among the sizable Muslim communities in the region, but stated that there was no corroborated information that these or other Islamic extremist groups had an operational presence in the area.

Allegations have linked Hezbollah to two bombings in Argentina: the 1992 bombing of the Israeli Embassy in Buenos Aires that killed 30 people and the 1994 bombing of the Argentine-Israeli Mutual Association (AMIA) in Buenos Aires that killed 85 people. In November 2006, an Argentine judge issued arrest warrants in the AMIA case for nine individuals: an internationally wanted Hezbollah militant from Lebanon, Imad Mughniyah, and eight Iranian government officials, including former Iranian President Hashemi Rafsanjani. Interpol subsequently posted a Red Notice for Mughniyah, and in November 2007, its General Assembly voted to approve notices for five of the Iranians wanted by Argentina (not including Rafsanjani). In February 2008, Imad Mughniyah was killed by a car bomb in Damascus, Syria.

Congress has continued to express concern about progress in the investigation of the AMIA bombing. H.Con.Res. 188 (Ros-Lehtinen), approved by the House by voice vote on July 30, 2007, applauded the Argentine government for increasing the pace of the AMIA investigation, and called upon the General Assembly of Interpol to issue red notices for five Iranians implicated in the bombing. H.Con.Res. 385 (Ros-Lehtinen), approved by the House by voice vote on July 15, 2008, condemned the AMIA bombing, and urged Western Hemisphere governments to take actions to curb activities that supported Hezbollah and other Islamist terrorist organizations. Another resolution, H.Res. 435 (Klein), approved November 5, 2007 by voice vote, expressed concern over the emerging national security implications of Iran's efforts to expand its influence in Latin America, and emphasized the importance of eliminating Hezbollah's financial network in the tri-border area of South America.

Cuba. Since 1982, the Department of State, pursuant to Section 6(j) of the Export Administration Act (EAA) of 1979, has included Cuba among its list of states sponsoring terrorism (the other states currently on the list are Iran, North Korea, Sudan, and Syria). Communist Cuba had a history of supporting revolutionary movements and governments in Latin America and Africa, but in 1992, then Cuban leader Fidel Castro said that his country's support for insurgents abroad was a thing of the past. Most analysts accept that Cuba's policy generally did change, largely because the breakup of the Soviet Union resulted in the loss of billions in subsidies.

The State Department's terrorism report maintains that Cuba has "remained opposed to U.S. counterterrorism policy, and actively and publicly condemned many associated U.S. policies and actions." It also noted that Cuba maintains close relationships with other state sponsors of terrorism, such as Iran and Syria, and has provided safe haven for members of several FTOs—the FARC, ELN, and Basque ETA from Spain. Colombia has publicly acknowledged that it wants Cuba mediation with the ELN. The terrorism report also maintained that Cuba permits U.S. fugitives from justice to live legally in Cuba, with many accused of hijacking or committing violent actions in the United States, although it noted that Cuba stated in 2006 that it will no longer provide safe haven to new fugitives who may enter the country. In April 2007, Cuba returned U.S. fugitive Joseph Adjmi, who was convicted of mail fraud in the 1960s. Cuba has called for the United States to surrender Luis Posada Carriles and three Cuban Americans that it accused of plotting to kill Castro and bombing a Cuban airliner in 1976. (Also see CRS Report RL33819, *Cuba: Issues for the 110th Congress.*)

Cuba's retention on the terrorism list has been questioned by some observers. In general, those who support keeping Cuba on the list point to the government's history of supporting terrorist acts and armed insurgencies in Latin America and Africa. They point to the government's continued hosting of members of foreign terrorist organizations and U.S. fugitives from justice. Critics of retaining Cuba on the terrorism list maintain that it is a holdover of the Cold War. They argue that domestic political considerations keep Cuba on the terrorism list and maintain that Cuba's presence on the list diverts U.S. attention from struggles against serious terrorist threats. (For background, see CRS Report RL32251, *Cuba and the State Sponsors of Terrorism List.*)

U.S. Policy

As in other parts of the world, the United States has assisted Latin American and Caribbean nations over the years in their struggle against terrorist or insurgent groups indigenous to the region. For example, in the 1980s, the United States supported the government of El Salvador with significant economic and military assistance in its struggle against a leftist guerrilla insurgency. In recent years, the United States has employed various policy tools to combat terrorism in the Latin America and Caribbean region, including sanctions, anti-terrorism assistance and training, law enforcement cooperation, and multilateral cooperation through the OAS. Moreover, given the nexus between terrorism and drug trafficking, one can argue that assistance aimed at combating drug trafficking organizations in the region has also been a means of combating terrorism by cutting off a source of revenue for terrorist organizations. The same argument can be made regarding efforts to combat money laundering in the region.

Although terrorism was not the main focus of U.S. policy toward the region in recent years, attention increased in the aftermath of the 9/11 terrorist attacks on New York and Washington. Anti-terrorism assistance has increased along with bilateral and regional cooperation against terrorism. Congress approved the Bush Administration's request in 2002 to expand the scope of U.S. assistance to Colombia beyond a counternarcotics focus to also include counterterrorism assistance to the government in its military efforts against drug-financed leftist guerrillas and rightist paramilitaries. Border security with Mexico also became a prominent issue in bilateral relations, with attention focused on the potential transit of terrorists through Mexico to the United States. The United States has imposed sanctions on three groups in Colombia (ELN, FARC, and AUC) and one group in Peru (SL) designated by the Department of State as FTOs. Official designation of such groups as FTOs triggers a number of sanctions, including visa restrictions and the blocking of any funds of these groups in U.S. financial institutions. The designation also has the effect of increasing public awareness about these terrorist organizations and the concerns that the United States has about them. As noted above, the United States has included Cuba on its list of state sponsors of terrorism since 1982, pursuant to section 6(j) of the EAA, and both Cuba and Venezuela are currently on the annual

Section 40A AECA list of countries that are not cooperating fully with U.S. antiterrorism efforts, lists that trigger a number of sanctions.

Through the Department of State (Diplomatic Security Office, Office of Antiterrorism Assistance), the United States provides Anti-Terrorism Assistance (ATA) training and equipment to Latin American countries to help improve their capabilities in such areas as airport security management, hostage negotiations, bomb detection and deactivation, and countering terrorism financing. Such training was expanded to Argentina in the aftermath of the two bombings in 1992 and 1994. Assistance was also stepped up in 1997 to Argentina, Brazil, and Paraguay in light of increased U.S. concern over illicit activities in the tri-border area of those countries. ATA funding is generally provided through the annual foreign operations appropriations measure under the Nonproliferation, Anti-terrorism, Demining, and Related Programs (NADR) account. In recent years, ATA for Western Hemisphere countries amounted to $8.9 million in FY2006, $7.3 million in FY2007, and an estimated $8 million in FY2008. For FY2009, the Administration requested $9.3 million in ATA for Latin America, with $2.8 million for Colombia and $3 million for Mexico, and the balance for other countries. Also under the NADR funding account, the United States began providing Terrorist Interdiction Program assistance for several Latin American countries in FY2008. An estimated $1.3 million is being provided to Panama, Brazil, and Nicaragua in FY2008, while the Administration requested $1.2 million for Latin America for FY2009.

The United States also works closely with the governments of the tri-border area—Argentina, Brazil, and Paraguay—through the "3+1 regional cooperation mechanism," which serves as a forum for counterterrorism cooperation and prevention.

Increased Regional Cooperation Since 9/11. Latin American nations strongly condemned the September 2001 terrorist attacks on the United States and took action through the OAS and the Rio Treaty to strengthen hemispheric cooperation against terrorism. The OAS, which happened to be meeting in Peru at the time, swiftly condemned the attacks, reiterated the need to strengthen hemispheric cooperation to combat terrorism, and expressed full solidarity with the United States. At a special session on September 19, 2001, OAS members invoked the 1947 Inter-American Treaty of Reciprocal Assistance, also known as the Rio Treaty, which obligates signatories to the treaty to come to one another's defense in case of outside attack. Another resolution approved on September 21, 2001, called on Rio Treaty signatories to "use all legally available measures to pursue, capture, extradite, and punish those individuals" involved in the attacks and to "render additional assistance and support to the United States, as appropriate, to address the September 11 attacks, and also to prevent future terrorist acts."

In the aftermath of 9/11, OAS members reinvigorated effort of the of the Inter-American Committee on Terrorism (CICTE) to combat terrorism in the hemisphere. The CICTE has cooperated on border security mechanisms, controls to prevent terrorist funding, and law enforcement and counterterrorism intelligence and information. At a January 2003 CICTE meeting, OAS members issued the Declaration of San Salvador, which pledged to strengthen hemispheric cooperation through a variety of border, customs, and financial control measures. At the February 2005 CICTE session held in Trinidad and Tobago, OAS members reaffirmed their commitment to deepen cooperation against terrorism and addressed threats to aviation, seaport, and cyber security. CICTE held its seventh annual regular session in Panama from February 28–March 2, 2007, which focused on the protection of critical infrastructure in the region.

OAS members signed the Inter-American Convention Against Terrorism in June 2002. The Convention, among other measures, improves regional cooperation against terrorism, commits parties to sign and ratify U.N. anti-terrorism instruments and take actions against the financing of terrorism, and denies safe haven to suspected terrorists. President Bush submitted the Convention to the Senate on November 12, 2002, for its advice and consent, and the treaty was referred to the Senate Foreign Relations Committee (Treaty Doc. 107-18). In the 109th Congress, the committee formally reported the treaty on July 28, 2005 (Senate Exec. Rept. 109-3), and on October 7, 2005, the Senate agreed to the resolution of advice and consent. The United States deposited its instruments of ratification for the Convention on November 15, 2005.

DOCUMENT NO. 7

U.S.-CHINA COUNTERTERRORISM COOPERATION: ISSUES FOR U.S. POLICY

CRS Report
RL33001

October 29, 2008

Shirley A. Kan

Summary

After the terrorist attacks on September 11, 2001, the United States faced a challenge in enlisting the full support of the People's Republic of China (PRC) in the counterterrorism fight against Al Qaeda. This effort raised short-term policy issues about how to elicit cooperation and how to address PRC concerns about the U.S.-led war (Operation Enduring Freedom). Longer-term issues have concerned whether counterterrorism has strategically transformed bilateral ties and whether China's support was valuable and not obtained at the expense of other U.S. interests.

The extent of U.S.-China counterterrorism cooperation has been limited, but the tone and context of counterterrorism helped to stabilize—even if it did not transform—the closer bilateral relationship pursued by President George Bush since late 2001. China's military, the People's Liberation Army (PLA), has not participated in the counterterrorism coalition. Still, for almost four years after the attacks on September 11, 2001, President Bush and other administration officials tended to praise the PRC's diplomatic and other support for the war against terrorism.

Since 2005, however, U.S. concerns about China's extent of cooperation in counterterrorism have increased. In September 2005, Deputy Secretary of State Robert Zoellick acknowledged that "China and the United States can do more together in the global fight against terrorism" after "a good start," in his policy speech that called on China to be a "responsible stakeholder" in the world. The summits of the Shanghai Cooperation Organization

(SCO) in 2005 and 2006 raised U.S. concerns. Since the summer of 2007, U.S. officials have expressed more concern about China-origin arms that have been found in the conflict involving U.S. forces in Afghanistan, as part of the broader threat posed by Iran and its arms transfers.

Congress has oversight over the closer ties with China and a number of policy options. U.S. policy has addressed: law-enforcement ties; oppressed Uighur (Uyghur) people in western Xinjiang whom China claims to be linked to "terrorists"; detained Uighurs at Guantanamo Bay prison; Olympic security in August 2008; sanctions that ban exports of arms and security equipment; weapons nonproliferation; port security; military-to-military contacts; China's influence in Central Asia through the SCO; and China's arms transfers to Iran.

In the 110th Congress, the House passed on September 17, 2007, **H.Res. 497**, noting that the PRC has manipulated the campaign against terrorists to increase oppression of the Uighur people, and has detained and beaten Rebiya Kadeer's children and imprisoned an ethnic Uighur Canadian. On May 22, 2008, Senator Sherrod Brown introduced the similar bill, **S.Res. 574**. On July 30, the House passed **H.Res. 1370**, calling on the PRC to stop repression of the Tibetan and Uighur peoples. The PRC's claims of "terrorist" threats from Uighurs have lacked clarity and confirmation. Some violent incidents occurred before and during the Olympic Games. On October 7, a judge ordered the release of the 17 remaining Uighurs held at Guantanamo, then an appeals court granted the Justice Department's request for a stay pending an appeal. This report will be updated as warranted.

Aftermath of the 9/11 Attacks

China has seen itself as a victim of terrorist attacks in the 1990s, thought to be committed by some Muslim extremists (ethnic Uighur separatists) in the northwestern Xinjiang region. Some Uighur activists reportedly received training in Afghanistan. China's concerns appeared to place it in a position to support Washington and share intelligence after the attacks of September 11, 2001.[1] In a message to President Bush on September 11, PRC ruler Jiang Zemin condemned the terrorist attacks and offered condolences. In a phone call with the President on September 12, Jiang reportedly promised to cooperate with the United States to combat terrorism. At the U.N. Security Council (UNSC) on the same day, the PRC (a permanent member) voted with the others for Resolution 1368 (to combat terrorism). On September 20, Beijing said that it offered "unconditional support" in

[1] See also CRS Report RL31213, *China's Relations with Central Asian States and Problems with Terrorism*, by Dewardric McNeal and Kerry Dumbaugh.

fighting terrorism. On September 20–21, visiting Foreign Minister Tang Jiaxuan promised cooperation, and Secretary of State Colin Powell indicated that discussions covered intelligence-sharing but not military cooperation. PRC counterterrorism experts attended a "productive" initial meeting on September 25, 2001, in Washington, DC. On September 28, 2001, China voted with all others in the UNSC for Resolution 1373, reaffirming the need to combat terrorism.

PRC promises of support for the U.S. fight against terrorism, however, were qualified by other initial statements expressing concerns about U.S. military action. China also favored exercising its decision-making authority at the UNSC, where it has veto power. Initial commentary in official PRC media faulted U.S. intelligence and U.S. defense and foreign policies (including that on missile defense) for the attacks. On September 18, 2001, in a phone call with British Prime Minister Tony Blair, China reported Jiang as saying that war against terrorism required conclusive evidence, specific targets to avoid hurting innocent people, compliance with the U.N. Charter, and a role for the Security Council. Also, observers were appalled at the reported gleeful anti-U.S. reactions in the PRC's online chat rooms after the attacks.

In Tokyo, on January 21, 2002, at a conference on reconstruction aid to Afghanistan, China pledged $1 million, in addition to humanitarian goods worth $3.6 million. But three days later, Jiang promised to visiting Afghan interim leader Hamid Karzai additional reconstruction aid of $150 million spread over four to five years. Of this $150 million, China offered $47 million by 2003 and offered $15 million in 2004.[2]

Policy Analysis

The extent of U.S.-China counterterrorism cooperation has been limited, but the tone and context of counterterrorism helped to stabilize—even if it did not transform—the closer bilateral relationship pursued by President Bush since late 2001. In the short-term, U.S. security policy toward Beijing sought counterterrorism cooperation, shifting from issues about weapons proliferation and military maritime safety (in the wake of the EP-3/F-8 aircraft collision crisis of April 2001).[3] Given the mixed state of bilateral ties after the collision crisis, Beijing's support met much of initial U.S. expectations. Testifying to Congress in February 2002, Secretary of State Colin

[2] "China to Offer $15m for Afghan Reconstruction," *Xinhua*, April 1, 2004.

[3] See CRS Report RL30946, *China-U.S. Aircraft Collision Incident of April 2001: Assessments and Policy Implications*, coordinated by Shirley Kan.

Powell praised Beijing's diplomatic support, saying "China has helped in the war against terrorism."[4]

Concerning other support, including any cooperation by the People's Liberation Army (PLA), the commanders of the Central and Pacific Commands, Gen. Tommy Franks and Adm. Dennis Blair, separately confirmed in April 2002 that China did not provide military cooperation (nor was it requested) in Operation Enduring Freedom in Afghanistan (e.g., basing, staging, or overflight) and that its shared intelligence was not specific enough, particularly as compared to cooperation from the Philippines, Singapore, and Malaysia.[5] The Pentagon's June 2002 report on foreign contributions in the counterterrorism war did not include China among the 50 countries in the coalition.[6] In December 2002, Assistant Secretary of State James Kelly confirmed intelligence-sharing, saying "we are sharing [counterterrorism] information to an unprecedented extent but making judgments independently."[7]

China's long-standing relationship with nuclear-armed Pakistan was an important factor in considering the significance of Beijing's support, especially with concerns about the viability of Pakistani President Pervez Musharraf's government. Some said that Pakistan's cooperation with the United States must come with PRC acquiescence, pointing to a PRC envoy's meeting with Musharraf on September 18, 2001. However, on September 13, 2001, Musharraf already had agreed to fight with the United States against bin Laden.[8] The PRC has reportedly provided Pakistan with nuclear and missile technology. China could provide intelligence about Pakistan's nuclear weapons and any suspected technology transfers out of Pakistan to countries like North Korea, Iran, and Libya.

In the long term, counterterrorism was initially thought by some to hold strategic implications for the U.S.-PRC relationship. However, it has remained debatable as to whether such cooperation has fundamentally transformed the bilateral relationship. Policymakers watched to see whether Beijing's leaders used the opportunity to improve bilateral ties, especially on weapons nonproliferation problems. In his State of the Union speech on January 29, 2002, President Bush expressed his expectation that

---

[4] Senate Foreign Relations Committee, hearing, *Fiscal Year 2003 Foreign Affairs Budget*, February 5, 2002.

[5] Foreign Press Center Briefing, General Tommy Franks, Commander, U.S. Central Command, Washington, April 11, 2002; Press Roundtable with Adm. Dennis Blair, Commander, U.S. Pacific Command, Hong Kong, April 18, 2002.

[6] Department of Defense, "Fact Sheet: International Contributions to the War Against Terrorism," June 14, 2002.

[7] Assistant Secretary of State for East Asian and Pacific Affairs, "U.S.-East Asia Policy: Three Aspects," Woodrow Wilson Center, Washington, December 11, 2002.

[8] First reported by Dan Balz, Bob Woodward, and Jeff Himmelman, "Thursday, September 13," *Washington Post*, January 29, 2002; and confirmed in the 9/11 Commission's report, *Final Report of the National Commission on Terrorist Attacks Upon the United States*, July 22, 2004.

"in this moment of opportunity, a common danger is erasing old rivalries. America is working with Russia and China and India, in ways we have never before, to achieve peace and prosperity." Nonetheless, Director of Central Intelligence George Tenet testified to Congress in February 2002, that the 9/11 attacks did not change "the fundamentals" of China's approach to us.[9]

The PRC's concerns about domestic attacks and any links to foreign terrorist groups, U.S.-PRC relations, China's international standing in a world dominated by U.S. power (particularly after the terrorist attacks), and its image as a responsible world power helped explain China's supportive stance. However, Beijing also worried about U.S. military action near China, U.S.-led alliances, Japan's active role in the war on terrorism, greater U.S. influence in Central and South Asia, and U.S. support for Taiwan—all exacerbating long-standing fears of "encirclement."

China issued a Defense White Paper in December 2002, stating that major powers remained in competition but that since the September 2001 attacks against the United States, countries have increased cooperation. Although this policy paper contained veiled criticisms of the United States for its military buildup, stronger alliances in Asia, and increased arms sales to Taiwan, it did not criticize the United States by name as in the Defense White Paper of 2000. However, the Defense White Papers of 2004 and 2006 again criticized the United States by name.

Since 2005, U.S. concerns about China's extent of cooperation in counterterrorism have increased. In September 2005, Deputy Secretary of State Robert Zoellick acknowledged that "China and the United States can do more together in the global fight against terrorism" after "a good start," in his policy speech that called on China to be a "responsible stakeholder" in the world. The summits of the Shanghai Cooperation Organization (SCO) in 2005 and 2006 raised U.S. concerns. Since the summer of 2007, U.S. officials have expressed more concern about China-origin arms that have been found in the conflict involving U.S. forces in Afghanistan, as part of the broader threat posed by Iran and its arms transfers.

Options and Implications for U.S. Policy

Summits and "Strategic" Ties

The counterterrorism campaign helped to stabilize U.S.-PRC relations up to the highest level, which faced tensions early in the Bush Administration in April 2001 with the EP-3 aircraft collision crisis and U.S. approvals of

[9] Senate Select Committee on Intelligence, hearing, *Worldwide Threats: Converging Dangers in a Post-9/11 World*, February 6, 2002.

arms sales to Taiwan. According to the Final Report of the 9/11 Commission issued in July 2004, President Bush chaired a National Security Council meeting on the night of September 11, 2001, in which he contended that the attacks provided a "great opportunity" to engage Russia and China. President Bush traveled to Shanghai in October 2001 for his first meeting with then PRC President Jiang Zemin at the Leaders' Meeting of the Asia Pacific Economic Cooperation (APEC) forum. Bush called the PRC an important partner in the global coalition against terrorists but also warned Jiang that the "war on terrorism must never be an excuse to persecute minorities."[10] On February 21–22, 2002, the President visited Beijing (a trip postponed in October), after Tokyo and Seoul. The President then hosted Jiang at Bush's ranch in Crawford, TX, on October 25, 2002, and Bush said that the two countries were "allies" in fighting terrorism.[11] By the fall of 2005, Deputy Secretary of State Robert Zoellick acknowledged that "China and the United States can do more together in the global fight against terrorism" after "a good start," in his policy speech calling on China to be a "responsible stakeholder."[12]

Law-Enforcement Cooperation

On December 6, 2001, Francis Taylor, the State Department's Coordinator for Counter-Terrorism, ended talks in Beijing that reciprocated the September 25 meeting in Washington, DC. He announced that the PRC agreed to give "positive consideration" to a long-sought U.S. request for the FBI to set up a Legal Attaché office at the U.S. Embassy, that counter-terrorism consultations would occur semiannually, and that the two sides would set up a Financial Counter-Terrorism Working Group. He reported that Beijing's cooperation has entailed coordination at the U.N., intelligence-sharing, law enforcement liaison, and monitoring of financial networks.[13] The PRC approved the FBI office in February 2002, and the first semi-annual meeting on terrorist financing was held at the Treasury Department in late May. The FBI attaché arrived at the U.S. Embassy in Beijing in September 2002. In November 2005, U.S. Attorney General Alberto Gonzales met with PRC Minister of Public Security Zhou Yongkang in Beijing. Visiting Beijing in June 2007, FBI Assistant Director for International Operations Thomas Fuentes said that he seeks "more information" from the PRC on terrorism.[14]

---

[10] White House, "U.S., China Stand Against Terrorism," Shanghai, China, October 19, 2001.

[11] White House, "President Bush, Chinese President Jiang Zemin Discuss Iraq, N. Korea," Crawford, Texas, October 25, 2002.

[12] Robert Zoellick, "Whither China: From Membership to Responsibility," September 21, 2005.

[13] Department of State, press conference, Beijing, December 6, 2001.

[14] Daniel Schearf, "U.S. Federal Bureau of Investigations Seeks Further Cooperation with China," *VOA News*, June 13, 2007.

Uighur People in Xinjiang and "Terrorist" Organizations

Questions concern the U.S. stance on the PRC's policy toward the Uighur (Uyghur) people in the northwestern Xinjiang region that links them to what the PRC calls "terrorist" organizations. Congress has concerns about the human rights of Uighurs. China has accused the United States of using "double standards" in counterterrorism in disagreements over how to handle the Uighurs.

Xinjiang has a history of unrest dating back before September 2001, particularly since the unrest in 1990. The PRC charges Uighurs with violent crimes and "terrorism," but Uighurs say they have suffered executions, torture, detentions, harassment, religious persecution, and racial profiling. Human rights and Uighur groups have warned that, after the 9/11 attacks, the PRC shifted to use the international counterterrorism campaign to justify the PRC's long-term cultural, religious, and political repression of Uighurs both in and outside of the PRC.[15] Since 2002, the PLA has conducted military exercises in Xinjiang with Central Asian countries and Russia to fight what the PRC calls "East Turkistan terrorists" and what it combines as the threat of "three evil forces" (of separatism, extremism, and terrorism). Critics say China has compelled extraditions of Uighurs for execution and other punishment from countries such as Uzbekistan, Kyrgyzstan, Kazahkstan, Nepal, and Pakistan, raising questions about violations of the international legal principle of non-refoulement and the United Nations Convention Against Torture.

The Uighurs are an ethnically Turkish people who speak Uighur and practice a moderate form of Islam. They say that their population totals 10–15 million people. Countering China's colonial name of "Xinjiang," meaning "new frontier," the Uighurs call their Central Asian homeland "East Turkistan." The land makes up about one-sixth of today's PRC. In 1884, the Manchurian Qing empire based in northern China incorporated the area as a province called "Xinjiang." Later, it was briefly the Republic of East Turkistan in 1933 and in 1944, and a Soviet satellite power from 1934 to 1941. In October 1949, the Communist Party of China set up the PRC and deployed PLA troops to occupy and govern Xinjiang. In 1955, the PRC incorporated the area as the "Xinjiang Uyghur Autonomous Region."[16] In addition to PLA forces, the paramilitary People's Armed Police (PAP) has imposed controls. Unique to Xinjiang are the paramilitary Production and Construction Corps (PCC) guarding, producing, and settling there; the past nuclear weapon testing at Lop Nur; and routine executions for what

[15] Amnesty International, "Uighurs Fleeing Persecution as China Wages its 'War on Terror'," July 7, 2004; Uyghur Human Rights Project, "Persecution of Uyghurs in the Era of the 'War on Terror'," October 16, 2007.

[16] James Millward, *Eurasian Crossroads: a History of Xinjiang*, Columbia University, 2007.

Uighurs say are political and religious dissent. Like Tibetans, Uighurs resent the Communist controls on religion, military deployments and exercises, increasing immigration of ethnic Han (Chinese) people, and forced birth control. PRC census data report Uighurs at 8.4 million and Hans at 40% of Xinjiang's population (up from 6% in 1953). In the early 1990s, the breakup of the Soviet Union and independence of neighboring Central Asian republics encouraged the Uighurs. In response to their dissent, the PRC regime routinely has held huge public sentencing rallies and executions of Uighurs, forcing thousands to watch (one in 1998 involved more than 20,000) and intimidating Uighurs by "killing one to frighten thousands," according to official PRC media.

As discussed above, Francis Taylor, the State Department's Coordinator for Counter-Terrorism, visited Beijing in December 2001. While he confirmed that there were "people from western China that are involved in terrorist activities in Afghanistan," he rejected the view that "all of the people of western China are indeed terrorists" and urged Beijing to deal politically with their "legitimate" social and economic challenges and not with counterterrorism means. Taylor stated that the United States did not agree that "East Turkestan" forces were terrorists. He said that the U.S. military captured some people from western China who were involved in Afghanistan with Al Qaeda (the terrorist group led by Osama bin Laden).

Nonetheless, while in Beijing on August 26, 2002, Deputy Secretary of State Richard Armitage announced that, after months of bilateral discussions, he designated (on August 19) the East Turkistan Islamic Movement (ETIM) as a terrorist group that committed acts of violence against unarmed civilians. China had issued a new report in January 2002, publicly charging ETIM and other East Turkistan "terrorist" groups with attacks in the 1990s and linking them to the international terrorism of Osama bin Laden's Al Qaeda.[17] The U.S. Embassy in Beijing suggested that ETIM planned to attack the U.S. Embassy in Kyrgyzstan, but no attack took place.[18] The State Department designated ETIM as a terrorist organization under Executive Order 13224 (to freeze assets) but not as a Foreign Terrorist Organization (under the Immigration and Nationality Act). E.O. 13224 defined "terrorism" as "activity that (1) involves a violent act or an act dangerous to human life, property, or infrastructure; *and* (2) appears to be intended to intimidate or coerce a civilian population; to influence the policy of a government by intimidation or coercion; or to affect the conduct of a government by mass destruction, assassination, kidnapping, or hostage-taking." At the same time, the United States, PRC, Afghanistan, and Kyrgyzstan asked the

---

[17] PRC State Council, "'East Turkistan' Terrorist Forces Cannot Get Away with Impunity," *Xinhua*, January 21, 2002.

[18] Philip Pan, "U.S. Warns of Plot by Group in W. China," *Washington Post*, August 29, 2002.

United Nations to designate ETIM under U.N. Security Council Resolutions 1267 and 1390 (to freeze assets of this group). Later, in 2004, the Secretary of State also included ETIM in the "Terrorist Exclusion List (TEL)" (to exclude certain foreign aliens from entering the United States), under Section 411 of the USA PATRIOT Act of 2001 (P.L. 107-56).

The case against ETIM—including even its name—has been complicated, in part by questions of the credibility of PRC claims that link "terrorism" to repressed groups like Uighurs, Tibetans, and Falungong. Moreover, there have been challenges in verifying the authenticity of Internet messages and websites ostensibly belonging to the Turkistan Islamic Party (TIP), apparently another name for ETIM, with possibilities that one or more messages were created by such a terrorist group, fabricated by the PRC to justify its charges, or made as a deception by a third party.

No group calling itself ETIM claimed responsibility for violent incidents in the 1990s. Although many Uighur or East Turkistan advocacy groups around the world have been reported for decades, the first available mention of ETIM was found in 2000. A Russian newspaper reported that Osama bin Laden convened a meeting in Afghanistan in 1999 that included the Islamic Movement of Uzbekistan (IMU) and ETIM, and he agreed to give them funds.[19] A Kyrgyz report in 2001 named ETIM as a militant Uighur organization with links to IMU and training in Afghanistan and Pakistan, but did not mention any links to Al Qaeda.[20] Detailed information on "three evil forces" written in August 2001 by a PRC scholar at the Xinjiang Academy of Social Sciences did not name ETIM.[21] Before the PRC government's public report of January 2002 on "East Turkestan terrorists," most were not aware of ETIM, and PRC officials or official media did not mention ETIM until a Foreign Ministry news conference shortly after the September 2001 terrorist attacks in the United States. But even then, the PRC did not blame ETIM for any of alleged incidents.[22]

In 2002, the leader of what China called ETIM, Hasan Mahsum, referred to his organization as the East Turkistan Islamic Party (ETIP) and said that it had no "organizational links" with Al Qaeda or Taliban (the extremist Islamic regime formed by former anti-Soviet Islamic fighters called Mujahedin that took over Afghanistan in 1994–1996). Moreover, he claimed that ETIM did not receive any financial aid from Osama bin Laden or Al Qaeda, although certain Uighur individuals were involved with the Taliban

[19] Yuriy Yegorov, "Color Green is Needed," *Nezavisimaya Gazeta*, July 26, 2000.

[20] Alisher Muradov, "East Turkestan is a Great State," *Moskovskiy Komsomolets v Kyrgyzstane*, September 6, 2001.

[21] Interview with Pan Zhiping in "Three Evil Forces Threatening Xinjiang's Stability," *Ta Kung Pao* [PRC-owned newspaper in Hong Kong], August 10, 2001.

[22] PRC Ministry of Foreign Affairs news conference, November 15, 2001.

in Afghanistan.[23] In November 2003, an organization calling itself the Turkistan Islamic Party (TIP) posted on the Internet its denial of the U.S. and PRC designations of ETIM as a "terrorist organization."[24]

In December 2003, the PRC's Ministry of Public Security issued its first list of wanted "terrorists," accusing four groups as "East Turkistan terrorist organizations" (ETIM, East Turkistan Liberation Organization (ETLO), World Uyghur Youth Congress, and East Turkistan Information Center) and 11 Uighurs as "terrorists," with Hasan Mahsum at the top of the list.[25] China demanded foreign assistance to target them. However, the list was intentionally misleading or mistaken, because Mahsum was already dead. Confirming his operational area at the Afghan-Pakistani border, Pakistan's military killed a multinational motley that included Mahsum on October 2, 2003, in Pakistan's South Waziristan tribal district.[26] In December 2003, the leadership of what it called TIP (having changed its name from ETIP in 1999 to be inclusive of non-Uighur Turkic peoples) posted on the Internet an eulogy of Mahsum. TIP reviewed his development of an organization in Afghanistan with the Taliban's support but not contact with Al Qaeda. The TIP announced that former Military Affairs Commander Abdulheq took over as the leader (amir).[27] However, the PRC Ministry of Public Security's list did not include Abdulheq. In 2004, the deputy leader, Abudula Kariaji, said that ETIM had sent militants trained in small arms and explosives to China and had met in 1999 with Osama bin Laden, who allowed some Uighurs to train in Afghanistan but did not support their non-Arab cause of over-throwing China's rule.[28] In January 2008, Al Qaeda in Afghanistan issued a book on 120 "martyrs" that included five who were Uighurs born in Xinjiang and fought with the Taliban in Afghanistan. One of them was said to have died fighting U.S. military forces that launched attacks in 2001.[29] In video messages since 2006, Al Qaeda's deputy leader, Ayman al-Zawahiri, on rare occasions, has mentioned the East Turkistan problem among various worldwide concerns. Beyond this awareness, he has not cited a relevant organization or action. In the video released on the eve of

[23] "Uyghur Separatist Denies Links to Taliban," *Radio Free Asia*, January 27, 2002. Also, a few Uighurs had been reported as studying at a Pakistani madrassa (religious school) and joining the Taliban in fighting in Afghanistan in 1999, as well as joining the Islamic fights in Chechnya and Uzbekistan (Ahmed Rashid and Susan Lawrence, "Joining Foreign Jihad," *Far Eastern Economic Review*, September 7, 2000).

[24] Turkistan Islamic Party, "Refute and Reminder of Accusations Published Around the World About Turkistan Islamic Party," November 24, 2003.

[25] "Eastern Turkistan Terrorist Groups, Individuals Identified," *Xinhua*, December 15, 2003.

[26] *Al-Hayah*, October 17, 2003; *AFP*, December 23, 2003; *Xinhua*, December 24, 2003.

[27] Turkistan Islamic Party, "Islam Tiger Hesen Mexsum (1964–2003)," December 31, 2003.

[28] David Cloud and Ian Johnson, "In Post-9/11 World, Chinese Dissidents Pose U.S. Dilemma," *Wall Street Journal*, August 3, 2004.

[29] Al-Qa'ida in Afghanistan, "Martyrs in Time of Alienation," January 31, 2008.

the 7th anniversary of the September 2001 attacks, he did not mention the East Turkistan cause or China in a litany of grievances.[30]

In 2003, Mehmet Emin Hazret, the leader of the East Turkistan Liberation Organization (ETLO), another organization targeted by the PRC's 2002 report as a "terrorist organization," denied that his group was responsible for violent incidents or had knowledge of an organization called ETIM, although he knew of its alleged leaders who had been in PRC prisons. Hazret also denied that ETLO had links to Al Qaeda. Nonetheless, he acknowledged that ETLO would inevitably set up a military wing to target the PRC government for its oppression of the Uighur people.[31]

The PRC government's own report of 2002 on "East Turkistan terrorists" claimed bombing incidents in Xinjiang from 1991 to 1998, with none after that year. That report did not discuss bombings outside of Xinjiang or call those other violent incidents "terrorism." The report alleged that some "terrorist" bombings occurred in February to April 1998 and injured 11 people. However, there were no PRC or non-PRC media reports of such incidents in 1998. Moreover, Xinjiang's Party Secretary Wang Lequan and Chairman Abulahat Abdurixit said in Beijing in early 1998 and 1999 that there were no major violent incidents in 1998. In April 1998, a PRC official journal published a comprehensive report on crime, cited bombings in 1997 but none in 1998, and stated that China had no terrorist organizations and had not been penetrated by any international terrorist groups.[32] In May 1998, Xinjiang's Vice Chairman Zhang Zhou told foreign reporters that there was an explosion near Kashgar earlier that year, but no one was killed or wounded.[33]

Before August 2008, the last bombing incident in Xinjiang reported by PRC and non-PRC media occurred in 1997, when three bombs exploded in three buses in Urumqi on February 25, 1997, while two other undetonated bombs were found on two buses. Many reports speculated that the deadly attacks were timed for the mourning period of PRC paramount ruler Deng Xiaoping who died on February 19.[34] However, the likely critical factor was the preceding major turmoil and crackdown in Xinjiang that occurred on February 5–6 in Yining (the western town Uighurs call Gulja), involving Uighur protests against executions, security crackdown, and perhaps hundreds killed and thousands arrested. Uighurs and Amnesty International called the

[30] Videos dated December 23, 2006; March 11, 2007; April 22, 2008; September 8, 2008.

[31] "Separatist Leader Vows to Target the Chinese Government; Uyghur Leader Denies Terror Charges," *Radio Free Asia*, January 29, 2003.

[32] *Zhongguo Guoqing Guoli*, April 28, 1998.

[33] *Ta Kung Pao*, March 13, 1998; *Zhongguo Xinwen She*, March 6, 1999; *South China Morning Post*, May 15, 1998.

[34] *AFP*, February 26 and March 5, 1997; *Reuters*, March 5, 1997; *Xinhua*, May 29, 1997.

incident the "Gulja Massacre."[35] Shortly after the incident on February 25, further bombings were reported in Urumqi on March 1, in Yining on March 3, in Beijing on March 5 and March 7, near Guangzhou on May 12, and in Beijing on May 13; but the PRC did not label the incidents outside of Xinjiang as "terrorist incidents." The incidents in 1997 occurred after the PRC government launched in 1996 the national anti-crime "Strike Hard" campaign that was carried out in Xinjiang and Tibet with crackdowns against those China called "separatists."

Uighur and human rights groups have expressed concern that the U.S. designation of ETIM as a terrorist organization in 2002 helped China to further justify persecution and violent repression against the people in Xinjiang. They also have noted distinctions between terrorism and armed resistance against military or security forces. They have pointed out that Uighurs have no anti-U.S. sentiments but rather look to the United States as a champion of their human rights.

In December 2002, Assistant Secretary of State James Kelly defended the action taken against ETIM as a step based on U.S. evidence that ETIM had links to Al Qaeda and committed violence against civilians, "not as a concession to the PRC." Moreover, Lorne Craner, Assistant Secretary of State for Democracy, Human Rights, and Labor, specifically traveled to Urumqi to give a speech at Xinjiang University as part of a visit for the U.S.-PRC Human Rights Dialogue. He said that "both President Bush and Secretary Powell have made very clear publicly and privately that the U.S. does not and will not condone governments using counterterrorism as an excuse to silence peaceful expressions of political or religious views." He added that the United States condemned the "Al Qaeda-linked" ETIM, but he was there to "reaffirm our friendship for the peaceful people of Xinjiang."[36]

The Congress and President Bush have expressed concerns about PRC repression of Uighurs, including imprisonment of the relatives of Rebiya Kadeer, a Uighur businesswoman who was detained in the PRC in

[35] There are conflicting reasons for the protest and paramilitary crackdown in Yining that occurred on February 5–6, 1997, as reported by the *Washington Post*, February 11 and 23, 1997; *Washington Times*, February 12, 1997; International Taklamakan Uighur Human Rights Association, February 15, 1997; *Far Eastern Economic Review*, February 27, 1997; *AERA*, May 26, 1997; and Amnesty International, "China: Remember the Gulja Massacre," February 1, 2007. Mass sentencing and execution rallies were reported afterwards. *AFP* reported on February 12, 1997, that about 100 Uighurs were executed. On April 24, 1997, a court held a rally with over 5,000 people to sentence 30 alleged offenders in the incident, sentencing three Uighurs to death, according to PRC official media. *Reuters* reported that when about 100 people rushed to rescue the 30 prisoners, People's Armed Police opened fire, killing two and wounding five. Again, on July 23, 1997, PRC media in Urumqi reported that a court sentenced 29 "terrorists and criminals" at a rally with over 4,000 people. The sentences included nine death sentences.

[36] James Kelly, Assistant Secretary of State for East Asian and Pacific Affairs, "U.S.-East Asia Policy: Three Aspects," Woodrow Wilson Center, Washington, December 11, 2002; Lorne Craner, Assistant Secretary of State for Democracy, Human Rights, and Labor, "The War Against Terrorism and Human Rights," speech in Urumqi, December 19, 2002.

1999–2005 and was nominated for the Nobel Peace Prize in 2006 after she gained freedom in the United States.[37] In October 2006, a staff delegation of the House International Relations Committee reported heightened congressional concerns about the Administration's designation of ETIM as a terrorist organization and the PRC authorities' beatings and detentions of Kadeer's sons, even during the staff delegation's visit in Urumqi.[38] In the 110th Congress, the House passed **H.Res. 497** (Ros-Lehtinen), noting that the PRC has manipulated the campaign against terrorists to increase cultural and religious oppression of the Muslim Uighur people and has detained and beaten Rebiya Kadeer's children. Passed on September 17, 2007, the resolution urged the PRC to protect the rights of the Uighurs, release Kadeer's children, and release a Canadian of Uighur descent, Huseyin Celil, who was denied access to Canadian consular officials. On May 22, 2008, Senator Sherrod Brown introduced the similar bill in the Senate, **S.Res. 574**. On July 11, Representatives Jim McGovern and Frank Wolf, Co-Chairs of the Congressional Human Rights Caucus, "strongly condemned" China's pre-Olympic crackdown on Uighurs, with the convictions two days earlier of 15 Uighurs (and immediate executions for two, suspended death sentences for three, and life imprisonment for the remaining 10).

In June 2007, President Bush met with Kadeer in Prague and criticized the PRC's imprisonment of her sons.[39] In July 2008, before going to the Olympic Games in Beijing in August, Bush addressed religious freedom and honored Uighur Muslims, Christians, and Tibetan Buddhists seeking religious freedom in China. He also met at the White House with five advocates for freedom in China, including Kadeer. Bush told her that he would seek the release of her two imprisoned sons.[40]

Policy options for Congress include:

- visits to Xinjiang by congressional or staff delegations;
- legislation to mandate appointment of a Special Envoy for Uighur affairs (in 1997, the House and Senate passed H.R. 1757 (ultimately not enacted) that included language on a Special Envoy for Tibet);

---

37 When Kadeer was arrested, she simply was going to meet one CRS analyst in Urumqi.

38 Dennis Halpin and Hans Hogrefe, "Findings of Staff Delegation Visit to Urumqi, PRC, May 30–June 2, 2006," Memorandum to Chairman Henry Hyde and Ranking Member Tom Lantos, October 30, 2006.

39 White House, "President Bush Visits Prague, Czech Republic, Discusses Freedom," June 5, 2007. Also: Rebiya Kadeer, "My Chinese Jailers," *Wall Street Journal*, May 30, 2007.

40 White House, "President Bush Honors the 10th Anniversary of the International Religious Freedom Act," July 14, 2008, and "Statement by the Press Secretary on President Bush's Meeting with Chinese Freedom Activists," July 29, 2008; Uyghur American Association, "Rebiya Kadeer Meets with President Bush at the White House," July 30, 2008.

- legislation to mandate appointment of a Special Coordinator for Uighur affairs (Under Secretary of State for Democracy and Global Affairs also serves as the Special Coordinator for Tibetan Issues);
- calls for the Assistant Secretary of State for Democracy, Human Rights, and Labor, and other human rights officials to visit Xinjiang;
- designation of Xinjiang as occupied territory (in 1991, Congress passed P.L. 102-138, citing Tibet as an "occupied country");
- review the Executive Branch's designations of terrorist groups;
- resolution of the fates of Uighurs detained at Guantanamo.

Detained Uighurs at Guantanamo

A related question pertains to the fate of Uighurs captured during U.S. fighting with Al Qaeda in Afghanistan and detained at Guantanamo Bay military prison since 2002. The PRC claimed them as its citizens for legal action as "suspected terrorists" and interrogated them at the prison. In May 2004, Amnesty International said that, in 2002, the United States allowed PRC officials to participate in interrogations and mistreatment of ethnic Uighurs held at Guantanamo. Then, in July 2004, Amnesty International urged the United States not to turn the 22 detained Uighurs over to China, where they would face torture and execution in China's campaign to repress the Uighur people in the name of "counterterrorism."[41] Other options have included sending them to a third country and resettling them in the United States.

Starting in late 2003, the Defense Department reportedly has determined that 15 Uighurs at Guantanamo could be released, including five who were picked up because they were in the wrong place at the wrong time and 10 who were considered low-risk detainees whose enemy was the PRC government. Seven others were determined to be "enemy combatants."[42] By 2004, U.S. officials told reporters that Uighurs detained at Guantanamo Bay had no more intelligence value, but the United States could not find a third country to accept them, while ruling out their return to China.[43] In August 2004, Secretary of State Colin Powell confirmed the dilemma and assured that "the Uighurs are not going back to China, but finding places for them is not a simple matter, but we are trying to find places for them."[44]

---

[41] "Group Says Chinese Saw Detainees," *Washington Post*, May 26, 2004; Amnesty International, "China: Fleeing Uighurs Forced Back to "Anti-Terror" Torture and Execution," July 7, 2004.

[42] Robin Wright, "Chinese Detainees are Men Without a Country," *Washington Post*, August 24, 2005; and *Asian Wall Street Journal*, August 25, 2005.

[43] Guy Dinmore and James Kynge, "China Torture Fears Curb Guantanamo Releases," *Financial Times*, June 23, 2004; and David Cloud and Ian Johnson, "In Post-9/11 World, Chinese Dissidents Pose U.S. Dilemma," *Wall Street Journal*, August 3, 2004.

[44] Secretary Colin Powell, "Roundtable with Japanese Journalists," August 12, 2004.

The United States has approached over 100 countries to accept the Uighurs, and the State Department reportedly had considered sending the Uighurs back to China instead of allowing them be resettled in the United States.[45]

On April 20, 2006, the Defense Department released a list of 558 people detained at Guantanamo, in response to a Freedom of Information Act lawsuit brought by the Associated Press. The list confirmed that there were 22 Uighurs with PRC citizenship being held. On May 5, 2006, the Pentagon announced the transfer from the Guantanamo Bay prison to Albania of five Uighurs, all of whom had been determined to be "no longer enemy combatants" during reviews in 2004–2005. The PRC then demanded that Albania extradite those Uighurs as "terrorists," but Albania refused. Their plight continues to raise a question of whether they should be resettled in the United States rather than stay confined in a camp in Albania.[46] Defense lawyers for remaining 17 Uighurs held at Guantanamo Bay have complained and testified that the Uighurs suffer in captivity of nearly total isolation at Camp Six.[47]

By mid-2008, U.S. policymakers began to grapple more urgently with the issue of whether and how to release the remaining Uighurs. In Congress, on June 4, 2008, at a hearing of the House Foreign Affairs Subcommittee on International Organizations, Human Rights, and Oversight, the Department of Justice's Inspector General, Glenn Fine, testified that U.S. military interrogators not only collaborated with PRC government agents to interrogate Uighurs at the prison, but that they also deprived them of sleep the night before by waking them up every 15 minutes in a treatment called the "frequent flyer program."[48] The Chairman and Ranking Member, Representatives Bill Delahunt and Dana Rohrabacher, then wrote a letter to Defense Secretary Robert Gates to request that the detained Uighurs promptly be transferred and paroled into the United States. The Members noted that the transfer would not automatically grant asylum, another option for policymakers.[49] In August 2008, the *Washington Post* called for President Bush to use his executive power to grant asylum to Huzaifa

[45] Demetri Sevastopulo, "U.S. Fails to Find Countries to Take Uighurs," *Financial Times*, October 28, 2004; "Uighurs Face Return to China from Guantanamo," *Financial Times*, March 16, 2005; "Detention Dilemma," *Washington Post* (editorial), May 3, 2005; Josh White and Robin Wright, "Detainee Cleared for Release is in Limbo at Guantanamo," *Washington Post*, December 15, 2005; Neil Lewis, "Freed From Guantanamo but Stranded Far From Home," *New York Times*, August 15, 2006; Josh White, "Lawyers Demand Release of Chinese Muslims," *Washington Post*, December 5, 2006.

[46] Tim Golden, "Chinese Leave Guantanamo for Albanian Limbo," *New York Times*, June 10, 2007; Jonathan Finer, "After Guantanamo, An Empty Freedom," *Washington Post*, October 17, 2007.

[47] R. Jeffrey Smith and Julie Tate, "Uighurs' Detention Conditions Condemned," *Washington Post*, January 30, 2007; Sabin Willett (lawyer for a detainee, Huzaifa Parhat), testimony before the House Foreign Affairs Subcommittee on International Organizations, Human Rights, and Oversight, May 20, 2008.

[48] House Foreign Affairs Subcommittee on International Organizations, Human Rights, and Oversight, hearing on the FBI's role at Guantanamo Bay prison, June 4, 2008.

[49] Bill Delahunt and Dana Rohrabacher, letter to Robert Gates, June 19, 2008.

Parhat and allow him to settle in the country.[50] In contrast, in October 2008, Senator Lindsey Graham, sponsor of **S. 3401**, the Enemy Combatant Detention Review Act, argued that while the Uighurs' case is "exceptional," their release in the United States would be a "dangerous precedent" and that detainees waiting release should be transferred to another country.[51]

In the courts, on June 12, 2008, the Supreme Court granted habeas corpus rights to detainees at Guantanamo and ruled that challenges to their detentions be moved to a civilian federal court. Then, undermining the evidence accusing Uighurs, on June 20, 2008, the U.S. Court of Appeals for the District of Columbia decided that in the case of Huzaifa Parhat, the Combatant Status Review Tribunal's determination of him as an "enemy combatant" was not valid.[52] On September 30, 2008, the Justice Department conceded in the D.C. District Court that the 17 remaining Uighur detainees were "no longer enemy combatants."

Then, at a hearing on October 7, Judge Ricardo Urbina ordered the release of the Uighurs into the United States, saying that "because the Constitution prohibits indefinite detention without cause, the Government's continued detention of Petitioners is unlawful." The Uighurs' attorneys sought their release, particularly with assistance promised by a Uighur community in the Washington, DC, area and by a religious community in Tallahassee, FL. One of their lawyers said that they should not be detained "just because it's politically expedient," while the Bush White House argued against setting a "precedent" for other detainees suspected of planning the 9/11 attacks.[53] On the day of the release order, the PRC branded the detainees as suspected "terrorists" and demanded that they be handed over to Beijing.

The next day, on October 8, the U.S. Court of Appeals for the District of Columbia Circuit temporarily blocked the order to release the Uighurs, as requested by the Justice Department which argued that they had received "military training." However, this claim about a danger undermined the State Department's efforts to find a country to accept the Uighurs as not dangerous, and Ambassador-At-Large Clint Williamson had to cancel an imminent diplomatic trip.[54] On October 20, the Court of Appeals granted the Justice Department's request for a stay of the order to release the Uighurs, in a 2-1 decision. In her dissent, Judge Judith Rogers wrote that "the fact that petitioners received firearms training cannot alone show they

[50] "A Home for a Detainee," *Washington Post*, August 16, 2008.

[51] Lindsey Graham, "A Dangerous Precedent," *USA Today*, October 14, 2008.

[52] U.S. Supreme Court, *Boumediene v. Bush*, June 12, 2008; and U.S. Court of Appeals, *Huzaifa Parhat v. Robert Gates*, decided June 20, 2008.

[53] Statements quoted by Del Quentin Wilber, "Uighur Detainees May be Released to U.S.," *Washington Post*, October 5, 2008; and William Glaberson, "Judge Orders 17 Detainees at Guantanamo Freed," *New York Times*, October 8, 2008.

[54] William Glaberson, "Release of 17 Guantanamo Detainees Sputters As Officials Debate the Risk," *New York Times*, October 16, 2008.

are dangerous, unless millions of United States resident citizens who have received firearms training are to be deemed dangerous as well."[55] The next hearing was set for November 24, 2008.

Olympic Security and Violent Incidents

There was congressional concern about whether China's tight security at the Olympic games in Beijing on August 8–24, 2008, would result in internal repression (including human rights dissidents, Uighurs, Tibetans) or harm to safety of American citizens (including those targeted by China for expressing concerns about Tibet, Darfur, Falungong, Taiwan, Burma, North Korean refugees, Xinjiang, etc.). U.S. officials and private firms (even major U.S. Olympic sponsors) faced difficulty in getting the PRC's plans for Olympic security. One policy implication concerns whether to support or oppose holding future international events in China.

In 2007, the PRC government reportedly intensified intelligence gathering of foreigners whom it suspected as protesting its policies in a range of areas, including various non-governmental organizations (NGOs).[56] Issues concerned the U.S. role, including how the State Department should warn and protect U.S. citizens who travel to Beijing. On April 30, 2008, the State Department issued a general "travel alert" to advise U.S. citizens that "any large-scale public event such as the upcoming Olympic Games may present an attractive target for terrorists. There is a heightened risk that extremist groups will conduct terrorist acts within China in the near future." However, while U.S. intelligence was concerned about PRC compromise of electronic equipment, like computers and cellphones, that Americans would bring to the Games (or other times), the State and Commerce Departments reportedly declined to issue a strong warning.[57] On July 30, 2008, Senator Sam Brownback introduced **S.Res. 633** on China's pre-Olympic clampdown, to express the sense of the Senate on the deterioration of respect for privacy and human rights.

Another question concerned the U.S. stance on the PRC's clampdown on security with greater repression before and during major events. Some were concerned about President Bush's attendance at the Olympic Games, involving the message it sent and any pretext for China's claimed need to tighten internal security for Bush's presence. U.S. policymakers knew about the PRC's record of rounding up dissidents, peaceful protestors, and other "undesirables" ahead of and during major international events, including

---

[55] U.S. Court of Appeals (DC Circuit), Jamal Kiyemba, Next Friend, et al. v. George W. Bush, October 20, 2008.

[56] Charles Hutzler, "China Gathering Intelligence on Activists It Thinks Might Disrupt 2008 Olympics," *Associated Press*, July 23, 2007.

[57] Siobhan Gorman, "U.S. Fears Threat of Cyberspying at Olympics," *Wall Street Journal*, July 17, 2008.

presidential summits. When President Bush visited Beijing on November 20, 2005, accompanying Secretary of State Condoleezza Rice acknowledged reports about crackdowns by the PRC's security forces on religious figures (with house arrests and detentions) in the days ahead of Bush's visit. Rice said that the U.S. side would raise those concerns "vociferously" with the PRC government.[58] On February 28, 2008, President Bush said he would raise concerns about human rights and religious freedom in China with its ruler Hu Jintao and at the same time "enjoy a great sporting event" as a "sports fan."[59]

As preparations intensified for the summer Olympics in Beijing, another issue concerned the extent to which the United States, including the military, should cooperate with the PLA or the paramilitary PAP, given concerns about China's internal repression surrounding international events. In March 2007, the PRC Minister of Public Security called for striking hard at "hostile forces" of "ethnic separatism, religious extremism, and violent terrorism" and "evil cults" like the Falungong to have "stability" for the Olympic games. A precedent was set in 2004, when various U.S. departments, including the Department of Defense, provided security assistance for the Olympic games in Athens, Greece, in 2004.[60] On June 22, 2006, at a hearing of the House Armed Services Committee, Brigadier General John Allen, Principal Director for Asian and Pacific Affairs, told Congress that the Defense Department might work with China on security cooperation for the Olympics. However, a year later, Deputy Under Secretary of Defense Richard Lawless testified to the House Armed Services Committee on June 13, 2007, that China did not accept assistance from the Defense Department for Olympic security.

In the lead-up to the Olympic Games, there was no clarity or confirmation about the PRC's claims of terrorist threats in China. The PRC regime has tended to selectively target violent incidents involving Uighurs and Tibetans as "terrorism" but not other violent attacks committed by Hans (ethnic Chinese people). After a Tibetan riot and security crackdown in Lhasa in March 2008, the PRC called the Tibetan Youth Congress "terrorist."[61]

In 2007, just as PRC preparations and propaganda for Olympic security intensified, the PRC claimed that on January 5, police destroyed a "terrorist training camp" run by ETIM in Xinjiang near the border with Pakistan,

---

[58] White House, Press Briefing by Secretary of State Condoleezza Rice on the President's Visit to China, Beijing, November 20, 2005.

[59] President George Bush, press conference, February 28, 2008.

[60] Such assistance included an anti-terrorism exercise held by the European Command in March 2004; exercise scenarios created by the Defense Threat Reduction Agency to defend against weapons of mass destruction; imagery collected by the National Geospatial-Intelligence Agency; and defensive barriers and facilities set up by deployed U.S. naval forces. See GAO, "Olympic Security: U.S. Support to Athens Games Provides Lessons for Future Olympics," May 2005.

[61] *Xinhua*, April 27, 2008.

killed 18 "terrorists," and captured 17 others (who were later sentenced to death, suspended death sentences, or life imprisonment). However, the civilian Public Security police reportedly carried out the action, not the paramilitary People's Armed Police (PAP). Visiting Beijing in June 2007, FBI Assistant Director for International Operations Thomas Fuentes said that the FBI was still assessing the validity of the PRC's claims about the terrorist threat.[62] The State Department reported that there were no acts of international terrorism in China in 2002, 2003, 2004, 2005, 2006, or 2007. The National Counterterrorism Center under the Director of National Intelligence did not report any terrorist attacks in the PRC in 2007. "Terrorism" was defined as "premeditated, politically motivated violence perpetrated against noncombatant targets by subnational groups or clandestine agents."[63]

The next year, the PRC claimed that police in January 2008 raided a house in Urumqi in Xinjiang, killing two people and capturing 15 others who were Uighur separatists carrying out "terrorist acts." Despite calling them "terrorists," the Xinjiang police found only axes, books, and knives (which are common traditional items in Uighur culture).[64] Again, the PAP was not involved in this reported raid by the civilian police. The U.S.-based Uyghur American Association called for an independent investigation of those claims and defended efforts of the Uighur people as peaceful. A reporter who visited the site of the raid in April found residents of the apartment building who reported that nothing dramatically dangerous had happened.[65] Then, in March 2008, the PRC claimed that a Uighur woman was an "East Turkestan element" who tried to blow up a plane flying from Urumqi to Beijing. A news article in New Delhi reported that the incident had a connection to terrorists in Pakistan, but the sophistication of that attempt remained disputable.[66] Also in March, soon after riots in Tibet, hundreds protested in the southern Xinjiang city of Khotan after police returned the body of a Uighur man who died in custody.[67]

However, just the next month in April, the city of Urumqi (including the airport and railroad station) and flights between Urumqi and Beijing were generally calm without stringent security. A few civilian policemen carried

[62] Daniel Schearf, "U.S. Federal Bureau of Investigations Seeks Further Cooperation with China," *VOA News*, June 13, 2007.

[63] State Department, "Country Reports on Terrorism," annual reports; and National Counterterrorism Center, "2007 Report on Terrorism," April 30, 2008.

[64] *Xinhua* and *Huanqiu Shibao*, February 18, 2008; *China Daily*, February 19, 2008; "Terrorist Attack Prevented for Olympics: Official," *Xinhua*, March 9, 2008.

[65] Dan Martin, "Residents Dispute PRC Official Account of Raid on Xinjiang Terrorists in January," *AFP*, April 8, 2008.

[66] Xinjiang Communist Party Secretary Wang Lequan quoted by *Zhongguo Tongxun She*, March 20, 2008; and Praveen Swami, "China's Mid-Air Terror Trail Leads to Pakistan," *Hindu*, March 22, 2008.

[67] *Radio Free Asia*, April 1, 2008; *AFP*, April 2, 2008.

sub-machine guns, and the airport banned small bottles of shampoo and other liquids in carry-on bags.[68]

In June 2008, the Olympic torch relay went though Xinjiang without terrorism, while there were security crackdowns in Xinjiang that prompted an attack on at least one police station.[69] In July, PRC and Hong Kong media reported tightened security checks for roads, railways, and airports throughout Xinjiang, amid a claimed need to protect the Olympics. Uighurs complained of racial profiling that targeted them at the airport or train station and that confiscated their passports to ban traveling.[70]

On July 9, 2008, official PRC media asserted in an English report that the police killed and arrested criminals in Xinjiang who were in a "holy war" training group. However, the original Chinese-language news article in Urumqi called them criminals and did not refer to any terrorist connections. On the same day, Uighur sources reported that the PRC regime forced about 10,000 Uighurs in Kashgar (Kashi) to watch a mass sentencing and execution rally.[71] On July 10, Urumqi's local Public Security officials claimed that they had cracked five "terrorist groups" and detained 82 "terrorists" in the first six months of 2008. On July 14, the local police in Kashi in Xinjiang claimed that they had eliminated 12 "terrorist" gangs.

Nevertheless, the PRC regime downplayed ostensible terrorist threats in videos posted on the Internet in 2008, citing Uighur grievances in China and targeting the Olympic Games. On June 26, 2008, a video was posted on YouTube with a message in Uighur threatening violence at the Olympic Games in Beijing issued under the name of the Turkistan Islamic Party (TIP), which could be ETIM, by a masked and armed man calling himself Seyfullah. However, instead of citing this to bolster its claims about the Uighurs, the PRC did not play up the development. Only a PRC official media report on July 3 cited a Vice Minister of Public Security as mentioning an "East Turkistan" threat on the Internet. Uighur leader Rabiya Kadeer reacted by supporting peaceful and successful Olympic Games in Beijing.[72] Again on July 25, TIP leader Seyfullah posted another video, claiming credit for bus bombings in cities in China from May to July and trying to stop the Olympic Games. Contrary to its usual hyping of an "East Turkestan" terrorist threat, the PRC government and its experts promptly denied the TIP leader's claims.[73] In another YouTube video dated August 1, a man

[68] Author's visit in April 2008.
[69] *AFP*, June 6, 2008; *Reuters*, June 16 and 17, 2008; *AFP*, June 19, 2008.
[70] *Xinhua*, July 29, 2008; *AFP*, July 31, 2008.
[71] Uyghur American Association, "Five Uyghurs Killed in Raid in Urumchi; Uyghurs Executed in Kashgar After Mass Sentencing Rally," July 10, 2008.
[72] Uyghur American Association, "Rebiya Kadeer Expresses Her Wish for a Peaceful Beijing Olympics and Urges Beijing to Cease its Harsh Repression of Uyghurs," July 18, 2008.
[73] *Xinhua*, July 26, 2008; *Zhongguo Xinwen She*, July 28, 2008.

identified as the head of TIP's Religious Education Department, Abdullah Mensur, warned Muslims against going to the Olympics in Beijing.

In those other bombings outside of Xinjiang, the PRC did not call them "terrorist" acts. On May 5, a bus exploded in Shanghai, killing three people. PRC authorities did not call the violent incident a "terrorist attack" and minimized the media's reporting.[74] On July 2, a man caused an explosion at a government office in Hunan province that injured 12 people, reported as "revenge."[75] On July 21, bombs exploded in two buses in Kunming city in Yunnan province, killing two people. The PRC Public Security authorities called the incident "sabotage," not terrorism.[76]

Then, on August 4, four days before the start of the Olympics in Beijing, in the western-most city of Kashgar (Kashi) in Xinjiang, two men drove a truck into a group of PAP Border Security Guards and threw two bombs, killing 16 of them. Immediately, PRC official media reported the violent incident as "suspected terrorism" and raised an alleged connection to "East Turkistan" terrorists. The police said they caught two Uighur men from Kashi, a vegetable vendor and taxi driver, who were found with "home-made" bombs, a hand-gun, and knives, and were waging a "holy war." Kashi's Communist Party Secretary said on August 5 that the incident was a premeditated "terrorist attack." However, the director of Xinjiang's Public Security Department said that the police did not have proof that a terrorist organization like ETIM was responsible for the incident. He also had to apologize to two Japanese journalists trying to cover the incident whom PAP guards detained and beat in a hotel, prompting Japan's diplomatic protest.[77] Foreign eye-witnesses reported that the attackers wore the same PAP uniforms as the security personnel.[78]

On August 10, according to PRC media, 15 male and female assailants exploded a series of home-made bombs in the town of Kuqa in Xinjiang that targeted the Public Security Bureau, government offices, and businesses. The bombs killed one security guard and one Uighur bystander. The police again prevented foreign news about what occurred by detaining Japanese reporters and deleting their photographs.[79] Then, two days later, on August 12, attackers stabbed to death three guards at a security checkpoint at Yamanya town near Kashgar, where an attack occurred on August 4. The authorities responded with police and paramilitary manhunts.

---

[74] *Xinhua, AFP*, May 5, 2008; PRC Foreign Ministry news conference, May 6, 2008.
[75] *Xinhua*, July 2, 2008; *South China Morning Post*, July 3, 2008.
[76] *Xinhua*, July 21, 2008; *Zhongguo Xinwen She*, July 22, 2008.
[77] *Xinhua, AFP*, August 4, 2008; *Kyodo, Xinhua*, August 5, 2008.
[78] *AFP*, August 5, 2008; *New York Times*, September 29, 2008 (also published pictures).
[79] *AFP*, August 13, 2008.

On August 13, the PRC Foreign Ministry quickly blamed "East Turkistan" forces even while reporting that the incidents were still under investigation. A PRC government intelligence-related analyst speculated to the media that the threats increased in Xinjiang.

However, these attacks were not the first time that coordinated multiple bombings occurred, that crude home-made bombs were used, that women allegedly were involved, or that suicide bombers committed the alleged acts. Such events were reported in the 1990s. Moreover, the three attacks in Xinjiang in August 2008 killed 21 people and targeted primarily security forces and not civilians, contrary to the bombings in 1997 in Urumqi and earlier in 2008 in Shanghai and Kunming.

In the violent incidents in 2008, the first reported bombings in Xinjiang since 1997, a critical factor could be the Taliban's resurgence in Pakistan and Afghanistan since mid-2006 that radicalized some disaffected Uighurs in that border area.[80] Many multinational militants have been known to operate in the area that also borders Xinjiang. Since 1997, if not earlier, Pakistani militants crossing into China have raised concerns in Beijing.[81] During the Olympics, the PRC arrested 35 Pakistanis accused of planning to attack the Games, which the Foreign Ministry did not deny.[82]

Alternatively, it is also possible that PRC security precipitated unrest in Xinjiang ahead of August 2008 for a pre-Olympic crackdown, similar to a suspected strategy employed in Tibet surrounding the March 2008 riots, so as not to upset its determined "successful" Olympics. PRC officials have cited the use of "preemptive strikes" in "stability maintenance" in Xinjiang. The violence also could have been reactions to the pre-Olympic security crackdowns that raised resentment. Some Uighurs might have taken advantage of the Games to publicize their plight.

Despite the Internet videos and incidents in Xinjiang, the Olympics took place on August 8–24, 2008, with no violence against the Games in Beijing. In the lead-up to the Games with increasing voices opposing PRC policies, some were concerned that the PRC would not be able to effectively maintain control and security at the Olympic Games. Nevertheless, as the PRC authorities severely tightened security around China, the regime showed a greater likelihood in over-reacting to any disturbances, even peaceful protests, by foreigners or PRC citizens. The PRC deployed immense security forces comprised of the military (PLA), paramilitary People's Armed Police (PAP), and civilian police and totaling 110,000 to tighten control. Those PLA forces include ground, air, and naval units. Indeed, while the PRC

80 On the Taliban resurgence, see CRS Report RL30588, *Afghanistan: Post-War Governance, Security, and U.S. Policy*, by Ken Katzman; and Ahmed Rashid, "A Taliban Comeback?", *YaleGlobal*, May 23, 2006.
81 Matt Forney, "Uighur Fire," *Far Eastern Economic Review*, February 27, 1997.
82 *Daily Times* (Lahore) and PRC Foreign Ministry news conference, August 20, 2008.

authorities exercised initial restraint against domestic and foreign protesters (who advocated for a free Tibet), agents violently beat up and detained some foreign reporters. In addition to the above-mentioned beatings and detentions by security forces of Japanese reporters in Xinjiang, PRC police beat up or forcefully detained Hong Kong reporters covering a sale of Olympic tickets in late July plus British and U.S. journalists covering pro-Tibet protests during the Games.[83]

On October 21, 2008, the PRC's Ministry of Public Security (MPS) issued its second list of alleged terrorists belonging to ETIM (after the first in December 2003), seeking to capture in China or abroad eight Uighurs wanted for having plotted "terrorist attacks" against the Olympic Games. Three days later, a video was posted to YouTube that identified itself as a message from TIP with a still picture of "Military Commander Seyfullah." The message in Uighur rebutted the MPS' charges, questioning the accuracy of the identification of suspects and defending the East Turkistan Muslim's "jihad" against "Chinese Communist invaders."[84]

Sanctions on Exports of Arms and Security Equipment

There has been congressional oversight of sanctions banning the export of crime control equipment to China. The President has the options of selectively or permanently waiving sanctions imposed after the 1989 Tiananmen Crackdown (Section 902 of the Foreign Relations Authorization Act for FYs 1990 and 1991, P.L. 101-246), which deny exports of defense articles/services (including helicopters), crime control equipment, and satellites. President Bush issued a waiver of those sanctions on January 9, 2002 (to export a bomb containment and disposal unit for the Shanghai fire department to prevent terrorist bombings) and again on January 25, 2002 (to consider export licenses for equipment to clean up chemical weapons in China left by Japan in World War II).

More presidential waivers were considered for exports of equipment for the Olympic games in Beijing in August 2008, but there were concerns about contributing to China's internal repression. In May 2005, China held its first exhibition on counterterrorism equipment, and over 200 U.S. and other foreign companies displayed their arms and equipment.[85] At a hearing of the Congressional-Executive Commission on China (CECC) on February 27, 2008, its chairman, Representative Sander Levin, expressed concerns that "any high-technology surveillance equipment will be left in the hands of China's public security and state security organ, who may use

[83] *Wall Street Journal*, July 26; *London Paper*, August 13; *AFP*, August 22, 2008.
[84] "China Identifies Alleged 'Eastern Turkistan' Terrorists," *Xinhua*, October 21, 2008; and "TIP Bayanati," dated October 23 and posted on October 24, 2008, translated by OSC.
[85] China's official *Xinhua* news agency, May 10, 2005.

them to monitor political activists, religious practitioners, and members of certain ethnic minority groups."[86] The Bush Administration reportedly approved the export of sensitive equipment and expertise to PRC security and PLA forces (for which no presidential waiver was needed, according to the State Department). The equipment included that used to detect explosives and radiation. Also, the Energy Department's National Nuclear Security Administration sent a Nuclear Emergency Support Team (NEST) to China to help in detection of a radiological bomb.[87] On June 30, 2008, President Bush notified Congress that he waived temporarily the sanction on munitions exports to allow athletes in shooting competitions to bring firearms and U.S. film crews to bring mobile high definition television camera systems with military gyroscopes to the Olympic Games, after which the equipment would be returned to the United States.

Weapons Nonproliferation

In his 2002 State of the Union speech, President Bush stressed the twin threats of terrorism and weapons proliferation, indicating a strong stance on proliferation problems with the PRC and others. PRC entities have reportedly transferred missile and/or chemical weapons technology to countries that the State Department says support terrorism, like Iran and North Korea. On numerous occasions, the Administration has imposed sanctions for weapons proliferation by PRC entities. However, the Administration has stressed China's cooperation at the Six-Party Talks on North Korea's nuclear weapons and at the U.N. Security Council on sanctions against Iran, rather than China's transfers.[88] China has not joined the Proliferation Security Initiative (PSI) announced by President Bush on May 31, 2003. In its Final Report issued on July 22, 2004, the 9/11 Commission urged that the United States encourage China (and Russia) to join the PSI, among many recommendations. The 110th Congress considered **H.R. 1**, the Implementing Recommendations of the 9/11 Commission Act of 2007. The House-passed bill of January 9, 2007, noted that the Commission called on China to participate in PSI. The Senate passed its bill on July 9 without such language. The Conference Report of July 25 adopted the House provisions on the commission's recommendations and on the sense of Congress that the President should expand and strengthen the PSI. The bill became **P.L. 110-53** on August 3, 2007.

[86] Congressional-Executive Commission on China, hearing on the Impact of the 2008 Olympic Games on Human Rights and Rule of Law in China, February 27, 2008.

[87] Bill Gertz, "China Gets U.S. Olympics Help," *Washington Times*, June 5, 2008; Daniel Pepper, "High-noise Device for Olympics Reviewed," *Washington Times*, June 6, 2008. Also, Bill Gertz, "U.S. Nuke Spotters Sent to China Before Games," *Washington Times*, June 20, 2008.

[88] See CRS Report RL31555, *China and Proliferation of Weapons of Mass Destruction and Missiles: Policy Issues*, by Shirley Kan.

Port Security

The Bush Administration also sought China's cooperation in the Container Security Initiative (CSI) of U.S. Customs and Border Protection. Launched in January 2002, CSI looked at PRC ports (Shanghai and Shenzhen) among the top 20 foreign ports proposed for U.S. screening of manifests and inspections of containers before U.S.-bound shipping. On July 29, 2003, China agreed to join CSI. However, only after this U.S.-PRC agreement did the Bush Administration discuss an agreement with Taiwan to cover the last of the 20 ports: Kaohsiung. The U.S. CSI team became operational in Shanghai in April 2005, and that CSI program underwent its first six-month review by late summer. That CSI program has been compared to the CSI experience with more cooperative and efficient customs authorities in Hong Kong, cooperation that became operational in 2002.[89] In November 2005, the United States and the PRC signed an agreement, as part of the Megaports Initiative of the Energy Department's National Nuclear Security Administration, to install equipment at China's ports to detect nuclear and other radioactive material that could be used for nuclear weapons and "dirty bombs."

Military-to-Military Contacts

While there have been no counterterrorism operations conducted with the PLA, the Pentagon has cautiously resumed a military-to-military relationship with China. In 2001, the Bush Administration limited contacts with the PLA after a Pentagon review started and the EP-3 aircraft collision crisis occurred. Then, for the first time under the Bush Administration, the Pentagon and the PLA again held Defense Consultative Talks (DCT) on December 9, 2002. There were visits by China's Defense Minister, General Cao Gangchuan, in October 2003 and the Chairman of the Joint Chiefs of Staff, General Richard Myers, in January 2004. Secretary of Defense Rumsfeld visited China in October 2005, the first visit by a defense secretary since William Cohen's visit in 2000 and long sought by the PLA for the resumption of a military relationship. Relevant legislation for congressional oversight includes the Foreign Relations Authorization Act for FYs 1990–1991 (P.L. 101-246); National Defense Authorization Act for FY2000 (P.L. 106-65); and National Defense Authorization Act for FY2006 (P.L. 109-163).[90]

However, there is a debate about the extent to which U.S. forces should help the PLA's modernization, including through combined exercises.

[89] Interviews with CSI teams in Shanghai and Hong Kong; CRS memo, "Congressional Staff Delegation's Visit to China, Hong Kong (August 2005), September 14, 2005, by Shirley Kan.

[90] For more discussion, see CRS Report RL32496, *U.S.-China Military Contacts: Issues for Congress*, by Shirley Kan.

Some have urged caution in military cooperation with China on this front of counterterrorism, while others see benefits for the relationship with China. Senator Bob Smith and Representative Dana Rohrabacher wrote Secretary of Defense Rumsfeld in late 2001, to express concerns about renewed military contacts with China. They argued that "China is not a good prospect for counter-terrorism cooperation," because of concerns that China has practiced internal repression in the name of counterterrorism and has supplied technology to rogue regimes and state sponsors of terrorism.[91] In contrast, a 2004 report by Rand urged a program of security management with China that includes counterterrorism as one of three components.[92]

Shanghai Cooperation Organization (SCO)

China has increased its influence in international counterterrorism cooperation through a Central Asian group. After the breakup of the Soviet Union in 1991, China in April 1996 sponsored a "Shanghai Five" meeting in Shanghai with Russia, Kazakhstan, Kyrgyzstan, and Tajikistan to sign an agreement on military confidence building measures. By 1998, at their meeting in Almaty, Kazakhstan, the countries added a ban on allowing the use of one's territory for activities that undermine the sovereignty, security, and social order of another. By 2000, when PLA General Chi Haotian, a Vice Chairman of the Central Military Commission, attended the first defense ministers' meeting and PRC ruler Jiang Zemin attended a summit in Dushanbe, Tajikistan, China shifted the five nations' counterterrorism approach to target what it mixed as the threat of the "three evil forces" of religious extremism, national separatism, and international terrorism. In Shanghai in June 2001, the group added Uzbekistan and became the Shanghai Cooperation Organization (SCO).

After the terrorist attacks on September 11, 2001, China's influence expanded in the SCO along with increased international attention to terrorism. China has granted military assistance to Central Asian countries. The PRC also has operationalized the fight with its military as it sought lessons for modernization. Since 2002, the PLA has conducted combined military exercises in Xinjiang with Central Asian countries and with Russia under the guise of combating terrorists.

However, the SCO summits in 2005 and 2006 raised U.S. concerns. In addition to Mongolia, the countries of India, Pakistan, as well as Iran were invited as observers in 2005. The SCO summit issued a declaration on

[91] Senator Bob Smith and Representative Dana Rohrabacher, letter to Secretary of Defense Donald Rumsfeld, December 17, 2001.

[92] Rand, "U.S.-China Security Management: Assessing the Military-to-Military Relationship," July 2004.

July 5, 2005, that called for a "deadline" for the counterterrorism coalition's "temporary" use of facilities and military presence in SCO countries, because major military operations against terrorists ended in Afghanistan, they claimed. U.S. armed forces were deployed at bases in Uzbekistan until 2005 and have maintained an airbase in Kyrgyzstan, raising China's suspicions about U.S. military deployments in Central Asia and a perceived U.S. encirclement campaign. PRC ruler Hu Jintao also argued that Central Asian countries could handle their own internal and regional affairs. General Richard Myers, Chairman of the Joint Chiefs of Staff, responded on July 14, 2005, that China and Russia were "trying to bully" the Central Asian countries. A week later, China's official *People's Daily* accused General Myers of showing "arrogance" and U.S. intentions to "permanently meddle" and be "strategically dominant" in Central Asia.

During the 109th Congress, on July 19, 2005, the House passed (by voice vote) Representative Tom Lantos's amendment to the Foreign Relations Authorization Act for FYs 2006 and 2007 (**H.R. 2601**). The language expressed the congressional concern that the SCO's declaration called for a deadline for deployments in Central Asia and called on the President and Secretaries of Defense and State to open a dialogue with SCO countries about the use of bases there. The House passed H.R. 2601 (by 351-78) on July 20, 2005, whereas the Senate did not vote on it.

The PRC hosted a summit of SCO members in Shanghai on June 15, 2006, that included Iran as an observer in an ostensibly counterterrorism group. The State Department criticized that inclusion of Iran, a state sponsor of terrorism, as running "counter" to the international fight against terrorism. Ahead of the SCO summit in Bishkek in August 2007, the PRC's official newspaper published an article calling for the U.S. military to withdraw from the base in Kyrgyzstan. Also, the Deputy Speaker of the Kyrgyz parliament said he expected pressure from Russia and China on his government concerning the use of the Manas air base by the U.S. military.[93] In August 2007, the PLA and Russian forces held a combined counterterrorism exercise called "Peace Mission 2007" under the SCO's sponsorship in Chelyabinsk in Russia's Ural Mountains and in Urumqi in Xinjiang. The exercise targeted what China called the "three evil forces." In 2008, Iran applied to be a SCO member.

PRC-Origin Weapons and Iran

Since the summer of 2007, U.S. officials have expressed greater concern about China-origin weapons that have been found in the conflicts involving U.S. forces in Afghanistan (and Iraq), as part of the broader threat posed

[93] *Renmin Ribao [People's Daily]*, June 15, 2007; *AKI Press*, July 10, 2007.

by Iran and its re-transfers to anti-U.S. fighters. PRC-made weapons found in Afghanistan, mainly small arms and ammunition, have included man-portable anti-aircraft missiles (such as the HN-5 missiles); armor-piercing ammunition; rocket propelled grenades; artillery rockets; sniper rifles; and components for weapons. In late 2001, PRC-origin (produced by the state-owned defense-industrial company, NORINCO) multiple rocket launchers (using 107 mm rockets) were found in Afghanistan. Also, in late 2001 to spring 2002, caches of PRC-origin HN-5 missiles, ammunition, and rocket propelled grenades were discovered. In June 2007, the Taliban used PRC-made HN-5 surface-to-air missiles in Afghanistan. In some cases, tracing to the producer of the arms is challenged by the intentional removal of serial numbers from the weapons or parts. Also adding to the challenge of identifying the source of weapons is the fact that Iran has manufactured an anti-aircraft missile, called the Misagh-1, that is similar to the QW-1 anti-air missile made by the PRC's state-owned, defense industrial company: the China Precision Machinery Import and Export Corporation (CPMIEC).[94]

Even while U.S. officials have pointed to China as the origin of some of the weaponry found in Afghanistan, another question concerns whether the supplies are new (since Operation Enduring Freedom began in 2001) or left over from the years when various countries transferred weapons to Mujahedin fighters in Afghanistan during its Soviet occupation in the 1980s or later in the 1990s. China's CPMIEC exported the HN-5 anti-aircraft missiles for years, and China previously supplied them to the Mujahedin in Afghanistan, Iran, and other countries.[95] Defense Secretary Donald Rumsfeld told reporters in August 2002 that Afghanistan is "filled with weapons" and that "you do find things from China, but you find them from country after country after country." He added, "a lot of it is quite old and probably not stable."[96] In September 2007, an Afghan Interior Ministry spokesman said that his government seized various types of arms, including PRC weapons, but did not have evidence of new PRC arms being transferred to the Taliban.[97] Aside from the explanation of left-over caches, PRC-made weapons are not the only type uncovered. In the same month, another Afghan official announced that arms made in China, Iran, and

[94] Bill Gertz and Rowan Scarborough, "Inside the Ring: China-al Qaeda Nexus," *Washington Times*, December 21, 2001; Bill Gertz, "China-made Artillery Seized in Afghanistan," *Washington Times*, April 12, 2002; "China-trained Taliban," *Washington Times*, June 21, 2002; Scott Baldauf, "Al Qaeda Massing for New Fight" and "How Al Qaeda Seeks to Buy Chinese Arms," *Christian Science Monitor*, August 9 and 23, 2002; *Jane's Land-based Air Defence 2003–2004*; Philip Smucker, "Taliban Uses Weapons Made in China, Iran," *Washington Times*, June 5, 2007; "Chinese Arms in the Hands of Taleban," editorial, *Kabul Times*, June 7, 2007; Bill Gertz, "China Arming Terrorists," *Washington Times*, June 15, 2007; Demetri Sevastopuloin, "U.S. Takes China to Task Over Iraq and Afghan Arms," *Financial Times*, July 9, 2007; *Jane's Armor and Artillery 2007–2008*.

[95] *Jane's Land-Based Air Defence, 1996–1997, and 2003–2004.*

[96] Briefing by Defense Secretary Rumsfeld and General Myers, August 9, 2002.

[97] *Tolu Television*, Kabul, September 4, 2007.

Russia were discovered in the city of Herat, near the western border with Iran.[98]

In its approach, the Bush Administration has focused concerns and questions on Iran, rather than China, and how the weapons ended up in Afghanistan (some through Iran), rather than where they were made (in China, Iran, or other countries). Focusing on Iran, Under Secretary of State for Political Affairs Nicholas Burns specifically said on June 13, 2007: "There's irrefutable evidence the Iranians are now [transferring arms to the Taliban in Afghanistan], and it's a pattern of activity."... "It's coming from the Iranian Revolutionary Guard Corps command, which is a basic unit of the Iranian government." After just retiring as Deputy Under Secretary of Defense, Richard Lawless told reporters on July 6 that "Identifying how [the weapons] came through Iran [into Afghanistan] and who is facilitating that transit through Iran is the key issue for us right now. It is really not the issue of where they ultimately were manufactured." Nonetheless, despite the primary focus on Iran, the Administration sent demarches to Beijing. Lawless confirmed that the United States expressed concerns to China about exercising greater care in its arms sales to Iran. Deputy Assistant Secretary of Defense for East Asia David Sedney also said at a meeting of the U.S.-China Economic and Security Review Commission on July 12, that the United States has "repeatedly asked China to stop its transfers to Iran of conventional weapons and technologies," but Beijing's response has been "irresponsible." He also warned, "partners do not provide weapons to people who support those who kill our troops and those of our allies." While in Kabul on September 11, Deputy Secretary of State John Negroponte acknowledged that he raised concerns with China about its arms sales to Iran and requested that China refrain from signing any new arms sales contracts with Iran.[99] The United Kingdom also asked Beijing about the Taliban's use of PRC weapons against U.K. troops in Afghanistan.[100]

It is uncertain as to whether China has stopped arms transfers to Iran or prevented any new arms sales contracts with Iran, as Negroponte urged. The PRC has not denied its arms sales to Iran and has conveyed a sense of "business as usual." In 2007, when questioned by reporters about PRC arms sales to Iran that have been found in Afghanistan (and Iraq), the PRC Foreign Ministry characterized its arms sales as "normal" military trade and cooperation with other countries. The ministry stated China's position

[98] *Pajhwok Afghan News*, Kabul, September 6, 2007; *AFP*, September 22, 2007.

[99] "Iran Arming Taliban, U.S. Claims," *CNN*, June 13, 2007; Richard Lawless, transcript of interview with Asahi Shimbum and other newspapers, July 6, 2007; Demetri Sevastopuloin, "U.S. Takes China to Task Over Iraq and Afghan Arms," *Financial Times*, July 9, 2007; Jim Wolf, "U.S. Faults China on Shipments to Iran," *Reuters*, July 12, 2007; John Negroponte, Press Roundtable in Afghanistan, Kabul, Afghanistan, September 11, 2007.

[100] Paul Danahar, "Taleban Getting Chinese Weapons," *BBC News*, September 3, 2007.

that its arms sales are beyond reproach and responsible because China follows these "principles" for arms exports: they are for legitimate self-defense; they do not undermine international peace and stability; they do not interfere in the internal affairs of the recipients; and they are exported only to sovereign countries. In addition, the Foreign Ministry claimed that China has stipulated another condition: no re-transfer to a third party without PRC permission. The ministry also argued that China has complied with international laws and United Nations Security Council (UNSC) resolutions.[101]

However, China could contend compliance with the letter of UNSC resolutions because China (along with Russia) objected to UNSC sanctions targeting Iran's arms imports. Thus, only after diplomatic negotiations on additional sanctions against Iran for its nuclear enrichment program (during which China and Russia objected to banning Iran's arms imports and export credit guarantees for doing business in Iran),[102] China voted with all other UNSC members on March 24, 2007, for Resolution 1747, which included a ban on Iran's arms exports (not imports).

Aside from the issue of whether the PRC has been responsive to U.S. concerns, the complicity of China's government in allowing or acquiescing in the arms flow to Iran is another question. Part of that question concerns whether the PLA has been involved. The arms manufacturers were PRC state-owned defense-industrial plants, rather than the PLA itself, although the PLA might have a role in any vetting of the arms exports. Regardless of whether the PRC government did or did not know about these arms sales to Iran or PRC weapons found in Afghanistan and Iraq, U.S. demarches have now raised the problem with Beijing.

Continuing into 2008, the Director of National Intelligence (DNI) testified to Congress that the PRC's arms sales in the Middle East are "destabilizing" and "a threat" to U.S. forces, while missile sales to Iran pose a "threat to U.S. forces in the Persian Gulf."[103] At a hearing in June 2008, Defense Department officials testified to Congress that although the United States demanded that the PRC stop transfers that violate U.N. sanctions, nonproliferation norms, and PRC law, U.S. efforts met with "mixed results." China's cooperation was "uneven" and it needs to act "responsibly." The officials testified that there are particular concerns about PRC sales of

[101] PRC Foreign Ministry news conferences, July 10; July 26; September 4, 2007.

[102] "Nations Closer to Deal on Iran Sanctions," *AP*, March 13, 2007; and Colum Lynch, "6 Powers Agree on Sanctions for Iran," *Washington Post*, March 16, 2007.

[103] Senate Select Committee on Intelligence, hearing on the DNI's annual threat assessment, testimony of J. Michael McConnell, February 5, 2008.

conventional weapons to Iran, a "country that supports terrorism and groups in Iraq, Lebanon, and Afghanistan that target and kill Americans and our allies."[104]

[104] House Armed Services Committee, hearing on recent security developments in China, prepared joint statement of James Shinn, Assistant Secretary of Defense for Asian and Pacific Security Affairs, and Major General Phillip Breedlove, USAF, Vice Director for Strategic Plans and Policy, Joint Chiefs of Staff, June 25, 2008.

DOCUMENT NO. 8

TERRORIST ATTACKS IN MUMBAI, INDIA, AND IMPLICATIONS FOR U.S. INTERESTS

CRS Report
R40087

December 19, 2008

K. Alan Kronstadt

Summary

On the evening of November 26, 2008, a number of well-trained militants came ashore from the Arabian Sea on small boats and attacked numerous high-profile targets in Mumbai, India, with automatic weapons and explosives. By the time the episode ended some 62 hours later, about 165 people, along with nine terrorists, had been killed and hundreds more injured. Among the multiple sites attacked in the peninsular city known as India's business and entertainment capital were two luxury hotels—the Taj Mahal Palace and the Oberoi-Trident—along with the main railway terminal, a Jewish cultural center, a café frequented by foreigners, a cinema house, and two hospitals. Six American citizens were among the 26 foreigners reported dead. Indian officials have concluded that the attackers numbered only ten, one of whom was captured.

The investigation into the attacks is still in preliminary stages, but press reporting and statements from U.S. and Indian authorities strongly suggest that the attackers came to India from neighboring Pakistan and that the perpetrators likely were members and acting under the orchestration of the Pakistan-based Lashkar-e-Taiba (LeT) terrorist group. The LeT is believed to have past links with Pakistan's military and intelligence services. By some accounts, these links are ongoing, leading to suspicions, but no known evidence, of involvement in the attack by Pakistani state elements. The Islamabad government has strongly condemned the Mumbai terrorism and offered New Delhi its full cooperation with the ongoing investigation, but mutual acrimony clouds such an effort, and the attacks have brought into question the viability of a nearly five-year-old bilateral peace process between India and Pakistan.

Three wars—in 1947–48, 1965, and 1971—and a constant state of military preparedness on both sides of the border have marked six decades of bitter rivalry between India and Pakistan. Such bilateral discord between two nuclear-armed countries thus has major implications for regional security and for U.S. interests. The Administration of President-elect Barack Obama may seek to increase U.S. diplomatic efforts aimed at resolving conflict between these two countries. The Mumbai attacks have brought even more intense international attention to the increasingly deadly and destabilizing incidence of Islamist extremism in South Asia, and they may affect the course of U.S. policy toward Pakistan, especially. The episode also has major domestic implications for India, in both the political and security realms. Indian counterterrorism capabilities have come under intense scrutiny, and the United States may further expand bilateral cooperation with and assistance to India in this realm. For broader discussion, see CRS Report RL33529, *India-U.S. Relations*, and CRS Report RL33498, *Pakistan-U.S. Relations*. This report will not be updated.

Introduction

An audacious, days-long November terrorist attack on India's most populous city, Mumbai, has deeply affected the Indian people and their government. Because the attackers appear to have come from, and received training and equipment in, neighboring Pakistan, the episode has led to renewed tensions between two nuclear-armed South Asian states with a history of war and mutual animosity. Seemingly incompatible national identities contributed both to several wars and to the nuclearization of the Asian Subcontinent, with the nuclear weapons capabilities of both countries becoming overt in 1998. In 2004, New Delhi and Islamabad launched their most recent comprehensive effort to reduce tensions and resolve outstanding disputes, an effort that has to date resulted in modest, but still meaningful successes. New Delhi acknowledges that a stable Pakistan is in India's interests. At the same time, however, Indian leaders are convinced that Pakistan has long been and remains the main source India's significant domestic terrorism problems. They continue to blame Islamabad for maintaining an "infrastructure of terror" that launches attacks inside India.

A central aspect of U.S. policy in South Asia is prevention of interstate conflict that could destabilize the region and lead to nuclear war. Since 2001, the United States has also been directly engaged in efforts foster stability in Afghanistan. Many analysts view this goal as being intimately linked with the India-Pakistan peace process. The Administration of President George W. Bush made Pakistan a key ally in the global "war on terrorism" while simultaneously deepening a "strategic partnership" with India. The Administration of President-elect Barack Obama may seek to increase U.S. diplomatic efforts aimed at resolving conflict between these two countries.

Potential issues for the 111th Congress with regard to India include legislation that would foster greater U.S.-India counterterrorism relations. With regard to Pakistan, congressional attention has focused and is likely to remain focused on the programming and potential further conditioning of U.S. foreign assistance, including that related to security and counterterrorism. Also, major U.S. arms sales to both countries are likely to be proposed, and these would require the (implicit) endorsement of Congress. This report reviews the most recent major incidence of terrorism in India and its possible connection to elements inside Pakistan. It then considers some implications for both countries, as well as for U.S. interests.

Attack Overview

At approximately 9:30 p.m. local time on the evening of November 26, 2008, a number of well-trained militants came ashore from the Arabian Sea on small boats and attacked numerous high-profile targets in Mumbai, India, with automatic weapons and explosives. By the time the episode ended some 62 hours later, about 174 people, including nine terrorists, had been killed and hundreds more injured. Among the multiple sites attacked in the peninsular city known as India's business and entertainment capital were two luxury hotels—the Taj Mahal Palace and the Oberoi-Trident—along with the main railway terminal, a Jewish cultural center, a café frequented by foreigners, a cinema house, and two hospitals.[1] Six American citizens were among the 26 foreigners reported dead. Indian officials have concluded that the attackers numbered only ten, one of whom was captured. Some reports indicate that several other gunmen escaped.[2]

According to reports, the militants arrived in Mumbai from sea on dinghies launched from a larger ship offshore, then fanned out in southern Mumbai in groups of two or three.[3] Each was carrying an assault rifle with 10–12 extra magazines of ammunition, a pistol, several hand grenades, and about 18 pounds of military-grade explosives. They also employed sophisticated technology including global positioning system handsets, satellite phones, Voice over Internet Protocol (VoIP) phone service, and high-resolution

---

1 Two detailed descriptions of the incident are "In Just Minutes, Mumbai Was Under Siege," *Washington Post*, and "India Security Faulted as Survivors Tell of Terror," *Wall Street Journal*, both December 1, 2008.

2 "Mumbai Attacks—City Fears Five Terrorists are 'Missing,'" *London Times*, December 2, 2008.

3 The Indian fishing vessel *Kuber* reportedly was hijacked by Pakistan-based terrorists in the Arabian Sea some two weeks before the attacks and its five-man crew executed ("Authorities Trace Final Voyage of the Kuber," *Wall Street Journal*, December 2, 2008).

satellite photos of the targets. The attackers were said to have demonstrated a keen familiarity with the Taj hotel's layout in particular, suggesting that careful advanced planning had been undertaken.

Home Minister Shivraj Patil (who resigned in the wake of the attacks) reportedly ordered India's elite National Security Guard commandos deployed 90 minutes after the attacks began, but the mobilized units did not arrive on the scene until the next morning, some ten hours after the initial shooting. The delay likely handed a tactical advantage to the militants.[4] According to a high-ranking Mumbai police official, the militants made no demands and had killed most of their hostages before being engaged by commandos on the morning of November 27.[5] Two full days passed between the time of that engagement and the episode's conclusion when the two hotels were declared cleared of the several remaining gunmen.

Indian Prime Minister Manmohan Singh apologized to the Indian people on behalf of his government for being unable to prevent the attacks. He said his government will pursue a three-level response to include (1) seeking to galvanize the international community to deal sternly with what Singh labeled the "epicenter of terrorism, which is located in Pakistan;" (2) taking a strong posture toward the Islamabad government in pressing it to end the use of Pakistani territory for staging terrorist attacks, and (3) recognizing that self-help measures to improve India's own domestic security are required.[6] On December 11, the country's new home minister, P. Chidambaram, announced major reform efforts for the country's security infrastructure to include the establishment of a new national investigative agency, a new Coastal Command, 20 new counterterrorism schools, and new regional commando bases.[7] The Indian Parliament passed a serious of stringent new anti-terrorism laws on December 17 (see below).

U. S. Response

Senior U.S. officials, including President Bush and President-elect Obama, joined the State Department in issuing immediate statements of support for and condolences to the Indian government and people.[8] H.Res. 1532, agreed to by unanimous consent on December 10, 2008, condemned the attacks, offered condolences and support to the people and government of

[4] "India to Restructure Security Services After Mumbai Failings," *Jane's Defense Weekly*, December 1, 2008.

[5] "'Our Mission Was Not About 10 Terrorists, It Was All About Saving Lives'" (interview with Mumbai's Joint Police Commissioner), Rediff.com, December 12, 2008; "Militants Lead Commandos in Deadly Dance in Mumbai," Reuters, November 28, 2008; "Terrorists Did Not Make Any Demands: NSG Chief," *Times of India* (Delhi), December 1, 2008.

[6] See http://www.indianembassy.org/newsite/press_release/2008/Dec/6.asp.

[7] "Indian Official Unveils Plan to Strengthen Security," *Washington Post*, December 11, 2008.

[8] See http://www.indianembassy.org/newsite/press_release/2008/Nov/11.asp.

India, and expressed U.S. congressional desire to improve coordination between the United States and India to combat terrorism and advance international security. The resolution also called upon the Pakistani government to cooperate fully with India in bringing the culprits to justice and to prevent Pakistan's territory from "serving as a safe-haven and training ground for terrorists."[9]

The Bush Administration claims to be carefully monitoring related developments and has sent FBI agents to Mumbai to assist in the investigation. On November 30, the Administration announced that it would dispatch Secretary of State Rice to India as "a further demonstration of the U.S. commitment to stand in solidarity with the people of India as we all work together to hold these extremists accountable."[10] Rice met with Indian External Affairs Minister Pranab Mukherjee on December 3 and was told that Indian officials have "no doubt that the terrorist attack in Mumbai was perpetrated by individuals who came from Pakistan and whose controllers are in Pakistan." Rice assured her interlocutors that the United States "stands in solidarity with the people of India," and she pledged full cooperation in bringing the perpetrators to justice and ensuring that future attacks are prevented.[11] She then traveled to Islamabad to convey to Pakistani leaders a U.S. expectation that Pakistan act quickly and resolutely to bring justice to any perpetrators on Pakistani territory.[12] Rice was followed in both capitals by other senior U.S. officials, including her deputy, John Negroponte, Joint Chiefs Chairman Adm. Mike Mullen, and Foreign Relations Committee Chairman-designate Senator John Kerry.

Suspected/Accused Culprits

Lashkar-e-Taiba

On December 9, Indian officials released the names or aliases of the nine suspected gunmen killed during the Mumbai siege, saying all were Pakistani nationals.[13] U.S. and Indian officials reportedly have used forensic evidence, including phone records, to establish solid links between the gunmen and elements inside Pakistan. Early indications pointed to the Lashkar-e-Taiba (LeT or "Army of the Pure"), which was outlawed by the Islamabad government in 2002, as being complicit.[14] The LeT denies involvement in the attack. Designated as a Foreign Terrorist Organization (FTO) under U.S. law in late 2001, the LeT is based in Muzaffarabad (in Pakistani Kashmir) and Muridke (near Lahore). The group seeks not only

9 H.Res. 1532.
10 See http://www.whitehouse.gov/news/releases/2008/11/20081130-1.html.
11 See http://www.state.gov/secretary/rm/2008/12/112622.htm.
12 See http://www.state.gov/secretary/rm/2008/12/112752.htm.
13 "India Police 'Name Mumbai Gunmen,'" BBC News, December 9, 2008.
14 See a profile of the LeT at http://www.cfr.org/publication/17882.

Islamic rule in all of Kashmir, but is also a proponent of broader anti-India and anti-Western struggles, and is the armed wing of a Pakistan-based, anti-U.S. Sunni religious organization formed in 1989. Its key leader is Hafiz Mohammad Saeed. The LeT is believed to have close links with both Al Qaeda and the Taliban, and over the years it appears to have taken a more expansive, global jihadi perspective.[15] The group even has some successes in efforts to recruit Westerners, especially Britons and Americans.[16] Under aliases and through front organizations, the LeT has operated more or less openly in Pakistan despite the 2002 ban, fueling pervasive doubts that Pakistan's security agencies will honor the promises of cooperation being made by Islamabad's civilian leaders.[17]

The LeT has been implicated in past, multiple-target attacks involving coordinated movements by well-armed gunmen who took hostages. The level of sophistication and training required to undertake the recent Mumbai attacks spurred many Indian and American analysts to name the LeT as a likely suspect.[18] Such suspicions appeared validated when Indian government officials announced that the sole attacker captured alive had confessed to being a Pakistani national trained in LeT camps. The 21-year-old militant, named as Azam Amir Kasab and said to be a native of Faisalabad in Pakistan's Punjab province, reportedly admitted that the Mumbai operation was launched from Pakistan's Karachi port.[19]

Jamaat-ud-Dawa (JuD), nominally a charitable organization established in 2005 (it provides education, health care, and emergency relief services in Punjab and Pakistani Kashmir) is identified as a continuation of the LeT with a new name. The Indian government claims the JuD operates 2,500 offices and 11 religious seminaries in Pakistan.[20] The JuD is viewed favorably by many Pakistanis for its charitable efforts. On December 10, at the request of the Indian government and with Washington's blessing, the U.N. Security Council took several actions related to LeT, including listing four of its members for targeted sanctions, adding JuD as an LeT alias, and adding aliases for the two Islamic trusts that have raised funds for LeT. Hafiz Saeed and Zaki-ur-Lakhvi were among those named, along with two

---

[15] Of three major Al Qaeda figures captured in Pakistan, one (Abu Zubaydah) was found at an LeT safehouse in Faisalabad, suggesting that some LeT members have facilitated the movement of Al Qaeda members in Pakistan (see http://www.state.gov/s/ct/rls/crt/2007/103714.htm).

[16] "Pakistan Militant Group Builds Web of Western Recruits," *Los Angeles Times*, December 8, 2008.

[17] "Mumbai Attack is Test of Pakistan's Ability to Curb Militants," *New York Times*, December 4, 2008; "Pakistan Army Link to Mumbai Suspects May Hurt Pledge," Bloomberg News, December 3, 2008.

[18] "U.S. Intelligence Focuses on Pakistani Group," *New York Times*, November 29, 2008; "US Official: India Attack May Have Pakistani Roots," Associated Press, December 2, 2008.

[19] "India Says All Attackers Came By Ship," *New York Times*, December 3, 2008.

[20] "India Raises Terror Issue at U.N.," *New York Times*, December 10, 2008. According to India's top diplomat, the JuD and the LeT are indistinguishable: "The headquarters are the same, the ideologies are the same, and the activities are the same" (see http://www.indianembassy.org/newsite/press_release/2008/Dec/10.asp).

men said to be key LeT financiers, one of them a Saudi national. The U.S. Treasury Department had in May 2008 designated these same four LeT "leaders."[21] One of the key "masterminds" of the Mumbai attacks is said to have been Yusuf Muzammil, a top LeT commander. Lakhvi, his lieutenant, reportedly took telephone calls from the Mumbai terrorists as the attack was underway. Both men, named by the captured gunman under interrogation, reportedly stage-managed the attacks in real time.[22]

Suspected Links With Pakistan's State Apparatus

Over the past two decades or more, the Pakistani government—its military and intelligence services, in particular—is widely believed to have used radical Islamist groups to forward its own regional policy goals. Reports link the LeT to Pakistan's main Inter-Services Intelligence (ISI) agency, which is likely to have facilitated its creation and early activities. Indian analysts emphasize evidence of a direct link between Pakistan-sponsored militancy in Kashmir and the wider assortment of radical Islamic groups active in Pakistan after 2001, with one going so far as to call the LeT a "wholly owned subsidiary" of the ISI.[23] Even Pakistan's current Ambassador to the United States has in the recent past commented upon Pakistan's "state sponsorship of jihad against India" and described the LeT as "backed by Saudi money and protected by Pakistani intelligence services."[24] In a 2005 book on the relationships between Pakistani Islamists and the Pakistani military, this diplomat wrote that, earlier in the decade, the ISI provided significant "severance pay" to jihadi leaders in return for their promise to "remain dormant for an unspecified duration." Among the alleged recipients of this ISI largesse were the LeT's Saeed, and Masood Azhar, chief of the Pakistan-based, FTO-designated Jaish-e-Mohammed (JeM).[25] The JeM, another Kashmir-focused militant group, was publically implicated by New Delhi (along with the LeT) for orchestrating a December 2001 attack on India's Parliament complex, an event that spurred a ten-month-long international crisis.[26]

On December 5, an unnamed, but ostensibly high-ranking Indian official claimed that his government has "clear and incontrovertible proof" the November Mumbai attack was planned by the LeT with training and other support from the ISI. U.S. officials have to date been more circumspect in

---

[21] See http://www.state.gov/r/pa/prs/ps/2008/dec/113087.htm and http://www.ustreas.gov/press/releases/hp996.htm.
[22] "Terror Attacks Traced to Two from Pakistan," *New York Times*, December 4, 2008.
[23] Quoted in "Beyond Control," *India Today* (New Delhi), December 8, 2003.
[24] Husain Haqqani, "The Ideologies of South Asian Jihadi Groups," *Current Trends in Islamist Ideology*, April 2005.
[25] Husain Haqqani, *Pakistan: Between Mosque and Military* (Washington: Carnegie Endowment for International Peace, 2005), p. 306.
[26] See http://www.state.gov/s/ct/rls/crt/2007/103714.htm.

their interpretation of evidence, but many are reported to believe that the LeT's recent growth in strength and reach has come only with active assistance from ISI elements, either active or "retired."[27] In mid-2008, U.S. intelligence officials apparently concluded that ISI elements were involved in a July car bombing of India's Embassy in Kabul, Afghanistan.[28]

Indigenous Indian Suspects

Indian authorities are holding at least four Indian nationals in possible connection with the Mumbai attack. One, Mumbai native Faim Ansari, was detained in February 2008 carrying maps with several Mumbai landmarks highlighted, including some of those attacked in November. Ansari reportedly confessed to having received training from the LeT and he may have been part of a foiled plot to attack Mumbai earlier in the year. A man arrested along with Ansari now stands accused of facilitating the infiltration of militants into India via Nepal. Two other Indians were arrested in early December: a native of Indian Kashmir who may have illicitly provided mobile phone cards to the attackers, and a Kolkata man suspected of providing him with those cards. The former figure appears to have been working as an undercover agent for Kashmir police seeking to infiltrate militant groups.[29]

Possible Motives

The gunmen's motives remain unclear, but most reports indicate that radical Islamist sentiments played a central role. One report included anecdotal evidence that the attackers were seeking vengeance for major attacks on Indian Muslim communities at Ayodhya, Uttar Pradesh, in 1992 and at Godhra, Gujarat, in 2002.[30] Some observers see evidence that the attackers were inspired, if not directed, by Al Qaeda's brand of global jihadi ideology.[31] A White House spokeswoman said the attack on a Jewish center "adds another layer of complexity" to the episode.[32] Secretary Rice has speculated that the goal of the attackers was "probably to stir up trouble between Pakistan and India."[33] Early reporting suggested that Westerners, especially Americans and Britons, were being singled out by the attackers,

---

[27] "Indian Official Points to Pakistan," *Washington Post*, December 6, 2008; "Pakistan's Spies Aided Group Tied to Mumbai Siege," *New York Times*, December 8, 2008.

[28] "Pakistanis Aided Attack in Kabul, U.S. Officials Say," *New York Times*, August 1, 2008.

[29] "Police Foiled Earlier Plot Against Mumbai," *New York Times*, December 6, 2008; "Police Say Indian Helped Smuggle Pakistani Gunmen," Associated Press, December 10, 2008; "Facts About Mumbai Attack Suspects in India," Reuters, December 7, 2008.

[30] "India Security Faulted as Survivors Tell of Terror," *Wall Street Journal*, December 1, 2008

[31] Bruce Riedel, "Terrorism in India and the Global Jihad," Brookings Institution, December 1, 2008; M.J. Gohel and Sajjan Gohel, "Were Mumbai Attacks Inspired by Al Qaeda?" (op-ed), *CNN.com*, November 30, 2008.

[32] See http://www.whitehouse.gov/news/releases/2008/12/20081201-2.html.

[33] See http://www.state.gov/secretary/rm/2008/12/112999.htm.

but subsequent eyewitness accounts did not appear to support the conclusion.[34]

A former Bush State Department official and South Asia specialist views the Mumbai attacks as an escalation of what he calls the "war for Pakistan": an ongoing and essentially civil-level battle to determine whether Pakistan will be a moderate or an extremist state.[35] At least one former senior U.S. counterterrorism official sees the attacks as part of a "goal-oriented" effort to advance an overall strategy to, in proximate terms, defeat the U.S. military and restore Taliban rule in Afghanistan. This strategy is assumed to be shared by Al Qaeda and the Taliban in both Afghanistan and Pakistan, as well as by the LeT.[36] Another expert agrees that LeT goals transcend the Kashmiri separatism that has been its primary motivation, and they are aimed at crippling the Indian state and conducting global war against a perceived "American-Zionist-Hindu" axis.[37] Conspiracy-minded regional analysts, including Iranians and Saudis, see the Mumbai attacks as part of a plot to draw New Delhi (further) into this alleged axis.[38]

Background

Domestic Indian Terrorism

As a vast mosaic of ethnicities, languages, cultures, and religions, India is difficult to govern. Of particular relevance in the current context are tensions between India and Pakistan rooted in unfinished business from the 1947 Partition of British India in which Pakistan was created as a homeland for South Asian Muslims, competing claims to the Kashmir region, and, in more recent years, "cross-border terrorism" in both Kashmir and major Indian cities. Terrorist attacks in India beyond Kashmir have been rampant in recent months and years, and include bombings in Jaipur in May (63 dead); Bangalore and Ahmedabad in July (46 dead); and New Delhi in September (18 dead). In 2008 many Indian officials came to realize that the capabilities of indigenous extremist elements had grown immensely. The newly emergent "Indian Mujahideen" (IM) group, widely believed to be an offshoot or pseudonym of the Students Islamic Movement of India (SIMI), has been found complicit in a number of recent bombings, even as government leaders continue to name Pakistan as an abettor of such

[34] "Top Indian Security Official Resigns as Toll Eclipses 180," *New York Times*, December 1, 2008.

[35] Daniel Markey, *Mumbai: A Battle in the War for Pakistan*, Council on Foreign Relations, Expert Brief, December 12, 2008, http://www.cfr.org/publication/17981/mumbai.html?breadcrumb=%2Fregion%2F279%2Fsouth_asia.

[36] Richard Clarke, "Plans of Attack" (op-ed), *Washington Post*, December 7, 2008.

[37] Ashley Tellis, "Terrorists Attacking Mumbai Have Global Agenda," *Yale Global*, December 8, 2008.

[38] Atul Aneja, "How West Asia Views Mumbai Attacks" (op-ed), *Hindu* (Chennai), December 17, 2008.

episodes. Mumbai itself has suffered several major terrorist attacks.[39] Some Indian experts assert that the IM's top operators, drawn mostly from SIMI's ranks, receive training at LeT camps.[40]

Indo-Pakistan Tensions

Decades of militarized tensions and territorial disputes between India and Pakistan arguably have hamstrung economic and social development in both countries while also precluding establishment of effective regional economic or security institutions. The nuclearization of the Asian Subcontinent became overt in 1998 when India and Pakistan both tested nuclear explosive devices. Since that time, a central aspect of U.S. policy in South Asia has been prevention of interstate conflict that could destabilize the region and lead to nuclear war. In 2004, New Delhi and Islamabad launched their most recent comprehensive effort to reduce tensions and resolve outstanding disputes. This "composite dialogue" process has to date resulted in modest, but still meaningful successes.

New Delhi acknowledges that a stable Pakistan is in India's interests. At the same time, however, many top Indian leaders are convinced that Pakistan has long been and remains the main source of India's significant domestic terrorism problems. They continue to blame Islamabad for maintaining an "infrastructure of terror" and for actively supporting terrorist groups that are held responsible for attacks inside India.[41] The latter half of 2008 saw a deterioration of India-Pakistan relations, especially after U.S., Indian, and Afghan authorities accused Pakistani state elements of being complicit in a lethal July car bombing at the Indian Embassy in Kabul, Afghanistan.[42] Some in New Delhi express frustration that the new

---

[39] In 1993 more than 250 people died in a series of bomb attacks across Mumbai believed to be retaliation for the demolition by Hindu radicals of a historic mosque at Ayodhya. A pair of August 2003 car bombings outside the Taj hotel killed 52 people. More recently, the serial bombing of Mumbai commuter trains in July 2006 killed nearly 200 people and injured many hundreds more. Indian authorities linked each of these attacks to Pakistan-based groups, although each may have been planned by indigenous elements.

[40] See, for example, Praveen Swami, "Pakistan and the Lashkar's Jihad in India" (op-ed), *Hindu* (Chennai), December 9, 2008.

[41] According to India's national security advisor, very few Indian Muslims have played major roles in domestic terrorism. He has asserted that, "Mostly, the [terrorist] activity has been generated from outside" and "the overwhelming majority" of India's terrorism problems emanates from the Pakistan-Afghanistan border region. Internal Indian government documents reportedly conclude that Pakistan's main intelligence agency has not changed its central objectives, which, according to these sources, include supporting anti-Indian militancy in Kashmir, Punjab, Assam, and along the India-Nepal and India-Bangladesh borders ("Negotiating War," *Outlook* (Delhi), May 28, 2008; "MK Narayanan" (interview), *India Abroad*, September 21, 2007; "ISI Still Helping Terror Groups Against India: Narayanan," *Times of India* (Delhi), March 26, 2008; "No Let Up in ISI Operations: Report," *Times of India* (Delhi), June 9, 2008).

[42] "Pakistan 'Behind Afghan Attacks,'" BBC News, July 14, 2008; "India Blames Pakistan in Embassy Bombing," Associated Press, July 21, 2008; "Pakistanis Aided Attack in Kabul, U.S. Officials Say," *New York Times*, August 1, 2008.

civilian leaders in Islamabad appear to exert little influence over Pakistan's powerful military and intelligence agencies, which historically have acted independent of civilian oversight.[43]

In December 2001, the United States designated the Lashkar-e-Taiba as a Foreign Terrorist Organization shortly after it was publically implicated by New Delhi for a gun and grenade attack on the Indian Parliament complex that killed nine people. This assault triggered a full Indian military mobilization along the India-Pakistan frontier. An ensuing ten-month-long standoff in 2002 involved one million Indian and Pakistani soldiers and was viewed as the closest the two countries had come to full-scale war since 1971, causing the U.S. government to become "deeply concerned" that a conventional war "could escalate into a nuclear confrontation."[44] Further lethal attacks on Indian civilians spurred Indian leaders to call for a "decisive war," but intense international diplomatic engagement, including multiple trips to the region by high-level U.S. officials and other considerations, apparently persuaded India to refrain from attacking.[45]

The Kashmir Issue

Although India suffers from several militant regional separatist movements, the Kashmir issue has proven the most lethal and intractable. Conflict over Kashmiri sovereignty has brought global attention to a potential "flashpoint" for war between nuclear-armed powers. The problem is rooted in competing claims to the state, which has been divided since 1948 by a military Line of Control separating India's Muslim-majority Jammu and Kashmir state and Pakistan-controlled Azad [Free] Kashmir. India blames Pakistan for supporting "cross-border terrorism" and for fueling a separatist rebellion in the Muslim-majority Kashmir Valley with arms, training, and militants. Islamabad, for its part, claims to provide only diplomatic and moral support to what it calls "freedom fighters" who resist Indian rule. New Delhi insists that the dispute should not be "internationalized" through involvement by third-party mediators and India is widely believed to be content with the territorial status quo. The longstanding U.S. position on Kashmir is that the issue must be resolved through negotiations between India and Pakistan while taking into account the wishes of the Kashmiri people.

[43] "India Frustrated by a Rudderless Pakistan," *New York Times*, August 12, 2008.
[44] Statement of Director of Central Intelligence George Tenet Before the Senate Armed Services Committee, "Worldwide Threat: Converging Dangers in a Post-9/11 World," March 19, 2002.
[45] See Polly Nayak and Michael Krepon, "US Crisis Management in South Asia's Twin Peaks Crisis" at http://www.stimson.org/southasia/pdf/USCrisisManagement.pdf.

Implications for India-Pakistan Relations

New Delhi's Response

On November 27, while multiple battles between militants and security forces still raged in Mumbai, Prime Minister Singh addressed the nation to denounce the "well-planned and well-orchestrated attacks, probably with external linkages," and noted evidence that the culprits were members of a group "based outside the country," an unmistakable reference to Pakistan. A day later, India's foreign minister said that preliminary evidence implicated "elements with links to Pakistan." On December 1, with bilateral tensions mounting, Pakistan's envoy in New Delhi was summoned and told the Indian government expected strong action to be taken against those Pakistani elements found to be responsible for the Mumbai attacks. Indian officials are not known to have presented any evidence, but suggested that such elements are still at large on Pakistani territory.[46] They submitted to Pakistan a list of 42 wanted fugitives believed to be on Pakistani territory.[47]

The Indian government is coming under ever-greater domestic pressure to ramp up bilateral and multilateral pressure on Pakistan as the alleged epicenter of global terrorism. Some in India call for military strikes against terrorist targets on Pakistani territory.[48] In claiming New Delhi has "strong evidence" that the attackers were trained in and came from Pakistan, India's deputy foreign minister said Islamabad must deliver on its 2004 commitment to end the activities of terrorists groups on Pakistani soil. External Affairs Minister Mukherjee has voiced New Delhi's insistence that Pakistan's actions against militant groups operating on Pakistani soil be taken to their "logical conclusion." This would include a total dismantling of the "terrorist infrastructure" inside Pakistan and the permanent outlawing of militant groups under whatever aliases. These steps were not, according to Mukherjee, taken following past episodes of Pakistani government assurances, and New Delhi has not been impressed with the efficacy of existing bilateral mechanisms designed to facilitate joint intelligence

[46] See http://www.indianembassy.org/newsite/press_release/2008/Nov/10.asp; "India Blames 'Elements' From Pakistan for Attack," Reuters, November 28, 2008; "On the Calling in of the High Commissioner of Pakistan Today Evening," Indian External Affairs Ministry press release, December 1, 2008; "In Wake of Attacks, India-Pakistan Tensions Grow," *New York Times*, December 2, 2008.

[47] These include LeT chief Hafiz Saeed; Indian criminal boss Dawood Ibrahim, who is accused of orchestrating serial bombings in Mumbai in 1993 and is suspected of residing in Karachi; and Masood Azhar, founder of the Pakistan-based Jaish-e-Mohammed terrorist group implicated in numerous anti-India attacks, among them a 2001 assault on the Indian Parliament. By some accounts, Ibrahim continues to live openly in Karachi ("Dawood Sitting Pretty in Karachi," *Times of India* (Delhi), December 4, 2008).

[48] "Indian Hawks Calls for Strike on Pakistan," *Financial Times* (London), December 19, 2008.

sharing and investigative cooperation in which "nothing has been produced."[49]

While New Delhi is believed to have ruled out direct military action for the time being, Indian officials immediately began considering a suspension of the ongoing bilateral dialogue with Pakistan.[50] On December 16, India's top-ranking diplomat announced what was already widely suspected: that the bilateral composite dialogue process was in "a pause" due to the Mumbai attacks. While senior India officials continue to press Islamabad to act more robustly against the Pakistani "elements" suspected of being behind the attacks, making this a requirement for "normal" relations, Defense Minister A.K. Antony stated that his country was "not planning any military action" at present.[51] Yet, on December 18, in the first concrete sign of deteriorating diplomatic relations, New Delhi canceled a planned January tour of Pakistan by India's national cricket team.

Islamabad's Response

The Islamabad government offered condolences and strongly condemned the terrorist acts in Mumbai. Pakistani leaders insist that India's fight against terrorism is their fight, as well, and they promised swift action against any Pakistani elements shown to be involved, expressing a willingness to deepen bilateral engagement while warning against the "blame game and knee-jerk reactions."[52] All of Pakistan's major political parties were unified in their condemnation of the attacks, but they also issued a joint resolution rejecting any "hasty allegations" against their country.[53] Pakistan at first offered to send its top intelligence official to India to assist in the investigation, then later reversed itself, offering to send a lower-ranking official. The episode was yet another embarrassment for civilian leaders in Islamabad who have sought to demonstrate their authority over Pakistan's security establishment with little success, and it may have further damaged the confidence of Indian leaders.[54] On December 2, Pakistan's foreign minister offered to establish a joint inquiry into the attacks and reiterated Islamabad's intention to cooperate fully.[55] Islamabad

---

[49] See http://www.indianembassy.org/newsite/press_release/2008/Dec/11.asp.

[50] "Pranab Rules Out Military Action," *Hindu* (Madras), December 3, 2008; "Cabinet Minister Resigns Amid Anger in India," *Washington Post*, December 1, 2008.

[51] "India-Pakistan Talks Stalled After Attacks—Delhi," Reuters, December 16, 2008; "Pranab, Antony Want Pakistan to Act," *Hindu* (Chennai), December 17, 2008; "Indian Defense Chief: No Plans for Military Action," Associated Press, December 16, 2008.

[52] See http://www.mofa.gov.pk/Press_Releases/2008/Nov/PR_363_08.htm; "Pakistan Wants India Tension Defused After Attack," Reuters, November 28, 2008; http://www.mofa.gov.pk/Press_Releases/2008/Nov/PR_367_08.htm.

[53] "Pakistan Parties Unite on Mumbai," BBC News, December 3, 2008.

[54] "Pakistan U-Turn on Sending Spy Chief to India," Associated Press, November 29, 2008; "Delhi Stiffens at ISI U-Turn," *Telegraph* (Kolkata), November 30, 2008.

[55] "Pakistan Offers to Aid India in Terror Investigation," *Washington Post*, December 2, 2008.

has repeatedly and emphatically condemned the attacks, promised "utmost cooperation and assistance" in bringing the perpetrators to justice, and offered to establish a joint investigative commission co-chaired by Pakistan's and India's national security advisors.[56]

Under pressure from foreign capitals and cognizant of the threat posed to domestic security, the Islamabad government launched a crackdown on Pakistan's indigenous religious militant groups on December 7. Security forces raided a main LeT complex in Pakistani Kashmir, taking control of several buildings and arresting at least six men, including Lakhvi and Zarrar Shah, both suspected of remotely commanding the Mumbai attackers. Country-wide raids on LeT and other militant compounds continued over ensuing days, leaving a total of 53 people in custody to date, according to the Interior Ministry. A JuD spokesman claimed that nine of the group's ten top leaders were among those detained. Pakistani officials reject calls for extraditing any of the fugitives sought by India, saying that any charges brought against such persons would be leveled in Pakistani courts only.[57] Islamabad also acted quickly in response to the U.N.-ordered sanctions on the JuD, reportedly detaining Hafez Saeed and directing banks to freeze all accounts held by the JuD. Eleven offices were shuttered in several cities. Pakistani authorities may find it difficult to track and seize LeT assets which were hidden in the public lead-up to U.N. action.[58]

Outlook for Bilateral Relations

In the face of domestic pressure from their respective publics, the leadership of both India and Pakistan have visibly sought to keep the situation from escalating. Yet political posturing could yet polarize the situation and reverse years of increasingly positive bilateral interactions.[59] Numerous Indian, American, and other observers have been jaded by a Pakistani history of "catch and release" in dealing with their indigenous extremists.[60] New Delhi welcomed Islamabad's December crackdown while also

[56] See http://www.mofa.gov.pk/Press_Releases/2008/Dec/PR_375_08.htm.

[57] "History, Dissent Cloud Pakistan's Mumbai Reaction," Associated Press, December 19, 2008; "Zardari Rules Out Returning Fugitives," *Hindu* (Chennai), December 4, 2008. JeM chief Masood Azhar was reported confined to house arrest at his compound in southern Punjab, but this report later was denied by a senior Pakistani official who said Azhar remains at large, his whereabouts unknown ("Masood Azhar Not Under House Arrest: Pakistan Envoy," *Times of India* (Delhi), December 17, 2008).

[58] "Pakistan Arrest Leaders of Charity Linked to Mumbai Attacks," *Washington Post*, December 11, 2008; "Money Eludes Pakistan's Crackdown on Accused Terror Group," *Wall Street Journal*, December 13, 2008.

[59] "India, Pakistan Tread Lightly After Mumbai Attack," Associated Press, December 2, 2008; "Public Anger Strains India-Pakistan Cooperation," *Christian Science Monitor*, December 5, 2008. In one example of heightened public emotion, tens of thousands of demonstrators gathered in southern Mumbai a week after the attacks began to express their anger, at times chanting "death to Pakistan" ("As Rice Presses Pakistan, Tens of Thousands Take to Streets in Mumbai," *New York Times*, December 4, 2008).

[60] "Pakistan Detains Extremist Leader," *Washington Post*, December 9, 2008.

pressing Pakistan to "shut down" the LeT entirely. One senior Indian government official called the Pakistani raids of LeT headquarters "eyewash" that did not address New Delhi's core concerns.[61] Meanwhile, skepticism about India's intentions and sincerity fuel nationalist cohesion in Pakistan, where such disparate groups as liberal businesspeople and Taliban commanders have rallied around the flag.[62]

Still, while visiting Islamabad in early December, just after meetings in New Delhi, Secretary Rice said she had "heard nothing but reasonable [and] responsible discussion" from authorities in both capitals. A week later, a spokesman for Pakistan's Foreign Ministry responded to the New Delhi-announced "pause" in the bilateral peace process with resignation and optimism that the "hiccup" in relations will be overcome.[63] A lengthy suspension could lead to a further deterioration of bilateral relations and a possible return to the crisis and near-war conditions of 2002. However, some analysts are sanguine, citing the resiliency of the five-year-old peace process, a new Pakistani leadership that has demonstrated keen interest in improved bilateral relations, and the weakened state of both countries' economies. Further reasons a bilateral war is considered unlikely include lessons learned during the 2002 crisis, and the existence of civilian (rather than military) leaders in Islamabad, and secular-minded leaders in New Delhi.[64]

Officials in Islamabad requested that India provide "credible information and evidence pertaining to the Mumbai attacks" without which they say Pakistan's own domestic investigation cannot move forward. Without provision of justiciable evidence, which Indian authorities have been hesitant to provide in past cases, it is not clear how long the detained alleged plotters will be held in Pakistan.[65] To date, Pakistani leaders continue to deny having seen any meaningful evidence that the attackers came from Pakistan. They also claim that Indian and Western intelligence agencies have offered no firm evidence that the attacks were orchestrated on Pakistani soil. Islamabad has denied requests from foreign governments to question its detainees.[66]

---

[61] "Shut Down LeT Operations, India Tells Pakistan," *Hindu* (Chennai), December 9, 2008; quote in "Pakistan Raids Aimed to Deflect Pressure—India Experts," Reuters, December 10, 2008.

[62] "Mistrust of India Forges Sense of Unity in Pakistan," *Washington Post*, December 6, 2008.

[63] See http://www.state.gov/secretary/rm/2008/12/112752.htm; "Pakistan Optimistic on India Talks Despite Pause," Reuters, December 17, 2008.

[64] "Pakistan Link to Mumbai Attacks Raises Tensions," *Jane's Country Risk Daily Report*, November 28, 2008; "India, Pakistan Keep Lid ion Tensions," *Los Angeles Times*, December 6, 2008.

[65] See http://www.mofa.gov.pk/Press_Releases/2008/Dec/PR_388_08.htm; "After Pressing Pakistan on Mumbai Attacks, India Now Pressured to Share Evidence With Rival," Associated Press, December 13, 2008.

[66] "Zardari Rejects Mumbai 'Claims,'" BBC News, December 17, 2008; "Pakistan Won't Let Foreigners Question Suspects," Reuters, December 15, 2008.

Many Indian commentators urge New Delhi to take a measured and unemotional approach toward Pakistan with the recognition that Islamabad, too, faces a serious terrorist threat, and that public pressure for decisive action may only exacerbate the situation. From this perspective, the Mumbai attacks could even serve as a catalyst for genuine progress in efforts to end the Pakistani military's alleged patronage of Islamist extremist groups.[67] However, skeptical Indian analysts insist that the Pakistani actions to date have been tactical moves aimed at creating "breathing space" for Islamabad. They remain convinced that the Pakistani military has yet to relinquish its the use of Islamist militant groups as "instruments of state policy."[68] Others conclude that the interests of the Pakistani military, Pakistan's conservative political parties, and Islamist extremists converge in ways that marginalize Islamabad's current civilian leaders, forcing the ruling political coalition there to "take a do-little, if not do-nothing, stance."[69] Dubious experts have long asserted that Pakistan's interest is to appear cooperative while continuing to pursue what is seen as a largely successful strategy of asymmetric warfare against India employing jihadi elements.[70]

Pakistani President Asif Zardari insists that Pakistan is a victim of the same kinds of terrorists who attacked Mumbai, arguing that their goals include weakening Islamabad's civilian government and derailing the India-Pakistan peace process. He has asked New Delhi to "pause and take a breath" in recognizing that India and Pakistan must work together with others to neutralize the mutual threat they face.[71] Pakistan's foreign minister expressed a desire that there should be no war between his country and India, but warned that Pakistanis "are fully prepared in case war is imposed on us."[72]

War fears are not unfounded, as escalatory dynamics in an atmosphere of mutual antagonism and insecurity are notoriously difficult to control. A Pakistani daily reported that Islamabad ordered its military forces to go on "high alert" on the weekend following the Mumbai attacks, when President Zardari received a "threatening phone call" purportedly made by Indian External Affairs Minister Mukherjee. Mukherjee issued a statement denying that he had made any such call and expressing worry that Pakistani

[67] See, for example, Siddharth Varadarajan, "India's Pakistan Problem is Pakistan's Problem Too" (op-ed), *Hindu* (Chennai), December 3, 2008.

[68] See, for example, Wilson John, *Action Against Jihadis, Too Little, Too Late*, Observer Research Foundation (New Delhi), December 10, 2008; Brahma Chellaney, "U.S. Must Stop Pampering Pakistan" (op-ed), *Japan Times* (Tokyo), December 17, 2008.

[69] "Denial or Worse?" (editorial), *Hindu* (Chennai), December 6, 2008.

[70] See, for example, Sumit Ganguly, "Pakistan Won't Cooperate With India" (op-ed), *Wall Street Journal*, December 5, 2008.

[71] Asif Ali Zardari, "The Terrorists Want to Destroy Pakistan, Too" (op-ed), *New York Times*, December 9, 2008.

[72] Quoted in "Pakistan 'Ready for War' With India After Mumbai," *Daily Telegraph* (London), December 10, 2008.

officials had "tried to give [the hoax] credibility" and even considered acting on it.[73] Reports based on the statements of Pentagon officials and others suggested that, in the immediate aftermath of the Mumbai attacks, Indian air force units were placed on alert for possible strikes on suspected terrorist camps inside Pakistan.[74] In mid-December, Islamabad issued a formal protest over two alleged violations of Pakistani airspace by Indian warplanes. Indian officials deny that any such violations took place.

Implications for India

Political Recriminations

Following the Mumbai attack, unity among Indian political leaders did not last even one day, and public anger toward them was reflected in a slew of recriminating media reports and public demonstrations.[75] Many ordinary Indians expressed anger at political leaders from both major national parties, whose alleged bickering and incompetence were seen as being at least partly responsible for allowing the attacks.[76] The Indian elite—mostly insulated from problems associated with the country's poor infrastructure and weak social services—found themselves the targeted victims of violence and now demand swift government action to provide public safety.[77]

The current, Congress Party-led United Progressive Alliance (UPA) ruling coalition has marked more than four years in power and overseen major economic growth in India. Yet Prime Minister Singh been criticized for perceived weak and ineffective leadership. The UPA government only barely won a vote of confidence in July 2008 and has lost numerous state-level elections, some to the opposition-leading, Hindu nationalist Bharatiya Janata Party (BJP), which held national power from 1998 to 2004. Although the UPA's constituent parties fared relatively well in several state-level elections in December, with national elections slated for May 2009 at the

[73] "A Hoax Call That Could Have Triggered War," *Dawn* (Karachi), December 6, 2008; http://www.indianembassy.org/newsite/press_release/2008/Dec/4.asp.

[74] "US: India's Air Force 'On Alert' After Mumbai Attacks," CNN.com, December 15, 2008; "Was India Mulling Air Strikes on Pak Camps?," *Times of India* (Delhi), December 16, 2008.

[75] "Mumbai Fallout: Will India's Government Survive?," *Time*, December 1, 2008; "In Anger Over Mumbai Attacks, Indians Vilify Their Politicians," *Washington Post*, December 5, 2008; "The Other Battle," *Frontline* (Chennai), December 19, 2008.

[76] "India Directs Anger at Politicians After Mumbai Attacks," Reuters, November 30, 2008. India has no overarching anti-terrorism laws. The Prevention of Terrorism Act (POTA) was promulgated under the BJP-led government of then-Prime Minister Atal Vajpayee in early 2002. POTA came under fire as providing the government a powerful tool with which to arbitrarily target minorities and political opponents. It subsequently was repealed by Singh's Congress-led coalition in 2004, only four months after the change of government. No new national anti-terrorism law was enacted to replace POTA, although the Unlawful Activities (Prevention) Act of 1967 allows the government to proscribe extremist groups.

[77] "Mumbai Terror Siege Politicizes an Upper Class Long Insulated," *New York Times*, December 7, 2008.

latest, the coalition remains at risk of succumbing to India's strong anti-incumbency tradition. The Mumbai attacks may make even more difficult a Congress Party victory at the national level and could fuel the Hindu chauvinism sometimes championed by the BJP.[78] In addition, India's already faltering economy may be further harmed by the Mumbai carnage.[79] At the time of this writing, three senior Indian officials—all from the Congress Party—have resigned in the wake of the attack. Home Minister Patil and the chief minister and deputy chief minister of the Maharashtra state, in which Mumbai is located, all acknowledged security lapses in tendering their resignations.[80] Former Finance Minister Chidambaram is now the new Home Minster.

Anti-Terrorism Law and Capacity Reform

Along with domestic political recriminations, the Mumbai attack has fueled already existing concerns about India's counterterrorism policies and capabilities. In the present case, the Mumbai attackers' extensive use of modern technology presented poorly equipped Indian investigators with a difficult challenge.[81] Reports have arisen indicating that some degree of warning was available to Indian authorities, although it is not clear how actionable such intelligence was.[82] U.S. intelligence agencies were reportedly among those warning Indian authorities of a potential attack "from the sea against hotels and business centers in Mumbai."[83] Past India counterterrorism investigations have realized only minor successes, usually producing insufficient evidence for prosecutorial action. Even if charges are levied, the

[78] See Brian Cloughley, "Who Benefits From Mumbai?" (op-ed), *Daily Times* (Lahore), December 17, 2008.

[79] "Attacks May Be Stern Test for Shaky Indian Markets," Reuters, November 26, 2008; "Slowdown Deepens in India, Attack Clouds Prospects," Reuters, December 1, 2008.

[80] "More Indian Officials Quit in Aftermath of Attacks," *Washington Post*, December 1, 2008. The BJP wasted no time in politicizing the tragedy even as it was still underway: controversial Gujarat Chief Minister Narendra Modi, a hardline Hindu nationalist and rising BJP star, gave a November 28 press conference at the Oberoi hotel in which he bashed the incumbent Congress-led government for failing to tackle the terrorism threat ("Crisis May Shift India's Political Landscape," *New York Times*, November 29, 2008).

[81] "Mumbai Attacks Show Up India's Technology Shortcomings," Reuters, December 11, 2008; "Mumbai Attackers More Tech Savvy Than the Police," Associated Press, December 14, 2008. In one stunning example of lax Indian security measures, two bombs were found in a pile of abandoned luggage at the train terminal nearly a week after they had been left there by the terrorists and days after the site had been re-opened to the public.

[82] In March 2007, India's then-defense minister warned Parliament of intelligence reports that militants might plan to infiltrate by sea. Subsequent parliamentary investigations found serious weaknesses in the ability of Indian security forces to protect against such infiltration. In mid-November 2008, India's foreign intelligence agency reportedly intercepted a telephone conversation between parties in Karachi, Pakistan, and Mumbai who discussed possible seaborne infiltration of India's west coast by LeT militants, but a preventive naval sweep was called off after five days ("Top Indian Security Official Resigns as Toll Eclipses 180," *New York Times*, December 1, 2008; "India to Restructure Security Services After Mumbai Failings," *Jane's Defense Weekly*, December 1, 2008).

[83] "U.S. Warned India in October of Potential Terrorist Attack," *ABC News* (online), December 1, 2008.

judicial system is badly hampered by painfully slow trials and obsolete technology.[84]

Efforts to reform the system come under criticism for being minor and slowly implemented. Only a few hundred Intelligence Bureau officials are said to specialize in counterterrorism—a seeming pittance in a country of more than 1.1 billion people—and the Indian Coast Guard employs less than 100 boats to patrol nearly 5,000 miles of shoreline. Indian police forces suffer from a dire lack of funding and training. Poor working conditions, archaic surveillance and communications equipment, and obsolete weapons further hinder their capacity.[85] One senior Indian terrorism analyst emphasizes the key role of local policing and he faults federal and state governments for maintaining a distressingly low police-to-population ratio of about 125 per 100,000, little more than half of the U.N.-recommended ration for peacetime policing.[86]

At an emergency meeting of major political parties on November 30, Prime Minister Singh vowed to establish a federal investigative agency, bolster maritime and air security, and create multiple new bases for commando forces.[87] On December 17, the Indian Parliament passed two major pieces of legislation in response to the Mumbai attacks, the National Investigating Agency Bill and the Unlawful Activities (Prevention) Amendments Bill. The latter is meant to facilitate investigations and trials of the accused in terrorism cases. Among other provisions, it would double (to 180 days) the detention period allowed for suspects and seek to restrict the flow of finances that abet terrorist activities. London-based Amnesty International warned that the provisions would violate international human rights treaties and should be rejected.[88]

Those who focus on (re-)establishing national anti-terror laws may be neglecting to acknowledge that such laws have at times been abused by those who implemented them, and that establishing a coherent national counterterrorism *strategy* may be the more urgent task.[89] Many observers cast doubt on the Indian state's capacity to effectively carry out its security overhaul plans, pointing to a severe lack of resources. Some warn that plans for a new national investigative agency may be too grandiose given New Delhi's past record with such undertakings, and that the role such an agency would play in the country's already dense bureaucracy is far from

[84] "India's Success Rate Lacks in Terrorist Prosecutions," *Wall Street Journal*, December 8, 2008.
[85] "Lack of Preparedness Comes Brutally to Light," *New York Times*, December 4, 2008; "'Rot' at the Heart of Indian Intelligence," BBC News, December 2, 2008.
[86] Ajai Sahni, "The Uneducable Indian" (op-ed), *Outlook* (Delhi), December 1, 2008.
[87] "Cabinet Minister Resigns Amid Anger in India," *Washington Post*, December 2008.
[88] "India Seeks to Sooth Public With New Terror Law," Reuters, December 18, 2008; Amnesty International, "India: New Anti-Terror Laws Would Violate International Human Rights Standards," press release, December 18, 2008.
[89] V. Venkatesan, "Short on Strategy" (op-ed), *Frontline* (Chennai), December 19, 2008.

clear. Others worry that expanding anti-terrorism commando forces will not resolve more fundamental problems within such forces, including what may be inadequate training and equipment.[90]

Implications for Pakistan

The Mumbai attacks have brought sharp attention to the ongoing problem of Islamism terrorism that emanates from Pakistan. Pakistani President Zardari faces the difficult task of avoiding open conflict with India while at the same time not alienating Pakistan's powerful military and intelligence services. Some analysts believe this balancing act may be doomed.[91] Substantively cracking down on the LeT/JuD—especially if it is seen to come under pressure from New Delhi, Washington, and other foreign capitals—poses the risk of a serious backlash among Pakistan's religious conservatives who are already vehemently opposed to Islamabad's cooperation with U.S.-led efforts to combat Taliban forces in Afghanistan and western Pakistan. This could result in even more violence and political instability in Pakistan. Yet this may also be a risk the civilian government and military must take in order to assuage now visceral anger in India and ever-increasing international skepticism about the true intentions of Pakistani leaders.[92] Some Pakistani commentators warn that Islamabad risks international isolation if it displays bravado rather than flexibility. Many, however, acknowledge that, while Islamabad's past use of Islamist proxy groups "may have been expedient," current geopolitical realities dictate that such policies are no longer viable.[93] Most independent analysts say only time will show how serious Islamabad is in its broader stated intention to neutralize indigenous militant threats.[94]

U.S. Policy

U.S. regional policy focuses foremost on fostering stability and precluding open conflict between two nuclear-armed powers; neutralizing the threat posed by religious extremists; democratization; and economic development.[95]

---

[90] Soutik Biswas, "Will India's Security Overhaul Work?" (op-ed), BBC News, December 11, 2008; Praveen Swami, "Mumbai Siege Turns Spotlight on Crisis Within NSG" (op-ed), *Hindu* (Chennai), December 12, 2008.

[91] See, for example, "Pakistan's President Zardari Attempts the Impossible," *Spiegel* (Hamburg), December 17, 2008.

[92] Daniel Markey, *Mumbai: A Battle in the War for Pakistan*, Council on Foreign Relations, Expert Brief, December 12, 2008, http://www.cfr.org/publication/17981/mumbai.html?breadcrumb=%2Fregion%2F279%2Fsouth_asia.

[93] See, for example, Khalid Ahmed, "Mumbai and Pakistan's 'Heroic Isolation'" (op-ed), *Friday Times* (Lahore), December 12, 2008, and Talat Masood, "In Our Own Interest" (op-ed), *Daily Times* (Lahore), December 18, 2008.

[94] See, for example, "India: Pakistan Must Sustain Resolve," *Christian Science Monitor*, December 11, 2008.

[95] For broader discussion, see CRS Report RL33529, *India-U.S. Relations* and CRS Report RL33498, *Pakistan-U.S. Relations*.

As noted above, the Bush Administration responded to the Mumbai attacks by reaffirming its commitment to close and supportive relations with India. Secretary Rice meanwhile has noted Pakistan's expressed willingness to assist in the investigation and she called this "a time for complete, absolute, and total transparency and cooperation," saying "the highest levels of cooperation" between New Delhi and Islamabad were extremely important.[96] While encouraging patience with the unfolding investigation, President-elect Obama responded to a question about the attacks by restating his view that sovereign states have a right to protect themselves from external threats.[97]

Fallout from the Mumbai terrorist attacks could further complicate U.S. policy in South Asia. President-elect Obama had shown signs that reconciliation between India and Pakistan would be a key foreign policy goal of his Administration in the interests of both regional and Afghan stability, and to reduce the likelihood of attacks by religious extremists. The new Centcom commander, Gen. David Petraeus, had voiced a similar interest, reasoning that a reorientation of Pakistan's strategic focus away from India and Kashmir, and toward militancy in Afghanistan and western Pakistan, would weaken the Afghan insurgency. Renewed tensions between New Delhi and Islamabad could easily derail such a tack while simultaneously intensifying pressure on the U.S. government to facilitate regional conflict resolution. One result could be a growing and increasingly sophisticated insurgency in Afghanistan and western Pakistan.[98] Any high-visibility U.S. government focus on the Kashmir issue specifically would likely evoke Indian resistance. It also would risk fueling Pakistani expectations of a future settlement favoring Pakistan, thus in turn providing a motive for Islamabad to sustain pressure by ramping up support for Kashmiri separatists. Some analysts point to this potential risk in encouraging President-elect Obama to appoint a special envoy who would deal with South Asia regional issues more broadly.[99]

One unnamed senior Pakistani security official reportedly said Pakistan would respond to any Indian military mobilization by withdrawing "all troops" from its border with Afghanistan and redeploying them along the frontier with India, as was done during the 2002 crisis. Some view such messages from Islamabad as a form of extortion and to argue that Pakistani leaders use such leverage to elicit U.S. pressure on New Delhi and to

---

[96] See http://www.state.gov/secretary/rm/2008/11/112474.htm.

[97] "India Has Right to Protect Itself: Obama," *Times of India* (Delhi), December 1, 2008.

[98] "India's Suspicion of Pakistan Clouds U.S. Strategy in Region," *New York Times*; "Pressure Increases on Obama for Regional Solution," *Wall Street Journal*, both November 28, 2008.

[99] See, for example, Lisa Curtis, *U.S. South Asia Regional—Not Kashmir—Envoy Needed*, Heritage Foundation WebMemo No. 2158, December 5, 2008, at http://www.heritage.org/research/asiaandthepacific/wm2158.cfm.

continue what may be an ongoing low-intensity proxy war against India.[100] Some analysts speculate that a bilateral India-Pakistan crisis could benefit Pakistan's security apparatus by shifting attention away from the U.S.-led "war on terror" that is deeply unpopular among the Pakistani people and that has caused the Pakistani army significant casualties and loss of domestic status.[101] Militancy in western Pakistan is identified as a major threat to U.S. interests.[102]

U.S.-India Relations

Washington and New Delhi have since 2004 been pursuing a "strategic partnership" based on shared values such as democracy, pluralism, and rule of law. One facet of the emerging partnership is greatly increased counterterrorism cooperation. The U.S. State Department's Country Reports on Terrorism 2007 identified India as being "among the world's most terror-afflicted countries" and counted more than 2,300 Indian deaths due to terrorism in 2007 alone.[103] This number is set to be equaled or exceeded in 2008. In late 2001, President Bush and then-Indian Prime Minster Atal Vajpayee agreed that "terrorism threatens not only the security of the United States and India, but also our efforts to build freedom, democracy and international security and stability around the world."[104] A 2006 session of the U.S.-India Joint Working Group on Counterterrorism ended with a statement of determination from both countries to further advance bilateral cooperation and information sharing on such areas of common concern as bioterrorism, aviation security, advances in biometrics, cyber-security and terrorism, WMD terrorism, and terrorist financing.[105] The Working Group has met a total of nine times since its 2000 creation, most recently in August 2008. Joint Chiefs Chairman Adm. Mullen was in New Delhi in early December to meet with senior Indian leaders, where he reiterated the U.S. military's commitment to work closely with Indian armed forces on counterterrorism.[106]

The Mumbai incident elicited more vocal calls for deepening U.S.-India counterterrorism cooperation that could benefit both countries. Such cooperation has been hampered by sometimes divergent geopolitical perceptions and by U.S. reluctance to "embarrass" its Pakistani allies by conveying alleged evidence of official Pakistani links to terrorists, especially those

---

[100] "Pakistan to Move Troops If Indian Tensions Worsen," Reuters, November 29, 2008; "US, India Face Pak Blackmail on Terror," *Times of India* (Delhi), December 1, 2008.
[101] "War-Mongering Militants Stoke India, Pakistan Crisis," Reuters, December 1, 2008.
[102] See CRS Report RL34763, *Islamist Militancy in the Pakistan-Afghanistan Border Region and U.S. Policy.*
[103] See http://www.state.gov/s/ct/rls/crt/2007/103709.htm.
[104] "Joint Statement of U.S., India on Terrorism, Bilateral Ties," U.S. Department of State Washington File, November 9, 2001.
[105] See http://usinfo.state.gov/is/Archive/2006/Apr/24-821244.html.
[106] See http://newdelhi.usembassy.gov/pr120408a.htm.

waging a separatist war in Kashmir. Mutual distrust between Washington and New Delhi also has been exacerbated by some recent clandestine U.S. efforts to penetrate Indian intelligence agencies. Despite lingering problems, the scale of the threat posed by Islamist militants spurs observers to encourage more robust bilateral intelligence sharing and other official exchanges, including on maritime and cyber security, among many more potential issue-areas.[107] U.S. law enforcement agencies possess specialized equipment that can trace voice-over-internet calls, along with other expertise for examining the global position and satellite phone systems used by the attackers. One unnamed senior Indian intelligence source was quoted as saying that FBI assistance in tracing VoIP calls will be a "test case for U.S. promises."[108]

U.S.-Pakistan Relations

U.S. officials expressed being pleased with Pakistan's most recent efforts to crack down on militant groups, lauding them as "important" and "great steps." Still, some reporting suggests that U.S. officials are thus far unsatisfied with the anti-terrorism measures taken by Islamabad government.[109] Secretary Rice also bucked widely-held perceptions when she claimed to have "heard nothing" in Pakistan suggesting any divisions between the army and the civilian government. While Pakistani officials are likely to have tailored their message to Rice to foster U.S. confidence, it is not clear if those officials can deliver on their promises, and some observers saw Rice's emergency diplomacy achieving nothing concrete.[110]

In a seeming response to President Zardari's repeated reference to the "nonstate" status of the LeT and other Pakistan-based militant groups, Secretary Rice told the Pakistani leader that Islamabad has a responsibility to "deal with those who used Pakistani territory even if they are nonstate actors." Rice added that she continues to believe Pakistan is "very committed to this war on terror." Following a December visit to Islamabad, Foreign Relations Committee Chairman-designate Senator John Kerry reported

---

[107] See Lisa Curtis, *After Mumbai: Time to Strengthen U.S.-India Counterterrorism Cooperation*, Heritage FoundationBackgrounder,December9,2008,http://www.heritage.org/Research/AsiaandthePacific/upload/bg_2217.pdf.

[108] Praveen Swami, "Key Test for Indo-U.S. Intelligence Ties" (op-ed), *Hindu* (Chennai), December 3, 2008; quote in "Terror Boat Was Almost Nabbed Off Mumbai," *Times of India* (Delhi), December 10, 2008.

[109] See http://www.state.gov/r/pa/prs/dpb/2008/113144.htm ; "Top US Military Official Says Pakistan Doing the Right Things After India Terror Attack," Associated Press, December 10, 2008. On potential dissatisfaction, see, for example, "Durrani Meets Rice in Washington," *Daily Times* (Lahore), December 20, 2008.

[110] See [http://www.state.gov/secretary/rm/2008/12/112877.htm]; "Rice's South Asia Trip Ends With Little Achieved," Associated Press, December 5, 2008.

feeling confident that Pakistani authorities recognize the need for a serious and harsh crackdown on religious extremist groups.[111]

In seeking to revamp U.S. South Asia policy, President-elect Obama and his advisors may face a key central question: Are conflictual relations between the region's two largest states primarily an India-Pakistan problem or are they mainly a Pakistan problem alone?[112] Among the options available to President-elect Obama when he takes office would be designating Pakistan as a state sponsor of terrorism under U.S. law, a drastic measure with regard to a "major non-NATO ally" that would have major implications, but one that is favored by some observers, especially in India.[113] Many independent analysts strongly urge the U.S. government to energetically support Pakistani leaders and work diplomatically to bolster international support for them if they choose the "dangerous path" of standing firmly against extremism.[114]

Many hardline Indian analysts, long convinced that the U.S. government coddles the Pakistani security establishment with major and largely unconditioned aid, assert that meaningful improvement will not come so long as Washington implicitly condones Islamabad's alleged double-game by "propping up" the Pakistani military. Even a former Indian national security advisor, a key architect of India's militarized response to the 2001 Parliament attack, suggests that the United States (and Britain) perpetuate the problem by continuing to underwrite the "instrument" (i.e., the Pakistan army) that abets terrorists who attack India.[115] Some in Pakistan worry that "pro-India" elements in the U.S. Congress will respond to the Mumbai attacks by seeking to curtail U.S. foreign assistance to Pakistan.[116]

Author Contact Information

K. Alan Kronstadt
Specialist in South Asian Affairs
kkronstadt@crs.loc.gov, 7-5415

---

[111] See http://www.state.gov/secretary/rm/2008/12/112752.htm; "Pakistan Sees Need for Crackdown After Mumbai," Reuters, December 16, 2008. In mid-December, the British Prime Minister held meetings in Islamabad (and New Delhi), where he promised to assist the Pakistani government with counterterrorism efforts and noted that three-quarters of the most serious terrorism plots investigated in Britain had links to Al Qaeda in Pakistan ("Brown Offers Pakistan Anti-Terror Aid," *Washington Post*, December 15, 2008).

[112] See "US to Probe New S Asia Strategy," BBC News, December 10, 2008.

[113] "Pak on Track to Being Named Terrorist State," *Times Of India* (Delhi), December 7, 2008.

[114] See, for example, Daniel Markey, *Mumbai: A Battle in the War for Pakistan*, Council on Foreign Relations, Expert Brief, December 12, 2008, http://www.cfr.org/publication/17981/mumbai.html?breadcrumb=%2Fregion%2F279%2Fsouth_asia.

[115] Brahma Chellaney, "U.S. Must Stop Pampering Pakistan" (op-ed), *Japan Times* (Tokyo)), December 17, 2008; "India Will Have to Fight Its Own Way" (interview with Brajesh Mishra), Rediff.com, December 15, 2008.

[116] "Move in US to Get Pakistan Aid Stopped," *Dawn* (Karachi), December 17, 2008.

SUBJECT INDEX

China

Colombia

Congressional Research Service (CRS) Reports

Counterterrorism

Defense Department Reports

FBI

Government Accountability Office (GAO) Reports

India

Intelligence

Latin America

Military – Role of

Pakistan

Taliban

Terrorism – International

Terrorist Incidents

Weapons of Mass Destruction

www.ingramcontent.com/pod-product-compliance
Ingram Content Group UK Ltd.
Pitfield, Milton Keynes, MK11 3LW, UK
UKHW051048150926
475595UK00005B/179